The Old Testament

A Literary History

Konrad Schmid

Translated by
Linda M. Maloney

Fortress Press
Minneapolis

THE OLD TESTAMENT
A Literary History

Cover image: Prophet from a Throne of Solomon. French or South Netherlandish. Made in: Bourges or Burgundy. Ca. 1390–1410. Colorless glass, silver stain, and vitreous paint. Overall: 9 x 4½ in. (22.9 x 11.4 cm). The Cloisters Collection, 1995 (1995.301). May have restrictions. Image copyright © The Metropolitan Museum of Art / Art Resource, NY The Metropolitan Museum of Art, New York, NY, U.S.A.
Cover design: Joe Vaughan
Book design: The HK Scriptorium, Inc.

Library of Congress Cataloging-in-Publication Data

Schmid, Konrad, 1965-
  [Literaturgeschichte des Alten Testaments. English]
  The Old Testament : a literary history / Konrad Schmid ; translated
by Linda M. Maloney.
    p. cm.
  Includes bibliographical references (p.   ) and indexes.
  ISBN 978-0-8006-9775-4 (alk. paper)
  1. Bible. O.T.—Criticism, interpretation, etc. 2. Bible.
O.T.—History. 3. Bible as literature. I. Title.
  BS1174.3.S3613 2012
  221.6'6—dc23
                                            2011042063

Manufactured in the U.S.A.

15 14 13 12   1 2 3 4 5 6 7 8 9 10 11

Contents

Preface   xi

**Part A. Purpose, History, and Problems of a Literary History
of the Old Testament**   1
  I. *Why Do We Need a Literary History
    of the Old Testament?*   1
    1. The Task   1
    2. History of Scholarship   4
    3. Place within Theology   12
    4. The Old Testament as a Segment of the Literature
      of Ancient Israel   13
    5. Hebrew Bibles and Old Testaments   15
    6. The Problem of an "Original Text"
      of the Old Testament   20
    7. Old Testament Literary History and Criticism
      within the Field of Old Testament Study   21
    8. Bases, Conditions, Possibilities, and Limitations
      of Historical Reconstruction   23
    9. Recent Trends in Old Testament Research
      and Their Consequences for a Literary History
      of the Old Testament   25

  II. *Language, Writing, Books, and Literary Production
     in Ancient Israel*   30
    1. Language and Writing   30
    2. Material Aspects of Literary Production   31
    3. Socio-Literary Aspects of the Production
      and Reception of Literature   32

    4. Authors and Redactors   36
    5. The Contemporary Audience
       for the Old Testament Literature   37
    6. Elements of Form-Critical Development   39

  III. *Methods and Presentation*   41
    1. The Cultural Impact of the Ancient Near
       Eastern Empires and the Periodization
       of Old Testament Literature   41
    2. Historical Contextualization   43
    3. Theological Characterizations   43
    4. Form-, Tradition-, and Social-Critical Distinctions
       in the Spheres of Tradition   44
    5. "Horizontal" and "Vertical" Relationships
       among Old Testament Texts and Writings   45
    6. Redaction as Inner-Biblical Reception   46
    7. Tradition and Memory   46

**Part B. The Beginnings of Ancient Israel's Literature
among the Syro-Palestinian City-States
before the Advent of the Assyrians
(Tenth–Eighth Centuries B.C.E.)**   49
  I. *Historical Backgrounds*   49
  II. *Theological Characterizations*   51
  III. *Spheres of Tradition*   52
    1. Cultic and Wisdom Traditions   52
      a. Literature at the Sanctuaries
         of the Northern Kingdom   52
      b. Literature of the Jerusalem Temple Cult   54
      c. Wisdom Traditions   56
    2. Annals and Narrative Traditions   57
      a. Northern Kingdom Traditions   58
      b. Literature of the Jerusalem Court   60

**Part C. The Literature of the Assyrian Period
(Eighth–Seventh Centuries B.C.E.)**   65
  I. *Historical Backgrounds*   65
  II. *Theological Characterizations*   67
  III. *Spheres of Tradition*   69
    1. Cultic and Wisdom Traditions   69
      a. Psalms   69

    b. Older Wisdom Literature   71
2. Narrative Traditions   72
    a. The Beginnings of the Deuteronomistic
        "Books of Kings"   72
    b. Traditions of the Judges (Judges 3–9)   78
    c. The Moses Story   79
    d. The Abraham-Lot Cycle   84
3. Prophetic Traditions   87
    a. Beginnings of Prophetic Tradition
        in the Books of Hosea and Amos   88
    b. The Earliest Isaiah Traditions
        and Their Josianic Reception   91
4. Legal Traditions   96
    a. The Book of the Covenant   96
    b. Deuteronomy   99

**Part D. The Literature of the Babylonian Period
(Sixth Century B.C.E.)**   **105**
   I. *Historical Backgrounds*   105
  II. *Theological Characterizations*   107
 III. *Spheres of Tradition*   111
    1. Cultic and Wisdom Traditions   111
       a. Lamentations as Anti-Psalms   111
       b. Laments of the People and the Collectivization
          of Individual Psalms   113
    2. Narrative Traditions   115
       a. The Hezekiah-Isaiah Narratives   115
       b. The Continuation of Samuel–2 Kings 23
          by 2 Kings 24–25   116
       c. The Origins of the Major Historical Work
          Exodus 2—2 Kings 25   117
       d. The Joseph Narrative   120
       e. The Patriarchal Narratives in Genesis   122
       f. The Non-Priestly Sinai Tradition   125
    3. Prophetic Traditions   126
       a. Beginnings of the Jeremiah Tradition   126
       b. Beginnings of the Ezekiel Tradition   130
       c. Deutero-Isaiah   131
    4. Legal Traditions   137
       a. The Decalogue   137
       b. The Deuteronomistic Deuteronomy   138

Part E. The Literature of the Persian Period
(Fifth–Fourth Centuries B.C.E.)   141

   I. *Historical Backgrounds*   141

  II. *Theological Characterizations*   145

 III. *Spheres of Tradition*   147

     1. Cultic and Wisdom Traditions   147
       a. The Priestly Writing   147
       b. Theocratic Psalms   152
       c. Job   154
     2. Narrative Traditions   155
       a. The Non-Priestly Primeval History   155
       b. Daniel Legends (Daniel 1–6*)   159
       c. The Origins of the Major Historical Work
          Genesis–2 Kings   160
       d. Ezra–Nehemiah   162
     3. Prophetic Traditions   164
       a. Haggai/Zechariah   164
       b. Continuations of Deutero-Isaiah
          and Trito-Isaiah   167
       c. Continuations of Jeremiah and Ezekiel   169
       d. The "Deuteronomistic" Theology
          of Repentance   174
       e. The Biblical Construction
          of Classical Prophecy   175
     4. Legal Traditions   176
       a. The Holiness Code   176
       b. The Book of Numbers   177
       c. The Formation of the Torah   178

Part F. The Literature of the Ptolemaic Period
(Third Century B.C.E.)   183

   I. *Historical Backgrounds*   183

  II. *Theological Characterizations*   184

 III. *Spheres of Tradition*   186

     1. Wisdom Traditions   186
       a. Proverbs 1–9   186
       b. Job 28 and Job 32–37   189
       c. Qoheleth   190
       d. The "Messianic Psalter"   192

EXCURSUS: THE RISE OF APOCALYPTICISM   193

2. Narrative Traditions 194
   a. Chronicles 194
   b. Development of the Balaam Pericope 197
   c. Hellenistic Elements in the Davidic Tradition 198
   d. Esther 198
   e. The Translation of the Torah into Greek 199
3. Prophetic Traditions 200
   a. Judgment-of-the-World Texts
     in the *Corpus propheticum* 200
   b. The Formation of a Comprehensive Book
     of Isaiah (1–62) 202
   c. The Devout and the Wicked in Trito-Isaiah 204
   d. Return from the Diaspora and Restoration
     of the Davidic Kingdom in Jeremiah 205
   e. Deutero- and Trito-Zechariah 206
   f. The Redactional Alignment of the Books
     of Isaiah and the Twelve Prophets 207
   g. The World Empires in Daniel 2 and 7 208

**Part G. The Literature of the Seleucid Period
(Second Century B.C.E.)** **211**
  I. *Historical Backgrounds* 211
  II. *Theological Characterizations* 213
  III. *Spheres of Tradition* 214
    1. Cultic and Wisdom Traditions 214
     a. Theocratization and Re-eschatologization
       in the Psalter 214
     b. Sirach and the Wisdom of Solomon 216
    2. Prophetic Traditions 218
     a. The Formation of the Nevi'im 218
     b. The Maccabean Book of Daniel 219
     c. 1 Baruch 220
    3. Narrative Traditions 221
     a. The Ages of the World in the Narrative Books 221
     b. Maccabees, Tobit, Judith, Jubilees 221

Part H. Becoming Scripture and the Genesis of the Canon **223**
  I. *Distinguishing "Scripture" from "Canon"* 223
    1. Josephus and 4 Ezra 14 224
    2. The Prologue to Sirach and
     "the Law and the Prophets" 225

II. *The Scripturalization of the Old Testament Literature within the Framework of Its History*   227

    1. The Biblical Presentation   227

    2. Religious Texts, Normative Texts, Sacred Scripture, and Canon   228

    3. Literary and Canonical History of the Old Testament   231

Notes   234

Bibliography   255

Index of Biblical Passages   310

Index of Authors   320

Preface

Sicut enim a perfecta scientia procul sumus,
lebioris culpae arbitramur saltem parum,
quam omnino nihil dicere.
Since, then, we are far from perfect knowledge,
we may be less guilty in daring such a leap
than in saying nothing at all.
> Jerome, *Commentary on Ezekiel* Part 3, 44, PL 25, 380B

This book is an English translation of my *Literaturgeschichte des Alten Testaments*, published by the Wissenschaftliche Buchgesellschaft, Darmstadt, in 2008 with an updated bibliography. It deals with the presuppositions, backgrounds, processes, and intertextualities making up the literary history of the Old Testament (for the relationship between "Old Testament" and "Hebrew Bible," see below, A.I.5). My aim is to present a history of the literature contained in the Old Testament that attends primarily to the lines of intellectual development and the textual relationships within it. It needs to be highlighted at the very beginning that this book intends to be nothing more than an introduction. Its purpose is not to treat its subject exhaustively. In the present state of research, with its multiple branches, that could scarcely be achieved, certainly not by a single individual and within a limited scope. At the same time, what follows is to be seen neither as merely a risky adventure nor as simply a fragment. It is true that nowadays the diffuse character of current research is often invoked, but from one point of view it is also often overestimated. Of course, Old Testament scholarship contains a great number of suggestions, often difficult to reconcile, regarding the origins and historical arrangement of the books and texts of the Old Testament, to which a literary history must, in principle, orient itself at least to a minimal degree. But the latest discussions among scholars have begun to reveal some contours of a new consensus that, while only partial and, perhaps, sometimes more representative of the European than the American academic context, nevertheless extends to some important basic conclusions. This emerging consensus thus supports such a project insofar as understanding the details at the same time requires the whole, just as comprehension of the whole depends on the details. In this regard, biblical scholarship, whose virtues do not always include an adequate measure of critical self-reflection, should not be less perspicacious than Schleiermacher.

Thus, broad perspectives are also important for the discussion of individual exegetical problems. In particular, the introduction of literary-historical considerations can either give crucial support to specific decisions in the exegetical sphere or show them to be improbable. In the present state of research, the literary-historical perspective cannot simply consist of a collection of already existing conclusions of scholarship on the subject of Old Testament introduction; rather, it is in a sense also a part, a continuation, and a reinforcement of that scholarship. Only an entirely positivistic approach to historical biblical scholarship could demand that the project of a literary history of the Old Testament be begun only after all the individual results of exegetical scholarship are completed. Those results are, in fact, only hypotheses to begin with, and their plausibility depends not only on themselves, but also on the frame of reference within which they are placed. If scholars don't want simply to rely on traditional assumptions, nothing dispenses us from paying attention to overarching questions such as the possibilities of literary-historical synthesis. Of course, it would be an equally positivistic misunderstanding to present these *vice versa* as determinants of what individual exegesis will then illustrate. Both approaches must be fundamentally open to revision, and addressing the question of combining their preliminary results remains an ongoing task of biblical scholarship.

Thus, this contribution sees itself neither as an end nor as a beginning of literary-historical scholarship on the Old Testament, but rather as an intermediate stopping place from which to pose the literary-historical question as such and to present some preliminary perspectives regarding content. It is neither intended nor able to offer an adequate evaluation and synthesis of the state of research on the history of the origins of the Old Testament, certainly not to summarize it. Its purpose, instead, is to reflect the historical-critical reconstruction of the conversation among the most important of its texts and textual corpora as the historical and theological task of scholarly research on the Old Testament.

The literary-historical framework that is discernible in the arrangement of this book, which presumes a series of classifying decisions, may appear problematic to some readers. On the most general level, literary-historical epochs are distinguished (pre-Assyrian, Assyrian, Babylonian, Persian, Ptolemaic, and Seleucid periods). A second level distinguishes different types of literature within these epochs (cultic and wisdom, narrative, prophetic, and legal traditions) while, finally, on a third level, the concrete literary works and positions are discussed. Most controversial will be the arrangements proposed on this third level, while the distinction of different eras in the literary history of the Old Testament according to the particular ruling powers in the Levant and their specific cultural impacts will probably encounter no fundamental dispute in the present state of the discussion. Likewise, the assignment of texts to the various spheres of literature (cultic and wisdom, narrative, prophetic, and legal traditions) will probably find little resistance, especially since these are of lesser significance regarding their content and serve mainly to facilitate an overview. As regards the concrete literary-historical classification of the Old Testament texts and writings, while we must readily acknowledge the uncertainties in scholars' discussions, there remain two things that should receive close consideration.

On the one hand, behind and alongside all confusion and disagreement, we can perceive a sufficient degree of historical ordering of parts of the Old Testament literature to make possible—and certainly not impossible—a reconstruction of the basic lines of an Old Testament literary history. This includes, within the Pentateuch, the delimitation and ordering of the Priestly writing; with some reservations, also the literary-historical core of Deuteronomy; among the Former Prophets, the identification, and recently also the redaction-critical distinction, of the "deuteronomistic" interpretive perspectives; among the Prophets, the distinction between First and Second Isaiah as well as the acknowledgment of the long-drawn-out history of the redaction of the prophetic books; likewise, in the Psalms and Wisdom literature, it does not appear hopeless from the outset to distinguish, for example, positions from the monarchical and post-monarchical periods. Of course, on the whole, more remains disputed than undisputed, but this is in the nature of a literary-historical project and cannot seriously be adduced against an attempt at the undertaking itself. In addition, a literary history of the Old Testament does not differ fundamentally in this regard from the task of commonly known "introductions to the Old Testament," the legitimacy of which is not disputed on the basis of the existence of controversial theories.

On the other hand, it should be emphasized that as a rule, the assignment of a position to a particular period of time is only relative. Many Old Testament texts and writings possess both an oral and a written prehistory as well as a post-history even within the Old Testament itself, so that discussing them in the context of one literary-historical epoch and not another need not mean that the material and texts that are used and worked over at this point were first conceived from scratch in this or that writing and were not altered thereafter. Rather, the Old Testament is in principle to be regarded as traditional literature, so that, for example, the treatment of the Moses-Exodus story in the context of the Neo-Assyrian period does not exclude, but instead includes the perspective that this narrative also makes use of older levels, just as it was later given a further substantial literary expansion. However, the Neo-Assyrian period is posited as the time of its first literary formation, and therefore it is discussed in that chapter and not elsewhere.

Information on historical matters in a detailed sense, given from time to time within the literary-historical exposition, is included only insofar as necessary for treating the literary-historical questions. For additional information and discussions, one should consult the recent works of introduction to the Old Testament and the history of Israel. The literary references in the text may appear rich, but in view of the breadth of the discussion of the subject they are merely examples.

Some passages in this book are revisions of essays previously published, modified here in different ways. The section on the history of research (A.I.2) is a shortened version of my essay, "Methodische Probleme und historische Entwürfe einer Literaturgeschichte des Alten Testaments."[1] In the reflections on the literary-sociological aspects of literary production and reception (A.II.3), the presentation in "Schreiber/Schreiberausbildung in Israel"[2] has been adopted and broadly expanded. The sub-chapter on the beginnings of the deuteronomistic books of Kings (C.III.2.a) is borrowed in part from "Das Deuteronomium innerhalb der 'deuteronomistischen Geschichteswerke' in Gen–2Kön,"[3] and some of the sections on the prophetic literature rest, sometimes shortening and sometimes lengthening, and wherever possible by means of literary-critical interconnections, on my introductory essay on the Later Prophets ("Hintere Propheten").[4]

Biblical passages marked with an asterisk denote a preliminary stage in the historical development of these texts: for example, Gen 28:10-22* refers to the original literary kernel of that pericope.

I am grateful to Fortress Press who made this translation possible. My thanks go especially to the translator, Linda Maloney, to my assistant Peter Altmann, to acquisitions editor Neil Elliott, and to Marissa Wold, who managed the project. In addition, I am also grateful to the Center of Theological Inquiry in Princeton, not only for the opportunity to enjoy a year's study in residence during which the German version of this book was produced, but also, and above all, for the intensive encounter with an American biblical scholarship that differs in a number of aspects from German discussions, as readers of this book certainly will notice. Nevertheless, I hope that this book will foster the dialogue between German and English speaking scholarship in biblical studies, which is still in need of further development.

Konrad Schmid
Zurich, September 2011

Part A

Purpose, History, and Problems of a Literary History of the Old Testament

---

I. Why Do We Need a Literary History of the Old Testament?

---

1. The Task

A literary history is an attempt to present and interpret literary works not simply in themselves but in their various contexts, linkages, and historical developments.[1] This task, despite the brevity of its description, presents both problems and possibilities for the writing of a history of literature. Quite rightly, discussion among literary scholars points out that the synthetic process of writing a literary history often includes at least a partial neglect of the individual works: "We must admit that most literary histories are *either* social history, histories of the thought revealed in the literature, *or* more or less chronologically ordered impressions and judgments of individual works."[2] According to René Wellek and Austin Warren we cannot have simultaneously a systematizing, literary-historical overview of various works from different periods and a book that also takes appropriate account of each individual work. Accordingly, in the end Wellek decided to abandon the project of a literary history altogether.[3] David Perkins also, in his book on the theory of literature, *Is Literary History Possible?* is inclined to answer the question in the title in the negative.[4] At the same time it is obvious that historical arrangements of particular works within their literary-historical contexts can indeed be advantageous for understanding them. In addition, a literary-historical overview as such—apart from the question of individual works—is a legitimate task, and one that furthers understanding, even if it is done at the cost of an abbreviated presentation of its constituent parts.

These discussions may here be set aside as they concern non-biblical literatures. But with regard to the Old Testament, it is obvious that the multiple points of contact between its texts make it extraordinarily apt for literary-historical examination. In fact, the Old Testament presents itself—in its various canonical arrangements and in different ways (see below, A.I.5)—as a literary history.[5]

But how should we approach the project of a literary history of the Old Testament as a critical, scholarly discipline?

This can be regarded as an attempt to bring together anew the previous sub-disciplines in Old Testament scholarship—not as a substitute for an existing sub-discipline, but as an augmentation of it. The closest relationship, in terms of fields of inquiry, is of course with the discipline of introduction, but the latter is seen, on the one hand, as integrally combined with elements of a history of Israel and a theology of the Old Testament (namely the discussion of the theological concepts in the Old Testament writings in their particular historical settings), while on the other hand—unlike an introduction—a literary history does not follow the sequence of the canon, but that of Israel's history.

Thus the texts of the Bible are first considered historically: they stem from particular eras and address particular periods, initially their own. But precisely in the case of the Bible the texts are also read anew in changed times, and they continue to be embellished by means of subsequent literary additions.[6] This process is highly significant for theology, a process to which we also owe the fact that we know the Old Testament at all: without the process of continual copying and expansion of the texts, the original editions would quickly have rotted away. Under normal conditions ancient scrolls did not survive for more than about two hundred years.

In accordance with this circumstance, a literary history of the Old Testament must treat not only the presumed primary figures in the Old Testament texts in their historical context of origin, but also their received images during the whole period during which the Old Testament was created. The book of Isaiah, for example, is relevant to nearly all epochs of Old Testament literary history—not only because it grew to its present form from the eighth to the second centuries B.C.E. and therefore combines texts from various historical situations, but also because its oldest components have been continually read and interpreted anew.[7] The historical view of the Old Testament literature may thus not be restricted to single-point investigations and orderings of individual pericopes. In addition—in some sense from a resultative point of view—it must consider how the traditional *and* the redactional parts of texts were understood together in the various phases of its literary growth and transmission.

The project of a history of Old Testament literature, with its historical perspective, grows out of the claims of Romanticism against the Enlightenment and refuses to consider the Bible as a picture book illustrating eternal truths. Yet it also moves beyond the implicit basic convictions of Romanticism by declining to adopt the latter's mania for origins and models of decadence. Instead, it attempts to understand its biblical object in a historically appropriate manner.

Posing questions historically also requires an awareness of factors beyond those of a mere history of events, including economic- and social-historical as well as geographical determinants of historical processes, similar to the propositions of the *école des annales*.[8]

Ultimately we should also resist the widespread tendency in attempts at historical contextualization of the Old Testament literature whereby its texts are regarded primarily as literary *reflections* of historical constellations—in terms of the history of philosophy, affirming Max Weber over against Karl Marx.[9] Texts not only reflect historical experiences but to the contrary also possess the power to move history. Coming to terms with the fall of Judah in the Babylonian period and the origin of ancient Judaism as a religiously determined *ethnos* is one example of such a process that cannot be plausibly explained in the absence of a corresponding basis in tradition.[10] On the other hand, the recent proposal that judgment prophecy must, historically speaking, be interpreted as *vaticinia ex eventu* in light of the Balaam inscription from Tel Deir Alla,[11] for example, is not necessarily convincing: *ex nihilo nihil fit*.[12] Without an anchor for a prophecy of judgment in statements or texts before their historical fulfillment, we do not have a comprehensive historical explanation of their origin. This does not exclude, however, but rather includes the possibility that in fact we may expect to find many prophetic texts whose perspective on the future was literarily construed *ex post facto*. Thus, for example, a major portion of the prophetic oracles against the nations directed at Israel's and Judah's Transjordanian neighbors does in fact give the impression that the intent was to rationalize their fall after the fact through judgment oracles.

A literary history of the Old Testament is not simply another introduction to the Old Testament, shaped historically rather than canonically. Rather, it broadens the traditional historical questions about the texts in various ways. Beyond the origins of Old Testament books and texts, it asks in particular how these are, on the one hand, located within historical strands of tradition, and on the other hand how they relate to presumably contemporary literary conversation partners in the Old Testament. Thus it must clarify both the diachronic and the synchronic linkages and references of a text. In doing so it attempts both to sharpen the profile of particular theological positions in the Old Testament by comparing them to competing positions, and also to reconstruct and clarify the theological-historical developments. It should already be noted here that the sketches of the development of the literary history of the Old Testament given in sections B to G are not always in a position to offer sufficient material bases for their claims. Literary-historical reconstruction of the Old Testament is not so new that such claims need to be substantiated for each step, as will be evident in the next section, but until now it has not been pursued intensively enough. At the same time, some more or less clear perspectives will emerge that will enable us to present the literary-historical connections among the Old Testament texts and writings in their historical contexts.

2. History of Scholarship

The literary-historical approach to the Old Testament is nothing new. What is its history of scholarship, and what possibilities and problems have been encountered to this point?[13]

Literary-historical inquiry presumes the beginnings of historical-critical research on the Old Testament and thus the awareness of the divergence between the Bible's self-presentation and historical reconstruction. Thus as early as 1670 Baruch Spinoza, in his *Tractatus theologico-politicus*, advocated for the necessity of literary-historical criticism of the Old Testament, since it presents the national and natural development of the spirit of the Hebrew people. Beginnings of literary-historical-critical investigation can be found also in the work of Richard Simon, Richard Lowth, Johann Gottfried Herder, and others.[14] However, in the decisive period of biblical criticism associated especially with the name of Julius Wellhausen, the reconstruction of the Old Testament's literary history remained closely tied to the biblical evidence, and—despite the vehement protest of Hermann Hupfeld in 1844 ("the sole and only correct name of the discipline [i.e. introduction] in its present sense is therefore history of the sacred Scriptures of the Old and New Testaments, or biblical literature, as R. Simon called it")[15]—no real literary-historical subdiscipline developed within Old Testament scholarship.

A proper literary history of the Old Testament, both designated as such and the product of methodical reflection, was first presented by Ernst H. Meier in his 1856 history of the poetic national literature of the Hebrews; however, this was regarded altogether as the work of an outsider and received scarcely any recognition.[16] That fate, and the fact that this literary history was the work of someone who was not an Old Testament scholar but an ancient Near Eastern scholar, can certainly be seen as a prophetic sign pointing to the almost complete marginalization of the literary-historical field in later Old Testament scholarship. In accord with his times, Meier approached the history of Old Testament literature firmly in terms of the question of a Hebrew "national" literature.[17] For him Hebrew literature, which he described more or less according to the Bible's depiction, fell into three epochs, a "preparatory epoch from Moses to the beginning of the kingship," which "described the emergence of the Hebrew state," a second epoch extending from "the creation of the kingship to the end of the exile," when "the national spirit achieved its true flowering," and a third epoch from "the beginning of the Persian period into the Maccabean era," this being also the period of "perfection and decline."[18]

Still closer to the biblical picture of the literary history of the Old Testament was the two-volume work of Julius Fürst, which was originally intended to include the New Testament as well, but in the end extended only to the treatment of the early Persian period.[19] Fürst followed the older documentary hypothesis in Pentateuch research; for him the Psalms are Davidic and the Proverbs originated with Solomon. The prophets, in this literary history, are essentially responsible for their entire books. But older source material has also been reworked in all these Old Testament writings. Therefore, for long stretches Fürst's literary history reads like a description of the older materials that had entered into the biblical books.

The two-volume work of David Cassel was moreso organized according to formal points of view.[20] The outline is not primarily chronological, but attempts to sort material according to genre. Cassel distinguished poetic, prophetic, legal, and historical literature. But his literary-historical description is carried out only for the first two of these groups, while—given the nature of the material—only the prophetic literature is truly differentiated historically. Cassel also noted the close relationships between the Hebrew Bible in its historical contexts, but as a rule considered the Bible to be on the giving end and not on the receiving end in explaining parallels to ancient Near Eastern texts.

Julius Wellhausen, who revolutionized historical biblical criticism with his late dating of the Priestly document, did not give the title "literary history" to any of his books, and yet both his *Prolegomena* and individual sections of his *Israelitischen und jüdischen Geschichte* contain features of a literary-historical approach.[21] One may argue that it was Wellhausen's historical-synthetic presentation of the results of biblical criticism that assured its success within Old Testament scholarship.

The well-known synthesis by Eduard Reuss saw itself programmatically as a continuation of the biblical criticism thus far achieved, especially after Karl Heinrich Graf, Julius Wellhausen, and Abraham Kuenen.[22] "For the best that has been done thus far is called a historical-critical introduction to the Old Testament; it is not the house itself but only a statistical report of the preparatory work in the construction shack and the workshop."[23] Reuss's own depiction is chronologically ordered and classifies the history of the literature somewhat schematically in four epochs, the "era of the heroes," the "era of the prophets," the "era of the priests," and the "era of the scribes."[24] Nevertheless, Reuss gave an indication of what would shape the presentations of the literary history of the Old Testament for several decades. He found in the hymns, such as the Song of Deborah, the pre-national beginnings of the Old Testament literature that were then continued by the great authors of the monarchical period, such as the Yahwist or Isaiah, and ended especially with the Priestly and legal literature of the post-exilic period. This three-step schema—individual ancient poetic texts as beginnings of literary history, the classical prophets and the early authors of the sources of the Pentateuch as the culmination, and the laws as the final notes—in some sense reflected the literary-critical "common sense" of the end of the nineteenth century and the beginning of the twentieth.

Gerrit Wildeboer's literary history appeared in 1893 in Dutch; two years later it was translated into German.[25] This was a broader synthetic overview of the origins of the Old Testament literature following the revolutions in Penta-teuch research brought about by Reuss, Kuenen, and Wellhausen, which were likewise of great importance for the overall picture of the literature of ancient Israel and its history. Wildeboer asserted in his introduction: "If we want to cor-rectly understand the value and significance of the history of Israel's literature we must above all be penetrated by the truth that not only was it post-exilic Judaism that transmitted this literature to us, but also that the authors of a major part of it are to be sought in that same period and, finally, that the trans-mission of older writings did not take place without alterations that were often quite extensive."[26] This statements sounds as if it would be programmatic for the work as a whole, but in its execution Wildeboer's book remained largely the prisoner of contemporary researchers' proposals for dating. Moreover, Wilde-boer profited very little from the literary-critical field as such: his description seems over long stretches to be a chronologically arranged introduction to the Old Testament.

We then find a brief description of Old Testament literary history in the work of Emil Kautzsch, first as an appendix to his translation of the Old Testa-ment, then "not without some original hesitations" as a separate publication.[27] This work divides the literary history into periods according to domestic politi-cal caesurae in the history of Israel ("the pre-monarchical era," "the period of the undivided monarchy," "the period of the divided kingdom to the destruction of Samaria," "from the destruction of Samaria to the exile," "the time of the exile," "the post-exilic period").[28] Despite its brevity, this book determined the starting point for literary-historical discussion to a certain degree for years after-ward. At the same time, the fact that Kautzsch's presentation was conceived as a short appendix was indicative of the shadowy existence of the literary-historical field in German-language scholarship; likewise, the later literary-historical proj-ects of Hermann Gunkel, Karl Budde, and Johannes Hempel appeared as parts of overarching presentations or series (Hermann Gunkel, "Die orientalischen Literaturen," in *Die Kultur der Gegenwart*, I/7; Karl Budde, *Die Literaturen des Ostens in Einzeldarstellungen*, vol. 7; Johannes Hempel in *Handbuch der Literaturwissenschaft*)—that is, they were generated in some sense by initiatives foreign to the subject itself.

If the project of a literary history of the Old Testament never became central to the field, nevertheless in the history of scholarship it is inextricably linked with the name of Hermann Gunkel, who undertook the broadest, most original, and—relatively speaking—the most significant efforts at its further development, even though in his own time he was only able to publish a brief sketch of fifty pages as a substantially developed presentation.[29] The field of form criticism, developed to a significant extent by him (though he did not call it that) played a special role: Gunkel conceived the literary history of the Old Testament as a history of its genres.[30] Behind this was the idea that the Old Tes-tament texts in general rest on oral pre-stages and that the intellectual history of ancient Israel was to be reconstructed by means of describing the genres of its theological discourses. Essentially, Gunkel's method of literary criticism was interested not in the texts themselves but in the formative elements behind them. Literary criticism as genre criticism sought the respective "Sitze im Leben" of genres and thus, at least in Gunkel's opinion, opened a window into Israel's religious and intellectual life. This methodological program was associated, in Gunkel's work, with an outline of the history of ancient Israel's literature that reveals a characteristic weighting. Gunkel distinguished three epochs: first he described "popular literature before the appearance of the great writers (to ca. 750)"[31]; this was followed by "the great authorial personalities (ca. 750–540),"[32] and finally "the imitators."[33] With this division Gunkel reproduced the separation, practiced especially in the nineteenth century, between pre-exilic, prophetic "Hebraism" and post-exilic, historical "Judaism." The religious geniuses to whom the great intellectual projects of the Old Testament can be traced belonged to the period between Isaiah and Deutero-Isaiah; after that there were only "epigones." Gunkel's proposal was not received favorably in his own time, which may have contributed to the continued shadowy existence of the literary-historical field he researched.[34] Apparently it was the relationship of the question of genres to the authorial personalities, which was unclear to those who studied his work, that for Gunkel enhanced the focus on genre, but that for his readers (as may be concluded from the reviews) put too much emphasis on it.

Karl Budde's presentation of literary history was conceived for a broader audience.[35] But Budde did not get beyond a summary of the results of a common introduction to the Old Testament; his book is a conclusion to his own work on the history of origins and does not mark a new beginning in scholarship.

In the English-speaking world, Harlan Creelman presented a chronological introduction to the Old Testament in 1917. Its claim to innovation was, indeed, comparatively modest: it was addressed to a broad audience and abandoned almost any ambition to offer its own historical judgment. Rather, it presents itself as a synthesis of previous research on the Old Testament. The overall view of Creelman's book was restricted very much to a critical perspective on the historical allocation of the biblical texts.

The introduction written in 1919 by Johannes Meinhold, which was frequently republished, was not conceived as a literary history but *de facto* it was more than the usual introduction, since it both discussed the literature of the Old Testament according to eras—and not according to the canonical sequence—and in addition it offered individual sections describing the historical epochs.

The literary-historical work of Julius A. Bewer was quite influential.[36] Bewer was a German-born Old Testament professor at Union Theological Seminary in New York who brought to American scholarship some important insights of German-language historical biblical criticism and genre research.

Perhaps the best known and most fully developed presentation of a literary history in twentieth-century German-language scholarship was the work of Johannes Hempel.[37] It was divided into an introductory chapter, "Premises" (1–23), which treated the history of scholarship in introduction to the Bible with special emphasis on Wellhausen as well as cultural-geographical determinants, and two major sections, "Forms" (24–101) and "The Course of History" (102–94). These last two clearly revealed the influence of Gunkel: the object of study was first approached in form-critical terms and only thereafter in terms of literary criticism. Hempel first treated the genres of Old Testament literature and their history, then the concrete texts in their historical sequence. What is noteworthy in Hempel's work is his conviction about the cultural-historical interweaving of the Old Testament: "The Israelite literature is to a great extent only understandable as part of 'ancient Near Eastern world literature.'"[38] But despite all the energy and innovative spirit that imbue this project it did not become constitutive for the genre: Old Testament literary-historical criticism still remained a marginal activity.

We should also mention, from the mid-twentieth century, the work of Adolphe Lods.[39] Lods asserted at the beginning of his presentation that the literary-critical field had long endured a shadowy existence within Old Testament scholarship.[40] He identified three essential reasons for this. First, the "composite character of the books themselves"[41] represented an elementary problem that was further exacerbated by the fact that scholarship was often only able to reconstruct the development of these books in uncertain fashion.[42] Ultimately, he pointed out, "we possess only minimal fragments of this literature."[43] However, according to Lods these aspects should not mislead us into abandoning the literary-historical questions, since it was inadequate simply to analyze the "composite character of the books themselves" in literary-critical fashion; the literary development of the Old Testament books must also be reconstructed synthetically. As regards the uncertainties in literary-historical reconstruction, Lods also emphasized that despite all difficulties in detail the fundamental information was altogether discoverable, and even the fragmentary character of ancient Hebrew literature was not basically different from that of Greek or Latin literature.

In literary-critical terms Lods was influenced by Wellhausen, in regard to religious history by Gressmann; accordingly he followed the documentary hypothesis in Wellhausen's version and emphasized the religious-historical contextualization of the ancient Hebrew literature. Three essential uniquenesses in Lod's presentation should be emphasized: for one thing, we are struck by the late starting point. Although keeping an eye on early poetic fragments and oral traditions, Lods began with the Assyrian period. In this he is remarkably modern, since recent scholarship finds that only from this point on was there a writing culture in ancient Israel that was developed enough to be able to produce longer texts. Then Lods's work, at least in some areas, clearly reveals an effort to describe intertextual influences. Thus, for example, he treats separately the prophetic influences on some additions to J or E.[44] Finally, we find in his work some broad discussions of parallel phenomena from ancient Near Eastern literature. Lods's book thus pointed clearly toward the future, but as a French Protestant Lods did not find much of a hearing in his own country or outside it.

From the beginning of the 1950s until the 1980s there was still greater silence on the project of a history of Old Testament literature. Klaus Koch wrote in 1964 that "the project of a literary history died unsung and in silence with the death of Gunkel and today is completely forgotten."[45] The concept of literary history scarcely appeared, and there were no new syntheses—and this in a period that is regarded, at least in German-language Protestant theology, as a time when Old Testament scholarship flourished.[46] A number of factors are probably responsible for this, though it remains striking: for one, literary-historical questions were at that time of marginal interest even within literary scholarship. Thus, for example, Hans Robert Jauss said in his introductory lecture at Constance in 1967:

> Literary history has in our time fallen more and more into disrepute, and by no means undeservedly so. The history of this honorable discipline unmistakably sketches a path of constant decline over the last 150 years. The high point of its contributions as a whole was in the early nineteenth century. To write the history of a national literature was seen in the times of Gervinus and Scherer, De Sanctis and Lanson as the crowning life achievement of a philologist. . . . This high-altitude path is a distant memory today. Literary history, as it has come down to us, endures only a miserable existence in the intellectual life of the present.[47]

In vogue, instead, was "work-immanent interpretation," for example in Emil Staigers's sense.[48] In addition, German-language Protestant theology clearly lay, together with biblical scholarship in general, under the influence of dialectical theology, for which literary-historical questions were of lesser interest. Finally, we should point out that after World War II a number of introductions to the Old Testament appeared in which the internal, apparently historically inspired structure, especially as regards the prophetic books, deviated only slightly from the canonical structure of the Old Testament, so that they could easily serve at the same time as functional equivalents to literary-historical presentations.[49] Even the epoch-making theology of Gerhard von Rad,[50] characterized in an early review as a higher sort of introduction, could be located, with some reservation, in this category.[51] Thus no particular need for a literary history as such was perceived.

However, this procedure in the organization of introductions to the Old Testament was possible and conceivable only as long as one could count on a broad agreement about presentation of the Bible and the course of Israel's history. In particular, the historical books Genesis to 2 Kings were regarded, especially in the epochal sequence of patriarchs, exodus, occupation of the land, period of the judges, and the monarchy, as fundamentally reliable, so that in this area introduction and literary history could run parallel. The prophets had to be slightly regrouped, especially as regards the location of the three "great" prophets, Isaiah, Jeremiah, and Ezekiel, in their historical times, while the Writings in general could be interpreted as the expression of post-exilic piety and theology. This harmonizing view of the Bible and literary history, which is also reflected in the proposed relationship of the Bible and the history of Israel, could be described, with Manfred Weippert, as "sub-Deuteronomistic."[52] Probably it is precisely this model of agreement, today regarded as so problematic at least in European biblical scholarship, that accounts in part for the flourishing of Old Testament research between 1950 and 1980.

Norman K. Gottwald's socio-historical interpretation of the Old Testament constituted a certain exception among the modified literary-historical introductions.[53] It is true that he made an effort at a historical presentation of the Old Testament literature, with a broadly sketched depiction of the pre-state traditions, but his presentation was subject to a certain biblicism and at the same time, because of some unconventional elements in his theoretical framework, its influence has been limited.

It was not until 1989 that a genuine literary history was again attempted. Georg Fohrer's brief book named his predecessors but judged them inadequate: "However, there was a lack especially of form criticism, which investigates the forms of discourse and genres, tradition criticism, which inquires about the pre-history of the writings, and redaction criticism, which concerns itself with the editing and revision of the written tradition."[54] For Fohrer, the previous proposals were methodologically too one-sided, too literary-critical in their direction—to the exclusion of the other exegetical methods. It is true that this accusation is formulated very broadly, but it is not wholly inaccurate. At the same time, we may ask whether this names the most important problem in the history of the discipline of "literary history of the Old Testament." Fohrer's criticism was aimed solely at the deficiencies in the method of historical allocation of biblical texts presented by the works he criticized, but he did not formulate any fundamentally different requirements for a "literary history of the Old Testament" than for the discipline of an "introduction to the Old Testament." Correspondingly, his literary history remained a chronologically arranged introduction and did not clarify any diachronic or synchronic textual relationships.

Not long after Fohrer's book, Otto Kaiser published his article on Old Testament literary history in the *Theologische Realenzyklopädie*.[55] For him the "literary history of the Old Testament" constitutes the "necessary companion to analytical introduction studies, which adopts its results and presents them in the organic context of the political, social, cultural, and especially the religious history of Israel and early Judaism."[56] It is all the more astonishing that Kaiser did not develop this program in his material sketch but essentially gave a short summary of an introduction to the Old Testament following the ordering of the biblical canon. Likewise in his collected volume, which has the concept of literary history in its title, he concerns himself essentially with questions of introductory scholarship.[57]

The long-desired project of a literary history not only of the Old Testament, but of the entire Christian Bible, has been attempted by the Biblische Enzyklopädie, whose publication began in 1996 and is being translated into English.[58] On the Old Testament side it is edited by Walter Dietrich. It does not, however, make prominent use of the term of "literary history."

> This is a series conceived in twelve volumes, nine of them devoted to the times and literature of the Old Testament, three to those of the New Testament. The various volumes are structured on a unified basic scheme: first, the biblical picture of the era to be discussed is given, and then is followed by an attempt at historical reconstruction of the period as well as a presentation of literature of the time, concluding with the question of the theological contribution. This very organization of the material shows that the interaction between history and its presentation in the Bible is the focus of the Biblische Enzyklopädie: it begins with the biblical presentation of history and compares it with historical findings, considered both in terms of literary history and of theology.
> On historical questions the volumes of the Biblische Enzy-klopädie—corresponding to the state of research, which is especially fluid in this area—offer a broad representation of the recent results of biblical criticism, archaeology, and ancient Near Eastern studies, a process that, however, does not lead to altogether compatible interpretations. For Lemche what the Bible says about the patriarchs Abraham, Isaac, and Jacob, or about Moses, is not history but fiction, "lovely sto-ries"[59] that in Lemche's opinion were created in the "fifth, fourth, or even the third century,"[60] that is, a full millennium later than the time in which the Bible locates them. Schoors, on the other hand, dates the beginnings of the patriarchal history to the eighth century,[61] while Diet-rich proposes origins for "parts of the patriarchal history, and in any case for the Moses story" before the early monarchical period; "for the primeval history and certainly for Sinai" he believes that pre-state primary forms are "scarcely to be excluded."[62] The readers of the Biblische Enzyklopädie are thus confronted with some problems of coherence. While these certainly reflect the disparity of the present state of discussion, their arguments are not related to one another within the series.
> The division into epochs proposed by the volumes of the Biblische Enzyklopädie presents a rough historical timeline that essentially follows the Bible's own portrait of history and thus—at least as regards this sequence of epochs—insinuates a fundamental correspondence between the Bible and history. But this is just what is under discussion: Are, for example, the patriarchal era and the period of the judges really two successive epochs, as the Bible has it, or are these not, especially in historical terms, to be seen as two portrayals of the same time period from different points of view?

One should also ask, especially if one puts so much weight on the question of the origins of the biblical literature, whether the weighting of the epochal division is correctly balanced: six of nine Old Testament volumes treat the pre-exilic period. In light of the evidence that there is a not a single book of the Bible that has come down to us in its pre-exilic form, we should be astonished at the relative dismissal of the Persian period, which is treated in only a single volume, even though this should perhaps be seen as the most important epoch of literary activity in the Old Testament.

The Biblische Enzyklopädie is a project that is indeed timely, but the "sub-Deuteronomistic" outline overall and the somewhat fragmentary agreement of the various volumes seems questionable.

Furthermore, the brief proposal by Christoph Levin should be mentioned.[63] This volume presents itself as an integrative literary, religious, and theological history. Levin's creed is that the Old Testament is a literary document of early Judaism containing documents from the pre-Persian period only in "fragments." The brevity of the presentation and the comprehensive scope, however, make it impossible for this little book to clearly evaluate the back-and-forth literary-historical influences among the various positions in the Old Testament.

From this overview of the history of research we can see that the project of a literary history of the Old Testament has not, on the one hand, been very frequently attempted.[64] On the other hand, most of these projects have attempted little more than an introduction to the Old Testament in historical rather than canonical order. But by that very fact such a presentation misses its genuine literary-historical-critical point: What is the material relationship of contemporary texts and writings in their historical context? Do they refer to one another? What positions develop from which literary-historical precursors? A literary history of the Old Testament makes sense only if it yields some additional value beyond the discussions within the discipline of introductory studies, which are in themselves entirely legitimate but have a different perspective.

3. Place within Theology

The application of the concept of a literary history to the Bible, which is also known of other ancient Near Eastern literatures,[65] follows from a particular basic theological conviction rooted in the beginnings of historical-critical biblical scholarship in the early modern period: that the Bible is literature like every other ancient literature and therefore is to be interpreted in the same way, without the application of any special sacred hermeneutics.[66] This means that the status of the Bible as sacred Scripture, grounded in its reception history, must not separate it from the critical approaches of reason. Instead, it can and must be investigated with those approaches, precisely with a theological rationale, namely, in order for interpreters to associate a *general* claim to truth with these writings and not grant to them the status of special literature accessible only to a particular group. Thus the declaration that the Bible is literature is not associated with an anti-theological impulse; on the contrary, it is not a matter of "degrading" the Bible from sacred Scripture to literature, but rather of locating its status as sacred Scripture in the texts themselves.[67]

Add to this the self-presentation of the Old Testament as literary history, which we have already mentioned and which deserves to be exegetically and theologically evaluated. Gerhard von Rad probably reckoned most seriously and thoroughly with this unique characteristic of the Old Testament. He represented the conviction that the most adequate form of a theology of the Old Testament was a narrative that retells the biblical story.[68] A literary history of the Old Testament can augment the theological retelling of the Old Testament especially by clarifying the discussions internal to the Bible itself. The question becomes more and more urgent precisely in a scholarly discourse that is indebted to von Rad in many ways, but also goes beyond him, especially in the question of the fundamentally salvation-historical shaping of the Old Testament, which no longer is seen as an overall or even prevalent characteristic of the biblical texts. In the current situation it needs therefore to be asked, what, on the one hand, were the Old Testament texts' own and distinct theological concepts, and how, on the other hand, is their plurality structured within the Old Testament itself.

4. The Old Testament as a Segment of the Literature of Ancient Israel

A literary history using the textual material of the Old Testament differs substantially, not in method but in its object, from other corresponding approaches to non-biblical literature such as, for example, a history of German literature. The reason for this is that the Old Testament does not comprehend the total literary heritage of ancient Israel, but only the part of it that on the basis of particular selection and/or reinterpretation has become the "Hebrew Bible" or the "Old Testament."[69] It is scarcely possible to determine the quantitative relationship between this subsequent canonical entity and the former literature of ancient Israel, but it is indisputable that a more extensive body of literature existed. We may think, comparatively, of the numerous ancient writings outside Israel of whose existence we know for certain only through mentions of or quotations from them by various ancient authors.

The surviving epigraphic text material, despite its fragmentary nature, if we include Israel's and Judah's trans-Jordanian neighbors, yields a very good idea of what we ought to imagine.[70] Perhaps most impressive, if still hard to understand, is the "Book of Balaam,"[71] a portion of which has been retained in a wall inscription in Deir Alla, located east of the Jordan river. Its *incipit*, "*spr*," indicates that this text was originally a scroll. The Mesha inscription is based on excerpts from annals and thus witnesses to the existence of an interpretive writing culture.[72] The Siloam inscription is also probably an excerpt, as seen from the lack of a dedication and the omission of the names of the sponsors of the building.[73] A piece of lyric poetry survived on a bronze bottle from Ammon, which reads as follows:

> The work of Amminadab, King of the Ammonites,
>   Son of Hassil'il, King of the Ammonites,
>   Son of Amminadab, King of the Ammonites:
>   the vineyard and orchard and the terrace walls and a water reser-
>   voir.
> May he rejoice and be glad for many days and years to come.[74]

We might, of course, hesitate to speak of "literature" in these examples, since the concept of "literature" implies a certain quantitative extent as well as a qualitative level in the texts in question. But on the basis of these findings, which are limited by the nature of the material on which the inscriptions are written, one may with good justification suppose that other and more extensive writings on papyrus and parchment existed in ancient Israel. These, with few exceptions, have not survived, but that other texts once existed is more probable than that they did not exist.[75] Indeed, the Old Testament itself mentions a few sources that are at least not entirely fictional. Thus, for example, we find allusions to (1) the Book of the Wars of YHWH, Num 21:14; (2) the Book of the Upright [Jashar] (yšr), Josh 10:13; 2 Sam 1:18;[76] (3) the Book of the Song [or Jashar] (šyr), 1 Kgs 8:53a (LXX); (4) the Book of the Acts of Solomon, 1 Kgs 11:41; (5) the Book of the Annals of the Kings of Israel, 1 Kings 14:19; (6) the Book of the Annals of the Kings of Judah, 1 Kgs 14:29.[77] The Book of the "Upright" and that of the "Song" are probably identical: the determinate title "of the Song," in itself hard to understand, probably arose from a mistaken writing of yšr, "upright" as šyr, "song."[78] We can sincerely doubt, in light of the modest cultural-historical development of ancient Judah at that time, that there was a Book of the Acts of Solomon. In any case, however, the reference to such a book makes it clear that in the Books of the Annals of the Kings of Judah and Israel there was probably nothing said about Solomon.

There were very likely other pre-exilic writings that did not survive or that were even deliberately set aside, especially after the catastrophe of Jerusalem in 587 B.C.E. We should especially mention prophetic traditions about salvation; we cannot exclude the possibility that they also existed in written form, even if scholars such as Kratz suggest that early written forms of prophecy especially arose out of judgment oracles.[79] In support, the Neo-Assyrian evidence shows that pure salvation oracles could be written down as well, although this did not lead to the phenomenon of an enduring tradition process of scribal prophecy as in Israel.[80] One may even suggest that the striking form-critical similarity between the oracles of salvation in Deutero-Isaiah and the Neo-Assyrian prophecies nearly a hundred years earlier (which could scarcely have been accessible any longer after the fall of the Neo-Assyrian empire),[81] prompts us to conclude that there were prophecies of salvation in monarchical Judah of the Neo-Assyrian type, and that these strongly influenced the prophecy of Deutero-Isaiah. After the writing of Isaiah 40–55, this text could then have replaced the older ones in the schools.

Thus the literary history of the Old Testament covers only a segment of the history of ancient Hebrew literature, and this segment can only be described *ex post*: the literary history of the Old Testament treats those texts that survived as texts available for use in the Jerusalem Temple school that later were recognized as sacred Scripture. Unlike, for example, a history of English literature, the Old Testament constitutes a corpus that is disparate in many regards and yet is to some extent coherent with regard to its content and especially to its history of reception. We can go so far as to say that the literary history of the Old Testament simultaneously documents the theological history of its texts, which managed to prevail as the "orthodox" ones. The literary history of the Old Testament does not directly reflect Israel's religious history, which can be reconstructed adequately in broad strokes, better on account of non-textual, archaeological evidence than of biblical evidence.[82] The difference between the perspectives of the Old Testament and Israel's religious history as a whole shows its theologically differentiated interpretation, which was subject to certain criteria of selection.

The Jewish texts from the middle Persian period preserved in Elephantine in Egypt, in contrast, with their partially polytheistic piety and the mention of a separate temple, offer an example of a religious-historical extension of the monarchical period: the beginnings of the colony go back, in all probability, to the sixth, perhaps even the seventh century B.C.E. The conditions of the pre-exilic period are apparently preserved "better" here than in the Judaism of the motherland.[83]

A literary-historical approach to the Old Testament thus opens a window to the most elite segments of religious reality in ancient Israel, the world of the priests, wisdom teachers, and others adept at writing. Correspondingly, in this book the religious-sociological level of the official state cult is given the greatest significance, while elements of the family, local, and regional cults that functioned non-literarily especially in the pre-Persian period play a role only insofar as they were received within the framework of the official cult to which the Bible witnesses in large degree.

5. Hebrew Bibles and Old Testaments

There is no such a thing as *the* Old Testament nor *the* Hebrew Bible; Jewish and Christian traditions recognize different organizations of the biblical books. In addition, the Christian tradition accepts different numbers of books in the different canons of the various confessions and churches.

Hebrew Bibles—in the sense of Judaism's sacred Scripture—in the usual standard order consist of three parts: Torah, Nevi'im, and Ketuvim, abbreviated as Tanakh. The Torah contains the books of Genesis, Exodus, Leviticus, Numbers, and Deuteronomy. The Nevi'im include the books of Joshua, Judges, 1–2 Samuel, 1–2 Kings, Isaiah, Jeremiah, and Ezekiel, as well as the Book of the Twelve Prophets. Finally, the Ketuvim is made up of the books of Psalms, Job, Proverbs, Ruth, the Song of Songs, Ecclesiastes (Qoheleth), Lamentations, Esther, Daniel, Ezra–Nehemiah, and 1–2 Chronicles. The following subdivisions are commonly used within the Nevi'im and Ketuvim: Joshua to Kings are taken together as the so-called "former prophets," Isaiah to Malachi as the "latter prophets." Within the Ketuvim, Ruth, Song of Songs, Ecclesiastes, Lamentations, and Esther make up the so-called "Megilloth," that is, the five "scrolls" assigned to particular feasts—something that, however, is only attested since the sixth century C.E. Ruth is for Shavuot, Song of Songs for Passover, Ecclesiastes for Sukkoth, Lamentations for the Ninth of Ab, and Esther for Purim.

But deviations in the order of books are attested in the manuscript tradition of Hebrew Bibles. What remain constant are the three canonical sections of Torah, Nevi'im, Ketuvim and the numbers of books contained in them. If we calculate the number of possible variations within these two constants we arrive at 120 for the five books of the Torah, 40,320 for the eight books of the Nevi'im (if, with ancient custom, we count the twelve minor prophets as a single book), and about forty million for the Ketuvim.

The tradition, however, did not come close to exhausting these possibilities. The Torah always has the same sequence. At least nine variations are attested for the Nevi'im, but all of them occur in the latter prophets (Isaiah—Malachi). Since Genesis to Kings represents a narrative, chronologically arranged presentation, it is therefore materially fixed. For the Ketuvim the order is rather fluid, with at least seventy different arrangements attested.

> The most important variants in the Nevi'im are found in the Babylonian Talmud (*b. B. Bat.* 14b-15a), which has the four books of the prophets in the sequence Jeremiah, Ezekiel, Isaiah, Twelve Prophets. This is founded on a theological consideration: Jeremiah is "all judgment," Ezekiel "half judgment, half consolation," and Isaiah is "all consolation." Of course, even a rapid reading of these books quickly shows that this is not an accurate summary: all three of the major prophetic books contain statements of judgment *and* salvation and to that extent are all "half judgment, half consolation." But why did the Babylonian Talmud arrive at this order? The answer is obvious if we consider the length of these four prophetic books: Jeremiah has 21,835 words, Ezekiel 18,730, Isaiah 16,392, and the Twelve Prophets 14,355. The arrangement in the Babylonian Talmud is thus clearly motivated by the size of the books, and the theological explanation represents a later rationalization of this arrangement by length.

In the Ketuvim the ordering sometimes varies greatly. At this point the following examples must suffice: the Codex Aleppo and the Codex Petropolitanus (B19A), two of the most important ancient manuscripts of the Hebrew Bible, from the years 950 and 1008 c.e., place Chronicles at the very beginning of the Ketuvim. Apparently Chronicles, which offers a broad narrative of the establishment of the Temple cult under David and Solomon, was thus understood as a "historical" introduction to the Psalms. The present standard ordering, on the other hand, places Chronicles at the very end of the Ketuvim, so that the important statement of a new exodus in 2 Chronicles 36:23b ("Whoever is among you of all his people, may YHWH his God be with him! Let him go up") closes the Tanakh.

As regards the Christian Old Testament, we must distinguish according to the different confessions. In current Protestant editions of the Bible the structure is as follows: the "historical books" are placed first under a single rubric: Genesis, Exodus, Leviticus, Numbers, Deuteronomy, Joshua, Judges, Ruth, 1–2 Samuel, 1–2 Kings, 1–2 Chronicles, Ezra, Nehemiah, Esther. Then come the "poetic books": Job, Psalms, Proverbs, Ecclesiastes, Song of Songs. Finally there are the "prophetic books" of Isaiah, Jeremiah, Lamentations, Ezekiel, Daniel, Hosea, Joel, Amos, Obadiah, Jonah, Micah, Nahum, Habakkuk, Zephaniah, Haggai, Zechariah, and Malachi.

This Old Testament thus also has a threefold division, but of a different nature from the Hebrew Bible. The first heading combines the Torah and the Former Prophets as "historical books," but the books of Ruth, Chronicles, Ezra, Nehemiah, and Esther, which are also narrative, are placed there as well. The second section ("poetic books") contains an important selection from the Ketuvim: Job, Psalms, Proverbs, Song of Songs. The third part ("prophetic books") contains the Latter Prophets of the Hebrew Bible (Isaiah, Jeremiah, Ezekiel, and the twelve minor prophets), but also Lamentations, which according to the Greek tradition was written by Jeremiah, and the book of Daniel, whose final shape belongs in the Maccabean period and that, probably for that reason, was not included in the Hebrew canonical section of Nevi'im, which had already been closed, and so had to be placed in the Hebrew Bible as a prophetic book among the Ketuvim.

Roman Catholic editions of the Bible have the same general structure, but they include seven additional books. Tobit and Judith are placed after Nehemiah; Esther is followed by the books of the Maccabees; and Wisdom of Solomon and Jesus Sirach are placed after the Song of Songs, while Lamentations is followed by Baruch. In addition, Esther and Daniel are several chapters longer (the so-called "Additions to Esther and Daniel"). The greater extent of the Old Testament in Roman Catholic Bibles is due to the fact that the Roman Catholic Church, at the Council of Trent in 1545, canonized the Vulgate, with its more extensive collection of books, as sacred Scripture—a decision that was made as part of the Counter-Reformation. This conciliar decision, incidentally, is the sole canonical decree in Judaism and Christianity. In other words, only the Roman Catholic Church has fixed its Bible, by means of an authoritative decision, as containing a certain number of books. The greater extent of the Vulgate Old Testament rests in turn on the so-called Septuagint, the ancient Greek translation of the Old Testament.[84] From it comes also the difference in sequence between Christian and Jewish Bibles:[85]

Hebrew Bible	Septuagint
Torah ("Law")	*Historical Books*
Genesis	Genesis
Exodus	Exodus
Leviticus	Leviticus
Numbers	Numbers
Deuteronomy	Deuteronomy
Nevi'im ("Prophets")	
Joshua	Joshua
Judges	Judges
	Ruth
Samuel	1–4 Kings
Kings	
	1–2 Chronicles
	Ezra–Nehemiah
	Esther
	Judith
	Tobit
	1–4 Maccabees
Isaiah	
Jeremiah	
Ezekiel	
Book of the Twelve (Hosea, Joel, Amos, Obadiah, Jonah, Micah, Nahum, Habakkuk, Zephaniah, Haggai, Zechariah, Malachi)	

Ketuvim ("Writings")	Poetic Books
Psalms	Psalms
Job	Proverbs
Proverbs	Qoheleth
Ruth	Song of Songs
Song of Songs	Job
Qoheleth	Wisdom
Lamentations	Sirach
Esther	Psalms of Solomon
Daniel	
Ezra–Nehemiah	
Chronicles	
	Prophetic Books
	Book of the Twelve (Hosea, Amos, Micah, Joel, Obadiah, Jonah, Nahum, Habakkuk, Zephaniah, Haggai, Zechariah, Malachi)
	Isaiah
	Jeremiah
	Baruch
	Lamentations
	Letter of Jeremiah
	Ezekiel
	Daniel

As in the Hebrew tradition, we must also differentiate within the Greek tradition according to its manuscripts. As regards the sequence of books in the major LXX manuscripts we may observe the following details: common to the great codices ℵ (Sinaiticus), A (Alexandrinus), and B (Vaticanus) is that, for one thing, they place Ruth, according to its setting a quite fitting location, between Judges and 1 Samuel and, in addition, they follow Genesis–Kings not with the *corpus propheticum*, but with Chronicles. Apart from that, ℵ, A, and B go their separate ways: in ℵ and B Chronicles are followed by Ezra–Nehemiah; ℵ then continues with Esther, Tobit, Judith, and 1–4 Maccabees, thus establishing a great historiographical corpus from Creation to the Maccabees. In ℵ there then follow the prophets and the remaining writings. B follows Chronicles–Esther–Nehemiah with Psalms, Proverbs, Qoheleth, Song of Songs, Job, Wisdom of

Solomon, Sirach, Esther, Judith, and Tobit, putting the prophets in the final position. In A, Ezra–Nehemiah are separated from Chronicles; there Genesis–Kings + Chronicles are followed by the prophetic books and then the remaining writings. The LXX thus reveals a certain effort to put the historical traditions together and order them chronologically. This is especially marked in ℵ, but B's ordering also seems to have been formulated according to this principle, since the historical presentations in Genesis–Kings + Chronicles–Ezra–Nehemiah are followed first of all by the books of "David" (Psalms) and "Solomon" (Proverbs, Qoheleth, Song of Songs and, interrupted by Job, Wisdom of Solomon). Then come Sirach, Esther, Judith, Tobit, and finally the books of the prophets. Chronological considerations seem also to have determined the internal ordering of the prophets: Hosea, Amos, Micah, Joel, Obadiah, and Jonah, and following them the other "minor prophets," are placed before Isaiah, Jeremiah, Ezekiel, and Daniel, which in the LXX is also counted among the prophets. The placing of the "minor" prophets before the "great" ones also has the effect of bringing Isaiah, Jeremiah, and Ezekiel, with their messianic prophecies, and especially Daniel, with its vision of the Son of Man in chapter 7, closer to the New Testament that follows.

The Protestant churches, with their humanistically motivated approach to the Hebrew Bible, demanded that only the originally Hebrew books in the Old Testament canon should be retained, and placed the remaining books of the Septuagint and Vulgate Old Testament among the so-called Apocrypha or deuterocanonical books, which, while worth reading, are to be subordinated to the other scriptures in theological rank and value.[86]

Beyond the larger canon of the Old Testament in the Roman Catholic Church, there are the still more extensive canons of the Eastern churches, especially Ethiopian Christianity, which also include Enoch and Jubilees in their Old Testament.

The following presentation will concentrate on the Hebrew Old Testament in its standard order and will give only summary treatment to the other writings in more extensive canonical collections, which stem primarily from the Hellenistic period.

6. The Problem of an "Original Text" of the Old Testament

Since the Qumran discoveries in particular it has become clear that the commonly held idea of an "original text" of the Hebrew Bible, established at the canonization of each of its books, must be thoroughly reconsidered.[87] The biblical manuscripts in Qumran as well as the ancient versions reveal a highly diversified tradition of differing forms of texts of the same biblical books, so that we must first of all agree with Blum that "there are, in effect, as many final forms as there are textual witnesses"[88]—*the* biblical text does not exist anywhere, certainly not established in one particular textual witness. The diversity of the textual tradition around the turn of the era can perhaps be imagined as something like the current existence of numerous translations of the Bible alongside one another: they are recognizably editions of the same books, but they are not always identical in their wording and arrangement.

In any case we must restrain ourselves from projecting the single-version, letter-for-letter fidelity of the textual tradition in the rabbinic period onto the Old Testament of previous times. The fact that the multiplicity of texts after 70 C.E. attested in Qumran gave way to a standard consonantal text, as witnessed by the Masoretic manuscripts from the early Middle Ages, is not due to any particular magisterial decision but rather, if not exclusively then primarily, to the fact that the (Pharisaic-) Rabbinic school, the normative strand of tradition in Judaism after the Jewish War, used and preserved what is now known as the Masoretic textual tradition.

However, we should not be deceived by the divergent traditions found in Qumran. Van der Woude in particular has quite rightly pointed out that the conditions in Qumran cannot be generally assumed for Judaism before 70 C.E.[89] The texts found in Masada and Wadi Murabba'at do not attest to the same multiplicity as those at Qumran;[90] rather, they reveal a consonantal text belonging to the proto-Masoretic textual tradition, and the Greek scroll of the Twelve Prophets from Naḥal Ḥever, which should be dated to the second half of the first century B.C.E., already reveals a revision of the LXX in a proto-Masoretic direction.[91] This means, however, that *alongside* the multiplicity of texts attested in Qumran we can also perceive a tendency in pre-70 C.E. Judaism that exercised pressure toward a standardized text of the Bible. Van der Woude believes that, especially in the Second Temple in Jerusalem, a relatively unified textual tradition was preserved, namely that of the later Masoretes.[92] Thus we can retain the idea of an "original text" of the Hebrew Bible in another sense: there was never a pure canonical form of the biblical text, since the establishment of the canon apparently did not mean preserving the literal text in every respect, but there were proto-Masoretic forms of the later standard text that were shaped and handed down by groups in the Second Temple period that played a definitive role in the origins of the Hebrew Bible.

Text-critical scholarship has clearly perceived that in a number of biblical books such as Joshua, Samuel–Kings, Jeremiah, and Ezekiel, the Hebrew *Vorlage* that remains perceptible through the Septuagint is closer to this proto-standard text than the later Hebrew editions of these books that developed subsequently.[93] Correspondingly, the boundaries between literary criticism of prior stages and text-critical scholarship have become quite fluid.

7. Old Testament Literary History and Criticism within the Field of Old Testament Study

Where should we locate the project of a literary history of the Old Testament within Old Testament scholarship? It is customary to distinguish three subdisciplines within the latter: history of Israel, introduction to the Old Testament, and theology of the Old Testament. During the twentieth century, each of these fields has been documented by multiple textbooks.[94] Alongside these there were also presentations of Israel's religious history, traditionally understood as a historical supplement to the theology of the Old Testament,[95] but more recently intended by some scholars to serve as a substitute for it,[96] a proposal that has neither been successful in this form nor deserves to be.[97] However, the religious history of Israel in its traditional dimensions has achieved an eminently more elevated significance within the interplay of the sub-disciplines of Old Testament scholarship. In the last thirty years, on the one hand, there have been numerous new or newly revealed archaeological discoveries in the Levant.[98] On the other hand the historical evaluation of the Old Testament writings has changed dramatically within the study of Old Testament introduction, partly in correlation to the archaeological finds.[99] It has thus become clear that we must depict the image of the religion(s) of ancient Israel very differently from what is portrayed in the Bible and in the rationalizing paraphrases of traditional biblical scholarship that have followed its lead.[100]

Contrasting with the increased significance of the religious-historical approach is a strange lack of clarity in the division of labor among the three traditional sub-disciplines named above. The model often followed in the past, taking the history of Israel and introductory studies as preliminary disciplines in aid of a theology of the Old Testament as the synthetic major discipline, has run into difficulties since the epoch-making *Theology of the Old Testament* by Gerhard von Rad,[101] namely as regards the possibility of a synthesis of theology of the Old Testament. This has occurred primarily because von Rad's abandonment of any attempt at systematization other than "retelling" for the presentation of a theology of the Old Testament has either been accepted or other types of solutions have proved less persuasive. The abandonment of a systematic presentation—which led in von Rad's major work, especially within his disciplinary context, to a highly appealing result—in some sense brought about the greatest crisis in the sub-discipline "theology of the Old Testament" since its origins because, when understood in this way, it could no longer be distinguished in principle from introductory studies.[102] An added problem was the discovery of theology (and thus, simultaneously, theolog*ies*) *within* the Old Testament.[103] This made the business of a unified theology of the Old Testament throughout its historical development much more difficult and presented it with quite new difficulties that cannot be regarded as having since been surmounted, not even in a preliminary sense.

It remains to be seen how these intra-Old Testament difficulties in the organization of the sub-disciplines will be resolved. Since the ensemble of Old Testament scholarship remains in an unsettled state, the project of an Old Testament literary history, not a new project but newly of interest, can, on the one hand, profit from this situation, since the construction of syntheses is not exclusively claimed by other sub-disciplines (nor should it be). On the other hand, however, the other sub-disciplines can expect to profit from an Old Testament literary history, since it makes suggestions for a historical overview of the literary and theological relationships among the Old Testament texts and books, but from a new perspective.

8. Bases, Conditions, Possibilities, and Limitations of Historical Reconstruction

The Old Testament is not a book but a library, and the "books" in this library are not books in the modern sense, traceable to one single author for each.[104] In accordance with ancient Near Eastern practice, the "books" of the Old Testament represent the literature of traditions, not of authors.[105] This circumstance was acknowledged within the Bible itself and was made an explicit topic. A particularly clear example is found in the narrative in Jeremiah 36, which speaks of the preparation of a second scroll containing the words of Jeremiah, after King Jehoiakim had burned the first scroll: "Then Jeremiah took another scroll and gave it to the secretary Baruch son of Neriah, who wrote on it at Jeremiah's dictation all the words of the scroll that King Jehoiakim of Judah had burned in the fire; *and many similar words were added to them*" (Jer 36:32). The passive formulation does not, of course, exclude the possibility that these "similar words" were again Jeremiah's, but it clearly opens the horizon for continuations post-Jeremiah. Thus we can discover in the book of Jeremiah itself that it is not the work of Jeremiah alone, but was later continued at considerable length by others.

A similar example of the process of ongoing writing that is made explicit in the Bible is in Isa 16:13-14. After a lament on the suffering of the neighboring people of Moab we find the following final note: "This was the word that YHWH spoke concerning Moab in the past." Then follows a clarification: "But now YHWH says: In three years, like the years of a hired worker, the glory of Moab will be brought into contempt, in spite of all its great multitude; and those who survive will be very few and feeble." Thus Isa 16:13-14 attempts to judge Moab from an altered cultural-historical context, seeing it no longer empathetically but critically. That this verse is a continuation of the writing is clear from the combination of closing signature (16:13) and new interpretation (16:14).

Corresponding to these findings, the first author of a biblical book who is known to us by name appears only around 180 B.C.E. in the person of Jesus Sirach (Sir 50:27-29). We can observe the beginnings of an authorial self-awareness some decades earlier, in the use of "I" by Qoheleth.[106] Of course, a number of Old Testament books are attributed to particular persons in their respective *incipits*, their introductory verses, but these are not historical attributions to authors; they are statements of the authority to whom the traditions presented in the book are to be traced.[107] Thus also the writing scene in Jeremiah 36—however legendary it may or may not be—presents the situation in such a way that we are led to understand that Jeremiah himself did not write a single word of his own book. The "words of Jeremiah" in the book of Jeremiah were not written down by the "author" Jeremiah, but by his secretary, Baruch. Thus Jeremiah is not the author; he is the authority for his book.[108]

Overall, the texts of the Old Testament—setting aside for the moment the probable oral stages in the different spheres of tradition[109]—were created over a period of about eight hundred years.

> Finkelstein and Silberman and Schniedewind place a one-sided literary-historical accent on the pre-exilic period for the genesis of Old Testament texts.[110] Of course, the seventh century B.C.E. played a particularly important role in the literary formation of the Old Testament, but it is impossible to argue that it was essentially already complete before or during this epoch. Historical-critical biblical scholarship has assembled enough evidence to show that the Old Testament books in their present form were clearly influenced by the theology of the Judaism of the Persian and Hellenistic periods,[111] which does not exclude the incorporation of older materials. At the same time, however, the discipline has made it clear that the decisive formative processes for the Old Testament literature belong to a later period than the seventh century B.C.E.

The earliest texts of the Old Testament retained in a fixed literary form probably come from the early monarchical period—though their oral prehistory may be a great deal older.[112] The most recent (datable) texts are found in the book of Daniel, from the Maccabean era, in the chronological notes in the historical books (especially Genesis 5 and 11, cf. Exod 12:40 and 1 Kgs 6:1), in a few possibly Hasmonean psalms, and in the Masoretic pluses in the book of Jeremiah (cf. Jer 33:14-26). We get the impression from the writings found at Qumran that the Old Testament existed in its essentially "finished" form around 100 B.C.E., not yet as regards its literal shape, but probably in its content.[113] In any case it is clear that the great majority of the books of the Old Testament are composite literature that grew over a long period into their current textual state. No book of the Old Testament has been retained in its pre-exilic, monarchical-period form. The Old Testament as we have it is the product of Persian-period and Hellenistic Judaism.

How can these preliminary literary stages of Old Testament books be reconstructed within the period framed by their earliest and latest possible datings? Old Testament scholarship has developed a subtle set of instruments for this purpose that cannot be described in detail here, but some remarks on selected problems are in order.[114] First we should say that no Old Testament texts have survived from the Old Testament period. Even the earliest biblical manuscripts from Qumran are later than the latest additions to the Hebrew Bible.[115] In addition, most of the biblical writings from Qumran have survived only in a very fragmentary condition. The oldest complete textual witness for the Old Testament remains the Codex Petropolitanus (B 19A) from the year 1008 C.E.

It accords with this state of the material evidence that reconstructions of prior stages of the text must for the most part be founded on internal arguments. Traditionally, Old Testament literary criticism discusses different stages of growth of the biblical books primarily on the basis of the observation of doublets, breaks, tensions, and contradictions in the text.[116] But solely formal, text-immanent procedures have proved inadequate. They are in danger of privileging literary-aesthetic ideals from the formative period of historical-critical biblical scholarship (for example, the text-genetic evaluation of literary redundancies must not be done mechanically, but is a process to be tested in historical perspective).[117] In addition to this is a consideration based on a calculation of probabilities: even if we may suppose that the reconstruction of a prior literary stage has an 80 percent probability, this rate declines for Stage II to 64 percent, for Stage III to 51.2 percent, and by Stage IV the value falls below 50 percent, that is, the reconstruction becomes arbitrary.[118] Therefore linguistic observations must be supplemented by theological-conceptual considerations in reconstructing prior literary stages, that is, literary criticism must be coupled with theological-historical reflection. In the textbooks this is discussed with regard to the independence of the exegetical methods, which in itself is an obvious aspect of exegetical work but in practice is often neglected.[119] For a presentation of the history of Old Testament literature, it is also of crucial importance to give material weight to the different stages of literary development. That, of course, does not mean evaluating theological positions in the Old Testament from current perspectives; material weighting means identifying theological positions in the Old Testament that have proved themselves historically to be shaping factors for the inner-biblical discussion.

Finally, we may point to the important function of archaeology in the Levant as a test: the quantity of the epigraphic and especially the iconographic primary evidence for Israelite religion, especially from the last thirty years, reveals, in its historical arrangement, certain possibilities and limits to what can and cannot be imagined for a particular epoch in the literary history of the Old Testament.[120] It is obvious that a literary history cannot be written on the basis of archaeology; non-textual material is silent, and epigraphic evidence is too minimal[121]—but neither can a literary history be written without taking into account the cultural-historical framework set by archaeology.

9. Recent Trends in Old Testament Research and Their Consequences for a Literary History of the Old Testament

At the present time we can observe a certain upheaval in Old Testament scholarship that is significant for a literary-historical approach and is occasioned especially by three factors. First is the view of the cultural circumstances of the origins of the Old Testament writings, particularly from a cultural- and religious-historical point of view, which has been substantially altered by new archaeological findings (see A.I.6 above). In addition, inspired not least by new religious-historical insights—especially in the study of the historical books, prophecy, but also the Writings, particularly the Psalms—new perspectives on the historical genesis of these books have emerged, distinguishing today's scholarship greatly from the customary assumptions of twentieth-century Old Testament scholarship.[122] Finally, theology as a whole has become more pluralistic. In particular the strong influence of dialectical theology has declined. In the middle of the twentieth century it led much of Old Testament scholarship astray into religious-historical projections onto Israel and its neighbors of the fundamental distinction between revealed and natural theology. The decline of its influence has made some less biased views of the literary and archaeological findings possible in ancient Israel, though of course the biases of these views may be pointed out by future scholars.

The framing presuppositions for an overall picture of a history of the literature of the Old Testament now beginning to emerge are not new discoveries. The problematic represented by the Old Testament, as essentially a document of the ancient Judaism of the Persian and Hellenistic period, has been well known since the nineteenth century. It measures Israel's history by the central religious concepts of monotheism, covenant, and law, which because of their overwhelming importance have been placed by the biblical authors at the beginning of Israel's history. This important difference between biblical and historical Israel, however, has only been appropriated with adequate seriousness in scholarship in recent years. Some forerunners have proved more a hindrance than a help to the discussion, by addressing the problem only in partial ways and using extremely late dating schemes.[123] Nevertheless, the most recent Old Testament scholarship appears again here and there to be in danger of distancing itself from historical probabilities through simplistic dichotomizing between the pre-exilic and post-exilic periods, between earlier polytheism and later monotheism, between ancient Israel and Judaism,[124] between natural religion and revealed religion, and similar pairings. But the fact that Old Testament scholarship has changed fundamentally is not altered by these dangers.

Changing perspectives in Pentateuch research have played a special part in this upheaval.[125] Well into the twentieth century, the documentary hypothesis was amazingly successful, according to which there was a successive interweaving of the three sources J, E, and P, all of which presented much of the same content but as literary phenomena arose independently of one another. Ultimately this success can only be explained by the fact that this hypothesis relied both in an elementary and quite exclusive way on the initial observations of historical biblical criticism—the alternation between YHWH/Elohim and the discovery of textual doublets—and enjoyed the benefits of long-enduring familiarity to biblical scholars. In fact, however, the documentary hypothesis implied a number of basic assumptions that, when regarded in a clear light, are extraordinarily problematic. First of all, its thesis was based on the conviction that the overarching syntheses stood at the beginning of the construction of the tradition: the "Yahwist" located by Wellhausen in the monarchical period and since von Rad even regarded as belonging to the "Solomonic" reign is supposed to contain a description of history extending from creation to the conquest of the Land. This thesis postulates a unique case within the Old Testament tradition: for the Former Prophets (Joshua–2 Kings) as well as the Latter Prophets (Isaiah–Malachi), as well as for the Writings, it is assumed without question that their final shape and outline are different from the concept of their earliest components. In the Pentateuch, according to the documentary hypothesis, things are supposed to be fundamentally different. The recognition that this is not the case has emerged slowly among scholars only in the wake of Blum's influential studies on the composition of the patriarchal history and the Pentateuch.[126] The latter have evoked some consensus at least in some strands of European scholarship to the extent that for the literary beginnings of the Pentateuch we should probably reckon with sources with a limited literary horizon, which only in the (exilic or) early post-exilic period were embedded in comprehensive contexts.[127]

Thus we can see today, and in a strand of research that is no longer only marginal, a "farewell to the Yahwist,"[128] a movement that seeks to explain the composition of the Pentateuch without a pre-Priestly master narrative, particularly one which already would have provided a link between the patriarchs and the exodus. Of course, it is not yet certain whether this approach will prove enduring. But for many alternative new models it is also obvious that the great salvation-historical blueprints in the Pentateuch do not lie at the beginnings of the construction of the tradition but arose only toward the end. The same is true for the credo-type summaries of salvation history which were so important for Gerhard von Rad's interpretation of the sources of the Pentateuch.[129] Israel's religion(s) in the monarchical period can thus no longer be interpreted according to the paradigm of discontinuity between Israel and its neighboring cultures so common in the wake of von Rad. The latter showed Israel as believing in the one God who could not be pictured,[130] a God who revealed himself in history, while the neighboring religions divinized the phenonena of nature through polytheistic extrapolation.[131] The most recent studies of the Pentateuch not only make it possible, but even positively compel us to depict Israel's pre-exilic religious history within that of the Near East,[132] though here also we should warn against the danger of axiomatically leveling it into its Near Eastern contexts.

In the realm of prophecy we can observe a similar upheaval, even though it seems less obvious.[133] Classic scholarship described the prophets as spiritually gifted individual geniuses who presented their addressees with the will of God, directly conveyed to them and sometimes imposed on them, without condition or compromise. This prophetic image was derived by exegetes of the nineteenth and twentieth centuries through a distinction between original prophetic sayings and secondary additions. The exegesis of the prophetic books consisted essentially of cleaning the "genuine" textual material from its "non-genuine" additions, resulting in the presentation of the prophets as religious geniuses.

In terms of intellectual history, this classic image of the prophets was inspired primarily by idealism and romanticism. It dominated the nineteenth century and was substantially advanced by Wellhausen's late dating of the law after the prophets (*lex post prophetas*), which freed the prophets from the burden of being interpreters of the law. The fundamental characterization of the prophets' message as not from this world was very useful to dialectical theology, which extended the notion of the prophets as religious geniuses into the twentieth century. The isolated status of prophecy as its central characteristic still appears clearly in the epochal *Theology of the Old Testament* by Gerhard von Rad.[134] According to von Rad prophecy cannot be associated with the other ideas of faith within Israel, and therefore in a second volume he treated it separately from all other traditions.

However, alongside this classical strand of research there were other early voices that deliberately inquired not only about the prophets and their "genuine" words, but about the secondary additions as such, seeking to make them plausible as interpretive work carried out within the Bible.[135] This direction of inquiry—the so-called redaction-critical approach[136]—achieved its breakthrough in Old Testament scholarship especially in Walter Zimmerli's commentary on Ezekiel.[137] Today it is among the dominant approaches in research on the prophets. It deliberately no longer inquires exclusively about the prophets' proclamation, but also investigates the different accents and directions conveyed in their books, which belong to the literary post-history of the prophetic sayings written there.

Research on the prophets in the late nineteenth and twentieth centuries could be described as a process that reduced the texts attributed by the books' superscriptions to the prophet behind them to a literary body whose content was "critically" supported (often based on questionable standards), but nevertheless was in accordance with self-witness of the book—the portion of the book of Isaiah that comes from "Isaiah," the book of Jeremiah from "Jeremiah," etc. In contrast, today the weight has shifted from the prophets to their books, from their sayings to the texts of the books. The prophetic books have taken on increased significance as entities conveying meaning *as books*, and no longer as merely accidental collections of so-called smaller units, in which the ongoing theological value was found. In this regard we can, in fact, speak of a paradigm shift in prophets research, even though the inquiry into original prophetic sayings must retain some importance.

The exegetical concentration on the passages in the prophetic books that have customarily been regarded as non-genuine makes it more and more clear that these are not only glosses and textual errors, but in many if not most cases are to be interpreted as later interpretations of existing textual materials that themselves convey meaning. We should therefore regard the "expanders" not as amateur glossators but as scribal redactors who in turn could be seen as "prophets." For one thing, their scribal activity reveals an astonishing innovative ability. Furthermore, in their anonymous subordination to the figures who gave their names to the books on which they worked, they reveal themselves by their own self-conceptualization to be people who worked prophetically.

Prophecy is thus increasingly seen as a collective and long-term phenomenon, and no longer as bound to a particular point in time and an individual genius, and it is again being taken seriously as written prophecy. Not all prophecy was originally oral; large parts of the prophetic books never existed except in written form.[138] For individual prophetic books such as Joel, Jonah, or Malachi we may even suggest that they are entirely attributable to scribal activity. Behind them there is probably no individual prophetic figure whose written proclamation formed the basis for the further redactional history of the book. Instead, these books appear to be altogether the products of scribal prophetic tradents.

Finally, it is helpful to confront the upheavals in the most recent research on the Psalms. From a literary-critical point of view the dating of the Psalms remains notoriously in dispute. But recent Psalms scholarship has been able to show how thoroughly the Psalter has been shaped into a theological book.[139] This does not exclude, but rather includes, the idea that older individual psalms originally used in the cult of the First and/or Second Temple have made their way into the book. But in its existing form the Psalter is a carefully structured literary whole whose *Sitz im Leben* is to be sought more in the scribal studio than in worship. Something comparable may be observed in the Wisdom literature in the narrow sense, for example, in Proverbs.[140]

In summary—despite all the reservations one must have about such slogan-like characterizations—we may observe the following tendencies in the most recent research on the Old Testament, especially when focusing on the European discussions:

1. The assumption of a salvation-historical shaping of Israel's religion from the beginning is untenable in its classic form. In particular, the hypothesis of a "Yahwist" that is so important as its foundation is unable to bear this weight.[141]

2. "Sub-Deuteronomistic" interpretations of the Old Testament that are based on a fundamental agreement between the sequence of epochs in biblical and historical Israel must be critically questioned.[142]

3. From a religious-historical perspective we can observe a certain (renewed) convergence in the description of Israel's monarchical-period religion(s) and neighboring religions.

4. In contrast to traditional ideas, the exilic and post-exilic periods are clearly being emphasized more as crucial phases in the formation of the Old Testament literature.

5. The "religious geniuses" so blithely proposed in the nineteenth and twentieth centuries are no longer believed to monopolize literary production in the Old Testament. Instead, it is apparent that the Old Testament literature, over broad stretches, is the literature of scribal interpretation.[143]

II. Language, Writing, Books, and Literary Production in Ancient Israel

1. Language and Writing

The Hebrew Bible (with Aramaic passages found in Ezra–Nehemiah and in Daniel; cf. also Jer 10:11) essentially falls into two subsections that can be called "classical/standard biblical Hebrew" and "late biblical Hebrew."[144] What is here called "classical biblical Hebrew" is essentially the language of the Torah and the Priestly and/or Deuteronomistic redacted literature in Genesis–2 Kings. "Late biblical Hebrew" can be found especially in Chronicles literature as well as Esther and Daniel, though these go their own way in some specific respects. The distinction between "classical biblical Hebrew" and "late biblical Hebrew" is essentially based on a comparison of biblical texts with two extra-biblical text corpora, namely the royal inscriptions and the Qumran literature.[145] "Classical biblical Hebrew" is a language of the learned, closely connected with the "Judahite-Hebrew" of the monarchical period and preserving it in a more and more Aramaic-speaking environment.[146] In accordance with its character as a language of scholars, "classical biblical Hebrew" has a relatively homogeneous form. "Late biblical Hebrew" can, in turn, be described as a further development of "classical biblical Hebrew." Contrary to the opinion frequently expressed that the transition from classical to late biblical Hebrew took place during the exile,[147] in view of newer research on Genesis–Kings we must instead presume that the most important biblical texts for "late biblical Hebrew" can scarcely be located earlier than 400 B.C.E.[148] In any case, the Hebrew of biblical texts is not solely determined by their chronology. Instead, the choice of language also indicates conceptual closeness to or distance from normative core traditions in the Torah: the books of Job or Qoheleth use a Hebrew that does not conform to the Torah because of their theological dissidence, while late Joshua or Judges texts can be closely paralleled with the classical biblical Hebrew of the Torah and the older parts of those same books.[149]

Hebrew, like Aramaic, is written in an alphabet of twenty-two characters. Inscriptions demonstrate that by the ninth century B.C.E. the direction of writing (from right to left) had been established. This is likewise an indication that longer texts requiring such conventions existed only from this point onward. Until the third century B.C.E. the old Hebrew script—in itself richly varied—was in use; it was also used occasionally in later periods, by the Samaritans for example. Some Qumran manuscripts are also written in old Hebrew, though these are only biblical manuscripts from the Torah and the book of Job, which was understood to be from the patriarchal era. The quadratic (Aramaic) writing probably began to spread as a result of the use of Aramaic for governmental documents in the Persian period. Its oldest attestation is in the inscription of *Iraq el-Emir* east of the Jordan (third century B.C.E.). Prior stages of this process can be observed in the texts from Elephantine.[150] In Qumran only a few scrolls (Torah and Job) were written in an archaic style, and sometimes the Tetragrammaton was written in old Hebrew script; otherwise quadratic writing predominated.

In antiquity Hebrew texts were unvocalized; only a few vowel letters (*matres lectionis*) appear in ancient Hebrew inscriptions, and mainly in the final position of the word. In Qumran, by contrast, they are very common and can also stand for short vowels within the word. The punctuation familiar today is the work of the Masoretes of the fifth to tenth centuries C.E. The customary Tiberian pointing was used interlinearly, while the Babylonian pointing, only familiar to scholarship since the nineteenth century, was supralinear.

2. Material Aspects of Literary Production

For historical inquiry about the origins of the Old Testament writings it is necessary to imagine the possibilities and conditions for the production of books and literature in the ancient world. Sources for this inquiry are information from the Old Testament (cf., for example, Ezekiel 1–3; Jeremiah 36) as well as the epigraphic evidence from Old Testament times and finally, and especially prominent, the scrolls from Qumran.[151] Despite the caution that must be exercised due to the lack of contemporary Old Testament textual evidence, we can say that books were commonly written in the form of scrolls (cf. Isa 34:4).[152] The codex, bound at the spine, appeared only in the Christian era. Writing was done on papyrus or parchment; papyrus was cheaper and was accordingly used most frequently. For longer texts—the Qumran text of the book of Isaiah fills a scroll eight meters long—only parchment was appropriate, since papyrus could not be rolled to any extent because of its brittle nature. From a purely technical standpoint much longer scrolls were possible; these may in some cases have extended to twenty-five meters.[153] The scrolls were made up of individual sheets sewn together and divided into columns before being written on (cf. Jer 36:23). When the scroll was read, only the column actually being read needed to be made visible, while the preceding and following content could remain rolled up.

In the Qumran trove the text is not in *scriptio continua*, but has spaces between words. There are also divisional marks such as longer spaces within the lines, *alinea* (indentation at the beginning of a new line), space at the end of lines, and blank lines, all serving to structure the text into meaningful units.[154]

3. Socio-Literary Aspects of the Production and Reception of Literature

For an understanding of the literary-historical emergence of the Old Testament it is indispensable to envision the circumstances: the texts were produced and received within a comparatively narrow circle that was adequately familiar with reading and writing and existed within a largely illiterate society.[155] Comparable material from Greece and Egypt points in the same direction.[156] Although the ability to read and write was restricted to a small portion of the population, the existence of a professional class of writers attests that the remainder of the people were not entirely illiterate. We should, rather, make a distinction: there is no precise boundary between literacy and illiteracy; the mastery of reading and writing was, then as now, a gradual process. A little note attesting to the delivery of goods like those appearing, for example, in the Samarian ostraca could undoubtedly be deciphered by a broader circle than the Siloam inscription or a prophetic book.

Contrary to the witness of the Old Testament itself, which asserts that some small sections of the Pentateuch were written by Moses (cf. Exod 17:14; 24:4; 34:28; Num 33:2), it appears that writing and scribal culture only developed in Israel in the ninth century B.C.E. (in Judah in the eighth century B.C.E.) to such an extent that we can reckon with the production of extensive literary works: "Hebrew literature, however, first flowered only in this period [i.e., the century from 850–750]."[157] This is indicated, in addition to general findings on the cultural-historical development of Israel and Judah that can be associated with scribal culture, by the historical distribution of old Hebrew inscriptions.[158] While there is no statistical basis on which to ground the assumption, nevertheless the distribution of inscriptions is related to the rise of literacy.

Numbers of Inscriptions in Israel[159]

Tenth century	4	inscriptions
Ninth century	18	inscriptions
Eighth century, first half	16	inscriptions
Eighth century, second half	129	inscriptions
Seventh century, first half	50	inscriptions
Seventh century, second half	52	inscriptions
Sixth century, beginning	65	inscriptions

The newly discovered abecedary from Tel Zayit can be dated to the late tenth century B.C.E. and is claimed by those who excavated the site as testimony to the establishment of schools in this period as a consequence of the increasing bureaucratization of Judah.[160] Whether it suffices to correct this general picture in fundamental ways remains questionable at the moment.

The opposite conclusion, that the lack of *Hebrew* inscriptions in the Persian period should cause us to think that the Old Testament was essentially created in the pre-exilic period,[161] has all the historical probabilities against it. Of course, the inscriptions of the Persian period were composed in the *lingua franca* of the time, namely Aramaic, but their number is materially greater than that of the Hebrew inscriptions.[162] In principle, the numerical total of the Persian-period inscriptions is further confirmation of the importance of the Persian epoch for the origins of the Old Testament literature rather than a refutation of it. In any case, the statistical findings must be interpreted with caution since most of the written texts from this period were inscribed on materials that have not survived the intervening centuries (papyrus in particular), and the surviving inscriptions, especially the ostraca, only fragmentarily reflect the writing culture. At the same time, the overall impression is significant, especially since it parallels two further observations.

For one thing, we should mention the fact that *written* prophecy in Israel and Judah appears only when there was the rise of a certain degree of literary culture, namely in the eighth century B.C.E. Wellhausen had already noted that not a single book of Elijah has been handed down, but there is one from Isaiah.[163] Between them lies the rise of a writing culture that included not only this Isaiah, but also Amos or Hosea and/or their tradents.

In addition, the fact that only from this point onward Israel and, somewhat later, Judah are recorded in ancient Near Eastern sources as states converges with the simultaneous rise of literary culture.[164] This in turn leads us to conclude that this stage of development includes also the development of a writing culture.

There is some evidence to the contrary, however: two of the most extensive inscriptions from the geographical area in question, the Mesha Stele[165] and the Balaam inscription from Tel Deir Alla[166] belong to the early period (ninth century B.C.E. and eighth/seventh centuries B.C.E.), and also—from a geographical point of view—come from the periphery. These findings caution against a too narrow and mechanical coupling of advanced state culture and writing, but in turn they should not be regarded as the sole valid parameters.

It is of further consequence for literary production that the Old Testament books were probably originally composed, as a rule, as separate and unique pieces. Their character as agglutinating interpretive literature points in this direction: it is scarcely imaginable that a multilevel continuous process of writing biblical books—and their different textual witnesses refute any attempts to dispute such a process—could have been carried out, simply from a technical standpoint, if numerous copies of the books had been in circulation.[167] This assumption can be further supported by information from the Old Testament itself. The instruction in Deut 17:18, for example, is significant: "When [the king] has taken the throne of his kingdom, he shall have a copy of this law written for him in the presence of the Levitical priests." This text does not demand that the king should have *a* copy of the Deuteronomic Law made; rather, it assumes that the copy the king will have made will remain the sole copy alongside the original. Likewise, 2 Chron 17:7-9; Neh 8:1-2; and 2 Macc 2:13-15 can be read similarly as pointing to a very limited circulation of Old Testament books during Old Testament times. 2 Maccabees 2:15 shows that in the second century B.C.E. even the Jewish community in Alexandria did not possess a complete Bible.[168] The limited spread of biblical writings is not surprising, given that their production was an arduous process and scrolls were correspondingly costly. In the rabbinic period a new scroll of Isaiah would have cost half the annual income of a scribe.[169]

It appears that the Jerusalem Temple played a special role in literary production. We may suppose that the model manuscripts were preserved there, forming the basis for an ongoing process of copying and augmentation.[170] Second Maccabees 2:13-15 speaks of a library in Jerusalem founded by Nehemiah; its contents ("the books about the kings and prophets, and the writings of David, and letters of kings about votive offerings"), however—as the striking omission of the Torah may show—were apparently described only eclectically, or in the sense of an "Enneateuch" (in which case the Torah would be the prophecy of Moses) and Latter Prophets and Psalms.[171] This would have been the library of the Jerusalem Temple. Similarly, the story of the finding of the book in the temple by the priest Hilkiah in 2 Kings 22, as well as 1 Sam 10:25, indicates that the Old Testament imagined a collection of books in the Temple. Its extent is hard to determine. Most libraries in the ancient Near East were selections and contained a modest number of texts.[172] For the temple library in Edfu some thirty-five titles are attested.[173] These libraries were not public, but were reserved to the use of the temple and its schools, so that in the ancient Near East there was often no strict division between library and archives. In addition it seems that there were, though much more rarely, library collections whose purpose was to bring together all the texts that could possibly be assembled. Examples of this sort are Ashurbanipal's library, the library of Alexandria, and probably also that in Qumran. It is difficult to determine the extent of the Jerusalem library: 2 Macc 2:13-15 indicates that it probably contained more than merely what would later be the Old Testament literature. This is further supported by the Qumran writings: it is hard to imagine that the library of Qumran, which extended far beyond the Old Testament, could have been larger than the temple library in Jerusalem.[174]

There is no reason to suppose that there was a homogeneous milieu of Jerusalem scribes. Although the groups responsible for the origins of the Old Testament books were probably very limited and located mainly in Jerusalem, at least from the Persian period onward, they appear to have represented a relatively broad spectrum of theological ideas. At any rate, the sometimes almost contrary viewpoints of the materials that now stand alongside one another in the biblical books point in that direction.

Our historical knowledge about scribes and scribal schools in ancient Israel is very limited.[175] That there were professional scribes is adequately attested both by the Bible itself and by surviving seal impressions from the monarchical period onward.[176] See, for example, 2 Sam 8:17; 1 Kgs 4:3; Jeremiah 32, 36, 43, 45 ("Baruch the scribe"); Ezra 7:6, 12-26 ("Ezra . . . a scribe skilled in the law of Moses that YHWH the God of Israel had given"); Neh 13:2-3; Sirach 38–39; Mark 11:27-33; Matthew 23. In the course of history their function shifted more and more toward that of scriptural scholarship, and they became a class that was responsible not only for writing (constantly needed because of the short lifespans of those handing on the texts), but also for the continued interpretation of the texts they produced and preserved (cf. Jer 36:32).[177]

Since August Klostermann it has usually been assumed that the scribes received their education in the schools associated with the temple or the royal palace.[178] However, there is scarcely any mention of these in the Bible (only Sir 51:23; Acts 19:9). Their existence is deduced from cultural-historical analogies, which is not fundamentally problematic in itself.[179] However, it does not seem like a good idea to draw a strict distinction between temple and palace schools: the temple was not an independent institution, but was dependent on the royal court.[180] The Talmudic tradition speaks of 480 schools in Jerusalem, which is probably an exaggeration.[181] But in any case there may well have been a number of schools from the Hellenistic period onward, especially in Jerusalem. We need not necessarily think of separate buildings for such schools; what was central to them was the teacher-pupil relationship (1 Chr 25:8; Prov 5:12-14; Ps 119:99). The students' instruction may have taken place in chambers within the temple or in the teacher's private rooms.[182]

Some scholars consider the very lack of attestation of schools in ancient Israel to be significant and attribute the education of scribes more to the handing on of knowledge within scribal "families." We should probably combine both ideas, as they are not mutually exclusive. This is suggested, for example, by the existence of the Jerusalemite Shaphanide family (cf. 2 Kgs 22:3; Jeremiah 36), which was closely associated with the royal palace and the temple.

4. Authors and Redactors

In earlier scholarship the distinction between authors and editors or redactors was highly important in discerning the origins of the Old Testament. Its literary substance was thought to come from authors, such as the Yahwist or Isaiah, and that substance was continued in texts by later "expanders" or "theologians," who were traditionally viewed negatively. Bernhard Duhm, for example, put forth the pointed opinion that they carried on their thinking "with very little authorial skill" and altogether "beneath the prophetic level."[183] While in spite of this they "occasionally" offered "quite significant ideas," it was nevertheless true that "these ideas were not created by those who present them to us; they are the result of the great intellectual history" in which their authors were only "passive participants." Even the important presentation by Herbert Donner defines the redactors simply as mediatory compilers of existing texts.[184] It was only recent redaction-critical research that has been able to show that this image is deficient. Of course, we can perceive a great many text complexes in the Old Testament that are purely compilations. But we will reach faulty conclusions if we limit textual redaction in the Old Testament to such processes: beyond these there are, among other things, broad redactional passages that develop their own concepts and theologies, so that a categorical distinction between author and redactor is often untenable.[185]

John Van Seters has offered an original discussion of the relationship between authors and redactors that is as eccentric as it is occasionally instructive. His conclusion "that there never was in antiquity anything like 'editions' of literary works that were the result of an 'editorial' process, the work of editors or redactors,"[186] is overdrawn and fails to recognize the current discussion among scholars about an objective view of the phenomenon of "redaction" in Old Testament literature.[187] Still, Van Seters rightly points to deficiencies and problems in form-critical and other historical attempts at clearer pictures of some supposed Old Testament "redactions." Closer scrutiny shows that Van Seters is not so far from the position he opposes, but he takes a very different perspective on the biblical texts and their genesis. While the redaction-critical research he attacks distinguishes a basic layer and later redactions, he investigates the supposed works within the Bible that he sees as the work of authors he characterizes as ancient historiographers ("Yahwist," "Deuteronomistic History," etc.), and about the traditions they incorporate but that, in his opinion, can no longer be extracted from the text but were "authorially" edited. One should also consider the fact that Van Seters almost exclusively considers the narrative traditions in Genesis–2 Kings and the historical work, as he proposes it, of the Yahwist and the Deuteronomist; he scarcely incorporates any of the literary relationships in prophecy and Psalms into his reflections.

The phenomenon of (authorial or) redactional work on the Old Testament must, in fact, be differentiated. First we must ask how earlier material became part of a particular text. Does it preserve memories of older, likewise oral traditions or traditional material that have entered into it but can no longer be reconstructed as prior levels of text?[188] Or does it edit existing material that can still be extracted as such from its present context by source-critical methods? In the second case it is helpful in principle to distinguish redactional insertions and editing according to their respective literary horizons: Is a particular redactional method directed only at the immediate surrounding context of the insertion, or does it apply to a section of the book, a whole book, or even a sequence of books? In any case these different possibilities must be considered. It is useless to declare that one or the other approach constitutes a general theory, since it is not difficult to demonstrate that in this regard different redactional methods were applied in the writing of the Old Testament. An example of an expansion that influenced only the immediate context is found in 1 Sam 9:9, where it is explained that r'h, "seer," is an archaic word for nby', "prophet." The superscriptions of Amos 3:1 and 5:1 have a larger section of the book in view: they serve to structure Amos 3–6 as a whole.[189] Isaiah 35, inserted as a bridge text between First and Second Isaiah, serves as part of a redaction of the entire book; it is the first step in creating the book of Isaiah as a whole, which was then in process.[190] Perhaps the clearest example of a redactional level that extends over several books, then, is found in the sequence of statements tracing the transfer of Joseph's bones from Egypt to Canaan in Gen 50:25; Exod 13:19; and Josh 24:32; which, thanks to their references forward and backward, are demonstrably unimaginable except as parts of a single literary layer.[191]

5. The Contemporary Audience for the Old Testament Literature

For whom were the Old Testament texts and writings composed? This question is very difficult to answer and must in large part remain open. Probably various narratives, sayings, or songs that were later incorporated in the narrative books, the prophets, Psalms, or Proverbs were delivered orally before a variety of audiences before or at the time they were recorded in writing. Publication through reading aloud, for example, is presumed by Hab 2:2: "Then

Yhwh answered me and said: Write the vision; make it plain on tablets, so that a runner may read it."[192]

But it is by no means the case that the whole Old Testament was intended from the outset or exclusively as oral literature or to be read aloud. This must be emphasized, in particular against the classic form-criticism of Gunkel and his followers. For texts that we may suppose that oral stages existed, we can say scarcely anything more than that it took place. The approach used here can restrict itself to the question of who read the texts of the Old Testament in their written form, whether they go back to prior oral stages or not. Even though we again cannot arrive at any sure conclusions, we can say with probability that over long stretches the Old Testament literature was written by scribes for scribes—whether these worked at the temple or the palace. In other words, the audience was essentially identical with the authors themselves. This seems especially likely because of the extreme degree of intertextuality in the Old Testament literature, which was evidently addressed to a particularly well-educated group of recipients.[193]

How ought we imagine the process of reading among ancient Israel's scribal class? Psalm 1:2 may give us a clue: the scribe described here "meditates" or, as we should more properly translate the Hebrew verb *hgh*, "mumbles" the Scripture day and night. Of course this is an exaggerated picture, but the reading process pictured here as a meditative "mumbling" is revealing inasmuch as "reading" in this cultural-historical context evidently did not simply mean reading through a text once from beginning to end, but studying it while reading it half aloud. Silent reading was very unusual in antiquity.[194]

This study of Scripture was the indispensable precondition for a scribe's activity: to judge by cultural-historical analogies, they were so embedded in tradition that when they were writing their texts, they did not always—in fact, probably very seldom—have at hand the written works on which they drew and to which they referred. Instead it appears that they were trained as scribes by immersion in classical literature, and that they memorized the essential texts.[195] The texts of the Old Testament were thus very present to the scribes of ancient Israel, but not necessarily in material form and more essentially in their minds. A particularly clear example of a scribal "patchwork" prophecy is found in Jer 49:7-22, which is most easily explained as a combination of several other prophetic passages (Obad 8-9; Jer 49:30, 32; Jer 25:8-11, 15-29; Obad 1-4; Jer 50:13, 40, 44-46; 48:40-41), which the author of Jer 49:7-22 recombined from memory.[196]

The degree to which reading and memorization were linked in Israel's writing culture can, finally, be illustrated by Ostracon III from Lachish, where a military commander boasts of being able to recite a letter from memory as soon as he has read it (ll. 10-13): "Every letter that comes to me, once I have read it, then I can recite it back in its entirety."[197]

6. Elements of Form-Critical Development

Even if a literary-historical description of the Old Testament cannot proceed today as Gunkel's once did, his question about the origins and history of the literary genres is still of enduring value,[198] so long as one does not attempt to use it as a vehicle for obtaining indirect insight into the spiritual and intellectual life of ancient Israel. Current research evaluates a great deal more of the textual material in the Old Testament as having been written from the beginning than was the case fifty years ago. Nevertheless, the traditional conviction in the wake of Gunkel and Scandinavian biblical scholarship in the first half of the twentieth century, that the Old Testament is essentially made up of written oral tradition, is still appropriate for the Old Testament inasmuch as the Old Testament seems to present itself in that way over broad expanses of the text. This is especially evident in the prophetic books and the Psalms. With the possible exception of Haggai, Jonah, and Malachi, the prophetic books appear to be collections of small units that were originally independent prophetic oracles—even if, in terms of literary history, this is only partly the case. We may even speculate whether the "small units" are a product of writing, since (except in the case of the Neo-Assyrian oracles of salvation) they are not clearly attested outside the Bible. It is possible that they are more representative of how people imagined prophets than of the way prophets actually spoke. In addition, we get the initial impression upon reading the Psalms that these texts are songs and prayers. That, too, is not false, but it is inaccurate as a general literary-critical evaluation. Something similar can be said, within the third part of the Hebrew canon, for the books of Proverbs, Lamentations, and Song of Songs. If we look at the historical books we can clearly see that, despite the more or less harmonious chronological and narrative progress from Genesis to 2 Kings, the substance of the tradition presented here also appears, at least, to rest on short narratives: individual pericopes are strung together, but in themselves they often reveal a striking narrative self-sufficiency or semi-autonomy.

Above all it is observations on the intertextual interweaving of many of these pieces, and their dependence on literary context, that make it impossible to conclude that they were originally oral material. But what seems to be historically inaccurate can certainly be the result of a deliberate literary presentation. The Old Testament intends to present itself not so much as a scribal literature but much more as originally oral. The reason for this choice is obvious in view of the respect for antiquity in the ancient world:[199] the Old Testament is intended as traditional, not innovative literature, and where it is innovative, then it does so in traditional garb.

If we look a little more closely at the tradition we can move beyond these general observations. The biblical books are indeed clearly more than (partly

constructed) florilegia of small units. Rather, they have experienced numerous thoroughgoing processes of shaping that have further developed their still
visible character as collections. Thus there are also points from which we can
see indications of the structuring of innovative genres that were literary from
the outset.

Thus, for example, in various prophetic books (or parts thereof), such as
Isaiah 1–39, the Septuagint translation of Jeremiah, Ezekiel, or Zephaniah we
find a comparable organization of the book according to the so-called "three-
part eschatological scheme,"[200] which embeds small textual units in larger
contexts and serves to establish the genre "prophetic book." The Psalter as a
whole is comprehensively structured in terms of the Chronicler's view of history.[201] The individual narratives and narrative cycles in the patriarchal history
were shaped in terms of the promises into extended compositions.[202] Impulses
leading to the construction of new major literary genres (at least in the Old
Testament) seem also to have come from without: Deuteronomy in its form as
"loyalty-oath" follows Neo-Assyrian form-critical conventions.[203] The Priestly
document may have been inspired by the royal inscriptions of the Persian
period. The book of Job seems virtually to rest on a form-critical combination of *Ludlul bēl nēmeqi*[204] and the Babylonian theodicy.[205] It remains difficult
to say how much the genre of the Joseph story was influenced by the Egyptian
narrative of the two brothers;[206] in any case it is striking that it clearly stands
apart from Genesis 12–36 as a well-rounded composition. In its novella form
it seems to have influenced the formation of books like Esther, Ruth, Judith,
and Tobit.

The formal literary language of the Old Testament is thus largely traditional, but also highly subject to intercultural influences. The overarching
processes of formation of the biblical books, in which from time to time
multiple "book forms" were layered on top of one another, were not based
on spectacular interventions on the surface of the texts.[207] Still, they are
perceptible and show an awareness among the Old Testament authors and
redactors that both books and parts of books could be the vehicles of theological statements.

Finally, the construction of a canon can be seen as the end point of the
form-critical development of the Old Testament literature, though—except
for the later New Testament—it remains without a genuine parallel in the
ancient world. As we will show later (in part H, sections I and II), there can
be no doubt that the canonical and literary histories of the Old Testament
are not phenomena that can be separated, certainly not as successive. Instead,
they are mutually interactive. The Old Testament canon is an entity that conveys meaning, and its overarching theological perspectives are anchored in
corresponding entries that are placed within the text itself, with a deliberate eye toward the canon (cf., e.g., Deut 34:10-12; Josh 1:7-8; Mal 3:22-24;
Psalm 1).

III. Methods and Presentation

1. *The Cultural Impact of the Ancient Near Eastern Empires and the Periodization of Old Testament Literature*

The question of periodization is a matter of widespread discussion in the fields of literary and historical theory.[208] At any rate it should be clear that epochs may not be stylized into quasi-hypostatic entities, nor can we do without the concept of epochs altogether if we are to understand historical or literary-historical processes in broad strokes. Therefore, for an Old Testament literary history the concept of epochs can neither be exalted nor altogether abandoned. Rather, it serves the elementary structuring of its development.[209]

The basic decisions about the reconstructed picture of a history of Old Testament literature are usually discernible from its overall structure: recall, for example, the distinctions chosen by Gunkel, who divided the Old Testament literature into the epochs of popular literature of the early period, that of the great authorial personalities, and that of the epigones. This reveals his high estimation of the literary geniuses from Isaiah to Deutero-Isaiah as the center of his proposed literary-historical triptych.

As easy as it is today to identify the limits of Gunkel's approach, it is equally difficult to go beyond them in any meaningful way without simply producing a new Procrustean bed for the intellectual and spiritual history of ancient Israel. The following consideration, however, seems in order: in accord with the recent sensitivity among Old Testament scholars to religious-historical factors, it seems appropriate to divide up and interpret the Old Testament literature on the basis of a cultural-historical comparison with the contemporary hegemonic powers in the Near East.[210] The Old Testament is to be understood not as an isolated entity, but primarily as a part of the ancient Near East. This insight justifies the decision to see the first step in a periodization of the Old Testament literature as starting from the cultural impact of the empires of the ancient Near East that were so central in Israel's history, especially from the Assyrian period onward.[211] When looking at the political history from the Assyrian to the Persian empires, it is clear that the military oppression that was still the central element in securing the imperial power of the Assyrian Empire was increasingly substituted with a culturalization of power that secured the existence of a great empire in an alternative fashion.[212] Correspondingly, the foreign rule of the Persians, for example, is regarded much more positively in the Old Testament than that of the Assyrians, not least, of course, because the culturalization of Persian power was essentially more pluralistic in orientation than the Assyrian propaganda.

Given the widely scattered archaeological findings, there is no doubt about the fundamental possibility of geographically far-reaching cultural contacts in the ancient Near Eastern.[213] The Babylonian Adapa myth is attested in Egyptian Amarna; in Ugarit (northern Syria) people were familiar with the Atrahasis epic; the epic of Gilgamesh was read in Megiddo in northern Israel; and as fragmentary evidence shows, an Aramaic version of the Iranian Behistun inscription was known on the Nile island of Elephantine. Cultural contacts within the ancient Near East were so close that Israel's central position and its almost constant political dependence on various great powers on the Euphrates and the Nile (within the so-called Fertile Crescent) from the eighth century B.C.E. onward made it not only possible, but highly probable that the then-current basic cultural and religious concepts were known in Israel and interacted with, whether through rejection or acceptance.

However, we should clearly emphasize that the Old Testament literature does not revolve around reactions (positive or negative) to ancient Near Eastern imperial ideologies in historical sequence. Every form of "parallelomania" should therefore be avoided.[214] But some of the crucial literary and theological concepts in the Old Testament can only be adequately described in historical terms if we compare them to their ancient Near Eastern counterparts.

To choose but a few examples from the presentation that follows: this is especially obvious, for example, in the fundamental idea of Deuteronomy and the tradition that followed it, which clearly borrows from Neo-Assyrian covenant theology that demanded unconditional loyalty from vassals toward the Assyrian monarch and reformulates it toward YHWH.[215] There is a comparable case in the anti-monarchical reception of the legend of the birth of Sargon, drawn from Neo-Assyrian tradition, in Exodus 2.[216]

The exilic interpretations of the Pentateuch's legal traditions may be directed against the Babylonian, monarchical tradition of law; in the Pentateuch the law is revealed by YHWH and promulgated by Moses.[217] The extended depiction of Solomon's building of the temple in 1 Kings 6–8 is to be interpreted against either an Assyrian[218] or a Babylonian background.[219] That kings are primarily temple-builders is a prominent *topos*, especially in Neo-Babylonian royal inscriptions. Furthermore, the evaluation formula in the book of Kings "he did what was right" has its closest parallels in the Neo-Babylonian chronicles.[220]

Similarly context-bound are the Priestly Document and texts allied with it that take up the Persian idea of a peaceful, yet culturally differentiated world order, reproducing it from an Israelite point of view.[221] Persian influences can also be seen in the idea of a succession of world empires in the older parts of the book of Daniel.[222]

Finally, the wisdom texts in Proverbs 1–9[223] or in Qoheleth, which are in dialogue with Greek popular philosophy,[224] cannot be adequately understood without their Hellenistic background.

Thus the current state of research offers both the possibility and the necessity of interpreting ancient Israelite literature in its ancient Near Eastern context, free from the pseudo-theological limitations of the period of the

"Babel-Bible controversy."[225] The originality of the Bible lies not in the immunity of its materials to analogy, but in their interpretations and transformations, none of which can be adequately understood without looking beyond the Bible itself.

2. Historical Contextualization

In the nature of the question itself a literary history of the Old Testament must consider its texts and writings against the background of Israel's history. Accordingly, the individual sections on the epochs of the Old Testament literature will be introduced by brief overviews of the historical backgrounds of each, intended only to point out some elementary framing circumstances of the experiences of that time period; these short remarks cannot manage more than that. The fact that they place a certain accent on political history without attempting to eliminate social- and economic-historical aspects is due to the fact that if not all, at least the central theological positions in Old Testament literature are formulated as "political theologies" (for example, the Jacob traditions, Deuteronomy, the Priestly Document, or the prophetic literature).[226] That is, from the Assyrian period onward these theologies were intimately connected with observation of the world events of the time, which often had radical consequences for Israel and Judah.

The methodological problem, that the reconstruction of Israel's history in itself rests at least in part on a critical analysis of the corresponding Old Testament writings and thus appears to present a certain circularity of argument as regards the interaction of history and literature in a particular epoch, must be kept in mind, but it should not be overestimated. In recent scholarship the reconstruction of Israel's history has been comparatively well supported by non-biblical sources and by archaeology, in particular for the historical overlap between Israel's history and the literary history of the Old Testament, which does not begin, in essence, before the eighth century B.C.E., so that from many points of view it is independently demonstrable.

3. Theological Characterizations

In accordance with its introductory character, the following presentation of the various literary-historical epochs of the Old Testament is not consistently analytical or deductive in its construction. Instead there is an attempt, prior to the description of the different individual literary-historical positions in an epoch, to sketch a subtle theological characterization of the literary witnesses of that epoch in historical terms. It should be noted that this is not about *religious*-historical findings but about *theological* positions that can be reconstructed from the Old Testament literature and their possible connections and oppositions.

When presenting some basic tenets of the theological character of the individual Old Testament writings, this will necessarily involve an element of anticipation in the argumentation. However, this is not meant to insinuate that prior or even final decisions have been made about them. The advantage of this method is that the various texts from a single epoch can be introduced through a rapid sketch, with the result that they can be interpreted within their literary-historical contexts.

4. Form-, Tradition-, and Social-Critical Distinctions in the Spheres of Tradition

Historical distinctions regarding a text's genesis belong, naturally, in the foreground of a literary-historical description of the Old Testament. But it should not be forgotten that separating different literary layers within a text presents, from among the many possible, significant, or necessary distinctions that could be made, only one of many ways that the Old Testament can be perceived as literature. After all, these texts and books were not only written, expanded, redacted, and edited in different time periods. Their authors also lived in different intellectual and social milieus, even when those milieus, at least from the Persian period onward, may have been very close geographically: the most important location for Old Testament literary production may at that time have been Jerusalem. While the Babylonian and especially the Egyptian diaspora in Alexandria developed as important centers of scribal learning, they are nevertheless of only secondary significance for the origins of the Old Testament itself.

The following presentation attempts to sort the Old Testament texts from each literary-historical epoch—essentially to facilitate understanding—according to their various spheres of transmission. Ideally, cultic, wisdom, narrative, prophetic, and legal traditions will be distinguished. This distinction is in the first place indicated simply by the respective textual "families" and thus rests on form-critical considerations in the broad sense. But as regards the question of the *Sitz im Leben* of the types of texts that classical scholarship associated with this effort, the highest degree of caution is in order. Since many Old Testament texts cannot (any longer) be regarded as the written records of originally oral units, the conclusion from a particular kind of text (or "genre") to a specific *Sitz im Leben* that lies behind it and to which it belongs is very uncertain. Rather, as a rule we must be content to say that many texts, as authorial products, only reveal their *Sitz im Leben* as a literary construct, and that the original *Sitz im Leben* of a particular genre can only be postulated hypothetically.

The distinction according to spheres of transmission does, however, permit an initial sorting of different tradition-historical channels.[227] Worship, wisdom, annals, prophecy, and law, while they cannot be perfectly distinguished, can be probed here and there for their different basic intellectual assumptions and backgrounds. But it should be kept in mind that in the course of the religious-historical transformations in the seventh to fifth centuries B.C.E., which took place during the rise of monotheism, the materials in these spheres of transmission were increasingly combined, and as a result we will often have to speak of processes of "theologization." In Israel's monarchical period the cult was not yet conceived as the absolute norm for the human world and human behavior. Subtle systems of wisdom and law were responsible in these domains as well. It was only with the turn to monotheism that cultically imbued traditions were extended in a spiritualizing and universalizing manner, also into the traditional spheres of wisdom and law.

Finally, social-historical distinctions must be kept in view. Do the texts in question reflect the official religion, do they mirror local piety, or can they only be understood in the context of family religion?[228] *Mutatis mutandis*, of course, the same is true here as in the case of form-critical questions: obviously ancient Israelite religion expressed itself in various ways in different social circumstances. But the texts of the Old Testament, even if we can still find in them traces of distinguishable social situations, only bear witness to these situations in a fragmented form. Religious expressions from the spheres of local and family religion are found in the Old Testament only in the forms in which they were officially received or rejected. Immediate access to them, though often sought and supposedly found, is in all probability rare.

5. "Horizontal" and "Vertical" Relationships among Old Testament Texts and Writings

The particular advantage of a literary-historical approach to the Old Testament over the normal structure of introductions is that it can make its "horizontal" and "vertical" linkages clear.[229] This refers to the question of presumably contemporary literary texts in conversation ("horizontal" relationships) as well as that of temporally sequential works that nevertheless address the same concepts and positions ("vertical" relationships). It will thus be important to regard Old Testament books and texts not only as discrete points but also in their literary and material ties to their Old Testament conversation partners and others within the ancient Near East.

It is well known that Old Testament texts interact with one another in multiple ways—affirming, correcting, or rejecting. But this interaction has by no means been exhaustively treated, and it will continue to occupy scholars for the foreseeable future. We can observe inner-biblical references especially in literary allusions and more or less literal quotations, though these are almost never demonstrable as such: one of the few explicit instances is Daniel 9.[230] The usual method of allusion, not directly introduced but discernible to scribal readers through the choice of words and themes,[231] again in its own way attests the probability of textual production and reception within narrow circles of learned scholars.

In addition, elementary material and linguistic links to ancient Near Eastern literatures show that the inquiry cannot be restricted to the Old Testament: "horizontal" and "vertical" references in Old Testament texts naturally do not stop at the borders of the canon, which in any case were drawn up after the Old Testament literature was finished.

6. Redaction as Inner-Biblical Reception

The argument for multiple interactions between the Old Testament texts and writings can be sharpened still further. Old Testament exegesis has, on the one hand, learned to regard the previously despised "expansions" in the biblical books as often being manifestations of inner-biblical scriptural interpretation and, on the other hand, has acknowledged that these "expansions" can be rather extensive texts, in many cases constituting the larger part of a book. Thus it has become ever more obvious that the literary growth of the biblical books was not merely marginal but has shaped their very substance.[232]

The redaction of biblical books was not an uncontrolled process of multiplication of texts but, as a rule, a textually productive process of inner-biblical *reception and interpretation* of existing textual material. In the Old Testament scriptures, text and commentary are usually combined; it was only after the closing of the canon that interpretation was placed outside the text itself. Redaction criticism can therefore be described as an examination of inner-biblical reception, whose reconstruction can bring to light the intra-biblical theological discourses in all their historical differentiations. Thus the literary-historical approach does not introduce something that is foreign to the books themselves; rather, it clarifies a deep structure that holds them together at the core.

7. Tradition and Memory

In any case, the unique character of the Old Testament texts as traditional literature makes it difficult and often even impossible to assign particular texts and their contents clearly and exclusively to *one* particular period. Many texts contain reworked traditions and memories that are older than themselves but did not exist in a fixed, written form.[233] Committing them to writing was then more than and different from a mere codification of these traditions and memories. Instead, the act of writing was already an initial process of interpretation. In turn, many texts were presupposed by subsequent posterior interpretations and were still regarded as valid in epochs that are sometimes to be located much later than their time of origin. Thus Old Testament texts can be "present" and literarily historically relevant in the modes of memory, tradition, and reception in different periods.

The dispute between maximalists and minimalists, between "early" and "late" dating is often carried on without regard for these distinctions.[234] Likewise in what follows, since it may appear from some scholarly perspectives as "late-dating," it should be kept in mind that the material treated may as a rule be traditional and older than the textual versions within which it is now embedded. What is critical for the ordering of particular texts and textual complexes in their respective literary-historical locations is their presumably earliest literarily and conceptually identifiable recording.

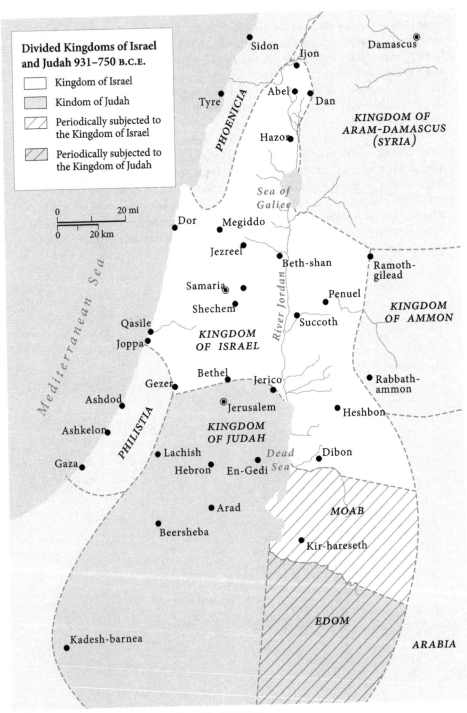

Divided Kingdoms of Israel and Judah 931–750 B.C.E.

Part B

The Beginnings of Ancient Israel's Literature among the Syro-Palestinian City-States before the Advent of the Assyrians (Tenth–Eighth Centuries *B.C.E.*)

I. Historical Backgrounds

In the late Bronze Age not only the southern[1] but also the northern part of Israel lay under Egyptian political influence.[2] Accordingly, Egyptian iconography was omnipresent, and remained so, despite the decline in the expansion of Egyptian power under the Ramesses pharaohs,[3] well into the tenth and ninth centuries B.C.E.[4] Thereafter we can observe a return to autochthonous Northwest Semitic religious concepts. It is only possible to conclude that there were contacts with the Philistines, now settling in the coastal plain,[5] because the Bible describes David as a mercenary allied with the Philistines,[6] but a more detailed description of the nature of these contacts is largely impossible because of the murky state of the sources.

As difficult as it is to reconstruct the political beginnings of Israel and Judah, probably initially as "patrimonial kingdoms"[7] and then, after the ninth/ eighth centuries B.C.E. as states,[8] it is clear to current scholarship that, as regards their cultural context, Israel and Judah were from the beginning integrated into the religious symbolic system of the Levant. That does not mean that Israel and Judah were completely dependent for their intellectual and religious history. But it also does not mean, as Old Testament scholarship in the twentieth century explicitly or implicitly supposed, that Israel and Judah developed religiously and intellectually as entities *sui generis*. While the history of Judah began to some degree in greater isolation than that of Israel, due to their respective geographical situations, neither of them ever existed in "splendid isolation."

In classical scholarship this retrenchment in the political influence of the ancient Near Eastern great powers in the early Iron Age[9]—in some places positively characterized as a power vacuum—was taken as an occasion and basis for developing the idea of a Davidic-Solomonic empire. Major portions of the Old Testament literature could then be located within that time period, especially the Yahwistic historical work, broad sections of the David traditions, and also wisdom texts and the similarly influenced Joseph novella.

However, viewed historically, we must now distance ourselves both from the political notion of a Davidic-Solomonic empire, projected by the Old Testament as a "Golden Age," and from the idea of a literary industry flowering in that period.[10] Although David was undoubtedly a historical figure and has been shown epigraphically by the Tel Dan inscription, which mentions the "House of David,"[11] to have founded a dynasty, archaeology has not yet been able to demonstrate the existence of the empire attributed to him, with the necessary administrative apparatus, and it is not out of order to suppose that this situation will not change significantly for years to come. There is no evidence of monuments or of a corresponding infrastructure in the capital, or indications of an extended territorial state such as would be expected.[12] Likewise, the remains of monumental architecture in Megiddo, Hazor, and Gezer, associated by traditional biblical archaeology with Solomon (on the basis of 1 Kgs 9:15), have in all probability been dated at least a century too early, even though the discussion concerning the so-called "low chronology"[13] has not yet been settled.

The idealization of the epoch of David and Solomon as an early flowering of Israel with corresponding political and cultural manifestations is thus not reflective of the contemporary historical circumstances; rather, it is the product of a later projection (or rather a retrojection) that subsequently influenced especially the historical picture in Chronicles and the completed Psalter, which saw the true foundational era of Israel in the time of David and Solomon. In line with this retrojection, the literary-historical interpretation inherent in the Old Testament itself attributed multiple writings to David and Solomon: Psalms, Proverbs, the Song of Songs, Qoheleth.[14] That written documents were produced under David, Solomon, and the early kings of Israel and Judah who followed them should be seen as no more than probable.[15] The Amarna letters[16] attest already centuries earlier to written correspondence in Jerusalem, but we are completely justified in doubting that this occurred in anything close to the measure asserted by the Bible, and biblical scholarship along with it until very recently.[17]

The cultural contexts that form the background for the beginnings of ancient Israel's literature are thus more modest than what is projected by the Bible and by biblical scholarship, at least in the first half of the twentieth century. Israel and Judah were, in the first place, small "patrimonial kingdoms" neighboring on politically and sociologically comparable realms such as Aram, which acquired a degree of power and ascendancy in the ninth century B.C.E., or like Moab and Ammon, which achieved statehood at about the same time as

Judah in the eighth century B.C.E., and Edom in the south, which attained state-hood only a century later than Judah.[18] Israel and Judah see themselves in their early traditions as existing in differing degrees of proximity to or distance from these states. The political uniqueness of these minor "states" is also recorded in the designation of Judah as "the house of David," as in the inscription from Tel Dan: the political commonwealth is regarded not as a territorial state but as a community adhering to a particular ruling dynasty. The classification "chief-dom," which has become common in recent scholarship,[19] is deceptive inasmuch as both Israel and Judah incorporated a traditional Bronze Age city culture.[20] At the same time, Israel in the tenth century B.C.E. was at least a century, Judah a good two centuries, from achieving a degree of statehood that would begin to make an *extensive* literary production possible on the basis of its associated cultural-contextual status.

II. Theological Characterizations

Accordingly, in the tenth to eighth centuries B.C.E. we cannot speak of anything more than the "beginnings" of Old Testament literature. Moreover, the histori-cal reconstruction is very uncertain, so that these "beginnings" are in turn often little more than "remnants" of themselves. Even if the judgments expressed here are accurate only in principle, still it should be acknowledged that in these texts we are largely in the realm of what can be called primary religious literature. The texts to be treated here are therefore not immediately to be characterized as *theological*. "Theology," understood here as a form of literary reflection on religious acts and concepts, presumes on the one hand a culture of scholarship that at that time existed, at best, only in rudimentary fashion, and on the other hand a wealth of experience within which what had previously been a matter of course is now in need of explication, development, and reflection in order that *theological* secondary literature may be created.

We must guard against separating the traditions of pre-exilic Israel and post-exilic Judaism in a radically dualistic fashion, as Kratz suggests.[21] Such dichotomization has a certain heuristic value, it is true, but the difficulty with applying such categories is evident especially in the dou-ble use of "secular," which represents sheer anachronism. The opposite of "theological" in the Old Testament is not "secular," most certainly not in the sense of an early stage of concepts that *later* became "theo-logical." We do better to speak of "implicit theology." Against a num-ber of all-too-boldly reconstructed literary-historical developments in the Old Testament we must in any case consider that many processes of redaction and reinterpretation did not simultaneously imply com-pletely new interpretations; often they served as explication of what was previously implicit in the content.[22] The processes of reception and reworking of sources from the monarchical period, which we can perceive as occurring often in the Old Testament literature from the Persian and Hellenistic periods, should be described in terms of continuity *and* discontinuity.[23]

If we consider the concrete contents of the written products of this epoch, which are to be addressed for the moment only in the limited terms of relevant "literature" for theological criticism, we can observe the common denominator in the various ideas of order they represent, which are by no means characteristic only of ancient Israel and Judah but were recognized throughout the ancient Near East.[24] The cultic and wisdom texts of this epoch—possibly still in large part oral—can be recognized through the elementary model of difference underlying the symbolic system they incorporate,[25] separating cosmos and chaos or, more precisely, life-supporting and life-diminishing powers, and seeing them as existing in constant conflict.[26] Cultic and ritual actions as well as politics and economics exist to fend off chaos and to support and expand cosmos. In some ancient Israelite inscriptions Asherah is mentioned as YHWH's consort.[27] Of course, one cannot conclude directly that this supports the existence of polytheism in monarchical Israel: YHWH and Asherah are not many deities, but only two, and their duality is due more to differentiation than to multiplication of the idea of divine agency.[28] Nevertheless, we should keep in mind the divinity of the deities of the neighboring peoples, the Moabites, Ammonites, and Edomites, which remained unquestioned: *cuius regio, eius religio.*

In analogy to the cultic traditions, the wisdom tradition sought to organize everyday life into an orienting grid of cosmos versus chaos. Likewise, the narratives in Genesis, which have political intent but are clothed in the guise of family circumstances, are ultimately subject to a comparable idea of order: they organize the different political communities within genealogically ordered relationships that structure the world of the minor states.

III. Spheres of Tradition

1. *Cultic and Wisdom Traditions*

a. Literature at the Sanctuaries of the Northern Kingdom

Although it seems unusual from a biblical perspective, the following should be placed in the foreground for the monarchical period up to the fall of the Northern Kingdom of Israel: because of its more significant geopolitical situation as well as climatic conditions, which enabled a better agricultural yield than was possible in semi-arid regions,[29] the Northern Kingdom initially developed more rapidly and was the more prominent kingdom. The north appears also to have been more densely settled than Judah or the land east of the Jordan.[30] We should therefore presume at the outset that literary production began to develop here, just as in the Southern Kingdom, though perhaps to a more significant degree, and that in both places it took place at the sanctuaries as well as the royal residences or, beginning with the Omrides, in the capital of Samaria.[31]

Certainly over long stretches we must content ourselves with this general proposition, since in the first place much was lost in the fall of Israel, and what remains exists only to the extent that it could be rescued by refugees from the Northern Kingdom[32] and was accepted in the milieu of Judah and Jerusalem, the latter being the decisive factor. The Bible of ancient Judaism does not include any sanctuary literature that acknowledges *genuinely* legitimate worship in any place but Jerusalem.

At the same time careful investigation enables us to obtain a few bits of information about the literature of northern Israel as it may have been transmitted at the sanctuaries in that region. Certainly we should be skeptical of the biblical view that traces the founding of the two sanctuaries at Bethel and Dan to Jeroboam I. For one thing, from Rehoboam to Asa the territory of Benjamin, including Bethel, was a disputed border region between Israel and Judah (cf. 1 Kgs 14:30; 15:7, 16, 32) and therefore quite unsuitable as the location for a royal sanctuary. Besides, the absence of archaeological evidence that Bethel was an economic center in the tenth and ninth centuries B.C.E. and the lack of any evidence of bull iconography in that period indicate that this sanctuary may first have been established under Jeroboam II. The biblical retrojection of it back to Jeroboam I would then be seen as the result of the biblical explanation of the bull images in Bethel and Dan as the "original sin" of the Northern Kingdom and of the competition between Jerusalem and Bethel in the seventh to fifth centuries B.C.E.[33]

We should still note that the literary beginnings of the Jacob traditions were handed on and cultivated at Bethel in the pre-Assyrian period. It has been suggested that individual psalms that were later adopted by Jerusalem originated in Dan, for example the Korah psalms or Psalms 29 and 68.[34] But they more probably belong to Bethel, since endogenous Israelite texts could scarcely have originated in Dan, given the inscriptional evidence found there, which is almost exclusively Phoenician and Aramaic. Finally, the sanctuary in Samaria, depicted negatively in the Bible as the temple of Baal, may have contained cultic statues,[35] but it might in fact have been dedicated to YHWH, as the inscriptions from Kuntillet Ajrud mentioning "YHWH of Samaria" suggests. We may therefore suppose that it had cultic literature of its own. It is possible that the royal Psalm 45* belongs here, since it celebrates the king's marriage to the daughters of foreign kings, which fits with the marital policies of the Omrides, who intermarried with Phoenicians.

It is not on the basis of the texts, which are very uncertain, but in light of geographical considerations that we may posit that the theology of the cultic literature in Bethel and Dan took a different course than that in Jerusalem. In

Jerusalem the royal residence and the palace sanctuary coincided; YHWH, who (in the local ideology) governed the whole world, legitimated the dynasty and its physical rule in Judah. In the North, YHWH was a local god (cf. 2 Kings 1)[36] and legitimated the Northern Kingdom of Israel as his own territory, separated from Judah, Aram, and Assyria by the border sanctuaries of Dan and Bethel.[37]

b. Literature of the Jerusalem Temple Cult

Differently from the case of the sanctuaries of the Northern Kingdom, the temple at Jerusalem endured a history that, despite its two destructions (587 B.C.E. by the Babylonians and 70 C.E. by the Romans), has allowed considerable elements of its cultic lyric and other traditional material to survive: the book of Psalms contains a group of texts that can be assigned on good evidence to worship at the First or Second Temple, though it should also be emphasized that the Psalms are not exhausted by that context and purpose.[38] There are psalms that had scarcely any cultic function (e.g., Psalms 1; 49; 73; 78; 104; 119; 136).[39] The Psalter as a whole is to be regarded in its present form as a meditation book for Torah devotees (cf. the opening Psalm 1)[40] and not as a liturgical book ("hymnal of the post-exilic community"), as Bernhard Duhm long ago observed:

> Many psalms were certainly never sung anywhere. Could any Jew have ever sung Psalm 119 through to the end, no matter how hard he might have tried? Likewise, most of the other alphabetical psalms, or those like Psalm 78, were read and perhaps memorized, but not sung. They served the purpose of private edification and instruction, some of them very much like the Proverbs of Solomon. The superscription of Psalm 102 sounds as if the psalm itself had been taken from a prayer book.[41]

That the Psalter contains poetic texts from very different time periods is not often disputed, but there is great uncertainty about even a tentative historical ordering of the texts. That is no accident; it relates to the themes the psalms themselves treat: songs of lament and thanksgiving, as well as hymns, necessarily contain few references to concrete contemporary historical circumstances. In fact, the character of these texts as liturgical formulae demands that they retain a certain openness so that different persons at prayer may find themselves reflected in the various situations they address.

In principle there is only one psalm that contains a contextual allusion open to historical evaluation, and that is Psalm 137 ("By the rivers of Babylon—there we sat down and there we wept when we remembered Zion"), whose *terminus a quo* therefore lies in the period of the exile. But the breadth of the spectrum of suggestions for dating beyond this psalm is evident from the fact that for Engnell this may be the latest psalm, while for Duhm it could be the oldest.[42]

Thus datings drawn from within the text itself are largely unfounded. Historical arrangements worthy of discussion can only be sought on the basis of reflections on the material profile of individual psalms. If we argue from that perspective we can posit as pre-exilic the early literary layers of the royal psalms 2:1-9; 18:33-46; 21:2-7, 9-13; 72:1-7, 12-14, 16-17?; 110:1-3?,[43] while Psalms 2* and 72*, as texts of the Assyrian period, should not be located within the tenth or ninth centuries B.C.E. As regards the rest of the so-called royal psalms, it is not very likely that they were created at a time when Judah had ceased to be a sovereign kingdom, even though, as projections of an ideal picture, they remained available for reception and tradition. In the Near Eastern context it is only to be expected that the temple cult legitimated and defended the earthly kingdom, so that corresponding texts are very much to be expected in such a setting.

It is also possible that some of the so-called individual songs of lament (cf. Psalms 6 and 13, *inter alia*) were originally royal texts, since in the monarchical period it was probably only the king who, with the exception of the priests, had full access to the worship of the temple.[44] After all, the temple, at least in Jerusalem, was located completely within the palace complex and to that extent was, like the sanctuary in Bethel, a "royal sanctuary, and a temple of the kingdom" (Amos 7:12; cf. 1 Kgs 12:26-27).[45] At any rate Psalms 56:8 ('*mmym*) and 59:6, 9 (*gwym*) regard the foreign peoples as the petitioner's enemies, so that a royal interpretation seems not improbable.[46] Fundamentally, one must keep in mind as regards the traditions of the first Jerusalem temple that the temple—architectonically speaking, at least—was nothing more than a branch of the royal court.[47]

In addition, for religious-historical reasons Solomon's speech at the dedication of the temple—handed down outside the Psalter—can be reconstructed from 1 Kgs 8:12-13 (LXX [1 Kgs 8:53]). It should be located in the pre-Assyrian period:[48] "Then Solomon said, 'YHWH has placed the sun in heaven; he himself has said that he will dwell in thick darkness. I have built you an exalted house, a place for you to dwell in, enthroned forever. So it is written in the book of the song.'" This text documents YHWH's taking possession of the Jerusalem sanctuary, probably dedicated in pre-Yahwistic times to the sun god. In the process, YHWH took on solar attributes.[49]

It is a matter of dispute whether the different texts of the pre-exilic temple cult should be regarded as pointing to a unified cultic tradition in Jerusalem: "The Jerusalem cultic tradition is taken to include the world-encompassing, intentionally closed concept that underlies most of the Psalms and whose essential elements are liturgically articulated, mutually augmenting and referring to one another, especially in the psalms of Zion, the creation psalms, the YHWH-is-king psalms, and the royal psalms."[50]

The idea of a Jerusalem cultic tradition developed within a scholarship that still generally interpreted the greater portion of texts in the Psalter as derived from the pre-exilic temple cult. Still, that assumption is not impossible even today,[51] since liturgical texts are, as a rule, conservative with regard to tradition, and even if their literary origins are later, they may reflect the traditions of earlier epochs. Probably the best example of this are the prophecies of Deutero-Isaiah, which undoubtedly stand within an already-existing liturgical tradition. It is probably accurate to say that the religious ideas in the psalms of the monarchical period reveal a certain convergence that can be interpreted in terms of the cosmos-chaos matrix. But contrary to Steck's traditional interpretation we should probably emphasize the diachronic dimension: the Jerusalem cultic tradition experienced a certain amount of historical development. At the same time, the interdependence of the themes in the Jerusalem cultic tradition remains a striking fact; it can be described as a complex of ideas differentiated within itself and existing in a certain proximity, as regards its content, with other Canaanite city theologies.[52]

c. Wisdom Traditions

Old Testament scholarship uses the term "wisdom" to designate a certain kind of spirituality[53] and (often without defining the difference) a particular group of books and texts shaped by that spirituality. The danger of this conflation is that one may perceive "wisdom" as a more distinct entity than it is in reality. Many of the "wisdom" sayings reflect a "common sense" that existed outside Israel as well and that cannot simply be defined as *a* separate segment in the intellectual and spiritual history of Israel.[54] Wisdom *literature* in ancient Israel was probably *the* educational literature *par excellence*, the tool with which students were instructed.[55] It is beyond question that so-called popular proverbs entered into the wisdom literature, just as they are handed down outside wisdom literature, for example in Gen 10:9; Judg 8:21; 1 Sam 10:12; 24:14; Ezek 16:44.[56] But it should be noted that such proverbs were not simply lumped together as wisdom literature without further ado; rather, they were combined into a larger composition that bore a meaning of its own, and their wording was probably reformulated as well.[57]

Proverbs 10:1-5, though it does not necessarily belong to the earliest literary-historical layers of the book, may furnish an example of the kind of meaningful relationships that can result from certain arrangements of sayings:

(1) A wise child brings joy to his father, but a foolish child grief to his mother.
(2) Treasures gained by wickedness do not profit, but righteousness delivers from death.
(3) YHWH does not let the righteous go hungry, but he thwarts the craving of the wicked.
(4) A slack hand causes poverty, but the diligent hand makes rich.
(5) A child who gathers in summer is prudent, but a child who sleeps in harvest brings shame.

These five verses from Proverbs 10 constitute a unit of sayings that at first may appear to be independent of one another but in fact are arranged into a deliberate composition. The thematic opposition between "wise" and "foolish" in 10:1 is made explicit in 10:5: the one who harvests in summer is "prudent," but the one who does not acts shamefully. Verse 2 makes a material connection to this explication and warns that paying attention only to economic efficiency can be dangerous; it emphasizes the necessity of acting rightly, because only property that is gained honestly is of any value. Verse 3 then deals with a problem that could arise from the position taken in v. 2: what happens when morally laudable action leads to economic difficulties? At this point, 10:3 introduces God into the argument: God will satisfy the righteous. Finally, v. 4 makes it clear that God's care does not make the individual initiative demanded in v. 5 superfluous: anyone who does not work will remain poor. So we can see that Prov 10:1-5 works out a subtle position with regard to the question of how wise action can be described in the concrete, and it secures this position against possible peripheral problems.[58] It is possible and even probable that Prov 10:1-5 was put together out of already-existing sayings, but the literary combination in itself brings essential new dimensions of meaning with it.

From a literary-historical standpoint we may ask how the theology of order in the cult related to that of the wisdom school.[59] There is fundamental agreement, since both worship and wisdom were concerned with constructing a world dedicated to life, but we can perceive some essential differences.[60] While the cult was in service to the "vertical" preservation of the world order, wisdom was concerned more with its "horizontal structure." The latter, however, was by no means as stable as people have been inclined to assume on the basis of classical definitions of the so-called cause-and-effect or act-consequence relationship, which was thought to serve as a kind of natural-law mechanism that sanctioned good and bad behavior as each deserved.[61] Instead, the social order protected by the phenomena subsumed in the concept of the "act-consequence relationship" was a fragile and vulnerable structure that could only be kept afloat through particular cultural activities. It was not created by these human actions, but people could act in accord with it or not, and thus help it to become a social reality or place obstacles before it.

2. Annals and Narrative Traditions

Old Testament research on this subject had become very extensive by the mid-twentieth century. The time of David and Solomon was regarded as the beginning and first high point of the composition of ancient Israel's literature. It was in this period that—according to the classical view—the Yahwistic work, the national epic of Israel, was created. Other works such as the Joseph story or large parts of the tradition now present in the books of Samuel were located in this time. The archaeological deconstruction of the Davidic-Solomonic empire as well as the reevaluation of the literary history of the Pentateuch have made this view impossible to maintain.[62] It is much more likely that what was present at the beginnings of the construction of this literature were not the great narrative syntheses such as supposedly existed in the Yahwist's historical work, but instead individual narratives and narrative cycles. These, in turn—contrary to the classical assumptions—were probably at least a century removed from David and Solomon. The reasons for this lie in the cultural-historical circumstances and the literary discoveries in the Old Testament itself, which allow us to see that the different blocks of tradition were not interwoven from the outset, but only secondarily.

Correspondingly, the traditional great literary works, the Pentateuch and the Former Prophets (Joshua–2 Kings) appear in the following description separated into their most important blocks of material. These stand alone not only in their content, but also in their literary character (for the most part, that is, except for the redactional links): the stories of the patriarchs, the Moses-exodus narrative, the Judges traditions, etc.[63] In addition, depending on the degree of their literary incorporation in larger contexts, they appear diachronically in a broad time span from the beginnings of the tradition's creation to its completion.

a. Northern Kingdom Traditions

As with the Psalms, so also the state of the annalistic tradition from the Northern Kingdom is unusually poor. There is not much evidence beyond repeated references to the "Book of the Annals of the Kings of Israel" (cf. 1 Kgs 14:19—2 Kgs 15:26). It may be that notes like "in his [Ahab's] days Hiel of Bethel built Jericho" (1 Kgs 16:34),[64] or "now King Mesha of Moab was a sheep breeder who used to deliver to the king of Israel one hundred thousand lambs, and the wool of one hundred thousand rams" (2 Kgs 3:4) are drawn from that book. In any case, it is not more than probable that the corresponding texts were composed and handed down in the Northern Kingdom. They may have disappeared by accident or been deliberately left out; in any case, scarcely anything is known of them now. We may think, for example, of lists like those in Joshua 18–19* for Naphtali, Zebulun, Issachar, and perhaps Asher, which may come from the time of Jeroboam II.[65] After Deuteronomy's theological designation of Jerusalem as the only legitimate place of worship, traditions from the Northern Kingdom survived, as a rule, only insofar as they were incorporated into the Judahite perspective and could thus be handed on there.

However, the patriarchal stories in Genesis retain a prominent block of narratives from the Northern Kingdom: the Jacob cycle in Genesis 25–35*.[66] The localities named in the cycle give us sufficient information about their geographic origins: Bethel, Shechem, Peniel, Mahanaim, Sukkoth, and Gilead were all part of the Northern Kingdom. Mesopotamian Haran, mentioned three times (27:43; 28:10; 29:4), probably owes its presence to a specific revision intended to link Laban to the rise of Haran as an Aramaic center in the seventh century B.C.E.[67] But as regards the localization, what is especially striking is the close connection of the cycle as a whole to Bethel, which is the starting and ending point of Jacob's wanderings (28:10-22*; 35:6-7), including the institution of an offering at the sanctuary (28:20-22). It appears, thus, that the Jacob tradition was handed down there. However, the North Israelite Jacob cycle may owe its literary survival primarily to the later redactional connection to the Abraham and Isaac traditions from Judah.

The Jacob cycle, extending from Genesis 25–35*, is an entity whose written form was subsequently expanded. Its core is seen to lie in the Jacob-Laban narratives (Genesis 29–31*), which are encompassed by the Jacob-Esau narratives (Genesis 25*; 27*; 32–33*). Inserted into this structure is the etiology of the sanctuary at Bethel (28:10-22*), and it may be that Genesis 32:23-33* also contains recollections of a further sanctuary etiology for Peniel, even though it can no longer be literarily reconstructed.[68] What is especially important is the observation that it does not seem possible any longer, by literary-critical means, to get behind the national-historical form of the Jacob cycle we now have, which is intended to equate Jacob with Israel and Esau with Edom, with Laban consequently standing for Aram.[69] This is primarily evident from the fact that the political blessings in Gen 27:29, 39-40 cannot be isolated from their context:

> *Let peoples serve you, and nations bow down to you.* Be lord over your brothers, and may your mother's sons bow down to you. Cursed be everyone who curses you, and blessed be everyone who blesses you! (Gen 27:29)

> Then his father Isaac answered him [Esau]: "See, away from the fatness of the earth shall your home be, and away from the dew of heaven on high. By your sword you shall live, and *you shall serve your brother; but when you break loose, you shall break his yoke from your neck.*" (Gen 27:39-40)

In addition to this, the one feature that is important to the development of the story, Esau's hairiness (*sʿr*, 27:11), also alludes to the geography of Edom/Seir (*sʿr*). This does not exclude the possibility that the material of the Jacob cycle had a pre-history that was not yet politically oriented,[70] but we lack sufficient secure anchors that might enable us to reconstruct any prior literary stage.

Thus, the national-historical perspective places Israel, Aram, and Edom in relationship to one another, but without any mention of a king. From a historical point of view there are two possible explanations: one is that the Jacob cycle should be located before the fall of the Northern Kingdom in 720 B.C.E. In that case the absence of a royal figure would be explained, on the one hand, by the fact that the Jacob cycle is anchored in the sanctuary at Bethel, which was not a royal seat. But on the other hand the fact that there never was an enduring dynasty in the Northern Kingdom that would have given the monarchy in the north the status enjoyed by the one in Judah may also be a factor here. Or else one may suggest that from the outset the Jacob cycle formulates a non-state etiology for Israel that relates post-monarchical Israel to its neighbors after 720 B.C.E.

In any case, the Jacob cycle's idea that Esau and Jacob were twins points to a period before 587 B.C.E. It evidently belongs to a time before the clash with Edom reflected in the many negative Edom texts in the prophetic tradition. The shift in the view of Edom was probably connected to the annexation by Edom of the Judahite southern territory as far as Hebron in the wake of the events of 597 or 587 B.C.E.[71]

Traditionally, the narratives surrounding the prophets Elijah and Elisha in 1 Kings 17–19, 21; 2 Kings 1–9, 13 are assigned to the ninth or eighth century B.C.E. But in recent years the evaluation of these texts has shifted dramatically.[72] Namely, the observations about the contextual embeddedness of 1 Kings 17–19 in the "Deuteronomistic" monarchical framework, as well as the texts' religious-historical profile, with its formulation of "monotheism," signaled already by the name of the protagonist, Elijah ("Yah[weh] is my God"), nourish the suspicion that these traditions, as literary texts, are more probably post- than pre-Deuteronomistic.

b. Literature of the Jerusalem Court

As in Israel, we may posit the existence of royal annals in Judah. The court literature was originally more important than that of the temple—in line with the fact that the function of the temple was subordinate to the court. The books of Kings speak of a "Book of the Annals of the Kings of Judah."[73] There are references to it from the description of Rehoboam's reign to that of Jehoiakim (cf. 1 Kgs 14:29 with 2 Kgs 24:5).[74] Alongside these we find references to a "Book of the Acts of Solomon" (1 Kgs 11:41). However, it is questionable whether these "books" ever actually existed. Before the eighth century B.C.E. Judah was "the house of David," a tribal state ideologically supported by a common basis in oral tradition by means of which the royal family and other influential families came to a mutual agreement. Only with the development of a genuine officialdom and a government apparatus could there have been an incentive for writing things down.

We should also mention lists (1 Sam 7:16; 14:47, 49-51; 30:27-31; 2 Sam 2:9; 3:2-5; 5:13-16; 8:16-18; 20:23-26; 23:24-39; 1 Kgs 4:1-6; 1 Kgs 9:17-18), largely in the form of names and perhaps already-existing literary blocks that were inserted into the respective contexts.[75]

It remains a matter of dispute whether behind the "Deuteronomistic" framework of the books of Kings, which essentially contain the regnal dates of the kings together with a synchronization between Israel and Judah and a theological judgment ("doing what is right/evil in the sight of YHWH"), we can reconstruct a separate set of annals.[76] The reworking of historical events in the books of Kings reveals a certain distance from the events themselves. Thus, the foreign political events that affected the Northern Kingdom appear to have been less familiar to the authors than those involving the history of Judah. Strikingly, the epigraphically important term *byt dwd*, "House of David," plays no part in the historical writing of the books of Kings.[77] But in any case the framework as it now exists, with its dates for the post-Solomonic monarchical periods in Israel and Judah, is historically reliable over long stretches and therefore was probably compiled from annalistic sources, whether or not the latter can still be detected in the text as we have it. This is evident in particular from the possibility of establishing cross-references between the biblical sources and Assyrian annals. The absolute date for the latter can be determined because of the reference to the solar eclipse of 763 B.C.E., and they also contain various references to Israelite and Judahite kings. The chronological relationship between the kings of Israel and Judah and with the Assyrian rulers is, apart from a few matters of detail, quite accurate.[78]

Occasionally it is suggested that both the description of Judah's territory in Joshua 15 and the list of Solomon's officials in 1 Kings 4 may retain older documents, but no certainty can be achieved in this matter.[79] In addition, Old Testament scholarship has often postulated narrative connections in the text between 1 Samuel 16 to 1 Kings 2 and located them in the time of David and Solomon. Attempts have been made to reconstruct the history of David's rise in 1 Samuel 16 to 2 Samuel 5 (7–8?). Also, since Leonhard Rost the idea of a history of succession to the throne (2 Samuel 6 [7 or 9] to 1 Kings 2, with the thematic question in 1 Kgs 1:20, 27: "who shall sit on the throne of my lord the king after him?") has been part of the traditional arsenal of theses in Old Testament scholarship.[80] It was also popular to reckon with a history of the Ark transmitted in 1 Samuel 4–6 + 2 Samuel 6.[81]

However, quite recently this picture has been sharply criticized.[82] In the first place, it is improbable, in cultural-historical terms, that such extensive works could have been completed in the early monarchical period. In addition, problems have been perceived on the literary level: the beginnings and/or conclusions of these narratives, which supposedly were originally independent, are not satisfactorily identifiable, and the reconstructed narratives reveal a whole series of interweavings, something that does not support the proposal that these three great source works existed with the separate boundaries that have been suggested.

John Van Seters has been the most radical critic of the history of succession (which he refers to as the "court history"): on the basis of the textual relationships in 1 Kings 2, where the passage from the "court history" in vv. 5-9 presumes its surrounding Deuteronomistic context in vv. 1-4, 10-12. He argues that we can conclude that the "court history" is post-Deuteronomistic and should most likely be set in the context of post-exilic efforts to combat messianic hopes for a restoration of the Davidic kingship.[83]

Walter Dietrich and Reinhard Kratz deal differently with the problems of the rise of and succession to the throne.[84] Dietrich does not separate the two complexes and instead proposes a "court narrative" extending from 1 Samuel 16 to 1 Kings 2 (or perhaps as far as 1 Kings 12), coming from the time between the fall of Israel and that of Judah, a narrative that nevertheless could incorporate older material.[85] For Kratz the solution to the problem lies in individual traditions that can still be reconstructed by literary-critical means and that deal with the origins of Saul's kingship (1 Sam 1:1-20 + 9:1-10, 16 + 11:1-15 + 13-14), as well as Judahite court narratives (2 Sam 11:1-27; 12:24b + 13:13 + 15:1-6, 13; 18:1-19, 9a; 20:1-22 + 1 Kings 1–2).[86] Conceptually, Saul and David at first had nothing more to do with each other than they did with the rulers in neighboring kingdoms. Only after 720 B.C.E. were David and Solomon declared to be successors to Saul through the literary combination of "their" traditions. As a result, only Judah was advanced as the sole legitimate heir of Israel.

The proposed existence of contemporary literary sources such as narratives of the ascension, the royal succession, and the Ark thus is scarcely satisfying as a sufficient explanation to the literary-historical problems in the books of Samuel. This theory seems to be inspired by source criticism of the Pentateuch rather than taking into account the actual content in the books of Samuel. We will be forced to reckon with more modest pieces of tradition. In their reconstruction the particular methodological preference will determine whether it is still possible to discern and discuss these shorter texts in literary-critical terms[87] or whether they are only perceptible as repeatedly reworked memories.[88]

The complexity of the questions regarding the history of origins that confronts us in evaluating the literature in the books of Samuel, especially their origins, is clear, for example, in the story of David and Goliath (1 Samuel 17). There are a considerable number of text-critical differences between its Greek and Hebrew versions.[89] But what is especially amazing is that there is a brief notice in 2 Sam 21:19 referring to the death of Goliath of Gath, and its description of Goliath's spear coincides word for word with 1 Sam 17:7 ("like a weaver's beam"): "Then there was another battle with the Philistines at Gob; and Elhanan son of Jaare-oregim, the Bethlehemite, killed Goliath the Gittite, the shaft of whose spear was like a weaver's beam" (2 Sam 21:19).

So who killed Goliath? David or Elhanan? Or is Elhanan "the Bethlehemite" another name for David, as the Targum of 2 Samuel 21:19 and *RuthR* 2:2 suppose? In any case this variant tradition, together with a number of small summary notes in 2 Sam 21:15-22; 23:8-39, shows that the authors of the books of Samuel apparently had at their disposal a great number of recollections that they were evidently able to shape into different forms, whether as summary notes in a collection of related brief descriptions of events or as long dramatic narratives like the one in 1 Samuel 17.[90]

In any case, there can scarcely be any doubt that the David narratives, while in literary terms clearly to be viewed as more recent than the events they describe, have preserved contemporary recollections. A particularly obvious example is found in the story about David's service to the Philistine king Achish of Gath (1 Samuel 27). It has been demonstrated archaeologically that Gath (*Tell eṣ Ṣafi*) was destroyed around the end of the ninth century B.C.E. Without a corresponding historical recollection, which in this case can be dated with sufficient certainty, this motif would scarcely have found its way into the tradition.[91] The criterion of "consistency with the milieu"[92] thus points to a contemporary background for many of the David traditions; however, socio-cultural considerations point to their later reworking into more extensive literary contexts, so that we may profitably distinguish between the age of the material and the time when it was committed to writing.

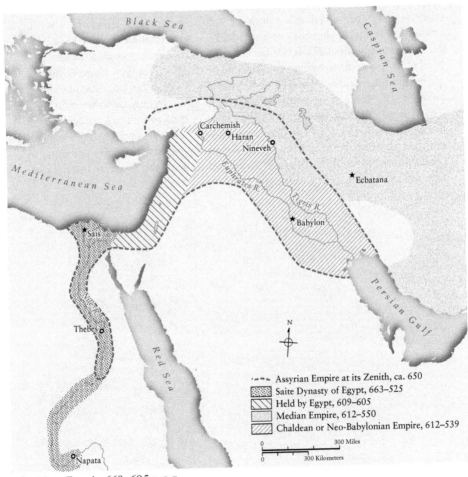

The Near East in 660–605 B.C.E.

Part C

The Literature of the Assyrian Period (Eighth–Seventh Centuries B.C.E.)

I. Historical Backgrounds

With the beginning of Assyrian dominance in the Levant, which may be dated to the ascent of the Assyrian king Tiglath-Pileser III to the throne in 745 B.C.E.,[1] the political and intellectual-spiritual situation in Israel and Judah was fundamentally altered.[2] The still nascent state structures of Israel and Judah began to separate in social-historical terms: the gulf between poor and rich opened dramatically, although in view of increasing productivity it may be supposed that the new poor were as well off as those who previously were considered rich. Israel and Judah also fell within the sphere of influence of an imperial great power that exercised extraordinary political, military, and increasingly also religious and cultural pressure. It is questionable, given the anachronistic connotations, whether one would want to use the term "class society" for this new social order.[3] To do so we would have to be able to demonstrate the existence of wholesale trade, manufacturing, and mining in Israel and Judah, but that is not the case for this period.

Assyria's tribute policy was an important factor in the political history of Israel and Judah in the eighth and seventh centuries B.C.E. That policy can be characterized as "military exploitation of surplus production."[4] Financing the expensive military apparatus and the building of imperial centers required regular annual campaign marches into the periphery of the empire. Those subject to tribute had two basic choices: either they paid their tribute on the arrival of the army and swore allegiance to the great king, or else the tribute would be taken by military force in the form of plunder. The Assyrian style of war, gruesome even by ancient Near Eastern standards, served the purpose of making a voluntary payment of tribute seem more attractive than being plundered by the army.

Their geographical situation made the states of Aram and Israel more exposed to the new situation in the Near East than Judah, and they were very quickly relegated to the status of tributaries of the Assyrian Empire. The payments must have been painfully high: according to 2 Kgs 15:20 a poll tax was therefore introduced in Israel. The painful tribute is the only explanation for the fact that these small states quickly allied themselves against the Assyrian hegemony and in their distress attempted militarily to force Judah (in 734/733 B.C.E.) to join their coalition. Judah resisted this pressure with the help of the Assyrians themselves; the immediate consequence was the annexation of Aram and Israel's relegation to vassal status (732 B.C.E.), followed later by the annexation and political destruction of the Northern Kingdom of Israel (720 B.C.E.). It is possible that we should posit two conquests of Samaria, since both Salmaneser V and his successor, Sargon II, boasted of this achievement.[5] It is probable, however, that a complex sequence of events is responsible for this impression: in 724 King Hoshea was taken prisoner and no successor was appointed; accordingly, Samaria could be considered "conquered," but the actual military conquest took place in 720.[6] From a literary-historical point of view what is especially significant is that this destruction of the state was apparently not accompanied by the immediate loss of all its traditions. Instead, it seems that some were saved by refugees who fled to Judah—for example, the traditions of Jacob, the Judges, and Hosea, although all these were reinterpreted in Judahite terms in the wake of the transfer, whether by insertions in the text (especially in Hosea) or incorporation into larger textual contexts (especially in Genesis and Judges). The immigration to Judah may be connected archaeologically to the original settlement of the southwestern hill of Jerusalem (the "new city" of 2 Kings 22) in the seventh century B.C.E.[7]

But in the course of these events Judah was not left unscathed. After rebellions in Ashkelon and Ekron in 705, and after Judah had begun to make compacts with Egypt, in 701 Sennacherib appeared in Judah and ultimately laid siege to Jerusalem.[8] We know about this event both from Sennacherib's annals[9] and from the books of Kings (2 Kgs 18:13-16). Sennacherib dealt a decisive military blow against Lachish.[10] The significance of this can be measured by the representation of the victory in the reliefs in Sennacherib's palace in Nineveh. Only by the payment of a huge tribute and the surrender (connected with the fall of Lachish) of the Shephelah was the Judahite king Hezekiah (725–697) apparently able to lift the Assyrian siege of Jerusalem.[11] This, however, did not deter the Old Testament from regarding the withdrawal of the Assyrians from Jerusalem in 701 B.C.E. as a mighty deed of deliverance by YHWH.[12] This is especially clear in the Isaiah tradition, which in its parallels to 2 Kgs 18:13-16 in Isa 36:1 omits verses 14-16 and so covers up Hezekiah's payment of tribute.

Hezekiah was followed on the Judahite throne by Manasseh (696–642), who proved himself a loyal vassal to the Assyrian overlords.[13] His fifty-five-year reign was long as a result. In the description in the books of Kings it is treated as one of the most shameful epochs in Israel's history. The historical background for abhorrence of this period on behalf of the redactor is the contemporary assimilation to the mighty cultural pressure from Assyria,[14] visible also in the smallest craftwork.[15] Historically, however, the reign of Manasseh may have seen an early flowering of Old Testament literature. It was, after all, contemporary with the monumental enterprise of the Assyrian king Ashurbanipal (669–631/627 B.C.E.) to establish a comprehensive cuneiform library in Nineveh containing more than 25,000 tablets.[16] A kingship inspired by contemporary Assyria would thus have included the advancement and collection of literary creations.

The parallel in Chronicles also reports Manasseh's repentance as the result of a period of imprisonment in Babylon, but this motif is inspired solely by the effort to create an appropriate theological foundation for the long reign of Manasseh. Only a pious king could have reigned as long as Manasseh did!

Geopolitically, the second half of the seventh century B.C.E. was marked by the decline of Assyrian power, sealed in 612 by the fall of Nineveh and in 610 by the destruction of the last bastion of retreat in Haran. From about 640 on, this decline was accompanied by the corresponding expansion of the Egyptian sphere of power in the direction of Syria and Palestine,[17] but that in itself was anything but stable. The Egyptians in turn were forced into retreat by the Neo-Babylonian victory at Carchemish (605 B.C.E.).

The reign of Josiah (639–609), in which Judah achieved a certain degree of prosperity, falls within this period. At that time Jerusalem may have been a flourishing metropolis with international contacts.[18] It is even possible that Judah expanded into the territory of the former Northern Kingdom and—something especially important as regards literary history—incorporated Bethel, with the traditions handed on there, including the Jacob cycle and the narratives of the judges.[19] The Bible attributes to Josiah a sweeping cultic reform that, in accordance with the central postulates of Deuteronomy, attended to the unity and purity of worship. However, the so-called reform account in 2 Kings 23, which is comprised of various diachronic stages, instead suggests that its basis lay in a description of purification measures in the temple, while the cultic centralization was added later. Still, whether we should make a fundamentally negative judgment on its historicity remains an open question.[20]

II. Theological Characterizations

When the preceding chapter addressed the pre-Assyrian-period "beginnings" of Old Testament literature, the implication was that the real starting point for a history of biblical literature is to be found in the Assyrian era. This can be grounded empirically in the corresponding cultural-historical findings, which indicate that before the Assyrian period Israel and especially Judah had not achieved a degree of statehood that would make an original literature likely. It was probably the cultural-historical influence of Assyria that encouraged the development of statehood in Israel and Judah, which could thus be regarded as "secondary states."[21] For Israel, of course, it was also military pressure from Assyria that brought this nascent state to its end only a few decades later. This very catastrophe, however, may have been of great significance from a literary-historical point of view, because reflection on this event led to the development of intellectual traditions in many areas. In Judah, then, at the end of the seventh century B.C.E. it was above all the establishment and definition of its own cultural and religious identity in contrast to Assyrian power, traditionally a very strong wielder of propaganda but now in decline, that left its mark in contemporary literature.

What can be said for the impetus for the literary history as a whole is likewise true, *mutatis mutandis*, for its theological perspectives. Contact and conflict with the literary exemplars of Assyrian propaganda, imbued with its national religion, which were "published" and imposed throughout the empire by means of vassal treaties, as well as the spiritual and intellectual assimilation of the experience of the fall of the Northern Kingdom, led for the first time in ancient Israel and Judah to the construction of a "theology"—if one is prepared to accept that there is something like a "theology" (or "theologies") in the Old Testament.[22] One might also describe the Assyrian counterparts as "theology."[23] These were significant for the intellectual processes in Israel and Judah inasmuch as here, for the first time in their history as states, there was cultural contact with imperial concepts that in themselves represented an enormous theological challenge.

If we consider the concrete concepts of Old Testament literature developed in the Assyrian period, we can distinguish four broad basic theological streams.

First to be named are the traditions that react to Assyrian threats and the subsequent fall of the Northern Kingdom by accusing not God, but the king and the people (the prophetic books, the books of Kings). These do not seem to restrict themselves to addressing the Northern Kingdom. Instead, processes of *relecture* in the literary production expand the accusations at the same time—if they were not applied to Judah from the start—as warnings to Judah, which worships the same God. Precisely because of this critical stance, these traditions may well have been of marginal significance in the Assyrian period itself. Only with the fall of Judah in the Babylonian period were they "verified" and "rendered orthodox." Special importance in this regard seems to belong to the Amos tradition, since it is the oldest prophetic conception that sees God as acting both strongly and decisively against his own people. The beginnings of the Isaiah tradition draw implicitly but clearly enough on the Amos tradition (e.g., Isa 9:7) and expand that book's prophecy of judgment to encompass Judah. It is especially important for an understanding of the Isaiah tradition in the Assyrian period to know that its message of judgment against Judah appeared to have been falsified by the experience of deliverance in 701 B.C.E., and the Isaiah tradition—at least as regards its judgment aspect—as well as the core of the book of Micah had to endure into the Babylonian period to some degree as "false prophecy."

Second, there is the literary production of "kingless" legends of Israel's origins, such as the Moses-exodus narrative or the traditions of the judges. These did not arise out of nowhere; they compressed existing traditions and recollections into a new, now literary conception of an Israel independent of a king—in the case of the judges traditions more pro-, in the case of the Moses-exodus narrative more anti-Assyrian.

Third, in a different direction, the materials in the wisdom and Psalms traditions appear to continue upholding the ideal of the monarchy. This perspective is not easy to interpret: either it represents a purely Judahite perspective celebrating the kingship that continued to exist in Judah, or else these are positions contra-factually related to the destruction of the neighboring kingdom already experienced and for that very reason clinging to the institution of the monarchy. These alternatives are not mutually exclusive.

Fourth and finally—probably only toward the end of the seventh century B.C.E., in the historical context of the fall of the Neo-Assyrian empire—we can perceive decidedly anti-Assyrian concepts that transfer the relationship of loyalty demanded by Assyria to Israel's own relationship with its God. Here we should mention especially the book of Deuteronomy, which can be approached as a subversive reception of Neo-Assyrian covenantal theology.

III. Spheres of Tradition

1. Cultic and Wisdom Traditions

a. Psalms

Although the question of dating in the Psalms is rendered difficult by the very nature of the material (since the individual and collective circumstances they describe reveal a certain invariability through time because of the genre itself), a few psalms may be assigned with reasonable probability to the Neo-Assyrian period. The psalms traditions from that era were probably always located within the traditional Zion tradition, if we are willing to retain this collective concept as a description of the national religious orthodoxy of the monarchical period. The theological promise of Zion's security based on the presence of YHWH received a strong impetus from Jerusalem's experience of rescue from the Assyrian siege of 701 B.C.E.

Thus, the basic form of the psalms of Zion 46* and 48* probably belongs to the Assyrian period.[24] For one thing, from the perspectives of the history of tradition and of compositional criticism they seem to be presumed by the texts of Isaiah and Jeremiah. In addition, their substantive theological statement about the impregnability of Zion would be hard to explain after 587 B.C.E.—as newly created promises, at any rate. Their literary shaping seems to presuppose at least the events of 701 B.C.E.[25] Interpreting them as hopeful post-exilic eschatological texts founders,[26] at least for Psalm 48, on the primarily past-tense forms. Instead, Psalms 46 and 48 are more easily understood against the background of the era of Manasseh.[27]

In addition, hymns like Psalms 24* or 93* are often counted among the older materials in the Psalter.[28] They probably reflect corresponding cultic activities.

In the cultic-historical interpretation of the Psalms represented primarily by Scandinavian scholars this approach seems forced, since it sought and found a corresponding festival behind almost every psalm. The fundamental problem of this interpretation was that the existence of these festivals cannot be otherwise demonstrated. On the other hand, it is indeed probable that some ritual texts for festivals are retained in the Psalter. The case of Psalm 24* presents a particularly clear example, since appropriate instructions for action ("lift up . . .") are present. Question-and-answer dialogues likewise point to cultic recitation by a number of persons.

> Lift up your heads, O gates!
>> and be lifted up, O ancient doors!
>> that the King of glory may come in.
> Who is the King of glory?
>> YHWH, strong and mighty,
>> YHWH, mighty in battle.
> Lift up your heads, O gates!
>> and be lifted up, O ancient doors!
>> that King of glory may come in.
> Who is this King of glory?
>> YHWH of hosts,
> he is the King of glory. (Ps 24:7-10)

The "processional theology" behind this text probably presupposes cultural contact with the Neo-Assyrian version of the *akitu*-festival, which suggests a location in the eighth or seventh century B.C.E.[29]

The reception at Jerusalem of Northern Kingdom psalms such as 29 and 68 may also belong to the period after 720 B.C.E.[30] But if we accept that these texts originated in the Northern Kingdom, they may only have been received, by way of the library in Bethel that was not disturbed by the catastrophe of 587 B.C.E., in the Babylonian or Persian period.

Finally, the supposed basic form of the royal Psalm 72 clearly reveals a Neo-Assyrian background. The thesis that Psalm 72* is directly dependent in its literary form on the coronation hymn of Ashurbanipal (669 B.C.E.) and was originally created as a coronation hymn for Josiah (639 B.C.E.)[31] is probably too bold.[32] The tradition-historical proximity to the Neo-Assyrian royal ideology, however, is accurately observed.[33] The king is portrayed as the ideal ruler, the wise judge, and the actor who determines the destiny of his people. His kingdom is depicted as a direct reflection of the Assyrian empire: "May he have dominion from sea to sea, and from the River [Euphrates] to the ends of the earth" (Ps 72:8). But despite all the similarities, the theological reversal in Psalm 72 is crucial: here law and justice are traced to God's own self ("your justice . . . your righteousness," v. 1),[34] and not, as was traditional in the ancient Near East, to the king as legislator.[35] Thus the sphere of justice is transposed "from the social and political into the theological sphere and [made] immediately subject to the will of God."[36] In that sense Psalm 72* is theologically very close to the basic intention of Deuteronomy, which was to transfer the Neo-Assyrian concept of loyalty from the great king to YHWH.

Given its treatment of Edom, Psalm 60* may also be dated with some degree of probability.[37] The text may have originated between 600 and 598 B.C.E., and thus is post-Neo-Assyrian.[38]

A counterpart to Psalm 72 in terms of content, which is described in verse 1 as a psalm of Solomon, is found in the extensive description of the governing system and reign of Solomon in 1 Kings 3–10, which praises him as the greatest, wisest, and wealthiest king in the whole world (1 Kgs 5:14; 10:23-24), ruling from the Euphrates to Gaza. This description would have originated as a presentation of the Solomonic kingship according to the Assyrian model,[39] even though the description of the temple in 1 Kings 6–7 includes later elements projected backward from the Second Temple.

Whether the psalms of the Neo-Assyrian period already constituted an "early stage" of the Psalter, that is, already made up a book, is hard to say, given the very complex structure of the Psalter in the received form. On the basis of the findings at Qumran we can see that the overarching structures of the Psalter were not yet firmly established in the second century B.C.E. Nevertheless, thematic collections of individual psalms during the Assyrian period are not improbable. Still, the method of their assembly remains inaccessible to attempts at reconstruction.

b. Older Wisdom Literature

Old Testament wisdom literature is traditional to a very high degree. Its materials were probably in many cases oral traditions that, given their nature as sayings, were relatively stable even without being shaped in written form. On the basis of their theological-historical profile it is supposed that the oldest parts of the text of Proverbs are to be found in chapters 10–29.[40] That at least some parts may have been collected in the monarchical period (at least during the Judahite monarchy), that is, in the Assyrian epoch, is seen from the fact that their redactional coherence is obtained by the inclusion of a series of statements about kings, which seems to presume the existence at least of the Judahite kingship (cf. Prov 14:28, 35; 16:10-15; 20:24-28; 21:1-2, 30-31; 25:6-7, etc.[41] If this is so, the collection and writing down of these sayings probably took place at the royal court. This also matches the self-attestation in Prov 25:1, which in itself—and read uncritically—has no historical reliability: "These are other proverbs of Solomon that the officials of King Hezekiah of Judah copied."[42]

However, we should take into account that in many texts the word "king" is simply used as a code for rule or leadership, so that an evaluation in terms of institutional history is not absolutely compelling. It is also possible that the texts that idealize the kingship were composed or handed down as a reaction to contrary experiences.

As regards the theological profile of Proverbs, contrary to previous attempts by scholars,[43] one should not lump all the YHWH-sayings together and evaluate them as secondary.[44] Ancient wisdom was by no means "secular." Rather, it was at least implicitly "theological," something that does not conceptually exclude a later "theologization." Instead we should pay attention to the specific concepts in the sayings. YHWH can be seen as the origin and guarantor of the so-called cause-and-effect or act-consequence relationship, but not in a systematically fixed manner.[45]

We can derive some especially interesting insights into the origins and composition of a partial collection within Proverbs from Prov 22:17—24:22,[46] since the texts found here apparently derive from Egyptian tradition and their reception most probably took place by way of the Phoenicians. They reveal close kinship with the teaching of Amenemope from the Ramesside period,[47] which in turn derive from older sayings collections. It is noteworthy that the process of partial citation and the adoption of motifs, themes, or concepts that characterize the reception of the teaching of Amenemope in Prov 22:17—24:22 were already part of the composition of the teaching of Amenemope itself. Thus the origins of Prov 22:17—24:22 reflect Egyptian school practices that were probably transmitted to the Levant by the Phoenicians.

In terms of literary history we may ask whether the origins of Israel's own wisdom literature can be associated with the process of distinguishing ethics from law.[48] In the seventh century B.C.E. ancient Israel saw the beginnings not only of wisdom literature but also of its own legal literature (the Book of the Covenant). As soon as law was solidified as a written entity in its own right, it is probable that ethics also took on written form such as we find in the beginnings of the wisdom literature.

2. Narrative Traditions

a. The Beginnings of the Deuteronomistic "Books of Kings"

If we take the books of Samuel and Kings together, as their content suggests we should and as is the case in the Septuagint,[49] it becomes clear that they represent, to some extent, a literary entity. Their beginning in 1 Samuel 1 already shows that, in contrast to what has preceded, something new is begun here, and it is not necessarily related to what is depicted in the books that now precede it in the canon: "There was a certain man of Ramathaim, a Zuphite from the hill country of Ephraim, whose name was Elkanah son of Jeroham son of Elihu son of Tohu son of Zuph, an Ephraimite" (1 Sam 1:1). Both thematically and theologically the beginning of 1 Samuel changes the tone of the historical picture: from now on the focus of interest is primarily on individual figures, no longer on the people as a whole. God's intervention in history takes place in a theologically normative fashion; it is dependent on the "right action" of the kings, though this has an effect on the people as well. The specific focus on the kings is established already at the beginning of the books of Samuel, in the clashes between Samuel and the people about the establishment of the monarchy in Israel (1 Samuel 8–12).

The literary form throughout Samuel–Kings, visible in Kings especially in the judgment texts but substantively related to the exposition in Samuel, is often associated by scholars with a direction in theological thought that arose probably toward the end of the seventh century B.C.E., in the time of Josiah. This thinking is reflected in the composition of the literary core of Deuteronomy, but it is also responsible for the collective interpretation of historical materials whose object is the monarchical period and its pre-history, now literarily combined in the Former Prophets (Joshua–2 Kings). In view of the substantive and linguistic relationship to Deuteronomy, scholars speak of the "Deuteronomic-Deuteronomistic tradition," with the adjective "Deuteronomic" applying to the theology of the literary core of Deuteronomy and "Deuteronomistic" to the further development of that theology as visible in the frame of Deuteronomy and especially in Joshua–2 Kings. Outside Deuteronomy + Joshua–2 Kings, "Deuteronomisms" are also found in other books of the Old Testament, especially Jeremiah and Exodus–Numbers.

The dating of the beginnings of this line of thought to the time of Josiah is more or less well founded, because in terms of its basic structure it is an Assyrian import. In accordance with the Assyrian idea of fidelity, it demands unlimited loyalty, in this case not toward the Assyrian king but toward Israel's own God, YHWH.[50] This demand is raised in a positive sense in Deuteronomy, while the books of Joshua–2 Kings (also Jeremiah) assert that Israel and its leaders failed to keep this obligation, resulting in the fall first of the Northern and then of the Southern Kingdom as a necessary theological consequence. With the linking of guilt and punishment within the framework of an overarching idea of order, the Deuteronomic and Deuteronomistic texts reveal a clear wisdom influence.[51] In addition, they show substantive parallels to the prophecies of judgment, which trace the cause of misfortune to guilt.

Though it previously proved tempting to narrow the time of origin of Deuteronomistic texts still further, to the time between the composition of Deuteronomy and the final scene in 2 Kings—the pardoning of Jehoiachin in 562 B.C.E.—it has now become clear that this theological perspective was at work for a much longer time in the literary history of the Old Testament.[52] Even texts as late as Daniel 9, 1 Baruch, and certain passages in Matthew and Luke are unmistakably shaped by Deuteronomistic thought. Thus Deuteronomism is a long-term phenomenon that acquired its identity by means of some basic theological tenets and a strikingly particular language. However, both these constitutive elements were naturally subject to a certain amount of change: in particular the theology of Deuteronomism reveals a development we will discuss further below. We must decisively distance ourselves from the picture of a school active in the early exilic period with a very limited focus. Likewise, the so-called proof from language is misleading: Deuteronomistic texts were previously thought to be recognizable with great certainty through the nature of their language.[53] To the contrary, we must assert that there are also "Deuteronomistic"-sounding texts that contain very un-Deuteronomistic content (e.g., Jeremiah 24 or 31:31-34). Linguistic usage is not a sufficient characteristic for identifying Deuteronomistic texts, which must instead be conceptually demonstrable as such.

How, then, are the beginnings of Deuteronomy in the books of Kings to be identified?[54] Even Wellhausen was of the opinion that "the real composition of the books of Kings took place before the exile and only subsequently was an exilic or (if not and) postexilic revision performed."[55] The substantive culminating point of the judgments on the kings is 2 Kings 22–23: "The author who constructed this skeleton of the book of Kings was utterly loyal to Josiah's reformation."[56] With Wellhausen, and then a broad current in scholarship following Frank Moore Cross,[57] and against the classical German-language "Deuteronomistic History" research in the twentieth century, strongly influenced by Noth,[58] we must ask whether the framework of the royal judgments was created within a pre-exilic edition of (Samuel*–)Kings*. The origins would then rest not on the need to explain the catastrophe of 587 B.C.E., but instead would ground the necessity of the Josianic reforms on the negative evaluation of all the kings of the north (and some of the south as well) and the fall of the Northern Kingdom, provided that one continues to hold to this position in one form or another. It may also be asked whether we should separate literary presentation and historical content in the judgment texts, so that Josiah and his—historically disputed—reform would not be posited as the *terminus ad quem*, but rather as the idealized image of both in the era of the Persian restoration of Jerusalem.

In any case, a glance at the basic statements of the framework can illustrate the substantive direction toward Josiah—or, if we take a skeptical view of 2 Kings 22–23, toward "Josiah." The kings of the north all receive negative censures, because they all cling to the "sins of Jeroboam":

> Nadab . . . did what was evil in the sight of YHWH, walking in the way of his ancestor and in the sin that he caused Israel to commit. (1 Kgs 15:25-26)

> . . . Baasha . . . did what was evil in the sight of YHWH, walking in the way of Jeroboam and in the sin that he caused Israel to commit. (1 Kgs 15:33-34)

> . . . Zimri . . . died—because of the sins that he committed, doing evil in the sight of YHWH, walking in the way of Jeroboam, and for the sin that he committed, causing Israel to sin. (1 Kgs 16:18-19)

> Omri did what was evil in the sight of YHWH; he did more evil than all who were before him. For he walked in all the way of Jeroboam son of Nebat, and in the sins that he caused Israel to commit, provoking YHWH, the God of Israel, to anger by their idols. (1 Kgs 16:25-26)

. . . Ahab . . . did evil in the sight of the LORD more than all who were before him. And as if it had been a light thing for him to walk in the sins of Jeroboam son of Nebat, he took as his wife Jezebel daughter of King Ethbaal of the Sidonians, and went and served Baal, and worshiped him. (1 Kgs 16:29-31)

. . . Ahaziah . . . did what was evil in the sight of YHWH, and walked in the way of his father and mother, and in the way of Jeroboam son of Nebat, who caused Israel to sin. (1 Kgs 22:51-52)

. . . Jehoram . . . did what was evil in the sight of YHWH, though not like his father and mother, for he removed the pillar of Baal that his father had made. Nevertheless he clung to the sin of Jeroboam son of Nebat, which he caused Israel to commit; he did not depart from it. (2 Kgs 3:1-3)

Thus Jehu wiped out Baal from Israel. But Jehu did not turn aside from the sins of Jeroboam son of Nebat, which he caused Israel to commit—the golden calves that were in Bethel and in Dan. . . . But Jehu was not careful to follow the law of YHWH the God of Israel with all his heart; he did not turn from the sins of Jeroboam, which he caused Israel to commit. (2 Kgs 10:28-31)

. . . Jehoahaz . . . did what was evil in the sight of YHWH, and followed the sins of Jeroboam son of Nebat, which he caused Israel to sin; he did not depart from them. (2 Kgs 13:1-2)

. . . Jeroboam . . . did what was evil in the sight of YHWH; he did not depart from all the sins of Jeroboam son of Nebat, which he caused Israel to sin. (2 Kgs 14:23-24)

. . . Zechariah . . . did what was evil in the sight of YHWH, as his ancestors had done. He did not depart from the sins of Jeroboam son of Nebat, which he caused Israel to sin. (2 Kgs 15:8-9)

. . . Menahem . . . did what was evil in the sight of YHWH; he did not depart all his days from any of the sins of Jeroboam son of Nebat, which he caused Israel to sin. (2 Kgs 15:17-18)

. . . Pekahiah . . . did what was evil in the sight of YHWH; he did not turn away from the sins of Jeroboam son of Nebat, which he caused Israel to sin. (2 Kgs 15:23-24)

. . . Pekah . . . did what was evil in the sight of YHWH; he did not depart from the sins of Jeroboam son of Nebat, which he caused Israel to sin. (2 Kgs 15:27-28)

. . . Hoshea . . . did what was evil in the sight of YHWH, yet not like the kings of Israel who were before him. (2 Kgs 17:1-2)

The last king, Hoshea (2 Kgs 17:1-2), is something of an exception. Probably this variation was motivated by the fact that beginning with verse 7 Israel is introduced as the subject of the sin, and therefore Hoshea is partially excused.

Of the thirteen kings of the south after Rehoboam (but cf. 1 Kgs 14:22 LXX) until Josiah, on the other hand, seven receive generally positive judgments, though these—except in the cases of Asa, Hezekiah, and Josiah—are all qualified with "but the high places were not taken away, and the people still sacrificed and offered incense on the high places." Exceptions within the sequence—marked in what follows by italics—are the six counterexamples of Abijam (1 Kgs 15:1-3), Jehoram and Ahaziah (2 Kgs 18:16-19, 25-27), Ahaz (2 Kgs 16:1-4), Manasseh and Amon (2 Kgs 21:1-3, 19-22); these are all condemned. Numerically, the positive and negative evaluations are thus almost equal. At the same time, in light of the context we may say that the negative judgments are "exceptions" because they rest on clearly identifiable circumstances: Jehoram and Ahaziah are related to the house of Ahab from the Northern Kingdom; he in turn, because of his marriage to Jezebel of Sidon, receives a particularly harsh condemnation. Jehoram and Ahaziah therefore, because of their relational ties, are subject to the general verdict on the Northern Kingdom. (Rehoboam as well as) Abijam, Ahaz, Manasseh, and Amon are guilty of particular cultic wickedness and for that reason cannot be evaluated positively.

> . . . *Abija(m)* . . . *committed all the sins that his father did before him; his heart was not true to* YHWH *his God, like the heart of his father David.* (1 Kgs 15:1-3)

> Asa did what was right in the sight of YHWH, as his father David had done. . . . But the high places were not taken away. Nevertheless the heart of Asa was true to YHWH all his days. (1 Kgs 15:11-14)

> Jehoshaphat . . . walked in all the way of his father Asa; he did not turn aside from it, doing what was right in the sight of YHWH; yet the high places were not taken away, and the people still sacrificed and offered incense on the high places. (1 Kgs 22:41-43)

> . . . *Jehoram* . . . *walked in the way of the kings of Israel, as the house of Ahab had done, for the daughter of Ahab was his wife. He did what was evil in the sight of* YHWH. *Yet* YHWH *would not destroy Judah, for the sake of his servant David, since he had promised to give a lamp to him and to his descendants forever.* (2 Kgs 8:16-19)

> . . . *Ahaziah* . . . *walked in the way of the house of Ahab, doing what was evil in the sight of* YHWH, *as the house of Ahab had done, for he was son-in-law to the house of Ahab.* (2 Kgs 8:25-27)

> Jehoash did what was right in the sight of YHWH all his days, because the priest Jehoiada instructed him. Nevertheless the high places were

not taken away; the people continued to sacrifice and make offerings on the high places. (2 Kgs 12:2-3)

. . . Amaziah . . . did what was right in the sight of YHWH, yet not like his ancestor David; in all things he did as his father Joash had done. But the high places were not removed; the people still sacrificed and made offerings on the high places. (2 Kgs 14:1-4)

. . . Azariah . . . did what was right in the sight of YHWH, just as his father Amaziah had done. Nevertheless the high places were not taken away; the people still sacrificed and made offerings on the high places. (2 Kgs 15:1-4)

. . . Jotham . . . did what was right in the sight of YHWH, just as his father Uzziah had done. Nevertheless the high places were not removed; the people still sacrificed and made offerings on the high places. (2 Kgs 15:32-35)

. . . *Ahaz . . . walked in the way of the kings of Israel. He even made his son pass through fire, according to the abominable practices of the nations whom YHWH drove out before the people of Israel. He sacrificed and made offerings on the high places, on the hills, and under every green tree.* (2 Kgs 16:1-4)

. . . Hezekiah . . . did what was right in the sight of YHWH just as his ancestor David had done. He removed the high places, broke down the pillars, and cut down the sacred pole. He broke in pieces the bronze serpent that Moses had made, for until those days the people of Israel had made offerings to it. . . . He trusted in YHWH the God of Israel; so that there was no one like him among all the kings of Judah after him, or among those who were before him. For he held fast to YHWH; he did not depart from following him but kept the commandments that YHWH had commanded Moses. (2 Kgs 18:1-6)

. . . *Manasseh . . . did what was evil in the sight of YHWH, following the abominable practices of the nations that YHWH drove out before the people of Israel. For he rebuilt the high places that his father Hezekiah had destroyed; he erected altars for Baal, made a sacred pole, as King Ahab of Israel had done, worshiped all the host of heaven, and served them.* (2 Kgs 21:1-3)

. . . *Amon . . . did what was evil in the sight of YHWH, as his father Manasseh had done. He walked in all the way in which his father walked, served the idols that his father served, and worshiped them; he abandoned YHWH.* (2 Kgs 21:19-22)

. . . Josiah . . . did what was right in the sight of YHWH, and walked in all the way of his father David; he did not turn aside to the right or to the left. (2 Kgs 22:1-2)

This overall survey of the judgments on the kings in 1 Kings 12—2 Kings 23 shows a thematic line extending from the destruction of the high places under Hezekiah (2 Kgs 18:4) through their reintroduction by Manasseh (2 Kgs 21:2) to their *enduring* profanation under Josiah (2 Kgs 23:8).

How should we date this framework? Favoring a beginning before the exile, besides the striking expression "to this day" as in 1 Kgs 8:8; 9:21; 10:12; 19:19; 2 Kgs 8:22, which possibly or apparently still presume the circumstances of the monarchical period,[59] are these arguments:

1. the remarkable circumstance that the books of Kings lack a special reflection on the fall of Judah in the style of 2 Kings 17 (and, strikingly, it has been inserted in 2 Kings 17 at v. 19) and

2. the apparently secondary attempts, in the passages about Manasseh in 2 Kgs 23:26; 24:3[60] and in the summary condemnations of all the kings in the judgments rendered on the kings after Josiah in 2 Kgs 23:32, 37 (cf. 2 Kgs 24:9, 19), to theologically annul the merits of Josiah's reforms.[61] After the fall of Judah, and corresponding to the ancient Near Eastern royal ideology, according to which the king was responsible for the well-being or misery of the state, the judgments on the kings were read by those who received them as reasons for the catastrophe. Correspondingly, the continuation of Samuel–2 Kings 23 by means of the last two chapters of 2 Kings would then have attempted *ex post facto* a general condemnation of all the Judahite kings as well.[62]

But it is also possible that the judgments on the kings stem from (post-) exilic efforts to present Josiah as the ideal monarch whose reign represented a relative high point in the history of the Israelite and Judahite kingdoms.[63] In that case, the post- and re-interpretations in 2 Kings 21 and 23–24 would be scribal theological disputes about historicized objects that should not be seen as immediately contemporary.

In any case, the Deuteronomistic edition of Samuel–Kings probably had recourse, in the books of Samuel, to a thoroughgoing portrayal of David that could have belonged to the seventh century B.C.E.,[64] while in the books of Kings the editorial work itself was much more influential in creating its own traditions.

b. Traditions of the Judges (Judges 3–9)

The Old Testament as we have it presents us with two spheres of tradition that offer narratives about pre-state Israel in its land: the stories of the patriarchs in Genesis and the narratives of the judges in the book of Judges. From a biblical point of view these are two epochs separated by centuries that included the relocation to Egypt, the exodus, the wandering in the wilderness, and the occupation of the land. Historically, however, these are much more likely to be narratives reflecting from different perspectives on life in the land without a state organization, something that can in principle be equally well interpreted as representing a pre-state or a post-state origin.

The literary form of the stories of the judges in Judges 3–9, as will soon be clear, may belong to the Assyrian period.[65] The fact that except for Othniel (Judg 3:7-11)[66] all the judges—Ehud, Shamgar, Deborah,[67] Barak, Gideon, and Abimelech—stem from the territory of the Northern Kingdom leads us to conclude that Judges 3–9 preserve specifically northern Israelite traditions. They propose and advocate the possibility within its non-state context of an existence for Israel without a king of its own—a figure ridiculed in the image of the bramble (Judges 9)—under Assyrian hegemony. In particular the episode of unsuccessful institutionalization attempted by Abimelech in Shechem (Judges 9), which historically seems to presuppose the destruction of Shechem in 722 B.C.E., warns Israel against having its own king. The circumstances surrounding the establishment of a Shechemite kingdom in Judges 9 could be read directly as a summary of the worst misdeeds of the rulers of the Northern Kingdom. The story of Abimelech in Shechem, we might say, concentrates two centuries of Israelite royal rule in a single literary chapter.[68] Even Israel's enemies in Judges 3–9 point to the Assyrian period: Moab first appears as a state capable of threatening Israel in 845 B.C.E. under King Mesha (Judg 3:12-14).[69] Something similar is true of the depiction of the conflicts with the Midianites, who seem to reflect Israel's experiences with the Arabs beginning in the seventh century B.C.E.[70]

Judges 3–9 should thus be approached as a post-monarchical programmatic writing that opposes an institutionalized kingship in Israel and favors a God-directed polity steered by charismatic savior figures. We get the impression that this intra-Israelite leadership need not necessarily conflict with overarching political-organizational structures. It is thus entirely imaginable that the political program of Judges 3–9 can be set within the framework of an orderly empire and to that extent—when seen within the cultural context—is pro-Assyrian in its orientation. In fact, the peaceful life of an Israel without a king in the face of its foes—the Moabites and Midianites—fits seamlessly within what we would expect in view of contemporary Assyrian propaganda toward Israel.[71] This program appears in Judges 3–9 in the guise of a description of Israel's pre-state times in order to secure the mythical quality of the concept as belonging to its origins. Judges 3–9 are, theologically and politically, not far removed from the contemporary Jacob cycle. Even Jacob, serving in Haran, who was never king in Israel, is not a figure who conflicts with Assyrian claims to hegemony.

c. The Moses Story

The Moses story, which in the current narrative sequence of the Pentateuch functions as the continuation of Genesis and with its natural end, the depiction of the occupation of the land in the book of Joshua, likewise points beyond the Pentateuch, was originally—both orally and as a written document—a separate complex of traditions.[72] This is evident, for one thing, from the fact that the Moses narrative is thematically and theologically independent, but also because the (textually fixed) history of the patriarchs in itself by no means leads organically to the Moses narrative. This forces us to conclude that the patriarchs and the exodus represent two previously independent complexes of tradition that were connected to each other in a secondary literary move. From this point of view Exod 1:6-8 is especially striking: "Then Joseph died, and all his brothers, and that whole generation. But the Israelites were fruitful and prolific; they multiplied and grew exceedingly strong, so that the land was filled with them. Now a new king arose over Egypt, who did not know Joseph." These three verses create an immediately obvious bridge between the Joseph story previously told and the exodus story that now begins: all memories of the rise of Joseph and his beneficial deeds for Egypt must be eradicated so that the motif of oppression can be plausibly introduced. Exodus 1:8 strains to make this sequence of events plausible: the new Pharaoh is supposed to have forgotten Joseph, who was second in command under his predecessors in Egypt. This difficulty is explained by the effort to tie the patriarchs and the exodus as tightly together as possible.

We can also see from Exod 1:6-8 that this link was created very late, namely by the Priestly document,[73] and that this is presumed by the non-Priestly text of Exodus 1: Israel's emergence as a people is reported only in Exod 1:7, a verse that is unanimously assigned to the Priestly document (cf. the intertextual connections with Gen 1:28; 9:6; 17:2), and this in turn is presumed by both the language and the substance of the subsequent text (Exod 1:9: "Look, the Israelite people are more numerous and more powerful than we"; cf. 1:20). But that also means that the non-Priestly text of Exodus 1 as a whole is dependent on the Priestly document and thus must be dated later than that writing, since the motif of Israel's becoming numerous and strong is present throughout Exodus 1.

Thus the Moses narrative was originally handed on independently, separated from the patriarchal history, and the two were only linked in the wake of the Priestly document. The literary Moses narrative originally began with Exodus 2, the story of the birth of Moses, which still betrays the fact here and there that it was created without knowledge of the genocide theme in Exodus 1. As the formulation in Exod 2:1 ("Now a man from the house of Levi went and took a Levite woman") shows by comparison to its closest biblical parallel, Hos 1:2 ("Go, take for yourself a wife of whoredom and [beget] children of whoredom"), the union of the parents, who are probably not left nameless by accident (the names Amram and Jochebed are contributed by the subsequent Priestly interpretation in Exod 6:20), was apparently an illegitimate liaison: Exodus 2:1 only speaks of "taking," not of "taking as a wife" [contra NRSV, NAB: "married"]. This, and not the threat of genocide, seems to have been the real reason for the child's exposure, especially since the Pharaoh's daughter is quite uninhibited in identifying it as "one of the Hebrews' children" (Exod 2:6), without seeming to know anything about her father's genocidal command.

This interpretation also matches the content of the closest ancient Near Eastern parallel to Exodus 2,[74] namely the Sargon legend that was traditional in Assyria, concerning the great usurper Sargon I (2350–2294 B.C.E.).[75]

> Sharrukin [Sargon], strong king, king of Akkad, am I. My mother was a high priestess, my father I do not know. My paternal kin inhabit the mountain region. My city [of birth] is Azupiranu, which lies on the banks of the Euphrates. My mother, a high priestess, conceived me, in secret she bore me. She placed me in a reed basket, with bitumen she caulked my hatch. She abandoned me to the river from which I could not escape. The river carried me along: to Akki, the water drawer. Akki, the water drawer, drew me out in his bucket. Akki, the water drawer, raised me as his adopted son. Akki, the water drawer, set me to his garden work. During my garden work, Ishtar loved me, [so that] for [five] four years I exercised kingship.[76]

Sargon reports that his mother was an *enitu* priestess, who was forbidden to marry. He did not know who his father was. But despite his doubtful descent he was chosen by the gods. The substantive profile in Exodus 2 is much the same: Moses' divine protection compensates for his illegitimate origin.

But above all the Neo-Assyrian background of the tradition reveals the critical, anti-Assyrian orientation of the Moses narrative, in sharp contrast to Judges 3–9. In place of the Assyrian great king, the non-monarchical figure of Moses appears as the one chosen by God to free Israel from imperial slavery. This reveals a remarkable perspective on the substantive closeness of the Moses narrative to the perhaps somewhat older but more pro-Assyrian traditions in Judges. Moses, too, is a savior of Israel, as is true of the "judges," but the Moses tradition is in clear competition with the Assyrian ideology. From this point of view the Moses narrative can be read as an anti-Assyrian condensation of the more pro-Assyrian traditions of the judges. We can scarcely regard too highly the importance of this stage of the construction of the Old Testament literature too highly: with the Moses narrative we have, for the first time in Israel, a clearly anti-imperial literary document that instead acknowledges God as the absolute "imperial" power. This basic motif of portraying God as the absolute sovereign, which coincides with the fundamental attachment of his people to him, will prove enduring throughout the history of theology, of central importance especially for the construction of monotheism. It rests on a reception from an Assyrian archetype, then transformed in an anti-Assyrian direction.

The Moses narrative, then, pointed toward the departure of the Israelites from Egypt—probably still without a developed plague narrative, but most likely including the motif of despoiling the Egyptians (Exod 11:1-3; 12:35-36). Its first climax was the depiction of the miracle at the sea. In the classic documentary hypothesis the plague narrative was excluded from the ancient J source, because as a whole it does not advance the flow of the narrative (only the killing of the firstborn is effective). In addition, by its miraculous nature it fundamentally anticipates the point of the rescue at the Sea of Reeds *as a miracle*, and thus in a sense constitutes a doublet to the latter, an observation that is relevant from a composition-critical point of view.

The great presentation of the calling of Moses at the mountain of God in Exodus 3–4 is, as a whole, an insertion into the context in Exod 3:1—4:18; the thread of the existing exodus narrative continues directly from Exod 2:23aα to Exod 4:19 (Exod 2:23aα is repeated before Exod 4:19 in the LXX). That Exodus 3–4 as a whole or at least in part already presupposes the Priestly document is suggested by a number of observations:

1. Israel's "crying out" in Exod 3:7, 9 points back thematically to Exodus 1–2, but its language is clearly related to Exod 2:23a, a "P" text.

2. In addition, Exodus 3–4 presupposes the call of Moses in the Priestly document (Exodus 6), and apparently integrates the problems resulting from the latter (the Israelites' "refusal to listen") into the call scene itself: In Exod 6:2-8 God speaks to Moses and Moses speaks to the Israelites (6:9a), but they do not listen to him (6:9b). In contrast, in Exod 3:1—4:17 God tells Moses in advance that Israel will "listen" to him (3:18), but Moses *immediately* responds, without having delivered his message at all, by expressing his fear that Israel will not "believe" him and will not "listen" to him (4:1).

3. Exodus 6, in accord with expectation and tradition (cf. Ezekiel 20), takes place in Egypt, while Exodus 3–4 seems to be secondarily localized at "the mountain of God, Horeb." According to Exodus 3–4—which apparently both draws upon and distances itself from Exodus 6—legitimate revelation takes place only at the mountain of God, and the essential content of revelation is the Hexateuch's salvation history (3:7-10, 16-18).

4. Exodus 4:1-9 presupposes the plague cycle in a form that is introduced by "P" (4:1-5; 7:8-13 "P"; transformation of the staff) and expanded by "P" (4:9; 7:14-24, the Nile's water is turned to blood ["J," the fish die]).

In its present context the Moses narrative comes to an initial, hymnic conclusion in Exodus 15; however, this psalm (the first in the reading sequence outside the Psalter) appears to contain no ancient traditional material. Pointing to the contrary is the Deutero-Isaianic coloring of the text; in addition, the description and interpretation of the miracle at the sea in Exod 15:8, 13 probably presupposes the Priestly document.[77] Exodus 15 is to be regarded as a literary means, external to the Psalms, to link the Psalter paradigmatically with the first crucial salvation-historical experience of Israel. But probably the Song of

Miriam in Exod 15:21b represents more ancient traditional material on which the composition of Exodus 15 was based, even though its liturgical form as an imperative hymn prevents us from saying that we can see here a contemporary document of the experience of rescue at the Sea of Reeds, whatever historical context we may assign to it.

Therefore the stations of the Moses narrative were probably: miracle at the sea, journey through the wilderness, occupation of the Land (probably Joshua 6*; 9–10*); the last was the natural goal of the narrative.[78] The description of the occupation of the Land is also nourished by Neo-Assyrian motifs.[79] But there have not yet been any methodologically persuasive attempts to reconstruct the precise literary history of the Moses narrative as a whole.

How should we characterize the Moses narrative in literary-historical terms? The most elementary indications appear, first of all, in that it formulates an allochthonous basis for the existence of Israel: it is Israel-from-Egypt and is not rooted from the beginning in its own land. Then it is striking that in this story there is neither an Israelite king nor does Moses have any explicitly royal features. Finally, the anti-Assyrian trajectory should be mentioned; this is visible especially at the beginning in Exodus 2. This indicates that the Moses-Exodus narrative would have received its oldest still perceptible literary form no earlier than the seventh century B.C.E., as also indicated by the archaeological findings regarding the political and geographical backgrounds reflected and reworked in it.[80]

From a literary-historical perspective the formation of the Moses narrative would have been influenced first of all by the prophecies of judgment in the eighth century B.C.E., because it presupposes the prophetically announced fall of the Northern Kingdom and formulates a legend of Israel's origins resting on a non-state basis. But that does not mean it was invented at that time. It is probably based on older oral tradition, as indicated by the anchoring of the exodus credo in various strands of tradition.[81] We can also see that the Moses narrative functioned in some sense as a foundation narrative for the Northern Kingdom, as the striking parallel designations of Moses and Jeroboam suggest (slave labor, intent to kill, flight).[82]

Furthermore, there is no question that the biblical exodus has some historical backgrounds. The question, however, has for a long time been approached with a certain exclusive naïveté, as if the sequence of events behind the biblical account could be reconstructed in quasi-linear fashion by use of the methods of historical-rationalizing paraphrase. But the Moses narrative is not a historical account; it is a collective narrative of origins.[83] That alone makes it probable that the building up of the tradition concentrated a number of events in one. It has been supposed that the expulsion of the so-called Hyksos, a series of generations of Semitic foreign rulers in Egypt (ca. 1730–1580 B.C.E.), forms the background for the biblical exodus narrative.[84] Alternatively, it has been suggested that the events surrounding the Syrian chancellor Bay (reported on the Elephantine stele of Setnakhte and in the great Papyrus Harris 1), who during the transition from the Nineteenth to the Twentieth Dynasty held power over Egypt for a time before being driven from the land by the Pharaoh Setnakhte (1186–1184 B.C.E), might represent the historical background for the Moses narrative.[85] In addition, we have known for a long time of Egyptian documents showing that there were various "eisoduses" and "exoduses" of Asiatics in the Nile Delta. Particularly eloquent is Papyrus Anastasi VI, 53-60, containing a letter from an Egyptian border official to his superiors:

> Another communication to my [lord], to [wit: We] have finished letting the [Shasu] tribes of Edom pass the Fortress [of] Mer-ne-Ptah Hotep-hir-Maat—life, prosperity, health!—which is (in) Tjeku, (56) to the pools of Per-Atum [of] Mer-[ne]-Ptah Hotep-hir-Maat, which are (in) Tjeku, to keep them alive and to keep their cattle alive, through the great ka of Pharaoh—life, prosperity, health!—the good sun of every land, in the year 8, 5 [intercalary] days, [the Birth of] Seth. . . . I have had them [the names of the tribes] brought on a copy of the report to the [place where] my lord is, as well as the other names of [the 60] days when the Fortress of Mer-ne-Ptah Hotep-hir-Maat—life, prosperity, health!—which is (in) [Tj]ek[u], may be passed . . .[86]

This document contains names that play an important part in biblical scholars' discussions of the historical exodus (Tjeku, Per-Atum [= Pithom], Shasu [Bedouin]), but the text is altogether clear in showing that movements by nomads ["Shasu tribes"] were being noted, apparently quite often. Finally, we should mention the decline of Egyptian power in Canaan in the twelfth and eleventh centuries B.C.E. as well as various movements for emancipation from later Egyptian claims to power, any of which might also be interpreted as an "exodus."[87]

Given the conditions under which ancient traditions of origins came into being, one is well advised not to interpret these points of contact as mutually exclusive, so that one must choose between them, asking "what is *the* historical background of the exodus?" Instead, it seems that all the experiences behind it have entered into the present literary form of the exodus event, which as such does not have one particular historical background, but many. We could say, to bring it to a point, that the depiction of the exodus is equally historical and non-historical. That Moses himself was a historical figure is suggested by his Egyptian name (cf. Thutmose, Ram[o]ses, etc.) and by the multiple traditions of his marriage to a foreign woman: neither would be expected if Moses were simply the product of legend.[88] But here, too, we must contend that so many later elements have been concentrated in the biblical figure of Moses that there are limits to what can be gained by insisting that he was a historical figure.

d. The Abraham-Lot Cycle

In the patriarchal stories in Genesis we can clearly see from the various geographical locations of the drama that, of the three patriarchs, Jacob originally belonged to central Palestine (Bethel, Shechem, etc.), while Abraham (Hebron, Mamre, etc.) and Isaac (Beersheba, Gerar) belonged to southern Judah. It is true that the patriarchal history depicts Abraham as the father of Isaac, which led Old Testament scholarship in the nineteenth century to regard Abraham as also the elder figure in terms of the history of the traditions. But, as Wellhausen already noted, the contrary is much more likely.[89] The present shadowy existence of Isaac alongside his "father" and the parallel traditions featuring Abraham and Isaac are more simply explained as borrowing from the less important Isaac in favor of the more important Abraham than the other way around: in the history of storytelling, motifs are as a rule transferred from minor to major figures. In addition the attestations for Abraham and Isaac outside the patriarchal history should be taken into consideration: for Isaac we can adduce two Amos passages indicating that in the monarchical period "house of Isaac" could be regarded as eponymous for the Southern Kingdom.

> . . . the high places of Isaac shall be made desolate, and the sanctuaries of Israel shall be laid waste, and I will rise against the house of Jeroboam with the sword. (Amos 7:9)

> Now therefore hear the word of Yhwh. You say, "Do not prophesy against Israel, and do not preach against the house of Isaac." (Amos 7:16)

For Abraham, by contrast, it is quickly apparent that no references to him from the monarchical period can be proven outside Genesis. None of the "Abraham" references in Isa 29:22; 41:8; 51:2; 63:16; Ezek 33:24; Jer 33:26; Mic 7:20; Pss 47:10; 105:6, 9, 42; 2 Chron 20:7; Dan 3:35 can be dated before the exile. We should not immediately conclude from this that the Abraham narratives are purely redactional constructions from the seventh or sixth century B.C.E.[90] or that their complete content is dependent on the Priestly document.[91] Rather, we may first of all posit that Abraham only became a prominent figure in the Old Testament tradition at a comparatively late date.[92] The present genealogical sequence of Abraham, Isaac, and Jacob as grandfather, father, and son is probably a basic reflection of the transformations in the political significance of these figures: with the fall of the Northern Kingdom and the dissolution of the sanctuary in Bethel the originally important figure from central Palestine, Jacob, gradually declined in significance in contrast to the Judahite figures of Abraham and Isaac, so that Jacob ultimately took his place at the end of the relational sequence.

That is to say, we can still see from Genesis 18 that the Abraham narratives are not simply a redactional extrapolation of the Isaac and Lot narratives. The story, which evidently derives from the *hieros logos* of the Terebinth sanctuary in Mamre, reveals a classic motif from the saga genre, namely a visit from gods who are hospitably received and reward the host with a gift, in this case the promise of a son. The reason for Isaac's name ("he laughed") in verses 10b-15

(Sarah "laughs") is inserted as a secondary climax in contrast to the high point of the story. The fact that this section is secondary within the narrative further clarifies the motif of Abraham and Sarah's advanced age, introduced after the fact in verse 11, as well as the fact that the identity of the divine visitors with YHWH, made explicit in the earliest layer of the narrative only on the story level, can now be shared also with the actors in the narrative as if it were a matter of course.

> And Sarah was listening at the tent entrance behind him. Now Abraham and Sarah were old, advanced in age; it had ceased to be with Sarah after the manner of women. So Sarah laughed to herself, saying, "After I have grown old, and my husband is old, shall I have pleasure?" YHWH said to Abraham, "Why did Sarah laugh, and say, 'Shall I indeed bear a child, now that I am old?' Is anything too wonderful for YHWH? At the set time I will return to you, in due season, and Sarah shall have a son." But Sarah denied, saying, "I did not laugh"; for she was afraid. He said, "Oh yes, you did laugh." (Gen 18:10b-15)

But this means that we can discover an Abraham narrative in Genesis 18 that originally lacked any reference to Isaac. The Isaac and Abraham traditions are thus probably not originally related as basic layer and expansion but as two sources alongside one another, so that the Abraham narratives, bit by bit, adopted motifs from the Isaac tradition and expanded them further.

The combination of Abraham and Isaac narratives was still probably completed in the monarchical period. At any rate, this seems indicated by the fact that in Genesis 13* and 18–19* (+ 21) we can perceive a formally coherent state-directed cycle constituted by two parallel strands. One of these, beginning with the figure of Abraham (13:2, 18), leads to the birth of the promised (v. 18) son Isaac (Gen 21:2).[93] The other draws a connection from Lot (13:5, 10-13) to the birth of his sons Moab and Ammon, who arise from an incestuous relationship with Lot's own daughters (Gen 19:30-38). Thus the relationship between Judah (cf. "Isaac" in Amos 7:9, 16) and the neighboring states of Moab and Ammon is theologically grounded and explained in this Abraham-Lot cycle.[94] The popular historical perspective of Genesis 13* + 18–19* (+ 21*) makes it clear that the Abraham-Lot cycle is also not to be interpreted as a family narrative, but formulates political theology. Even the material preceding this cycle, as the example of Genesis 18* shows, is already politically motivated: the promise of a son connected to the sanctuary at Mamre may originally have served as a legitimation of the immediately adjacent city-kingdom of Hebron before it was transferred to Abraham.

As was likewise the case with the Jacob cycle, a monarchical figure is absent from the Abraham-Lot cycle. If we locate it within monarchical-era Judah this finding might be connected to the handing on of this tradition in circles associated not with the royal court but with the Judahite landed gentry, who were an independent power factor in Judah.[95] But as a literary entity it could also presume the first deportation under Jehoiachin and document the hegemonial claims of the landed Judahite elite who came to the fore after the Judahite royal court was transferred to Babylon in 597 B.C.E. The attitude of the population remaining in the land, as referenced in Ezek 33:24, suggests that they referred to Abraham as their patron, something that makes a corresponding narrative of origins likely: "Mortal, the inhabitants of these waste places in the land of Israel keep saying, 'Abraham was only one man, yet he got possession of the land; but we are many; the land is surely given us to possess.'" At any rate, Ezek 33:24 does not seem to presume any literary connection between the Abrahamic and exodus traditions; instead, the one can be used to argue against the other.

3. Prophetic Traditions

Prophecy was not a phenomenon limited to ancient Israel.[96] Comparable phenomena are known from Mari (eighteenth century B.C.E.) and the Neo-Assyrian empire (seventh century B.C.E.).[97] Likewise, the dominant idea of the prophecies of judgment, that a deity turns against his or her own worshipers because of their guilt and history of sinfulness, is not unique,[98] although the idea that the deity expresses and decrees such retribution in advance through prophetic proclamations appears to be confined to ancient Israel. In cultural-historical terms, written prophecy presupposes the institution of the monarchy, since the prophets describe themselves as messengers of divine decrees that in their form are reminiscent of the proclamations of royal decrees, and they transform the royal messenger service into a relationship between God and the prophet.

What is without analogy, however, is the specific form of ongoing written prophecy,[99] known and indeed attested by the Old Testament (Jer 36:32).[100] It is true that in the Neo-Assyrian realm there were anthology tablets with prophetic sayings from different periods,[101] but the redactional processes that produced these anthology tablets were restricted to compilation and thus were not themselves forms of literary production.[102] Whether they had the potential for such development can no longer be empirically verified or falsified because of the fall of the Neo-Assyrian Empire and the scholastic tradition associated with it at the end of the seventh century B.C.E. Nevertheless, a significance over time is attributed to them (though it is restricted to a relatively short period): under Ashurbanipal (668–631/627? B.C.E.) positive oracles to his father, Esarhaddon (680–669 B.C.E.), were collected and assembled to legitimate the rule of Ashurbanipal, who, as in the case of Esarhaddon himself, was not the eldest son and therefore problematic in terms of dynastic succession.

But it was primarily in ancient Israel that prophecy was not understood to be valid only at a particular historical point in time; it was handed on through different periods and re-interpreted in terms of those new times, and this was done through a continued expansion of prophetic texts within the Bible itself.

Accordingly, the literary history of the prophetic books takes place throughout the whole literary history of the Old Testament and cannot simply be treated within the epoch of the protagonist that gave each particular book his name.

This perspective is no reason to doubt *in principle* the historicity of the biblical prophetic figures under whose names prophetic books have survived. On the basis of the literary evidence it is only in the cases of Joel, Jonah, or Malachi that one could be led to assume that these are purely literary products. Very disputed, however, is the question of how one should concretely imagine the prophets and their earliest proclamation. That discussion can only be pursued from the perspective of analytical redaction criticism and synthetic literary historical criticism: a corresponding dissection of the text of a prophetic book makes it possible, by drawing retrospective conclusions, to make clear what may be reasonably posited as its earliest form. It is difficult to determine the degree to which the prophets who gave their names to the books were themselves active as authors and redactors of their own books, but as a rule it is rather improbable. Their words were likely collected from the beginning by anonymous authors and redactors and assembled into books.[103]

If we survey the prophetic books of the Old Testament, it quickly becomes clear that the beginnings of the construction of prophetic traditions must lie in those books whose protagonists belong both biblically and historically to the Assyrian period: Hosea, Amos, Micah, and Isaiah. The following reflections will be confined to the books of Hosea, Amos, and Isaiah.

a. Beginnings of Prophetic Tradition in the Books of Hosea and Amos

Written prophecy begins with the books of Hosea and Amos,[104] and "written" prophecy as such may originate in the experience of the fall of the Northern Kingdom.[105] Whatever may be the oral stages preceding the catastrophe to which it can be traced, the crucial motivating factor in their being committed to writing can be seen *ex post facto* in their interpretation of the past. There can scarcely be any value in doubting the literary beginnings of written prophecy in the pre-exilic period. Evidence like Isa 8:1, 16-18; Jer 29:1; or the Lachish ostracon III, 20-21 presumes prophetic writers before 587 B.C.E.[106] In addition, the quotations from Mic 1:2 in 1 Kgs 22:28 and Mic 3:12 in Jer 26:17-19—perhaps not accidentally adoptions of the beginning and end of the presumable literary core of the Micah tradition—must be evaluated in historical terms.

It is true that Amos may have appeared as a prophet before Hosea, but it seems that the Hosea tradition was the first to be given a fixed form, and the prophecy of Amos was assembled in its literary form only under the influence of Hosea. In turn, the book of Amos had retroactive influence on the book of Hosea, as the verses 4:15; 7:10; 8:14; 11:10 in the latter book show, using language and themes from the book of Amos and thus interpreting both books as proclaiming one and the same will of God.[107] That the Hosea tradition has a certain priority from the literary point of view may be connected with the fact that the tradents of Hosea's accusations, which are more cultically accented, wanted to put them before the critique in the book of Amos, which is more strongly social in its orientation.

In Hosea, because of the allusive style, which leaves a great deal unclear to later readers, we can see how much the individual texts in the book still belong to the beginning phases of written tradition: they presume a good deal of knowledge on the part of the readers.[108] At the same time the core of the book of Hosea, chapters 4–9, seems to have been formed from the outset as a continuous text.[109] There are no superscriptions or closing formulae, and the book as a whole makes no use of the messenger formula; the formula of divine speech is found only in 2:15, 18, 23, and 11:1. The current presentation of the book of Hosea thus places no value on the original smaller units. Instead, the imperatives in 4:1; 5:1, 8; 8:1; 9:1 that provide its structure indicate a dramatic sequence illustrating the approach, inbreaking, and consequences of judgment. A composition of this sort can scarcely be imagined before 720 B.C.E.

> Differently from the second part of the book in Hosea 4–9(ff.), the three chapters Hosea 1–3 appear to have originated independently of each other and may even at first have been handed down separately, though that would not exclude mutual references or influences. This appears, for one thing, in the striking fact that each of the three chapters contains its own secondary positive conclusion (2:1-3; 2:16-25; 3:5), which hints at original independence. Besides this, there are notable form-critical differences: Hos 1:2-9 is an account in the third person; its point lies primarily in the naming of Hosea's children from his marriage to the prostitute Gomer: "Jezreel," "No Pity," and "Not My People." Hosea 2:4-15 is a continuous divine speech, while Hos 3:1-4 is Hosea's own account of his (different?) marriage to an adulterous woman who images the relationship of God to Israel.[110]

While the Hosea tradition was probably addressed first to the Northern Kingdom of Israel—though this has been disputed recently[111]—it was apparently redirected to Judahite readers in the seventh and sixth centuries B.C.E., as shown on the one hand by the naming of Judahite kings as well in the book's superscription, and on the other hand by a series of clear insertions of statements about Judah. The Judahites are, in the first place, warned in a way that could point to a contemporary situation in the seventh century B.C.E.: "Though you play the whore, O Israel, do not let Judah become guilty. Do not enter into Gilgal, or go up to Beth-aven, and do not swear, 'As YHWH lives'" (Hos 4:15). But other Hosea texts seem to be aware already of the fall of Judah and set it parallel with the fall of the Northern Kingdom: "Israel's pride testifies against him; Ephraim stumbles in his guilt; *Judah also stumbles with them*" (Hos 5:5). It seems obvious, then, that Hosea's message has been literarily updated for Judah in order to make it impossible for readers there to historicize the text and to force them to apply Hosea's tradition to themselves as well.

The book of Amos contains the oldest prophecy in Israel, one that became a cornerstone of written prophetic tradition. Because of its social-critical acerbity and Amos's independence of any institutional group of court or cultic prophets (for Amos those are "the prophets," cf. Amos 7:14), we may suppose that at first this prophecy had scarcely any chance of becoming theologically influential. There were probably two primary moments of historical resonance in the Amos tradition that were important for its influence. For one thing, the superscription of the book, literarily constructed in stages (the dating with the names of kings—from Israel and Judah!—collides with the precise note of an earthquake), shows that the earthquake that took place under Uzziah, still known to Zech 14:5 and to Flavius Josephus may have been understood to be an early affirmation of the truth of Amos's prophecy:[112] "The words of Amos, who was among the shepherds of Tekoa, which he saw concerning Israel *in the days of King Uzziah of Judah and in the days of King Jeroboam son of Joash of Israel*, two years before the earthquake" (Amos 1:1). The earthquake motif then becomes prominent in the proclamation contained in the book of Amos:

> So, I will press you down in your place, just as a cart presses down when it is full of sheaves. (Amos 2:13)

> I saw YHWH standing beside the altar, and he said: "Strike the capitals until the thresholds shake, and shatter them on the heads of all the people; and those who are left I will kill with the sword; not one of them shall flee away, not one of them shall escape." (Amos 9:1)

In addition, the fall of the Northern Kingdom in 720 B.C.E. would have aided the reception of the Amos tradition in its breakthrough so that it was expanded to include Judah.[113] The book of Amos itself seems to reflect on these problems in the visions in chapters 7–9.[114] The visions, with their structure toward a climax, played out in some sense in a private communication between YHWH and Amos and not supplied with any kind of command to proclaim them, apparently serve to show that Amos's prophecy of judgment was forced on him by God and did not arise of his own will. Amos functions in the first place as an advocate, but through the third vision he has to acknowledge the inevitability of the judgment that will mean the "end [of] my [i.e., God's] people Israel" (Amos 8:2-3). We can speculate whether the specific terminology of Israel as God's people already presumes the fall of the Northern Kingdom as a state and reflects on its post-national existence.[115]

The middle section of the book of Amos, probably somewhat older, in chapters 3–6, in any case reveals a different linguistic usage: "Hear this word that YHWH has spoken against you, O *people of Israel*" (Amos 3:1)—"Hear this word that I take up over you in lamentation, O *house of Israel*" (Amos 5:1). But these two verses are significant from another point of view. Apparently the two imperatives serve to divide the whole complex of Amos 3–6: Amos 3:1 addresses the "people of Israel" with divine words that were spoken to Israel in the past; these are followed, according to Amos 5:1, by prophetic words that are now directed in the present time to the political entity "house of Israel" (= Northern Kingdom of Israel) and at the same time are declared to be a "burial lament." Thus Amos 3–6 as a whole expresses the idea put forth in Amos 5:1, which laments prospectively the fall of the Northern Kingdom as a state because the people of God, without exception, have failed in carrying out the will of God.

Amos 5:1 also displays a rather typical feature of Old Testament prophecy. The proclamation of judgment is expressed in language drawn from the traditional lament over a corpse, but characteristically transformed: for one thing, the lament is raised over a collective, the house of Israel, and not over an individual; for another, this collective still exists, at least as presented in the book. The song treats Israel as if it were already dead. Amos 5:1 thus defamiliarizes a traditional speech pattern and so generates prophetic language.

From a literary-historical point of view, the beginnings of the Hosea and Amos traditions are of special significance inasmuch as they do not interpret the Assyrian threat in terms of the traditional thought patterns of the Jerusalem cultic tradition, as a chaos to be averted. Instead, they relate this threat to the cosmic-creative action of their own God: the fall of Israel brought about through the Assyrian military power is a means whereby God reacts to the evil cultic and social conditions in Israel, which in terms of domestic policy are rooted in social-historical processes of distinction and discrimination that are in turn grounded in a growing state capitalism. Hosea and Amos link domestic political and foreign political perspectives as cause and effect. The theological legitimacy of the fall of Israel that they proclaim is, however, not a matter of taking a position in favor of Assyria. The Assyrian empire remains, as shown by the imagery applied, a catastrophe-causing power, but implicitly its might is temporally restricted to its use as God's instrument of judgment.

> The book of Amos was apparently subjected at a later date to a Deuteronomistic revision, not very extensive but still well-defined (e.g., 1:1, 9-12; 2:4-5, 10-12; 3:1, 7; 5:25-26).[116] The book was apt for revision in a "Deuteronomistic" sense because Amos—like Jeremiah at the catastrophe of the Southern Kingdom—was the prophet who was active at the time when the Northern Kingdom fell.

b. The Earliest Isaiah Traditions and Their Josianic Reception

One of the earliest discoveries of modern biblical scholarship was that the sixty-six chapters of the book of Isaiah do not all come from the eighth-century B.C.E. Isaiah who gave his name to the book, but that words from that Isaiah are to be expected only within chapters 1–39.[117]

Within Isaiah 1–39 the ancient literary cores are sought especially in Isaiah 1–11, 28–32,[118] a procedure made plausible by the principle of exclusion: Isaiah 12 is an eschatological song of thanksgiving, and in Isaiah 13–23 we find sayings about foreign peoples, only a portion of which, in Isaiah 17, could go back to the eighth century B.C.E. Isaiah 24–27 contains a proto-apocalyptic vision of a world judgment that should probably be dated even to the post-Persian period, and in Isaiah 33–35 we find various bridging elements to the subsequent tradition of Deutero-Isaiah; Isaiah 36–39 contain stories about Isaiah taken from 2 Kings 18–20.

Where exactly the oldest texts in the book are to be found is a matter of dispute.[119] Of primary importance for a decision is the interpretation of the so-called memoir of Isaiah in chapters 6–8*.[120] Above all, the step-by-step origins of Isa 8:1-4, 5-8 reveal that Isaiah at first only pronounced judgment against the Syrian-Ephraimite coalition (cf. Isa 17:1-6), while the theologized pronouncement of judgment against Judah in 8:5-8 is secondary.[121]

> Then YHWH said to me, Take a large tablet and write on it in common characters, "Belonging to Maher-shalal-hash-baz [The spoil speeds, the prey hastens]," and have it attested for me by reliable witnesses, the priest Uriah and Zechariah son of Jeberechiah. And I went to the prophetess, and she conceived and bore a son. Then YHWH said to me, Name him Maher-shalal-hash-baz; for before the child knows how to call "My father" or "My mother," the wealth of Damascus and the spoil of Samaria will be carried away by the king of Assyria. (Isa 8:1-4)

> The LORD spoke to me again: Because this people has refused the waters of Shiloah that flow gently, and melt in fear before Rezin and the son of Remaliah; therefore, YHWH is bringing up against it the mighty flood waters of the River, the king of Assyria and all his glory; it will rise above all its channels and overflow all its banks; it will sweep on into Judah as a flood, and, pouring over, it will reach up to the neck; and its outspread wings will fill the breadth of your land, O Immanuel. (Isa 8:5-8)

If the pronouncement of judgment in Isa 8:5-8 belongs in the context of the events of 701 B.C.E., Isaiah himself had become a prophet of judgment against Judah. If it was created as a reflection on the fall of Judah and Jerusalem in 587 B.C.E., "Isaiah" would first have stood up against Judah in the additions of later tradents. But against this is the theological outline of the call vision in Isaiah 6, most probably from the monarchical period, which from the outset is shaped by a theology of judgment[122]—even if one believes the charge to provoke obstinacy in Isa 6:9-10 to be secondary.[123] Already on the basis of its idea that God is resident in the temple (rather than in heaven), Isaiah 6 cannot be a text from the exile or later.[124] Likewise, the concentrically structured and therefore evidently literarily unified section in Isa 1:21-26, which in light of the exilic later interpretation in 1:27-28 is itself most probably pre-exilic, suggests that Isaiah was a prophet of judgment, though he also developed a perspective beyond judgment.[125]

> How the **faithful city** has become a whore! She that was full of *justice, righteousness* lodged in her—but now murderers!
>> Your silver has become *dross*, your wine is mixed with water.
>> Your princes are rebels and companions of thieves. Everyone loves a bribe and runs after gifts. They do not defend the orphan, and the widow's cause does not come before them.
>>> Therefore says the Lord YHWH Zebaoth, the Mighty One of Israel:
>>> Ah, I will pour out my wrath on my enemies, and avenge myself on my foes!
>> I will turn my hand against you; I will smelt away your *dross* as with lye and remove all your *alloy*.
> And I will restore your *judges* as at the first, and your counselors as at the beginning. Afterward you shall be called the city of *righteousness*, **the faithful city.** (Isa 1:21-26)

> Zion shall be redeemed by justice,
> and those who return to her, by righteousness.
> But rebels and sinners shall be destroyed together, and those who forsake YHWH shall be consumed. (Isa 1:27-28)

There is therefore much to be said for the traditional view that the proclamations of judgment in Isaiah 1–11 contain material handed down from the prophet Isaiah,[126] even though the concentric arrangement of the chapter possibly belongs to the post-Isaianic, though still pre-exilic period:

1:21-26	Vision of justice
5:8-24	Woes against Judah
5:25-30	Refrain poem
6–8	Memoir
9:7-20 (10:4)	Refrain poem
10:1-4	Woes against Judah
11:1-5	Vision of justice

A dating that falls within the monarchical period is indicated, on the one hand, by the fact that the section from the time of Josiah, 8:23; 9:1-6 appears to play no part in this structure and therefore probably did not exist at this point.[127] On the other hand, the domestic-political orientation of the profile of the "messianic promise" in 11:1-5 is clearly different from its exilic counterparts in Jeremiah and Ezekiel.

The "refrain poem" receives its name from the recurring refrain in Isa 5:25; 9:11, 16, 20; 10:4: "for all this his anger has not turned away; his hand is stretched out still." Favoring a location of the composition of Isaiah 1–11 in the seventh century B.C.E. is, on the one hand, the motif of the command to provoke obstinacy in Isa 6:9-10, which evidently identifies the effect of Isaiah's preaching with its content ("keep listening, but do not comprehend; keep looking, but do not understand!") and so presumes a certain distance from Isaiah's prophetic activity, if not even from the lifting of the Assyrian blockade without much consequence for Jerusalem in 701 B.C.E.[128] This event caused Isaiah's prophecy of judgment to seem false for a century or more, until it was finally verified in the destruction of Jerusalem by the Babylonians in 587 B.C.E.

How should these beginnings of the Isaiah tradition be interpreted in literary-historical terms? If we maintain this coherence within Isaiah 1–11, Blum's observation seems decisive: the Isaiah tradition does not begin a new prophecy but connects, through quotation, with the older Amos tradition.[129] The crucial statement is found in the so-called refrain poem, in Isa 9:7-8: "Yhwh sent a word against Jacob, and it fell on Israel; and all the people knew it—Ephraim and the inhabitants of Samaria—but in pride and arrogance of heart they said: 'The bricks have fallen, but we will build with dressed stones; the sycamores have been cut down, but we will put cedars in their place.'" Contrary to many Bible translations, this verse is clearly formulated in the perfect tense: the divine word has already been fulfilled against the Northern Kingdom. This is not a matter of future prophecy, but of interpretation of the past. That this saying is about the prophecy of Amos is not explicitly stated, but it can clearly be discerned from the context. For one thing, the judgment on the Northern Kingdom is evidently being described as an earthquake ("the bricks have fallen"), as suggested also by Isa 5:25 in the first part of the refrain poem: "Therefore the anger of Yhwh was kindled against his people, and he stretched out his hand against them and struck them; *the mountains quaked*, and their corpses were like refuse in the streets. For all this his anger has not turned away, and his hand is stretched out still." Earthquake as judgment is a basic element of the prophecy of Amos (cf. Amos 1:1; 2:13; 9:1). In addition, the refrain poem—by its very genre, cf. the matching form of Amos 4:6-12— reveals further links to the book of Amos. Particularly noteworthy is Isa 9:12, with the motifs of "not turning back" (cf. Amos 4:6, 8, 9, 10, 11), "striking" (Amos 4:9), and "not seeking" (Amos 5:4, 5, 6, 14): "the people *did not turn* to him who *struck* them, or *seek* Yhwh of hosts." In view of this resemblance it seems necessary to conclude that Isaiah 5; 9–10 allude to the book of Amos. As to the content, this means that for the early book of Isaiah the threat of judgment against Judah is not a new oracle of judgment by God but an extension of the judgment originally imposed on the Northern Kingdom. Thus Isaiah does not proclaim anything other than what Amos had predicted; the only difference is that it now extends Amos's message to Judah.

If these observations regarding the refrain poem are correct, it is also highly likely that we should connect Isaiah's call vision in chapter 6 with Amos's visions in Amos 7–9. As Amos, within the narrative course of the visions, must first of all accept that the judgment is inevitable,[130] so Isaiah in chapter 6 must learn that the assignment God has for him is such that, because of its content, whoever freely accepts the mission must expect to be rejected in the strongest possible way.

Still in the pre-exilic period, probably during the reign of Josiah, the Isaiah tradition was subjected to a crucial reinterpretation, as worked out especially by Hermann Barth, who called it the "Assyrian" redaction.[131] This reinterpretation, for one thing, extended the judgment that, according to Amos and Isa 9:7, had already fallen upon the Northern Kingdom and then, according to the Isaiah tradition, had affected Judah, to now include the divine instrument, Assyria itself:

> YHWH of hosts has sworn: As I have designed, so shall it be; and as I have planned, so shall it come to pass: I will break the Assyrian in my land, and on my mountains trample him under foot; his yoke shall be removed from them, and his burden from their shoulders. This is the plan that is planned concerning the whole earth; and *this is the hand* that is stretched out over all the nations. For YHWH of hosts has planned, and who will annul it? *His hand is stretched out*, and who will turn it back? (Isa 14:24-27)

The fact that the judgment on Assyria is an extension of the judgment on Israel and Judah is evident from the quotation of the refrain from Isa 5:25; 9:11, 16, 20; 10:4, in 14:26-27 ("his hand is stretched out"). At the same time, the fall of Assyria introduces the time of salvation for Judah, as it was experienced in the prosperous time of Josiah:

> . . . In the former time he brought into contempt the land of Zebulun and the land of Naphtali, but in the latter time he will make glorious the way of the sea, the land beyond the Jordan, Galilee of the nations. The people who walked in darkness have seen a great light; those who lived in a land of deep darkness—on them the light has shined. You have multiplied the nation, you have increased its joy; they rejoice before you as with joy at the harvest, as people exult when dividing plunder. For the yoke of their burden, and the bar across their shoulders, the rod of their oppressor, you have broken as on the day of Midian. For all the boots of the tramping warriors and all the garments rolled in blood shall be burned as fuel for the fire. For a child has been born for us, a son given to us; authority rests upon his shoulders; and he is named Wonderful Counselor, Mighty God, Everlasting Father,

Prince of Peace. His authority shall grow continually, and there shall be endless peace for the throne of David and his kingdom. He will establish and uphold it with justice and with righteousness from this time onward and forevermore. (Isa 8:23; 9:1-6a)

The grateful look backward to the birth of a royal child in Isa 9:1-6—contrary to later church reception, this section, because of its formulation in the perfect tense, is demonstrably not a messianic promise—in all probability refers to Josiah, who ascended to the throne of Judah at the age of eight (2 Kgs 22:1-2). Thus Isa 9:5 is formulated as a fulfillment of the statement in Isa 7:14, which in turn was understood messianically, contrary to its original sense:

9:5 For a child has been <u>born</u> for *us*,	7:14 Look, the young woman is with child and
a <u>son</u> given *to us*.	<u>shall bear</u> a <u>son</u>, and shall name him
	Immanuel [God with *us*].

The fall of the Assyrian power was thus explained as a prospect of salvation for Judah and judgment against Assyria.

The book of Isaiah is a strikingly "un-Deuteronomistic" prophetic book.[132] Probably it was above all its orientation to a strong traditional Zion theology that made it subsequently impregnable to Deuteronomistic interpretations such as those that affected, for example, the books of Amos and Jeremiah.

4. Legal Traditions

The Pentateuch contains three large bodies of law (the Book of the Covenant [Exodus 20–23], the Holiness Code [Leviticus 17–26], and Deuteronomy). Of these, the Book of the Covenant is rightly regarded as the oldest. The relationships among the three corpora (all of which, of course, were subjected to literary expansions) can be quite clearly determined on the basis of the internal biblical interpretive relationships: Deuteronomy can be understood over long stretches as a reinterpretation of the Book of the Covenant,[133] while the Holiness Code in turn accommodates material from Deuteronomy to the Priestly document.[134]

a. The Book of the Covenant
Exodus 20:22–23:33 contains a corpus of legal statements that, because of Exod 24:7 ("Then he [Moses] took the book of the covenant, and read it in the hearing of the people"), is known as "the Book of the Covenant." There is the broadest possible consensus that this corpus represents a literary entity that grew over time. However, in the last ten years the evaluation of the basic theological tendency of the Book of the Covenant has shifted dramatically. While Jörn Halbe determined

the core of the Book of the Covenant to consist of religious laws as in Exodus 34,[135] the newer work of Eckart Otto, Ludger Schwienhorst-Schönberger, Yuichi Osumi, Ralf Rothenbusch, Reinhard Kratz, and Rainer Albertz agrees that, on the contrary, the components of "secular law" (*mishpatim*) stemming from ancient Near Eastern legal tradition are earlier, and they regard the "theologizing" of this material as secondary.[136] This conclusion is based partly on a new evaluation of the literary development of Exodus 20–23, but also on changed religious-historical perspectives on the Old Testament that have rendered impossible the classic approach of legal history following Albrecht Alt.[137] Alt and his followers generally distinguished between apodictic and casuistic legal statements and saw in apodictic law, which formulates categorical prohibitions without differentiating punishments in different cases ("you shall not . . ."), the genuine nomadic heritage of Israel, whereas the casuistic provisions, which associated particular punishments with particular offenses ("if . . . then . . ."), were thought to have been adopted from Canaan. It has now become clear that neither the division of apodictic and casuistry between Israel and Canaan nor the thesis of Israel's exclusively nomadic origins can be maintained.

The theologizing of the law was accompanied by a completely altered conception of law. We must be clear that the traditional ancient Near Eastern law collections were—contrary to what they have been called—not "codices," but law collections.[138] That is, these are not prescriptive texts, but descriptive, representing "an aid for applying the law, but not a rule."[139] The legislative authority in the ancient Near East was not a written rule of law but the monarch.[140] That in pre-Hellenistic Egypt there were no written law codes, with the exception of a decree by King Horemheb in the Eighteenth Dynasty,[141] is thus not an exception but only a consistent illustration of this situation, which found its material expression in the Greek and Roman idea of the king as *nomos empsychos* or *lex animata*.[142] Accordingly, we should see the older "secular law" rules in the Book of the Covenant as model cases that aided legal scholars but were not binding on them as such. One example of this kind of legal statement, formulated in the third person, is found in Exod 22:4-5:

> When someone causes a field or vineyard to be grazed over, or lets livestock loose to graze in someone else's field, restitution shall be made from the best in the owner's field or vineyard. When fire breaks out and catches in thorns so that the stacked grain or the standing grain or the field is consumed, the one who started the fire shall make full restitution.

That this kind of statement is not simply a matter of "secular" law is clear from the subsequent verses, Exod 22:6-8:

> When someone delivers to a neighbor money or goods for safekeeping, and they are stolen from the neighbor's house, then the thief, if caught,

shall pay double. If the thief is not caught, the owner of the house shall
be brought before God, to determine whether or not the owner had
laid hands on the neighbor's goods. In any case of disputed ownership
involving ox, donkey, sheep, clothing, or any other loss, of which one
party says, "This is mine," the case of both parties shall come before
God; the one whom God condemns shall pay double to the other.

In cases that could not be decided, an ordeal could be prescribed in order to
make the determination. In any case it is evident that in these texts God is not
the legislator but at most the judge.

This changes the moment the Book of the Covenant, especially through
the introduction in Exod 20:22—21:1 and the insertion of the second person,
becomes "divine law" and thus simultaneously the standard for the rest of the
further history of law in the Old Testament, which as a consequence necessarily becomes an interpretation of the more ancient divine law. The law is
detached from the traditional royal authority and is, so to speak, "excarnated"
into written form.[143] For that reason about half of all Old Testament statements of law are equipped with an introduction containing an explanation
of the law's origins, a promise for those who keep this law, a reason for it, a
threat, or a clarification of its meaning. This can be explained by the fact that
these laws no (longer) had an authority that would see to it that they were carried out. Instead, they apparently rest on their authority as divine law alone.[144]
This is clearly evident, for example, in Exod 22:20-23:

You shall not wrong or oppress a resident alien, for you were aliens in
the land of Egypt. You shall not abuse any widow or orphan. If you do
abuse them, when they cry out to me, I will surely heed their cry; my
wrath will burn, and I will kill you with the sword, and your wives shall
become widows and your children orphans.

As regards the content of this Book of the Covenant, now as divine law, it
is striking that it is no longer the model character of complex legal situations
that shapes the tradition, but instead the central theological statements of law,
justice, and mercy,[145] which are in the foreground of the prophetic proclamation of Hosea, Amos, Micah, and Isaiah.[146] "The shattering of all obvious
certainties bemoaned by the prophets of the late eighth and early seventh centuries B.C.E., which they later declared to be divine judgment on an unfaithful
people, is taken up by the Book of the Covenant in such a way that positive
divine law is derived from the laments and accusations of the prophets."[147] In
fact, there are striking relationships between the prophetic tradition and the
Book of the Covenant that can be interpreted accordingly.[148] Compare, for
example, Amos 2:6-8 with the statement of divine law (in the second person)
in Exod 22:24-26:

Amos 2:6-8	Exodus 22:24-26
Thus says YHWH: For three transgressions of Israel, and for four, I will not revoke the punishment; *because they sell the righteous for silver, and the needy for a pair of sandals*—they who trample the head of the poor into the dust of the earth, and push the afflicted out of the way . . . they lay themselves down beside every altar on <u>garments taken in pledge</u>; and in the house of their God they drink wine bought with fines they imposed.	*If you lend money to [one of] my people, to the poor among you, you shall not deal with them as a creditor; you shall not exact interest from them. If you take <u>your neighbor's cloak in pawn</u>, you shall restore it before the sun goes down; for it may be your neighbor's only clothing to use as cover; in what else shall that person sleep? And if your neighbor cries out to me, I will listen, for I am compassionate.*

Besides the reception of the prophetic tradition, be it only the content or literary,[149] we can discern a second element in the interpretations of divine law in the second person in the Book of the Covenant: they reveal a prominent shaping by the exodus tradition. The redactional beginning of the Book of the Covenant with the prohibition of images in Exod 20:23 and the motif of liberation of slaves in Exod 21:2 already awaken strong associations with that tradition:

> You shall not make gods of silver alongside me, nor shall you make for yourselves gods of gold. (Exod 20:23; cf. 23:13b)

> When you buy a male Hebrew slave, he shall serve six years, but in the seventh he shall go out a free person, without debt. (Exod 21:2)

Something similar can be said of the historicizing passages within Exodus 21–23 and the epilogue of the Book of the Covenant:

> I will hand over to you the inhabitants of the land, and you shall drive them out before you. You shall make no covenant with them and their gods. They shall not live in your land, or they will make you sin against me; for if you worship their gods, it will surely be a snare to you. (Exod 23:31b-33)

This complex of exodus motifs indicates that it was first within the framework of the interpretation of the Book of the Covenant as divine law that these motifs were inserted into the narrative context in which they now reside; still, it is not very likely that the divine law passages in the second person are all to be assigned to a single literary level.

b. Deuteronomy

The name "Deuteronomy" for the last book of the Pentateuch, which is the result of a misunderstanding on the part of the Greek translator of Deut 17:18 ("second law" instead of "copy of the law"), is appropriate in terms both of the history of its origins and of its narrative context: considerable parts of Deuteronomy were created as a new edition of the Book of the Covenant appropriated for the advancement of cultic centralization.[150] In its current location in the Pentateuch, Deuteronomy is meant to be read as nothing but the proclamation by Moses of the lawgiving at Sinai in the land east of the Jordan.[151] The literary core of the law of centralization itself, in Deut 12:13-14, is literarily dependent on the law for the altar in the Book of the Covenant in Exod 20:24 and directly cites it:[152]

Deuteronomy 12:13-14	Exodus 20:24
Take care that you do not offer your burnt offerings <u>at any place</u> you happen to see. But only at the place that Yhwh will choose in one of your tribes—there you shall offer your burnt offerings and there you shall do everything I command you.	You need make for me only an altar of earth and sacrifice on it your burnt offerings and your offerings of well-being, your sheep and your oxen; <u>in every place</u> where I cause my name to be remembered I will come to you and bless you.

But the individual laws are also reformulated in the service of cultic centralization:

Deuteronomy 15:12-18	Exodus 21:2-7
<u>If a member of your community, whether a Hebrew man or a Hebrew woman, [sells himself or herself to you]</u> and works for you six years, in the seventh year you shall set that person free. *And when you send a male slave out from you a free person, you shall not send him out empty-handed.*	<u>When you buy a male Hebrew slave,</u> he shall serve six years, *but in the seventh he shall go out a free person, without debt. . . .*
. . . But if he says to you, "I will not go out from you," because he loves you and your household, since he is well off with you, then you shall take an awl and thrust it through his earlobe into the door, and he shall be your slave forever. You shall do the same with regard to your female slave. Do not consider it a hardship when you send them out from you free persons, because for six years they have given you services worth the wages of hired laborers; and Yhwh your God will bless you in all that you do.	But if the slave declares, "I love my master, my wife, and my children; I will not go out a free person," then his master shall bring him **before God.** He shall be brought to the door or the doorpost; and his master shall pierce his ear with an awl; and he shall serve him for life.

The reformulation of the slave law from Exod 21:2-7 in Deut 15:12-18 shows in exemplary fashion a whole series of new interpretations: slavery as such is regarded in Exodus 21 as a matter of course ("when you buy a male slave"); in Deuteronomy it is accepted but is regarded critically ("sells himself or herself to you," that is, "has to sell himself or herself to you"; "member of your community [lit.: 'brother']"). When the slave is set free, in Deuteronomy 15 she or he is equipped in such a way that the former slave can construct an independent existence and will not immediately fall back into slavery. But if the slave wishes to serve in the master's house for life, it is sealed by a ritual that in Exodus 21 is evidently sacred in nature ("before God"), while in Deuteronomy 15 it appears in a secular form. Especially striking, finally, is the closing passage in Deuteronomy 15, which on the one hand formulates a motivation for releasing the slave and on the other hand places in view the divine blessing to be had by keeping this commandment: apparently the law in Deuteronomy attempts to validate itself through empathy, not by executive power.

At any rate, support for locating the first edition of Deuteronomy in the time of Josiah has been based, as a rule, on the connection, apparent since W. M. L. de Wette's *Dissertatio Critica*,[153] between the depiction of Josiah's reform in 2 Kings 22–23 and the main aim of Deuteronomy. Josiah's reform, with its maxims of "unity of worship" and "purity of worship," incorporates the elementary demands of Deuteronomy, and as a result scholars have described it as the document underlying the reform.

However, the historicity of Josiah's reform is disputed.[154] In addition, the connection between Deuteronomy and the reform can scarcely find an adequately secure historical grounding in the controversial literary criticism of Deuteronomy and 2 Kings 22–23. We are in danger of arguing in a circle if the connection that must first be demonstrated by literary criticism is already presupposed.[155]

At the same time, the historical location of the basic content of Deuteronomy in the late Assyrian period may be accurate, even though this has become fluid again in the course of academic discussion.[156] The crucial argument lies in the observation that Deuteronomy is completely molded in the style of an Assyrian oath of fidelity (*ade*), though it requires unconditional loyalty not to the Assyrian monarch but to YHWH. We do not need to grasp at the overdrawn thesis that Ur-Deuteronomy (containing Deuteronomy 13* + 28*) is nothing more than a translation of *VTE* §10.56 and further elements.[157] Against this are (1) the internal literary criticism of Deuteronomy, which makes it very unlikely that Deuteronomy 13* represents a literary core, as well as (2) the by-no-means literal transposition of *VTE* into the passages mentioned.[158] The Neo-Assyrian background of Deuteronomy can be grasped with sufficient clarity from a tradition-critical point of view: Deuteronomy is a subversive reception of Neo-Assyrian vassal-treaty theology.[159] Likewise, the program of cultic centralization, which appears unique, has a parallel in the Neo-Assyrian realm in the binding of the god of Assyria to the Assyrian capital city, and it may well have been at least motivated by that parallel.[160]

If we retain the idea of an Ur-Deuteronomy in the time of Josiah, we must then inquire about its literary-historical linkages. We have just mentioned the intercultural reception of Neo-Assyrian treaty theology, which seems to have exercised the strongest influence on Deuteronomy. Thus the Deuteronomic theology of the "love of God" is not drawn from Hosea, as was popularly supposed by those who followed Alt, but is an ancient Near Eastern form of speech that in international treaty law refers to political loyalty: "If you do not love Assurbanipal, the crown prince of the succession, the son of Esarhaddon, the king of Assyria, your Lord, as yourself . . ." (*VTE* 24, 266–68), then the sanctions listed in the following section of curses will come to pass.[161]

And yet Deuteronomy also reveals strong ties to Israelite traditional material. We have already mentioned the fact that Deuteronomy represents a "centralized" update of the Book of the Covenant. In its reformulation of that book Deuteronomy makes an effort to find solutions for daily life in relation to a centralized cult. Thus, for example, in Deuteronomy 12 secular local slaughtering of animals is permitted, and the permanent dedication of slaves at house or local sanctuaries (Exod 21:6) is also secularized (Deut 15:17). Finally, the establishment of cities of refuge (Deut 19:1-13) takes the place of the previous asylum function of local sanctuaries (Exod 21:12-14).

The construction of a solidary ethos of kinship is also clearly evident in Deuteronomy.[162] This is to be explained theologically through the mutuality of God and people established in the Deuteronomic covenant theology and historically by the influx of refugees into Judah from the Northern Kingdom in the seventh century B.C.E. We should perhaps reckon with the possibility that it was only after the fall of the Northern Kingdom that the idea of a consciousness of unity and of the existence as a single people encompassing northern Israel and Judah was fully established.[163] At any rate, texts from the period when there were still two kingdoms clearly distinguish between the "house of Israel" and the "house of Judah," while the theologized discourse of the "people of God" is apparently grounded in the loss of the independent statehood of at least the Northern Kingdom.

If these considerations are accurate, then the possibilities for a specific religio-political interpretation of the *Shema* (Deut 6:4) arises. The demand is: "Hear, O Israel: Yhwh, our God, in one Yhwh!" The most probable translation and interpretation of the original meaning of this command is that reason is given for the oneness of Yhwh in the sense of a restriction of the legitimate manifestations of Yhwh to the Yhwh of Jerusalem, as the demands in Deuteronomy 12 for a centralization of worship correspondingly require for ritual praxis.[164] The interpretation of Deut 6:4 in the sense of the first commandment sometimes advocated is, rather, to be addressed as an early form of reception history of the *Shema*, contemporary with the first commandment, and not as its original meaning.[165]

In addition, Deuteronomy is clearly shaped by wisdom traditions.[166] Besides certain individual points of contact, we should mention above all the

Deuteronomic translation of the act-consequence model into the sphere of divine law: if Israel keeps the commandments given to it, it will receive blessing; otherwise curses will come upon it. The influence of prophecy on Deuteronomy as we now have it[167] seems to be the product of its later literary history.[168]

The significance of Deuteronomy from a literary-historical perspective can scarcely be overstated. Its domestic and intercultural hermeneutic, which adopts and reinterprets both the Book of the Covenant and Assyrian treaty theology in subtle ways, lends it a unique character distinguished both by tradition and by innovation.[169] This exegetical mediation and interweaving of tradition and innovation can, from a formal point of view, be witnessed repeatedly as a fundamental impulse in the literary history of the Old Testament, even in other text complexes. From the point of view of its content, Deuteronomy's influence was both formative and provocative: the Deuteronomic-Deuteronomistic tradition would accompany the growth of Old Testament literature to its end and beyond, and during that span of time this strand of tradition repeatedly evoked counter-conceptions, the most prominent of which was formulated in the Priestly document.[170]

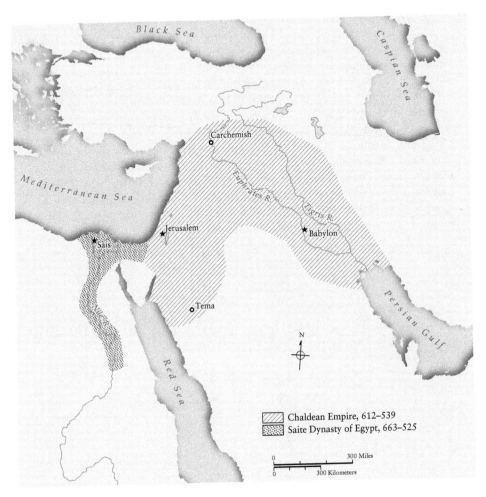

The Near East in 580 B.C.E.

Part D

The Literature of the Babylonian Period (Sixth Century B.C.E.)

I. Historical Backgrounds

Perhaps even before the fall of Nineveh in 612 B.C.E. and the remnant of the Assyrian state in Haran in 610 B.C.E., but definitively after the death of Josiah in or before Megiddo in 609 B.C.E. (the battle is a literary construct of 2 Chr 35:20-24),[1] Judah fell under Egyptian hegemony.[2] The Assyrians handed domination of the Levant to their former vassals and new allies. The Egyptian Pharaoh Necho II deposed Josiah's son Jehoahaz, who had been crowned by the Judahite landed gentry immediately after the death of Josiah, and elevated his older brother Eliakim/Jehoiakim (608–598) to the throne. However, this Egyptian-dominated episode did not last long: with the victory of Nebuchadnezzar II, then still the crown prince of Babylon, over the Egyptians at the battle of Carchemish (605 B.C.E.) began the "seventy-year" hegemony (cf. Jer 25:12; 29:10) of Babylon in the ancient world of the Near East. It thus encompassed a relatively modest time period, but politically and theologically it was of crucial importance, especially for Jerusalem and Judah—or at any rate for the producers of literature and their audience among the elite circles—due to the fall of the monarchy, the state, and the temple, and the survival, nevertheless, of the religion and culture.

After 605 B.C.E. Judah became a Babylonian vassal state for three years under Jehoiakim. In the wake of Nebuchadnezzar's advance against Egypt in the year 601 B.C.E., which had a disastrous outcome, it seemed to Jehoiakim that the time had come to dissolve his nation's vassal status. The retaliatory act from Babylon came a few years later, in 597 B.C.E., and fell on Jehoiakim's successor, his son Jehoiachin.[3] The Babylonian army captured Jerusalem, deported the upper classes and artisans (who could make weapons)—according to 2 Kgs 24:14 the "upper ten thousand"—and set in place a puppet king, another of Josiah's sons, Mattaniah/Zedekiah. The number "ten thousand" is probably an exaggeration. Jeremiah 52:28-30 speaks of the deportation of 3,023 Judahites in 597. It is possible that Zedekiah's secession from Babylon, the political motivation for which cannot be clearly discerned, was associated with the shift of power in Egypt from Psammetichus II to Apries.[4] In any case the Babylonian army reappeared in Judah, now apparently under the leadership of the great king himself, and conquered Jerusalem in 587 B.C.E. The Babylonians' political motive is probably to be sought in its desire to eliminate Judah as a gateway for Egyptian influence in the Levant.[5] City and Temple were destroyed; the king was deported and his sons killed.[6] Once again there was a deportation, and the books of Kings create the impression that it encompassed a considerable majority of the population.

> In the fifth month, on the seventh day of the month—which was the nineteenth year of King Nebuchadnezzar, king of Babylon—Nebuzaradan, the captain of the bodyguard, a servant of the king of Babylon, came to Jerusalem. He burned the house of YHWH, the king's house, and all the houses of Jerusalem. . . . Nebuzaradan the captain of the guard carried into exile the rest of the people who were left in the city and the deserters who had defected to the king of Babylon—all the rest of the population. But the captain of the guard left some of the poorest people of the land to be vinedressers and tillers of the soil. (2 Kgs 25:8-12)

The portrait in Chronicles goes still further and speaks of a complete emptying of the land:

> Therefore he [YHWH] brought up against them the king of the Chaldeans, who killed their youths with the sword in the house of their sanctuary, and had no compassion on young man or young woman, the aged or the feeble; he gave them all into his hand. . . . He took into exile in Babylon those who had escaped from the sword, and they became servants to him and to his sons until the establishment of the kingdom of Persia, to fulfill the word of YHWH by the mouth of Jeremiah, until the land had made up for its sabbaths. All the days that it lay desolate it kept sabbath, to fulfill seventy years. (2 Chr 36:17-21)

However, from a historical perspective these two parallel accounts are not very trustworthy because both the archaeological discoveries about the structure of settlements in Judah and Jer 52:28-30, which speaks of three stages of deportation (597 B.C.E.: 3,023 Judahites; 587 B.C.E.: 832 Judahites; 582 B.C.E.: 745 Judahites) suggest a quite different picture. The greater part of the population remained in the land, even though the decline of population due to the deportations must have been far-reaching in its effects.[7] The theory of the "empty land," represented especially by Chronicles but secondarily anchored in Kings as well as in the Jeremiah and Ezekiel traditions,[8] derives from the perspective of the exilic community, stemming especially from privileged circles that regarded themselves as the legitimate heirs of monarchical Israel and imagined the land as a "vacuum" during the exile, a place waiting only for them and no one else.

After the deportation of the Judahite king and the destruction of Jerusalem, it appears that Nebuchadnezzar established an administration (or, and this is less likely, a successor kingship)[9] under Gedaliah, with its seat in Mizpah. However, Gedaliah was murdered soon after. The reason for this bloody deed may be found in the fact that Gedaliah, a non-Davidide, might have laid claim to royal status. This, however, is disputed.[10] Thereafter Judah ceased to exist as an independent political entity and was probably added to the province of Samaria.[11]

Literary and theological life continued, both in the land and in the Babylonian exile.[12] Unlike the deportation practices of the Assyrians, the exiled Judahites were settled by the Babylonians in separate colonies and thus were able not only to maintain their uniqueness but to develop it quite considerably.[13]

However, the Babylonian world hegemony was brief. It did not long survive the death of Nebuchadnezzar II (562 B.C.E.). Amel-Marduk (562–560 B.C.E.) and Neriglissar (560–556 B.C.E.) were followed by Nabonidus (556–539),[14] whose peculiar religious and cultic preferences made him so despised by the influential Babylonian priesthood of Marduk that they welcomed the rise of the Persian king Cyrus, whose rise had been observable since the fall of Lydia in 546 B.C.E., and even greeted him as the liberator of Babylon when, in 539 B.C.E., he captured the city without a fight.[15]

II. Theological Characterizations

The Babylonian period in the history of Old Testament theology is characterized by some fundamental disruptions, though we should make an important distinction at the outset: Old Testament perspectives are not to be interpreted simply as responses to historical experiences but also within the framework of longer-term intellectual, spiritual, and cultural developments, and should be examined in terms of their own historical influence. The intellectual-historical developments in the seventh century B.C.E. must have been of crucial significance for the fact that the religion of Judah did not also disappear in the wake of the catastrophe that struck Judah and Jerusalem, as was the standard outcome in comparable situations in the ancient Near East. The texts and writings created in this period had had to deal in no small way with the experience of the demise of the Northern Kingdom, and thus they began to develop conceptions of "Israel" that were not determined by statehood and political sovereignty but bore accents of promise (the preliminary editions of the patriarchal history), election (the Moses narrative, the stories of the judges, the "books of Kings"), or covenant theology (Deuteronomy). The intellectual construct of Israel as the people of God—and not a people whose identity was determined by its land— was probably something intellectually available at least a century beforehand.[16]

It has rightly been pointed out that in the ancient Near East the notion that a deity would turn against his or her own worshipers was not limited to Israel.[17]

There are examples in the Mesha stele (lines 4-5: "Omri was king of Israel, and he oppressed Moab many days, for Kamosh was angry with his land")[18] and in a Babylonian text edited by Lambert that traced the destruction of Babylon by the Elamites to Marduk's wrath at Babylon.[19] We could also mention, for example, the "Curse of Akkad"[20] or the Weidner Chronicle.[21] Finally, we should point to ancient Near Eastern interpretive texts that trace the destruction of temples to the fact that the respective gods had abandoned their temple.[22] Nevertheless, the idea of complete divine judgment on God's own people in ancient Israel remains without a real parallel in the ancient Near East.

After experiencing their own catastrophe, indeed, texts like Jeremiah 50–51 and Isaiah 47 developed a corresponding expectation of judgment on Babylon, the power that had destroyed the Jerusalem temple. These kept alive the hope that the city of Babylon would be destroyed, something that was not historically realized.[23] Accordingly, Jeremiah 50–51 and Isaiah 47 can be dated with some probability as still belonging to the Babylonian era. The judgment expected against Babylon is interpreted in Jeremiah 50–51 as a prolongation of the judgment on Judah that had already happened and had been carried out by Babylon itself. Correspondingly, individual sections within Jeremiah 50–51 adopted judgment sayings against Judah word for word from the first part of the book of Jeremiah and readdressed them to Babylon (but cf. Jer 10:12-16//51:15-19):[24]

Jeremiah 6:22-24	Jeremiah 50:41-43
Thus says YHWH: See, a people is coming from the land of the north, a great nation is stirring from the farthest parts of the earth. They grasp the bow and the javelin, they are cruel and have no mercy, their sound is like the roaring sea;	Look, a people is coming from the north; a mighty nation and many kings are stirring from the farthest parts of the earth. They wield bow and spear, they are cruel and have no mercy. The sound of them is like the roaring sea;
they ride on horses, equipped like a warrior for battle, against you, O daughter Zion! "We have heard news of them,	they ride upon horses, set in array as a warrior for battle, against you, O daughter Babylon! The king of Babylon heard news of them,
our hands fall helpless; anguish has taken hold of us, pain as of a woman in labor.	and his hands fell helpless; anguish seized him, pain like that of a woman in labor.

Of course, the prior intellectual and spiritual history of Israel and Judah in the seventh century B.C.E. did not in and of itself furnish the instruments for enduring theological interpretations of the catastrophe. Rather, what existed in the moment were conditions that made it possible to discover such interpretations. As the texts of the Babylonian period show, these interpretations were wrested in painful processes that, on the one hand, took leave of traditional ideas, but on the other hand had to engage with competing concepts as well.

Most likely texts of lament were the first texts produced. These were, be it noted, not simply intuitive religious expressions but involved formulating theological positions: the laments, for example, in Lamentations and Jeremiah 4–10 are intellectual confrontations with pre-exilic Zion theology, reflecting on the collapse of the former orthodoxy with the methods of internal biblical exegesis.

More or less at the same time, or perhaps somewhat later, positions were formulated that associated the national collapse with a specific critique of the kings. These are to be found in the prophetic texts that are critical of the monarch, such as those in Jeremiah (chs. 21–23), but primarily in the addition of 2 Kings 24–25, with their summary condemnation of all the kings, to the preceding description of the monarchical periods in Israel and Judah, and finally also in the texts at the beginning of 1 Samuel that are critical of monarchy and in some sense serve as a prelude to the end: the heart of the sanctuary, the Ark, is lost to the Philistines (1 Samuel 4–6), and the institution of monarchy is condemned as such even before its inception (1 Samuel 8, 12).

This view that assigns guilt to the kings, however, was immediately transformed and expanded in that the accusations were now transferred to the people as a whole. This process presumes a solid conviction that the monarchy is irretrievably lost. This popular perspective is especially obvious in 2 Kgs 17:9-20 and in the reinterpretation of the account of the creation of two images of calves by Jeroboam I (1 Kings 12) in the episode of the golden calf (Exodus 32). The efforts toward a theological history in Samuel–Kings have a certain parallel in the interpretations of the past in Neo-Babylonian texts, for example those that ground the destruction of Babylon by Sennacherib (689 B.C.E.) and the removal of the statue of Marduk to Assyria in Marduk's wrath against his own people.[25]

But it was not only in the realm of reinterpretation of theology of history that the Babylonian period brought crucial changes; the same was true regarding the understanding of God. The withdrawal of God from the sanctuary to a dwelling in heaven, observable in many texts,[26] is only one of a number of decisive reformulations we can perceive and that—in this case—drew crucial momentum from the experience of the temple's destruction. However, there is a need for subtle differentiation: God does not move from earth to heaven, because even in texts from the monarchical period, God, despite having his throne in the temple, can act from heaven. Yet it was the exilic period that first developed the notion of a heavenly sanctuary that explicitly names a divine throne.

The literary development of 1 Kings 8 can be read in exemplary fashion in terms of the literary-historical withdrawal of God's dwelling into heaven: in 1 Kings 8, beginning at verse 22—apparently in a development of the older traditional idea in verses 14-21—the dominant view is that God's presence is not bound to the temple; God himself is enthroned in heaven. The new beginning of the prayer in verse 22 has Solomon extend his hands "toward heaven" and in what follows he speaks explicitly of God's heavenly throne:

O hear in heaven your dwelling place; heed and forgive. (1 Kgs 8:30)

. . . whatever prayer, whatever plea there is from any individual or from all your people Israel, all knowing the afflictions of their own hearts so that they stretch out their hands toward this house; then hear in heaven your dwelling place . . . (1 Kgs 8:38-39)

If your people go out to battle against their enemy . . . and they pray to YHWH . . . then hear in heaven their prayer and their plea, and maintain their cause. (1 Kgs 8:44-45)

Still more basic are the beginnings of an explicit formulation of a monotheistic program in the Deutero-Isaiah tradition. In the Babylonian period, for the first time, we can find explicitly monotheistic statements in the Old Testament: "I am YHWH, and there is no other; besides me there is no god" (Isa 45:5). Of course, biblical monotheism was not born from scratch in the exile; it had developed gradually in Israel since the Assyrian period.[27] The political theology of the books of Isaiah and Deuteronomy would have been especially important in this process: ideas like those from Isaiah 10, that Assyria is the rod of divine wrath, the wrath of the God of Israel, were not first formulated in the wake of the Assyrian period, and the shaping of Deuteronomy as an exclusive oath of loyalty to God (and not to the Assyrian monarch), with Deut 6:4 as the programmatic introductory statement, both reveal elementary features of a universal, politically determined idea of God as we find conceptualized in the exilic monotheistic texts, especially the Deutero-Isaiah tradition. Of course, we should note here already that the establishment of a monotheistic theology at a later time through the construction of an angelology (Daniel), the development of a Satan-figure (Chronicles, Zechariah, Job), or a personified pre-existent figure of Wisdom was in a certain sense "counterproductive" to the development of monotheism.[28]

The Babylonian epoch in Old Testament intellectual and spiritual history was also marked by the reception of scientific and cosmological materials from Babylonian intellectual culture. Notions of the origin of the world—apparently mediated by the cultural contacts between the exiled Judahite priests and Babylonian scholars—would henceforth be shaped by adoption and critical discussion of Babylonian concepts: the world arose through the splitting of ancient floods, called in Babylon Tiamat[29] and in the Bible (without an article) *těhōm*

(Gen 1:2). It is true that this new view of the origins of the world was first given its full formulation in the contemporary scholarly discussion during the early Persian period in the texts of the primeval history, especially in the Priestly document.[30] But the adoption of this material, given its origins, should be located in Babylon.

Finally, the experience of the loss of the monarchy had far-reaching consequences, apparently evoking a literary reflection on the *conditio humana*. We must presume for the monarchical period of ancient Israel what has traditionally been regarded as true of the whole of the ancient Near East: only the king was a human being in the "later" full sense of the word. He alone possessed spirit, responsibility, and self-determination, and by means of these gifts he guided his subjects. Accordingly, we have suggested above in discussing the songs of individual lament that these were originally monarchical texts. With the loss of the kingship in Judah, accompanied by the intellectual and spiritual survival of Israel, a reflective anthropology began to arise in place of the royal ideology. This process, like that of cosmological reflection, had its beginnings in the Babylonian period and developed during the Persian and Hellenistic periods to form a broad strand of tradition.

III. Spheres of Tradition

1. Cultic and Wisdom Traditions

a. Lamentations as Anti-Psalms

Even though the Jerusalem Temple was destroyed in 587 B.C.E., that did not mean that all cultic activities ceased. We may conclude from Jer 41:5 that sacrifice could be offered at the site of the former temple as before.[31] In addition (depending on how one judges the historicity of the cult centralization under Josiah) we may suggest that worship was conducted at other sanctuaries within the land, such as Bethel. At the same time, naturally, the rupture caused by the loss of the temple was massive, especially for the group of the Jerusalem elite who were the vehicles of tradition.

This is especially clear in the book of Lamentations, the Old Testament text that in its earliest form is most clearly to be located in the wake of the catastrophe of 587 B.C.E., perhaps immediately after, but at any rate before Deutero-Isaiah.[32] It is comprised of songs of lament that were attributed to Jeremiah in the Septuagint (probably on the basis of a midrashic interpretation of 2 Chr 35:25 and Lamentations 3). This conclusion cannot be sustained from the Hebrew text. Formally they are acrostics (this applies only to Lamentations 1–4), that is, the lines of poetry follow the Hebrew alphabet. Lamentations 5 falls outside the acrostic structure but it has the same number of lines as the Hebrew alphabet has letters, namely twenty-two.

In terms of the structure of its content, Lamentations borrows from the typical three-part structure of psalms of lament, containing the elements of lament, petition, and praise (cf., e.g., Psalms 6 and 13), but giving them distinctive alterations.

Lamentations 5

Lament:

> Remember, O YHWH, what has befallen us; look, and see our disgrace!
> Our inheritance has been turned over to strangers, our homes to
> aliens.
> We have become orphans, fatherless; our mothers are like widows.
>
> . . .
> Slaves rule over us; there is no one to deliver us from their hand.
> We get our bread at the peril of our lives, because of the sword in the
> wilderness.
> Our skin is black as an oven from the scorching heat of famine.
> Women are raped in Zion, virgins in the towns of Judah.
> Princes are hung up by their hands; no respect is shown to the elders.
> Young men are compelled to grind, and boys stagger under loads of
> wood.
>
> . . .
> Woe to us, for we have sinned!
> Because of this our hearts are sick, because of these things our eyes
> have grown dim: because of Mount Zion, which lies desolate;
> jackals prowl over it. (Lam 5:1-18)

Petition:

> But you, O YHWH, reign forever; your throne endures to all generations.
> Why have you forgotten us completely? Why have you forsaken us
> these many days?
> Restore us to yourself, O YHWH, that we may be restored; renew our
> days as of old . . . (Lam 5:19-21)

Praise:

> unless you have utterly rejected us, and are angry with us beyond
> measure.

What is most striking here is the fact that the traditional closing praise in the genre "individual song of lament" has been replaced by an anxious question: is God's rejection final, will things ever be different? Consequently a kind of doxological element appears in the petition section, intended to motivate God's intervention. Finally we should note that the lament section also contains expressions of sinfulness. Differently from previous psalms of lament, then, there is an insistence that the evil that has befallen the people is a severe punishment for their own sin. The petition is for an end to the judgment that has already lasted so long.

Of primary importance for the theology of Lamentations is that it markedly places the sin of Jerusalem in the foreground.

> How lonely sits the city that once was full of people!
> How like a widow she has become, she that was great among the
>   nations!
> She that was a princess among the provinces has become a vassal.
> She weeps bitterly in the night, with tears on her cheeks;
>   among all her lovers she has no one to comfort her;
>   all her friends have dealt treacherously with her, they have become her
>   enemies. . . .
> Her foes have become the masters, her enemies prosper,
>   because YHWH has made her suffer *for the multitude of her
>   transgressions*;
>   her children have gone away, captives before the foe.
>   . . .
> *Jerusalem sinned grievously*, so she has become a mockery;
>   all who honored her despise her, for they have seen her nakedness;
> she herself groans, and turns her face away. (Lam 1:1-8)

It has become clear in recent scholarship that the sin of the city Jerusalem is not simply to be equated with the sin of her inhabitants; here the city itself as an entity is in view.[33] As in Jeremiah 4–10 (see below), it is no longer the unassailable mountain that is the image of Zion-Jerusalem, as was common in the Jerusalem cultic tradition (cf. Psalm 48), but the woman who has betrayed her husband ("for they have seen her nakedness"). In accord with ancient Near Eastern metaphorical language this refers to making treaties with foreign powers (and thus also with foreign gods). As regards Jerusalem, the reference is probably to the shifting policy of allying with Babylon and then with Egypt in the final years before its fall, which is interpreted theologically as "adultery" and "whoredom."

Deutero-Isaiah, only a few years later, would react in particular against the statements of sin in Lamentations, taking its literary and substantive starting point from the idea that Jerusalem's penalty "is paid, that she has received from YHWH's hand double for all her sins" (Isa 40:2).

b. Laments of the People and the Collectivization of Individual Psalms
Besides the familiar individual songs of lament that, given the conditions of the cult, we may suspect were originally envisioned only for the king, the Psalter also contains so-called laments of the whole people, such as Psalms 44, 90, or 137.[34] In terms of form-critical logic, a *Sitz im Leben* was identified for these laments in collective rituals of mourning. But with the growing insights into the

literary character of many parts of the Old Testament text, we should perhaps posit that these popular laments had no direct cultic function; they were literary productions from the outset. If it is possible that the pre-exilic individual songs of lament were royal texts, the shaping of the genre of popular songs of lament can be understood as a transformation of the royal ideology. In Psalm 90, for example, we can see that the text is not solely concerned with offering a generalized plaint over the limitations and mutability of human life. Rather, the problem that collective situations of suffering can last longer than a human life, so that the sufferers may not experience relief, is considered theologically.[35] Thus Psalm 90 does not seem to be simply a cultic text; it is a piece of theological reflection.[36]

Also worthy of consideration from a historical point of view is the main difference between the popular songs of lament and the book of Lamentations: "They do not lament so much as they demand."[37] Probably they reflect an already advanced state of reflection on the catastrophe and move deliberately beyond lament to an accusation against God, something we can also perceive in the book of Jeremiah.

It is likely that in the Babylonian period—under the shadow of the fallen monarchy—other processes of collectivization of the Psalter began. These were achieved either by corresponding redactional entries in older individual psalms or by compositional combinations.[38] That, of course, does not mean that all the collective utterances in the Psalter should be assigned to this later period. Instead, it seems that in many places, in the wake of the loss of the kingship, existing statements that referred to an individual person (the king?) were expanded secondarily.

The compositional arrangement of Psalms 3–14, for example, seems by its content in particular to be pursuing the goal of collectivizing individual psalms:[39]

Psalms 3–7	Psalm 8	Psalms 9–14
Laments/petitions of an individual	Hymn	Laments/petitions of groups
3:6 Morning		9/10 (acrostic)
4:9 Evening		11
5:4 Morning		12
6:7 Night		13
7:12 Day		14

This is evident, on the one hand, from the coupling of Psalms 9–14, with their statements about the "poor" and "needy" (characterized as a group), with Psalms 3–7 and their petitioners designated as individuals. This makes it clear that both individuals and groups may fall victim to similar fates. On the other hand, the evident *inclusio* established by Psalm 3:9 and Psalm 14:7 with the motif of help for Israel shows that the collective perspective is the interpretive frame for the whole composition. At the same time it gives us a point of reference from which to date the situation of suffering that is presupposed: the catastrophe of Judah and Jerusalem constitutes a probable *terminus a quo*:

> <u>Deliverance</u> belongs to YHWH;
>> may your blessing be on your people! (Ps 3:9)
> O that <u>deliverance</u> for Israel would come from Zion!
> When YHWH restores the fortunes of his people,
> Jacob will rejoice; Israel will be glad. (Ps 14:7)

The interplay of individualization and collectivization is also addressed at the center of the composition, in Psalm 8, which concerns divine care for the "human"—something that can be interpreted as applying to both the species and the individual.

2. Narrative Traditions

a. The Hezekiah-Isaiah Narratives

The Hezekiah-Isaiah narratives in 2 Kings 18–20, with parallels in Isaiah 36–39 (though with some characteristic deviations, such as the omission of 2 Kgs 18:14-16 in the context of Isaiah 36) speak of the events surrounding the threat to Jerusalem from the Assyrians in the year 701 B.C.E. The provocative speech of the Assyrians is contrasted with an oracle of Isaiah in favor of Jerusalem, celebrating the power of the God of Judah, which causes the withdrawal of the Assyrians. While 2 Kings 18–20 and the parallel in Isaiah 36–39 take place in the Assyrian period, some elements in the presentation betray the fact that these narratives apparently also rework experiences from the time after 597 B.C.E. and project them back into the situation of the siege of Jerusalem under Hezekiah. First of all, it is striking that the sequence of events in 2 Kgs 18:13-19 does not agree with the presentation in the annals of the Assyrian king Sennacherib:[40] while in the latter the sequence is (1) laying siege to the cities of Judah, (2) laying siege to Jerusalem, (3) tribute, in the Old Testament the presentation of tribute (2 Kgs 18:14-16) happens before the siege of Jerusalem (2 Kgs 18:17-19). Further, in 2 Kgs 19:9 Tirhakah, a Pharaoh of the "Cushite dynasty," is mentioned in the course of the events of 701 B.C.E.; he is supposed to come to Judah's aid. But in fact Tirhakah was only nine years old at the time and did not ascend the throne until 690 B.C.E.[41] Finally, 2 Kgs 19:36 relates Sennacherib's murder and the succession of his son Esarhaddon to the Assyrian throne taking place immediately after 701 B.C.E. Historically, however, those events occurred in 681 B.C.E.[42]

These discrepancies, as Christof Hardmeier in particular has suggested, can be explained by events from the time of the Neo-Babylonian siege of Jerusalem at the beginning of the sixth century B.C.E.[43] That the tribute is paid before the siege agrees with the presentation of the tribute from the treasures of temple and palace in the year 597 B.C.E. before the subsequent siege of Jerusalem. The expectation of help from the Egyptians is also attested for that period by Jer 37:3-10 and explains the mention of the Egyptian Pharaoh Tirhakah in 2 Kgs 19:9. Finally, the anticipation of Sennacherib's death by twenty years in the depiction in 2 Kgs 19:36 may have been motivated by the expected death of the great king of the Babylonians.

Accordingly, Hardmeier interprets the Hezekiah-Isaiah narratives in 2 Kgs 18:9—19:9, 32-37 as a propagandistic presentation during the pause between sieges in 588 B.C.E. (cf. Jer 37:5), when the national religious party in Jerusalem sought to legitimate their desire to hold out against the Babylonians by looking back to the siege of Jerusalem in the time of Hezekiah and accordingly polemicized against the preaching of judgment in the Jeremiah and Ezekiel traditions, branding them as defeatist.[44]

We can see in the Hezekiah-Isaiah narratives a special feature that is otherwise known primarily from the prophetic tradition: just as in prophecy, a word of judgment can be fulfilled more than once in history. Accordingly the authors of 2 Kings 18–20 and the parallel Isaiah 36–39 apparently regard the history of Judah as a repetitive continuum in which comparable things can take place at different times.

b. The Continuation of Samuel–2 Kings 23 by 2 Kings 24–25

If we suppose a "Deuteronomistic" depiction of the monarchical period from the time of Josiah, ending with 2 Kings 23 (see above), then in view of the present extended context in the books of Kings, incorporating the monarchical history after Josiah as well, we must conclude that this description of the time of Josiah was subsequently expanded to include the last four kings of Judah. We would have here the first continuation of the "Deuteronomistic" theology in the exilic period. As Gottfried Vanoni has shown, the altogether negative judgments on the kings after Josiah reveal a distinctively different orientation than the approach applied to the preceding monarchs.[45] This is evident from the fact that the last four evaluations all conclude with the refrain "just as all his ancestors had done" (2 Kgs 23:32, 37; cf. 24:9, 19, "just as his father Jehoiakim had done"). Thereby the dynasty of the Judahite kings is altogether disqualified, in parallel with the existing total rejection of the rulers of the Northern Kingdom: all kings have sinned. Therefore the same fate confronts the Judahite kings as had befallen those of Israel as portrayed in the books of Kings: in the reception they are condemned *qua* their belonging to the institution of the kingship.[46]

It is a matter of dispute whether 2 Kgs 23:32, 37 are to be read as total condemnations.[47] But the sole parallel formulation, in 1 Kgs 15:9, of the expression "just as all his ancestors had done," used in 2 Kgs 23:32, 37, confirms the sweeping horizon of the latter, for in 2 Kgs 15:9 Zechariah is in view as the last representative of the Jehu dynasty. Correspondingly, 2 Kgs 23:32, 37 consider the whole of the Davidic dynasty. This probably also explains the different formulations in the cases of Jehoiachin ("his father," 24:9) and Zedekiah ("Jehoiakim," 24:19), who could no longer be regarded as fully valid representatives of the Davidic dynasty after the arrival of the world sovereignty of Nebuchadnezzar.[48]

Altogether in line with ancient Near Eastern royal ideology, the texts condemning the last four kings of Judah therefore attributed the fault for the national catastrophe to the primary persons responsible, the kings. The theological logic of the presentation thus noetically links the events experienced in the past to the corresponding qualifications of the kings: *because* Judah has fallen, *therefore* we must assume that the kings failed, and not the other way around. If one is more inclined from the outset towards a post-monarchical origin of the framework of the books of Kings, with its judgmental texts, the corresponding perspectives in 2 Kings 24–25 would have been written to counter exilic hopes for a restored kingship; according to these texts the kingship is *per se* an institution that has rightly fallen.

We should certainly expect that the perspective of a negative evaluation of all the kings would also be anchored redactionally at the beginning of the depiction of the monarchical period. At any rate there is a good possibility that we should read the texts in 1 Samuel 8, 12, which reject the kingship as an institution and frame the older, positive view in 1 Samuel 9–11,[49] together with the perspective we have described in 2 Kings 24–25. In addition we may also propose that the loss of the Ark in 1 Samuel 4–6[50]—at least in certain thematic accents— is tied to 2 Kings 24–25. The fate of the Ark sanctuary prefigures in a certain sense the fall of the temple. Thus, for example, at the very beginning of the history of Israel's kings 1 Sam 4:22 states: "The glory has departed from Israel." Also, the beheading of the statue of the god Dagan of the Philistines, reported in 1 Sam 5:3-4, strongly recalls the polemic against idols in Deutero-Isaiah.

Remarkably enough, the great dynastic promise to David in 2 Samuel 7, if it is not entirely of exilic origin,[51] has not been fundamentally revised except through some conditional statements. It continued to be handed on as an unconditional promise, which suggests that the "Deuteronomistic" movement was quite interested in the continuation of the Davidic kingship during the Babylonian period.[52] Haggai's position (Hag 2:21-23) follows conceptually on this.

c. The Origins of the Major Historical Work Exodus 2—2 Kings 25

In a further step that (on the basis of the "Babylonian" and not "Persian" conclusion in 2 Kings 25; cf. to the contrary 2 Chronicles 36) should probably also be located in the Babylonian period, the "Deuteronomistic History" centering on and growing around 2 Kings 24–25 to encompass the books of Samuel through 2 Kings 25, was knit together with the depiction of the exodus and the occupation of the land in Exodus–Joshua. The result was the creation of a major historical work extending from Exodus 2 through 2 Kings 25—probably, though, without the book of Judges, which was still independent.[53] The last four verses, 2 Kgs 25:27-30, which constitute a striking *inclusio* with elements of the Joseph story (Genesis 37–50) and probably are already familiar with the prior placement of Genesis, were most likely not yet a part of this presentation.[54]

What are the indications that there was a major exilic historical work made up of Exodus 2–2 Kings 25? First, there is a thematic and linguistic coherence in Exodus–2 Kings that goes clearly beyond the language that holds this material, along with Genesis, together. We are talking about the so-called "Deuteronomisms" in the historical books of Exodus–2 Kings; while these are not wholly absent from Genesis, they are to be assigned there to later literary-historical strata that probably belong within the realm of the post-Priestly redactions of the Pentateuch.[55] In addition, Exodus–2 Kings clearly conceives of Israel as coming out of Egypt (and not stemming from the patriarchs). Above all, the reception of the account of Jeroboam I's creation of two royal sanctuaries with statues of calves (1 Kings 12) in the story of the golden calf (Exodus 32)[56] shows that Exodus–2 Kings as a literary whole was subjected to a redactional revision and was conceived as a major historical work. Exodus 32:4b obviously adopts 1 Kgs 12:28b: the plural formulations found also in Exodus 32 ("These are your gods, O Israel, who brought you up out of the land of Egypt!") can only be understood in light of 1 Kings 12, which, in contrast to Exodus 32, is actually about the making of *two* calf images. It is clear that Exodus 32 thus transfers the classic originary sin that brought about Israel's destruction, namely the sin of Jeroboam, the first monarch of the Northern Kingdom, which was continued by all his successors, to the people themselves: it is not the kings who are guilty; the people themselves are at fault for the catastrophe:

> He [Aaron] took the gold from them, formed it in a mold, and cast an image of a calf; and they said, *"These are your gods, O Israel, who brought you up out of the land of Egypt!"* (Exod 32:4)

> So the king took counsel, and made two calves of gold. He said to the people, "You have gone up to Jerusalem long enough. *Here are your gods, O Israel, who brought you up out of the land of Egypt.*" (1 Kgs 12:28)

However, Exodus 32 appears to have been shaped not only in light of 1 Kings 12, but also from the older textual material reflecting on the fall of the Northern Kingdom in 2 Kings 17. This is evident especially from the motif of "great sin," which appears in the Old Testament almost exclusively in Exod 32:21, 30-31 and 2 Kgs 17:21 (and otherwise only in Gen 20:9):

On the next day Moses said to the people, "You have sinned *a great sin*. But now I will go up to YHWH; perhaps I can make atonement for your sin." So Moses returned to YHWH and said, "Alas, this people has sinned *a great sin*; they have made for themselves gods of gold." (Exod 32:30-31)

When he had torn Israel from the house of David, they made Jeroboam son of Nebat king. Jeroboam drove Israel from following YHWH and made them commit *great sin*. (2 Kgs 17:21)

Thus, as it had done in its reception of 1 Kings 12, Exodus 32 takes up a motif from 2 Kings 17 belonging to the figure of Jeroboam and applies it to the people. Apparently the whole theologically negative history of the kings is now to appear only as an appendix to a history of the nation that already prefigures it. Accordingly, it seems probable that we should conclude that the corresponding interpretive passages in Exodus 32 were in fact inserted into a literary complex that also contained the history of the kings.

The perspective on the people found in Exodus 32 then, interestingly enough, left its traces also in the redactional history of 2 Kings 17 itself:[57] the older statements in 2 Kgs 17:21-23 insist that the guilt of Israel is rooted in the sin of Jeroboam, while the long and apparently secondary introduction in verses 7-20 makes it clear that the people themselves are the primary bearers of responsibility.

This occurred because the people of Israel had sinned against YHWH their God, who had brought them up out of the land of Egypt from under the hand of Pharaoh king of Egypt. They had worshiped other gods and walked in the customs of the nations whom YHWH drove out before the people of Israel, and in the customs that the kings of Israel had introduced. (2 Kgs 17:7-8)

When he had torn Israel from the house of David, they made Jeroboam son of Nebat king. Jeroboam drove Israel from following YHWH and made them commit great sin. The people of Israel continued in all the sins that Jeroboam committed; they did not depart from them until YHWH removed Israel out of his sight, as he had foretold through all his servants the prophets. So Israel was exiled from their own land to Assyria until this day. (2 Kgs 17:21-23)

Thus the great complex of Exodus–2 Kings (probably still without Judges) witnesses to an advanced reflection on sin and guilt, which with its accusation against the people already reveals a clear distance from the loss of their own kingdom.

This major historical presentation lies within the intellectual and spiritual environment of the "Deuteronomistic" writing, which refers back constitutively to Israel's being led out of Egypt as its foundational theological datum and emphasizes the covenant theology that links YHWH and Israel (YHWH is Israel's God, and Israel is YHWH's people), and that makes the relationship between God and God's people an exclusive one. Egypt, by contrast, is a typical example of the pagan world of the nations: the offense of the Egyptian Pharaoh that evokes the plagues consists precisely in not being a worshiper of YHWH and not wanting to be one (Exod 5:2-3). That world threatens Israel, but it is powerless against the might of YHWH, which is on Israel's side. The plague cycle that probably lies at the base of Exodus 7–12 shows that it is precisely the Egyptian "theologians" who, in view of YHWH's signs and wonders, are left with no choice but to acclaim "This is the finger of God" (Exod 8:15) and capitulate.

The antagonism between Israel and the nations then continues with comparable acerbity in the transfer and description of the occupation of the land. The law corpora of the Old Testament are located in the period of Israel's desert wandering, and in prominent places they forbid all alliances with the inhabitants of the land (Exod 23:32; 34:12; cf. Deut 12:29-31), who are considered "enemies" (e.g., Deut 25:19). Instead, their cults are to be destroyed (Exod 34:13-15) and they themselves killed (Deut 20:16-17; cf. Exod 23:33).

Theologically, this exclusivist religio-political character matches the argumentation for exclusive worship of YHWH. It is no accident that, in literary terms, it is embedded in this great Exodus tradition: in consequence of his action in choosing and rescuing Israel from out of the world of the nations YHWH presents himself as a "jealous" God who permits no worship of other deities, though their very existence is not (yet) disputed (Exod 20:5; Deut 5:7). It is this demand that Israel assume a special position within the world of the nations that causes Israel to collapse and fall, since in the monarchical period it chose the forbidden way of the nations and worshiped their gods instead of its own God.

The sharp contrast between Israel and the nations in Exodus–2 Kings has its contemporary cultural background in the increased pressure to define the identity of "Israel" in the absence of a state, a land, or a kingship. The harsh sayings against the nations and the powerful images of conquest in the book of Josiah stand as contrafactual to and not parallel with the historical experiences behind them.

d. The Joseph Narrative

The Joseph narrative (Genesis 37–50) is fundamentally different from the preceding traditions of the patriarchs in Genesis 12–36 because it presents a story spanning fourteen biblical chapters rather than individual scenes in loose connection. It has therefore become common to call the Joseph story a "novella." It tells of the conflict between Joseph and his brothers, Joseph's rise in Egypt, and the reconciliation between Joseph and his brothers. Unlike the patriarchal narratives in Genesis 12–36 (see below), we cannot assume that the Joseph narrative grew slowly from blocks of material to its present form. Instead, it seems to have been conceived from the beginning as a dramatic cycle and then redactionally attached to Genesis 12–36.[58]

The present function of this narrative within the Pentateuch is to explain how the ancestors of what later became Israel arrived in Egypt, so that the people could subsequently leave there. But the Joseph narrative was not written for that purpose, as is clear simply from the fact that in Genesis 50 Israel goes to Canaan to bury Jacob and is only returned to Egypt by means of a single verse (Gen 50:14). Add to this the fact that the Joseph narrative contains some tensions with the subsequent presentation in Exodus that substantially affect the picture of the Pharaoh and Israel, so that the first task of Exodus 1 is to set the Joseph story aside (Exod 1:6-8).

Within the framework of the Documentary Hypothesis people were convinced that the earliest layers of the Joseph narrative were embedded in the overall project of the Hexateuch made up of J and E. Julius Wellhausen stated: "It is to be supposed that this work [Genesis] is here [in Genesis 37–40] made up, as elsewhere, of J and E; our previous results force us to this position and would be seriously shaken if it could not be demonstrated."[59] This statement is correct insofar as in fact the plausibility of the source model depends to a great degree on exegesis of the Joseph narrative.[60] If the ancient Hexateuch sources J and E cannot be shown to be present in Genesis 37–50, then their reconstruction lacks any link between the patriarchal and exodus traditions, which literary criticism would consequently have to keep separate. Today it is primarily the second part of Wellhausen's statement that has proved true: many scholars now interpret the Joseph narrative without refering to J and E; to be sure, the "shaking" of the Documentary Hypothesis has been caused in large part by literary discoveries in the Joseph narrative.[61]

But what is the substantive statement of the Joseph narrative if its bridge function to the Exodus event is secondary? We may mention a number of perspectives here: first, the positive image of Egypt portrayed in the Joseph story is striking. The Pharaoh is a wise ruler; Joseph, a non-Egyptian, is able to advance rapidly at the Egyptian court and even marry an Egyptian woman. Thus the Joseph story presents itself as a kind of "anti-Deuteronomistic" historical work that—contrary to the goal envisioned by the large text complex of Exodus–2 Kings—presents life in the diaspora not as a catastrophe, but as a theologically legitimate possibility.[62] Also in its theology of sin the Joseph narrative distances itself from Deuteronomism: the sin of the brothers is not punished, but forgiven (Gen 50:19-20).

It should also be noted that the Joseph narrative is not only about Joseph, but also about Joseph and his brothers in relation to their father Jacob. Even though we should not too hastily make a historical allegory of Genesis 37–50, it is still inviting to inquire into the relation of this constellation to the identity of Israel: apparently the Joseph story, written from a diaspora perspective—and about that point of view there can be no doubt, given the rise of the Israelite Joseph in a foreign royal court[63]—presents an option for all Israel, which must be redefined after the loss of its sovereign statehood. Its definition of Israel is not in the sense of an independent territorial nation but as a nation bound by a common purpose, a nation that remains united even after the "death" of "Jacob."

Finally, the enlightened theology of the Joseph narrative should be taken into account. Since Gerhard von Rad it has been common to speak of the wisdom nature of the Joseph story,[64] although (contrary to von Rad) this certainly does not point to the "Solomonic Enlightenment" he posited as the time of its origin. On the one hand we can discern features in the story that are critical of Joseph (cf. Gen 37:10: this dream is not verified by his father's bowing down).[65] He thus does not easily fulfill the ideal image of the wise man. On the other hand, as regards the deeds of the brothers and their consequences (they escape punishment for their crimes against Joseph) we find here a fundamental disruption of a basic element of the traditional ideas of wisdom as regards the connection between act and consequence. God's secret guidance for the well-being and survival of Israel is superior to the punishment of the evildoers.

> Whether the contacts between the Joseph narrative and the Egyptian tale of the two brothers,[66] which in any case are scarcely literary in nature, would allow us to conclude a particular familiarity of the novella with Egyptian traditional material is something that must remain open. A rootedness of the authorship of Genesis 37–50 in the Egyptian diaspora is not improbable, given the background of the scene.

e. The Patriarchal Narratives in Genesis

In accord with the shifts in Pentateuch research in the last decade, and especially since the epochal work of Erhard Blum,[67] it no longer seems out of line to locate the most important literary layers of the composition of the patriarchal narrative in the exilic period.[68] These layers include the linking together of the already-existent major narrative cycles about Abraham–Lot and Jacob as well as the incorporation of the Joseph novella. The break with the traditional interpretation of the patriarchal narratives, however, is radical: within the theoretical framework of the Documentary Hypothesis their interpretation was entirely in terms of the salvation history of the Hexateuch, which, according to the "short historical credo" (Deut 26:5-9), provided the structure of the tradition. The patriarchal narratives were thus from the very beginning merely a prelude to the great history of God with Israel, from the departure from Egypt through the desert wandering to the occupation of the land.

But the credo text in Deuteronomy 26:5-9 is not ancient, either in its formulation or in its substance,[69] which, as regards the formulation, even von Rad himself admitted.[70] It even contains language borrowed from the Priestly document. Through the work of Rolf Rendtorff, Erhard Blum, and Matthias Köckert the conviction was established that the Hexateuch's historical picture was created not at the beginning, but rather at the end of the redactional editing of the traditions in the first six books of the Bible, and from a literary-historical perspective it cannot constitute the primary horizon of interpretation for the patriarchal narratives.[71]

This means that the patriarchal narratives were not originally a prelude, but an independent tradition of origins for Israel that did not always move toward the portrayal of the exodus and find its continuation there. The independence of the patriarchal narratives was apparent in the traditional approach as well: on the basis of Alt's influential reconstruction of a religion of the gods of the fathers these narratives were located in Israel's misty nomadic prehistory.[72] However, the idiosyncratic nature of the patriarchal narratives has less to do with a distant prehistory[73] than with their independent literary history, in which it continued as an independent body of tradition into the exilic period.

The core of the story of the patriarchs as it now stands can be found in the Jacob narratives (Genesis 25–35*); however, the Abraham (Genesis 13* + 18–19*) and Isaac (Genesis 26*) traditions each have their own independent basis as well. The Joseph narrative (Genesis 37–50*) is another major building block with its own character. An overarching patriarchal narrative containing Genesis 12–50* would first have been created in the exilic period by means of the redactional joining of these existing cycles plus the Joseph narrative.[74] The units of tradition are held together, on the one hand, by the genealogical linking of the protagonists Abraham, Isaac, Jacob, and Joseph as grandfather, father, son, and grandson, already suggested for Abraham and Isaac (eponymous for the Southern Kingdom) in Genesis 13* + 18–19* but probably redactional in itself, as well as by the promises. Gerhard von Rad argued:

> Although the great narrative complexes covering the call of Abraham down to the death of Joseph consist in the coalescence of a great variety of traditional material, the whole has nevertheless a scaffolding supporting and connecting it, the so-called promise to the patriarchs. At least it can be said that this whole variegated mosaic of stories is given cohesion of subject-matter . . . by means of the constantly recurring divine promise.[75]

However, the promises are different in nature, both in their content and in terms of the history of their origins. They have two sources in the history of tradition: one in the Abraham narrative in Genesis 18, the only pre-Priestly patriarchal story with an integral promise (of a son, v. 14b), the other in the theme of blessing in the Jacob narratives.

Especially important for the compositional unity of the patriarchal narratives are the promises in Gen 12:1-3; 13:14-17; 28:13-15; 46:2-4.[76] These contain the assurance of progeny and of land. Both these themes were of acute importance for Israel and Judah in the seventh to fifth centuries B.C.E., as the Assyrian and Babylonian deportations, together with economic problems, led to a major decline in population in a region no longer subject to its own monarchical rule.[77] The promises should be understood contextually against their counterfactual background. We can perceive another important element in the theological-historical profile in Gen 12:1-3:

Genesis 12:1-3	Psalm 72:17

Now YHWH said to Abram, ". . . I will make of you a great nation, and I will *bless* you, and make your **name** great, so that *you will be a blessing. . . . and in you* <u>all the families of the earth</u> *shall be blessed.*"	May his [the king's] **name** endure forever,
	    his fame continue as long as the sun.
	May <u>all nations</u> *be blessed* in [his *name*];
	    may [all peoples] pronounce him happy.

With the motif of the "great name" and its function as mediator of salvation Gen 12:1-3 absorbs significant elements of the royal ideology as expressed, for example, in Psalm 72:17, and transfers them to the ancestor of the people, Abraham. These "democratizing" tendencies are scarcely imaginable at the time when the state was still in existence. Instead, Gen 12:1-3 is close to the corresponding perspectives in Isaiah 40–55, where exiled Israel is addressed as "Abraham" or "Jacob" and can also be portrayed in royal dignity.

We should also notice that the system of promises in Gen 12:1-3; 13:14-17; 28:13-15; 46:2-4 is associated with notices about movement: "Go from your country" (12:1); "do not be afraid to go down to Egypt" (46:2), and so on. This is a sign that the people of God is independent of geography: Israel is Israel because of its relationship to God and not because it is settled in its land.

For Gen 12:1-3 and 46:2-4, in fact, still later dates have recently been proposed, and with very good reason. These proposals see the texts as subsequent in their literary history to the Priestly document.[78] However, it is also possible that the contacts with "P" adduced here can be explained by the fact that "P" adopted a theology of promise that already existed; this would also explain its renewed theological accentuation of the patriarchal history. In particular, the contacts between Gen 12:1-3 and the Priestly refrain in the table of the nations in Gen 10:5, 20, 31-32 ("nation," "family," "land")[79] can be plausibly arranged diachronically so that the Priestly view of the world in Genesis 10 is determined by the inheritance promised as blessing to Abraham.[80]

The aggressive and exclusive orientation of the exodus tradition is absent from the patriarchal narratives in Genesis. Instead, from a political point of view their pacifism is impressive. The ancestors coexist peacefully with different *ethnoi* and groups in the land and make agreements with them, something that was strictly forbidden according to the exodus narrative. Their inclusivism is also striking. The patriarchs, in their wanderings and journeys, come in contact with a whole series of divinities who reveal themselves under various names and to whom they erect cultic shrines in different places. It is, of course, clear to readers of the patriarchal narratives that behind these deities is always one and the same God, namely YHWH. For the actors in the narratives it is not so clear, and their uncertainty undoubtedly has a historical background: behind the narratives of the ancestors are memories or oral traditions that originally spoke of more and other deities and their sanctuaries, and not only of YHWH. The ancestors, on their journeys, proclaim the same thing that the course of tradition had yielded, namely the identification of different local deities with the one God of Israel. The narratives of the ancestors reflect an independent, alternative concept of the assimilative and autochthonous origins of Israel in its land alongside the exodus tradition, which located Israel's origins in Egypt and accordingly defended Israel's identity vehemently and exclusively against other national-religious identities.[81]

f. The Non-Priestly Sinai Tradition

It is striking that in the present narrative sequence of the Pentateuch the progress of the story largely stagnates from Exodus 19 to Numbers 10: Israel remains stationary at Sinai, and most of the textual material consists of instructions received by Moses from God. It has long been acknowledged that most of the material in the so-called Sinai pericope (Exodus 19–Numbers 10) belongs within the historical compass either of the Priestly document or expansions of it, whether as a still-independent source document or after combination with the non-Priestly Pentateuch. This is essentially true of the instructions for the construction of the "tent of meeting" and their execution (Exodus 25–31; 35–40), the cultic law materials of the book of Leviticus, and the so-called ordering of the camp in Numbers 1–10. To be excluded from this material are the texts in Exodus 19–24; 32–34. Scholars are not in agreement on their literary-historical setting. All that is clear is that these texts either presuppose the Priestly document or react to it, but they cannot be a part of it.[82] If—with good reason—we reckon with a Sinai pericope prior to the Priestly document, with text sections that now constitute Exodus 19–24; 32–34,[83] a number of elementary observations suggest that its basis should no longer be located in the pre-exilic period: the tradition of the mountain of God is very sparsely attested outside the Pentateuch. The oldest extra-Pentateuchal text that mentions the exodus and Sinai together is found in Nehemiah 9. In addition, it has long been observed that, as far as the narrative is concerned, the Sinai pericope interrupts the sequence of actions in the Moses-exodus story, and the scenery and geography represent an enormous detour. It has therefore been suggested that the Sinai pericope should be read as a literary reaction to the annulment of the indigenous "mountain of God tradition" in Judah, the Zion theology.[84] With the removal of God's dwelling place from Jerusalem to the mythic mountain region—even 1 Kgs 19:8 no longer knows the location of Sinai, other than that it can be reached in a journey of "forty days and forty nights" from Beersheba—it is withdrawn from all political turmoil and danger and made theologically enduring. It must at present remain a matter of speculation whether behind the Sinai tradition, which in any case is literarily late, some older and even pre-state memories like those we may posit for the exodus tradition lie hidden. In essence, a conclusion would have to be achieved by way of an investigation of the inner-biblical horizons of Exodus 19–24: if it seems probable that this literary presentation is an interpretation of existing texts and materials, a negative response would be most appropriate.

If it is also probable that this Sinai pericope included the making of a covenant (Exodus 24), and the object of this covenant-making was the so-called Book of the Covenant[85] (Exodus 20–23)—"a Sinai theophany without a Law would result in nothing but theatrical thunder on an empty stage"[86]—then additional theological-historical developments would be evident here. The pre-exilic covenant theology of Deuteronomy seems indeed to be taken up in Exodus 24, but now as "decentralized": the making of the covenant between God and Israel no longer depends on a central sanctuary in Jerusalem because that has been lost. Here we can perceive the beginning of the central argument of the later Torah: Israel's identity no longer depends on the land, but on the law. Second, by this means the Book of the Covenant would be given authority in its original sense and against its Deuteronomic interpretation. This theological victory of the older Book of the Covenant over the newer Deuteronomy can still be perceived in the present narrative sequence of the Pentateuch: the Book of the Covenant is presented as divine discourse at Sinai, while Deuteronomy is a discourse by Moses in the land east of the Jordan.

3. Prophetic Traditions

a. Beginnings of the Jeremiah Tradition

The literary beginnings of the book of Jeremiah are especially eloquent in a literary-historical view. The Jeremiah tradition probably began with the laments in Jeremiah 4–10 (which can be traced to the historical prophet Jeremiah), not yet associated with an accusation, and historically this could scarcely have happened except in immediate association with the catastrophe of Judah and Jerusalem in 587 B.C.E.[87] Othmar Keel in particular has pointed to the unusual world of ideas in the Jeremiah tradition. The difference from the book of Ezekiel is striking: here we are entirely in the realm of rural-agricultural metaphors, with scarcely any influence from the great sweep of ancient Near Eastern pictorial symbolism.[88]

In the text as it now stands, Jeremiah 4–10 appears as a sweeping accusation, but this impression is due to a series of additions, which can easily be distinguished both in form and in substance. These accusations are directed against an entity addressed in the second person singular feminine, easily identified as Jerusalem (cf. "Jerusalem," 4:14).

Look! He comes up like clouds, his chariots like the whirlwind; his horses are swifter than eagles—woe to us, for we are ruined!

O Jerusalem, wash your heart clean of wickedness so that you may be saved. How long shall your evil schemes lodge within you?

For a voice declares from Dan and proclaims disaster from Mount Ephraim. (Jer 4:13-15)

At the noise of horseman and archer every town takes to flight; they enter thickets; they climb among rocks; all the towns are forsaken, and no one lives in them.

And you, O desolate one, what do you mean that you dress in crimson, that you deck yourself with ornaments of gold, that you enlarge your eyes with paint? In vain you beautify yourself. Your lovers despise you; they seek your life. (Jer 4:29-30)

Thematically these second-person-singular-feminine accusations circle around the reproaches of whoredom and adultery (cf. also Jer 2:19-25, 32-33). In the ancient Near East these were common metaphors for infidelity to a covenant.[89] This means that the accusations that Jerusalem has sinned are directed at Judah's bad covenantal policy. In the last years of the Judahite kingship efforts were apparently made (as 2 Kings 24–25 reveal) to make an arrangement between the great powers of Babylon and Egypt. Ezekiel 17, for example, explicitly testifies to such a seesaw policy of Judah between Babylon and Egypt:

Then the word of YHWH came to me: Say now to the rebellious house: Do you not know what these things mean? Tell them: The king of Babylon came to Jerusalem, took its king and its officials, and brought them back with him to Babylon. He took one of the royal offspring and made a covenant with him, putting him under oath (he had taken away the chief men of the land), so that the kingdom might be humble and not lift itself up, and that by keeping his covenant it might stand. But he rebelled against him by sending ambassadors to Egypt, in order that they might give him horses and a large army. Will he succeed? Can one escape who does such things? Can he break the covenant and yet escape? As I live, says the Lord YHWH, surely in the place where the king resides who made him king, whose oath he despised, and whose covenant with him he broke—in Babylon he shall die. (Ezek 17:11-16)

The accusation of whoredom thus means that Jerusalem has not trusted in its God, YHWH, but has made pacts with foreign great powers (especially Egypt), who themselves—or rather their gods—appear in the second-person-singular-feminine texts as "lovers" who now, however, abuse Jerusalem and even rape her.

Against the notion that the oldest texts of the book are to be found in the laments it has been objected that mere laments over misfortune could not have formed the basis for a tradition. It is said that these offer no explanation of how the written text came to be. The act of lamenting is, of course, to be expected historically, but not its documentation. This objection is overcome, however, by noticing that the oldest laments in the book of Jeremiah represent a definite theological position and by that very fact the construction of a tradition can be shown to be plausible. Apparently these laments are aimed directly at the Jerusalem-Zion theology, the national religious orthodoxy at the First Temple based on the idea that because of the presence of Yhwh Zion was unassailable. This is especially clear in the subversive adoption of Psalm 48 in Jeremiah 6:

Psalm 48:2-7, 9, 13-15	Jeremiah 6:22-26
His holy mountain, beautiful in elevation, is the joy of all the earth, Mount Zion, in the far <u>north</u>, the city of the great King. Within its citadels God has shown himself a sure defense. Then the kings assembled, they came on together. As soon as they saw it, they were astounded; they were in panic, they took to flight; trembling *took hold* of them there, *pains as of a woman in labor* . . . As we have heard, so have we seen in the city of Yhwh of hosts, in the city of our God, which God established forever. . . . **Walk about Zion, go all around it** and count its towers, consider well its ramparts, go through its citadels, that you may tell the next generation that this is God, our God forever and ever. He will be our guide forever.	Thus says Yhwh: See, a people is coming from the land of the <u>north</u>, a great nation is stirring from the farthest parts of the earth. They grasp the bow and the javelin, they are cruel and have no mercy, their sound is like the roaring sea; they ride on horses, equipped like a warrior for battle, against you, O daughter Zion! "We have heard news of them, our hands fall helpless; anguish has *taken hold of us, pain as of a woman in labor.* **Do not go out into the field, or walk on the road;** for the enemy has a sword, terror is on every side." O my poor people, put on sackcloth, and roll in ashes; make mourning as for an only child, most bitter lamentation: for suddenly the destroyer will come upon us.

For Psalm 48, Zion is secure against all attacks. The very sight of Zion causes the hostile kings to panic and flee. In Jeremiah 6 the horrors foreseen for the enemies fall on the inhabitants of Zion itself. The metaphorical world also changes completely: the "*mountain*" of Zion in Psalm 48 is in Jeremiah 6 "*daughter* Zion" rolling in ashes. The reception of Psalm 48 in Jeremiah 6 seems thus to be directed by an effort to deal theologically and metaphorically with the collapse of the Zion theology.

To the oldest lament texts in Jeremiah 4–10 should probably the added the sayings about foreign nations in Jeremiah 46–49, since the latter are very close in both language and theme to the texts in chapters 4–10. The distress that came with the Babylonians affected not only Judah and Jerusalem, but the neighboring peoples as well, and this circumstance found its literary expression in Jeremiah 46–49.[90]

The laments in Jeremiah 4–10, redactionally expanded by texts using the second person singular feminine with reference to Jerusalem, would probably have been quickly augmented by the so-called prophetic symbolic actions, which already presuppose the theology of sin and guilt and further interpret the judgment explicitly as divine judgment (Jeremiah 13, 16, 18, 27–28, 32). These symbolic actions show that they belong here because (with the exception of Jeremiah 27) they are formulated in the first person singular. Otherwise the book speaks of Jeremiah in the third person. We should probably see in the symbolic actions an older stage of the book that as yet contained no external accounts.

Finally, the older texts of the book include the statements about the kings in Jeremiah 21–23:[91] Jeremiah appeared as a critic of the royal house of Judah. That these texts are in part contemporary can be seen, for example, in the saying against Jehoiakim, the third-last king of Judah:

> Therefore thus says YHWH concerning King Jehoiakim son of Josiah of Judah: They shall not lament for him, saying, "Alas, my brother!" or "Alas, sister!" They shall not lament for him, saying, "Alas, lord!" or "Alas, his majesty!" With the burial of a donkey he shall be buried—dragged off and thrown out beyond the gates of Jerusalem. (Jer 22:18-19)

The prediction that Jehoiakim would not be buried after his death was not fulfilled; 2 Kgs 24:6 says of Jehoiakim's death: "So Jehoiakim slept with his ancestors; then his son Jehoiachin succeeded him." The expression "slept with his ancestors" describes a regular burial. There is no reason to suppose that 2 Kgs 24:6 does not offer reliable information. Since Jer 22:18-19 contains a prediction that was not fulfilled, we have good reason to suppose that it is ancient, because after the actual burial of Jehoiakim it is unlikely that anyone would have formulated a prediction of judgment that ran contrary to the actual historical events.

Ultimately the book of Jeremiah was also subjected to Deuteronomistic redactional activity, even though the degree of intervention must be estimated differently from the findings in Thiel's work.[92] Particularly worth mentioning are some minor entries in Jeremiah 1–25 that abandon the tenor of the context and in their language and substance formulate clearly Deuteronomistic accusations:

> My joy is gone, grief is upon me, my heart is sick. Hark, the cry of my poor people from far and wide in the land: "Is YHWH not in Zion? Is

her King not in her? *"Why have they provoked me to anger with their images, with their foreign idols?"* "The harvest is past, the summer is ended, and we are not saved." For the hurt of my poor people I am hurt, I mourn, and dismay has taken hold of me. Is there no balm in Gilead? Is there no physician there? Why then has the health of my poor people not been restored? (Jer 8:18-23)

In terms of theological development, what is especially significant in these beginnings of the Jeremiah tradition is that the move from lament to accusation, and thus the development of a theology of sin and guilt, can be adequately perceived by composition-critical means. The oldest lament texts in the book of Jeremiah thus appear to have been secondarily, but very quickly, augmented by statements of guilt like those in Lamentations. In the prophetic traditions the guilt-and-punishment paradigm was no longer unassailable during the Babylonian period, even though the older prophetic books from the Assyrian period had expressed themselves in those terms in relation to the fall of the Northern Kingdom. But this is precisely what is to be expected in light of Deuteronomism: the oldest levels of Deuteronomic thinking in the books of Kings probably only rejected the cultically illegitimate Northern Kingdom along with tendencies toward apostasy in the Southern Kingdom. The idea that Judah as a whole had also become guilty in the eyes of God had to be reconceived in light of the actual catastrophe, which called for a theological basis. In addition, it is worth considering that the judgment sayings against Judah, especially in the books of Isaiah and Micah, represent rather implausible reference points in the late pre-exilic period since for nearly a century, as their warnings remained unfulfilled, they had been suspected of being false prophecies.

b. Beginnings of the Ezekiel Tradition

The beginnings of the Ezekiel tradition are more difficult to understand than those of the Jeremiah tradition. The question is above all whether one considers it possible or not to reconstruct a stage of the book prior to the one favoring the exiled people, which belongs to the early Persian period. The book of Ezekiel is clearly the mouthpiece of the interests of the "first Golah" (group of exiles) who were deported with Jehoiachin in 597 B.C.E. and included Ezekiel himself. The Babylonian stamp on the book of Ezekiel is perceptible not least in its metaphorical world, which is clearly inspired by the international standard "dominant culture" of Mesopotamia.[93]

For example, Karl-Friedrich Pohlmann sees a pre-Golah-oriented book with texts primarily from Ezekiel 4–24*; 31*; 36*, structured according to a two-part sequence of judgment and salvation, though the view of salvation in this first book of Ezekiel was still subdued and the extent of the text very narrow.[94] Pohlmann sees the earliest individual texts of the book in the poems in Ezekiel 19*/31*, which still lament the catastrophe that has occurred without any reference to YHWH. He traces these to Jerusalem circles close to the royal court. In those terms, then, the oldest book of Ezekiel would have had a substantive approach similar to the early Jeremiah tradition. But the literary-historical reconstruction of the book of Ezekiel is less clearly delineated and more disputed as a result.

In any case, the origins of the book of Ezekiel appear to lie in the Babylonian period and not the Persian period, though the book's own testimony is not in itself a reliable historical argument for that assumption. But the great vision in Ezekiel 8–11, which speaks of the departure of the "glory of YHWH" from the Jerusalem temple, sees that "glory of YHWH" as withdrawing not to Babylon (as the Golah-oriented perspective in Ezekiel 1–3 presumes), but only a few hundred meters away to the Mount of Olives, indicating that pre-Golah-oriented textual elements are to be found in the book of Ezekiel: "And the glory of YHWH ascended from the middle of the city, and stopped on the mountain east of the city" (Ezek 11:23).

Nevertheless, there can be no doubt that the book of Ezekiel was very soon and very thoroughly "Babylonized." Its dating system is based on 597 B.C.E. Ezekiel is described solely as a prophet of the Jehoiachin Golah and the land of Israel is presented as altogether desolate and without any hope for the future independent of the return of the exiles. The vision in Ezekiel 40–48, probably critically utopian in its orientation, is a literarily complex structure, with its bases probably extending back to the Babylonian period.[95] Favoring this position could be the absence of the third dimension in the descriptions of the building of the new temple as well as the divergences from the Priestly document's theology of the sanctuary as found in Exodus 25–40. This would point to pre-Priestly origins for Ezekiel 40–48, which for a considerable time made it impossible for the book of Ezekiel to be granted a place among the standard writings of Persian-period Judaism. The Temple Scroll found in Qumran, but probably older, attempts to reconcile Exodus 25–40 with Ezekiel 40–48.[96]

c. Deutero-Isaiah

Among the most solid results of historical-critical biblical scholarship is the hypothesis that the second part of the book of Isaiah, chapters 40–66, had no historical connection with the eighth-century B.C.E. prophet who gave his name to the book. "Isaiah" is not mentioned; the prophetic proclamation concentrates on promises of salvation; and the historical setting presumes the sixth century B.C.E. at the earliest, as shown by the explicit mention of the Persian king Cyrus. The basic content of Isaiah 40–66 can probably be traced to a sixth-century-B.C.E. prophet whose name is unknown and who is generally called "Deutero-Isaiah" by scholars.[97] Against the recently presented idea that Isaiah 40–66 is only a continuation of the prophecy and cannot be traced to the work of an individual prophetic figure[98] is the form-critical shaping of the material in Isaiah 40–55, which makes the thesis of a prophet "Deutero-Isaiah" as plausible as ever.

Isaiah 45:1-2 allows for a relatively accurate dating of the writing down of the message of "Deutero-Isaiah."[99] This passage originally anticipated a violent seizure of power in Babylon by Cyrus ("I will break in pieces the doors of bronze") and was only subsequently edited to match the historical events, the capture of Babylon without a fight ("to open doors before him"): "Thus says Yhwh to his anointed, to Cyrus, whose right hand I have grasped to subdue nations before him and strip kings of their robes, *to open doors before him—and the gates shall not be closed.* I will go before you and level the mountains, I will break in pieces the doors of bronze and cut through the bars of iron" (Isa 45:1-2).

Pointing in the same direction is the fact that Isaiah 40–66 argues strongly that prophecy is identified on the basis of the fulfillment of its claims.[100] The truth of the prophetic message is to be seen in the fact that it was proclaimed beforehand. This argument would not be so prominently anchored in the Deutero-Isaiah tradition if its historical beginnings did not lie before the fall of Babylon:

> I declared and saved and proclaimed, when there was no strange god among you; and you are my witnesses, says Yhwh. I am God . . . (Isa 43:12-13)

> Who told this long ago? Who declared it of old? (Isa 45:21)

> The former things I declared long ago, they went out from my mouth and I made them known; then suddenly I did them and they came to pass. (Isa 48:3)

> I declared them to you from long ago, before they came to pass I announced them to you, so that you would not say, "My idol did them, my carved image and my cast image commanded them." (Isa 48:5)

The oldest comprehensive, still early-Persian edition of the prophecy of Deutero-Isaiah seems visible mainly in Isaiah 40–48*, where the passages 40:1-5 and 52:7-10 may be interpreted as Prologue and Epilogue.

Isaiah 40:1-5	Isaiah 52:7-10
Comfort, O comfort my people, says your God. Speak tenderly to <u>Jerusalem</u>, and cry to her that she has served her term, that her penalty is paid, that she has received from Yhwh's hand double for all her sins. A voice cries out: *"In the wilderness prepare the way of Yhwh, make straight in the desert a highway for our God. Every valley shall be lifted up, and every mountain and hill be made low; the uneven ground shall become level, and the rough places a plain.* Then the glory of Yhwh shall be revealed, and <u>all people shall see it together</u>, for the mouth of Yhwh has spoken."	How beautiful upon the mountains are the feet of the messenger who announces peace, who brings good news, who announces salvation, who says to Zion, "Your God reigns." Listen! Your sentinels lift up their voices, together they sing for joy; for in plain sight they see *the return of Yhwh to Zion.* Break forth together into singing, you ruins of Jerusalem; for the Yhwh **has comforted his people**, he has redeemed <u>Jerusalem</u>. Yhwh has bared his holy arm before the eyes of all the nations; and <u>all the ends of the earth</u> shall see the salvation of our God.

This first edition of Deutero-Isaiah stands apart from all Israel's previous written prophecy now found in the Old Testament by the fact that its content is unlimited salvation and happiness. Probably it was reacting against the consolidation of Persian power evident no later than the reign of Darius I, but it does not seem yet to anticipate extensive return movements, since the Prologue and Epilogue celebrate only the return of God's own self to Zion-Jerusalem as the saving event. Jerusalem's sin, still in the foreground of Jeremiah 4–10 and Lamentations, has been paid for. For Deutero-Isaiah this salvation has not yet broken forth in its full effect everywhere, but God has firmly resolved to do it, and its earthly realization is imminent. This difference between heavenly decision and earthly realization has its linguistic precipitate in the so-called "salvation perfects" in Deutero-Isaiah: In chapters 40–66 certain saving decrees not yet in effect can be spoken of in the perfect because they are already sealed by God.

Thus God's judgment on his people is past. For the subsequent period Deutero-Isaiah envisions the beginning of a new salvation history for Israel, one with quite different characteristics from the former one. What is probably most striking is that no king is expected for Israel in the future; the integration within the Persian empire is accepted as part of the divine deliverance.

The evocation of the Persian king Cyrus as "YHWH's anointed" (Isa 45:1) is something new in the framework of ancient Near Eastern and thus also ancient Israelite religious history. Traditionally, ancient Near Eastern religions operated within the framework of national-religious concepts that counted everything foreign as part of the realm of chaos. When the Deutero-Isaiah tradition regards Cyrus as a legitimate ruler with God's favor it takes a qualitative leap that completely explodes the traditional framework of a national religion.[101] YHWH, the God of Israel, is thus advanced as the sole ruler of the world who also installs the Persian monarch or, possibly, deposes him as well.

With regard to the sayings about Cyrus in Isaiah 40–66, it has been common to refer to the so-called Cyrus cylinder, a Persian document from the time of the fall of Babylon in 539 B.C.E. On this document Cyrus had the following inscribed:

Marduk . . . ordered that he [Cyrus] should go to Babylon. He had him take the road to Tintir (Babylon), and, like a friend and companion, he walked at his side.

His vast troops whose number, like the water in a river, could not be counted, were marching fully-armed at his side. He had him enter without fighting or battle right into Shuanna; he saved his city Babylon from hardship. He handed over to him Nabonidus, the king who did not fear him. . . . As for the population of Babylon . . . I soothed their weariness; I freed them from their bonds(?). Marduk, the great lord, rejoiced at [my good] deeds. . . .[102]

There is a structural similarity between Isaiah 40–66 and the Cyrus cylinder in that the Persian Cyrus can also be regarded in the Cyrus cylinder as the elect of a foreign god, here the primary Babylonian god, Marduk. Differently from Isaiah 40–66, what we have here is a statement by Cyrus himself, who thus presents himself as a ruler in Babylon who is also legitimated by the local gods. In contrast, Isaiah 40–66 goes a step further: the description of Cyrus as YHWH's "anointed" is a foreign statement of Judeans that adopts the Persian Cyrus in place of the shattered Davidic dynasty. Correspondingly, then, in statements in the book of Jeremiah that probably stem from the Persian period, such as Jer 25:9; 27:6; 43:10, Nebuchadnezzar is called God's "servant," which otherwise in the Old Testament is primarily a title of David.[103] Also comparable are the acknowledgments of the God of Israel by foreign rulers in Daniel 1–6, which are likewise close to this concept.

The Deutero-Isaiah tradition represents a strict monotheism, acknowledging YHWH alone as God; all other deities worshiped by the nations are nothing: "I am YHWH and there is no other" (Isa 45:6). We can call this monotheism exclusive—the class of divinities is restricted to one element, YHWH—in contrast to inclusive concepts such as, for example, those in the Priestly document, which also reckon with only one God but are altogether able to admit that this God can be called upon and worshiped in various forms. In this view the class of gods also includes only one element, but that one can be called YHWH, Ahuramazda, Zeus, etc.

Deutero-Isaiah's monotheism marks an elementary and radical change in the religious history of Israel.[104] Exclusive faith in one God finds an explicit presentation here for the first time. It is formulated by adopting and sharpening the first commandment of the Decalogue, which forbids the worship of other gods but does not exclude their existence, instead continuing to presume it as before:

Isaiah 45:6-7	Deuteronomy 5:6-7
I am YHWH, and there is no other. I form light and create darkness, I make weal and create woe; I YHWH do all these things.	I am YHWH your God, who brought you out of the land of Egypt, out of the house of slavery; you shall have no other gods before me.

Both texts begin with the self-introductory formula customary in ancient Near Eastern polytheism: "I am YHWH," the means by which a self-revealing deity traditionally identified himself or herself. The first commandment then defines "your God," that is, Israel's God, "who brought you out of the land of Egypt, out of the house of slavery." The universal concept applied in Deutero-Isaiah drops the description and moves directly to the complementary negative statement: "and there is no other." This sharpens decisively the Decalogue's prescription, "you shall have no other gods before me," and also carries the self-introductory formula *ad absurdum*. Then, however, with the provision that "I form light and create darkness, I make weal and create woe," Isa 45:6-7 offers a thematic complement to the statement of the first commandment about God's bringing Israel out of Egypt. Isaiah, however, does not formulate a pure statement of salvation, but—with a consistent monotheism—explicitly attributes both salvation *and* destruction to divine action. In fact, the term *br'* used in connection with the concept of "woe" refers exclusively to divine action, so that God is not only designated explicitly as the cause of the woe but this depiction is even emphasized.

The monotheistic portrayal in Deutero-Isaiah is directly and substantively connected with its concept of the ruler: if the world ruler Cyrus is to govern Israel as a divinely legitimated king as the earthly representative of God, it is in turn clear that God himself governs the whole world. We can thus suspect that the rise of monotheism in Israel emerges from a political background.

If God is only one, and as such is the creator and ruler of the world, this implies that God's action in the world must be thought of differently from what was the case in the older literature of the Old Testament. A new direction in Deutero-Isaiah is that all divine action is fundamentally regarded as creative action. This is especially easy to see in the hymns that structure Deutero-Isaiah, appearing at high points in the course of the book to praise the creator God and thus make clear that God's deeds in history are creative actions.

Deutero-Isaiah's historical situation, after the fall of Judah and Jerusalem, made it necessary to reflect critically on the older foundational traditions of Israel. As regards the exodus of Israel out of Egypt, it is clear that for Deutero-Isaiah it no longer had any present relevance for salvation. The old exodus from Egypt had obviously produced a history of perdition that culminated in the loss of the land. The relationship between Israel and its God could no longer rest on the exodus as the justification for its existence. Deutero-Isaiah counters: there will be a new exodus, now out of Babylon, that will far surpass the old one. First, YHWH himself will leave Babylon, and the people will follow. And on the basis of this new exodus, which creates a new relationship between God and the people, the old one can be forgotten without regret.

It is noteworthy that the new exodus will also witness a "water miracle," but not one that destroys the enemy like that in Exodus 14. Instead, YHWH will give water in the desert to assuage his people's thirst.[105]

> Thus says YHWH, who makes a way in the sea, a path in the mighty waters, who brings out chariot and horse, army and warrior; they lie down, they cannot rise, they are extinguished, quenched like a wick: Do not remember the former things, or consider the things of old. I am about to do a new thing; now it springs forth, do you not perceive it? I will make a way in the wilderness and rivers in the desert. The wild

animals will honor me, the jackals and the ostriches; for I give water in the wilderness, rivers in the desert, to give drink to my chosen people, the people whom I formed for myself so that they might declare my praise. (Isa 43:16-21)

Deutero-Isaiah deals with the patriarchal traditions very differently from the exodus material. Because of the tradition of the promise of the land that is anchored there, the patriarchal tradition is the only theologically relevant tradition of salvation. Therefore it is taken up and broadly augmented:

But you, Israel, my servant, Jacob, whom I have chosen, the offspring of Abraham, my friend; you whom I took from the ends of the earth, and called from its farthest corners, saying to you, "You are my servant, I have chosen you and not cast you off"; do not fear, for I am with you, do not be afraid, for I am your God; I will strengthen you, I will help you, I will uphold you with my victorious right hand. (Isa 41:8-10)

The people Israel can be addressed with the names of the ancient ancestors, who here appear outside Genesis, at least as regards the line from Abraham to Jacob, in genealogical sequence. Deutero-Isaiah thus activates the theology of promise from the patriarchal history in Genesis, which describes Israel as a people to whom God has unconditionally promised possession of the land. Unlike the exodus tradition with its embedded "Deuteronomistic" theology of the law, the patriarchal tradition thus exercises an important orienting function given Israel's exiled status.

The application of the patriarchal terminology to the people in Deutero-Isaiah is associated with the transfer of statements about the kings to the people itself: both the designation as servant of Yhwh and the notion of election, and finally also the command "do not be afraid!" stem from the sphere of royal ideology. That ideology is thus placed on the common level and the people are assigned the privileged place of the king.

In the course of time the basic Deutero-Isaiah writing was expanded repeatedly.[106] The various additional layers, which took place essentially within chapters 40–55, can be fundamentally distinguished from those in the broader scope of chapters 40–66; finally, some redactional operations extended to the whole book and must be considered within the overall Isaianic horizon.

Thus within chapters 40–55 we can identify with some certainty the polemic against other gods (40:19-20; 41:6-7; 42:17; 44:9-20; 45:16-17, 20b; 46:5-8; 48:22) as a particular kind of addition.[107] Likewise, the Zion texts in chapters 42–55 (especially 49:14-26; 51:9-10, 17, 19-23; 52:1-2; 54:1) seem to have entered the book in succession. Finally, we should also mention the Servant Songs, which in the traditional view were first created independently but now are more frequently thought also to be redactions added to the main text.

In the broader scope of chapters 40–66 we find the Trito-Isaiah continuations of Deutero-Isaiah in chapters 56–59 and 63–64. And above all in Isaiah 65–66 we can perceive the concluding redaction of Isaiah as a whole, bringing the entire book of Isaiah to an end and therefore also constructing a tight *inclusio* with Isaiah 1.

4. Legal Traditions

a. The Decalogue

The basic features of legal-historical development in the wake of the first edition of Deuteronomy can be quite clearly observed in the first part of the frame of Deuteronomy in chapters 4–6. This apparently grew from the outside in, in onion-like layers: In Deuteronomy 6:4, the so-called *Shema Israel* ("Hear, O Israel") one finds, correctly, the original introduction to Deuteronomic law code, aimed at the centralization of the cult, since the *Shema Israel*, with its probably originally mono-yahwistic point ("Hear, O Israel, YHWH, your Lord, is one YHWH") formulates the fundamental theological program of the centralization of worship. YHWH is only *one* YHWH, that is, there are no legitimate manifestations of YHWH (such as those we know, for example, from the epigraphy of the monarchical period: "YHWH of Samaria"; "YHWH of Teman")[108] apart from the YHWH of Jerusalem.

The Decalogue, by contrast, is a later construction, though it may have reworked older materials.[109] While it was popular to suppose, following Alt,[110] that the apodictic formulation of its legal provisions pointed to its great antiquity, it has now become clear that the specific form of the Decalogue should be viewed not in terms of the history of its origins but in light of its function. The Decalogue is in the first place a scribal, condensed reflection on legal themes, not a cornerstone of law.[111]

The possibility that the *Shema Israel* was understood in the sense of the first commandment, considered by many to be the original intention,[112] first emerges on the one hand by prefacing it with the first commandment in Deuteronomy 5, which establishes the framework for what follows, and on the other hand from the insertion of the love commandment in 6:5 ("You shall love YHWH your God with all your heart, and with all your soul, and with all your might"), which against the traditional ancient Near Eastern background uses the "love" metaphor to refer to unconditional loyalty to YHWH.[113] The secondary nature of the Decalogue in contrast to the *Shema Israel* can be recognized from the elevated central position of the Sabbath commandment, which undergirds the identity of exiled Israel, while the demand for a centralization of worship, which can be carried out only in the land itself, is strikingly absent from the Decalogue.[114]

That the Decalogue is to be located in the Babylonian period and prior to Deutero-Isaiah is shown by the polytheistic frame of reference for the first (and, depending on how the commandments are numbered, the second) commandment: the prohibition against worshiping other gods does not exclude their existence but rather presumes it. It is clear how drastically the state of the discussion has shifted in the course of theological development from the *Shema Israel* (Deut 6:4-9) to the Decalogue if we see that the *Shema Israel* is still entirely focused on internal politics and intra-Israel discussions ("one Yhwh"), while the Decalogue, with its prohibition of foreign gods and images apparently presupposes intensive international contacts and dangers to Israel's identity, such as we may assume existed especially in the Babylonian exile.[115]

The extensive discussion about whether the Exodus Decalogue (Exodus 20) or the one in Deuteronomy (Deuteronomy 5) has priority need not and cannot be summarized here.[116] As far as the double tradition itself is concerned, it is in any case noteworthy that the two great proclamations of the law, at Sinai and in the land east of the Jordan, are introduced by the Decalogue, so that the substantive identity of their meaning must be emphasized. On the redactional level the establishing of a relationship between the Sinai revelation and its reformulated promulgation by Moses in Deuteronomy makes it clear that the Torah is characterized and can be summarized "decalogically."[117]

b. The Deuteronomistic Deuteronomy

The placement of the Decalogue at the beginning of Deuteronomy is programmatically representative of its "Deuteronomistic" interpretation in the Babylonian period. Deuteronomy was now reshaped into a constitutional project and "decalogically" restructured.[118] The superscription in Deut 12:1 restricts the validity of the subsequent laws to Israel's life in its land, while the Decalogue claims universal validity. In chapters 16–18 Deuteronomy contains laws for offices and a royal law, though one that reduces the king to the status of a mere scribe.[119] The Deuteronomistic Deuteronomy remains a utopian project; the historical realization of a sabbatical year is attested only for 162 B.C.E. (1 Macc 6:49, 53).

This placement of the Decalogue at the front also corresponds to the specific conception of revelation in Deuteronomy 5, namely that the Decalogue was made known to the whole people at Sinai, while the laws in Deuteronomy 12–26 were first proclaimed to the people by Moses in the land east of the Jordan. If we are inclined to think that Deuteronomy 12–26 was originally a discourse by Yhwh, this block may have been reshaped into a Moses-discourse in the course of the redactional process.

The Deuteronomistic Deuteronomy probably owes its origin to the redactional insertion of Deuteronomy 6–28 into the larger context of the narrative books. Deuteronomy now becomes the projected constitution of Israel after the occupation of the land. It is primarily at the level of the first commandment that the formulations in the Former Prophets, now including Joshua and perhaps Judges, agree with those in Deuteronomy. These accordingly point to a literary interweaving that probably already extended back beyond Deuteronomy at least to Exodus, since Deuteronomy offers a beginning that is satisfying syntactically, but scarcely so in its substance. On the other hand, however, the double tradition in Exodus 20 and Deuteronomy 5 prominently locates the work "decalogically" in relation to the continuing narrative context of Exodus–Numbers.[120]

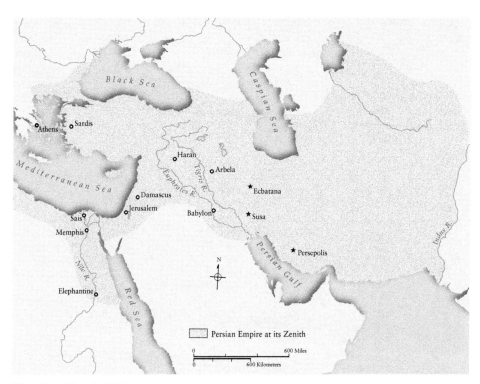

The Near East in 500 B.C.E.

Part E

The Literature of the Persian Period (Fifth–Fourth Centuries B.C.E.)

I. Historical Backgrounds

If, as in this book, the history of Israel is divided into periods not from an endogenous point of view as monarchical period, exilic period, and so-called "post-exilic" period, but exogenously according to the influence exercised by the respective hegemonial powers in the ancient Near East, then the common notion that the exile ended with the Persians' assumption of power is quickly exposed as a fiction. The exile did not end in 539 B.C.E. when Babylon was conquered without a struggle, nor did it cease with the waves of returnees in the succeeding decades. The diaspora continued, even without compulsion from a foreign power. The deportees, especially those belonging to the second and later generations, seem in the meantime to have achieved respect and prosperity in Mesopotamia and Egypt, as attested indirectly by the documents of the banking house of Murašu, which contain a number of Jewish names,[1] by the legends of the rise of Joseph and Daniel,[2] and by the high positions of Judahites such as Zerubbabel, Nehemiah, and also—though hard to pin down historically—Ezra.[3] As a result, the will and impulse to return may not always have been well developed. We can even interpret the so-called "murmuring" stories in Exodus and Numbers (cf. especially Exodus 16; Numbers 11; 14; 16) in which the people resist entering into the promised land against this background. It is possible that they are a critical reflex, anchored in previous history, against the problem of refusal to return, virulent in the early Persian period.[4] The exile had apparently changed in the interim from a place of banishment to a new homeland. Israel's diaspora existence influenced the Old Testament so fundamentally that—apart from the role of the patriarchs as guests and foreigners in their own land—the Torah formed in the Persian period takes place entirely outside Israel.

Speaking of the "restoration" is as misleading as reference to the "post-exilic period," because there was no restoration of the conditions of the monarchical era; instead, Judah found its way "under the pressure of the political circumstances to a new form of community life . . . that was more oriented to the structures of the pre-state period"[5]—or, as was more likely the case, found its model in the structures projected for the pre-state era.

In this connection we should discuss whether the beginning of "Judaism" should be placed in the Persian period. This was a common notion in the nineteenth century, however often with a pejorative coloring,[6] but also in the twentieth century, with a value-neutral or positive intention.[7] Sometimes the break is seen as having occurred in the time of Alexander.[8]

> The problem of defining epochs is, of course, such that definitions are imposed on the historical phenomena from without and will differ depending on the perspective applied. Those who prefer to restrict the idea of Judaism to the rabbinic Judaism after 70 C.E. will see as the crucial difference the loss of the Second Temple and the subsequent complete transformation of Judaism to a book religion. This opinion is necessarily connected to a more uniform notion of Judaism, which one may perhaps regard as the most profound caesura of the events of 70 C.E. English-language scholarship has advanced the rather awkward but substantively justified expression "Judaisms" for the time before 70 C.E.[9]
>
> In any case, however, there is significant continuity between the "Judaism" of the Second Temple and rabbinic "Judaism," especially concerning its post-state existence and the decisive fundamental theological formulations of monotheism, covenant, and law, so that the broadly recognized concept of "ancient or classical Judaism" is meaningful and justified if one adequately considers the internal differentiations within it.[10]

The historical circumstances that framed Persian-period Israel were established, on the geopolitical level, by the Persian empire, which now encompassed nearly the entirety of the world known to the ancient Near East. The rise of the first great Persian king, Cyrus, began with a successful conquest of his Median opponent Astyages in 550 B.C.E. and became unmistakable especially with his sweeping military success against the Lydian king Croesus in 546 B.C.E. The decisive step to world power happened later, however, in 539 B.C.E. with his unopposed occupation of Babylon, made possible especially by the peculiar religious politics of the last Babylonian king, Nabonidus, in his opposition to Marduk.[11] Cyrus was apparently received with the same measure of enthusiasm by the Babylonian priesthood of Marduk[12] as the contempt they had previously expressed for Nabonidus.[13]

For Judah, however, this geopolitical break was of little importance at the time. The change in the central government was at first associated with few perceptible changes in the Levant. From that point of view the beginning of the rule of Darius I, with the introduction of the satrapies, a new fiscal system with coined money, and the rigorous repression of the Babylonian revolts in

522/521 B.C.E. were more important. Here also we can observe shifts in material culture.[14]

Add to this that the building of the temple, while prepared for under Cyrus by the commissar Sheshbazzar who was sent for the purpose (Ezra 5:14-16),[15] was only begun and carried out in the time of Darius. The beginning of the temple building project in the reign of Darius II (423–404 B.C.E.) rather than that of Darius I (522–486 B.C.E.)[16] does have the peculiar sequence of Persian kings in Ezra 1–6 on its side, but it can scarcely be reconciled with Haggai and Zechariah 1–8.[17] Especially important for Judah's perception of the political change, however, was the fate of Babylon itself. While according to Jeremiah 50–51 and Isaiah 47 there was hope and longing for the destruction of Babylon, it did not happen under the Persians; in fact, Babylon became a location of one of the Persian king's residences. Here, too, it is probably the reign of Darius I, during which Babylonian revolts were violently repressed, that should be seen as the historical turning point.

Unlike the Assyrians and Babylonians before them, the Persians did not aim to break down the local structures by means, for example, of deportations that affected mainly the elite. Instead they strengthened local autonomy under supervision from the central administration. It is even possible that at first a figure like Zerubbabel, a Davidide (1 Chr 3:16-19), may have acted as governor of Judah (Hag 2:2).[18] However, as two seals from the Persian period that can be associated with the descendants of Zerubbabel referred to in 1 Chr 3:16-19 ("Hananiah," "Shelomith") attest, the Davidides appear to have been gradually pushed out of the gubernatorial office.[19]

On the whole, however, it is not astonishing to learn that the Persians are viewed in a strikingly positive light throughout the whole of the Old Testament. It should always be kept in mind that not a single national oracle against the Persians appears in the texts of the Old Testament.[20] The Persian imperial ideology of a peaceful state made up of many peoples, each retaining its own cultural and religious uniqueness, as expressed, for example, in the Behistun inscription of Darius I,[21] which—as confirmed by examples of its Aramaic version found in Elephantine—also circulated as a text for scribal education, was adopted positively in various concepts within the Old Testament literature of the Persian period and made Israel's own, for example in the Priestly document or Chronicles.

Finally, the first waves of returning exiles took place in the reign of Darius I, that is, the returnees were members of the second and third generations of those originally exiled. Ezra 2 and Nehemiah 7 contain lists of returnees naming 42,360 people with their belongings. "But the list in Ezra appears not to be a real list of returnees, but a census list. The author of the Chronicler's historical work apparently found significance in the idea that the destruction of Jerusalem in 587 had left an empty land behind, and that the returnees thus reported were identical with the existing population."[22] Behind the theory of the total deportation of Judah and this literary manipulation are conflicts arising in the wake of the return of the deportees.[23] The portion of the population taken to Mesopotamia as a result of the Neo-Babylonian occupation was certainly a tiny minority in comparison to those who remained in the land, but they were drawn from the upper class. Their descendants in the second and third generation would have insisted on being restored to correspondingly privileged positions, so quarrels were nearly impossible to avoid.

Besides the enmities between the returnees and those remaining in the land there were also conflicts with the neighbors, the Samaritans, which affected the whole experience.[24] The Samaritans were, in fact, the descendants of survivors from the Northern Kingdom, which had collapsed in the Assyrian period, but on the one hand they were ethnically mixed with transplanted, exogenous groups of people as a result of the Assyrian practice of deportation;[25] on the other hand, they had probably been cultically independent since the sixth century B.C.E. The historical beginnings of a Samaritan sanctuary on Mount Gerizim are nowadays placed much earlier than was the case even ten years ago, when essentially the presentation in Flavius Josephus was accepted as the framework of what could be historically expected.[26]

The major point of contention was Jerusalem. The rebuilding of the city, in view of the political and economic weight of the reconstructed temple, had led to unpleasant competition from the perspective of the larger and more important Samaria.[27] The power struggles delayed the building of the city and the wall, as well as a resettlement capable of making the city function, until the time of Nehemiah. A palpable impression of the desolate condition of Jerusalem, which would be eloquent enough simply as a literary composition, is found, for example, in Neh 2:11-15:

> So I came to Jerusalem and was there for three days. Then I got up during the night, I and a few men with me; I told no one what my God had put into my heart to do for Jerusalem. The only animal I took was the animal I rode. I went out by night by the Valley Gate past the Dragon's Spring and to the Dung Gate, and I inspected the walls of Jerusalem that had been broken down and its gates that had been destroyed by fire. Then I went on to the Fountain Gate and to the King's Pool; but there was no place for the animals I was riding to continue. So I went up by way of the valley by night and inspected the wall. Then I turned back and entered by the Valley Gate, and so returned.

The conflict with Samaria over the rebuilding has been a long-underestimated factor in the political and religious history of Persian period Judah.

The missions of Ezra and Nehemiah fall into the middle of the period of Persian rule over Syria-Palestine. While, according to the biblical presentation, the scribe Ezra was in charge of cultic matters, the governor Nehemiah was responsible for organizing the construction and the social restoration of Jerusalem and Judah. Of these two figures, however, only Nehemiah can be clearly located historically. According to Neh 1:1; 2:1 he came to Jerusalem in the twentieth year of Artaxerxes (probably Artaxerxes I, 465–425, that is, the twentieth year would have been 445 B.C.E.). Ezra, on the other hand, according to Ezra 7:7, would have reached Jerusalem already in the seventh year of Artaxerxes, thus thirteen years before Nehemiah. In the opinion of the books of Ezra–Nehemiah this was certainly the same Artaxerxes, but historically that is scarcely possible: Ezra, according to Ezra 9:9, found Jerusalem already surrounded by the walls that Nehemiah was supposed to rebuild. On the other hand, Nehemiah seems to have paid no attention to the Ezra returnees in developing his own resettlement policies, even though they must have arrived previously. In the biblical tradition Ezra, as a priest and scribe, must have been superior to the political functionary Nehemiah on theological grounds. But as a historical figure Ezra remains merely vague.[28]

It appears, then, that in the fourth century B.C.E. Jerusalem was again surrounded by walls in the sense of an ideal restoration of monarchical-period Jerusalem, but it still possessed only a modest number of inhabitants.[29] Nehemiah 5 documents serious social problems,[30] which present an eloquent background for the social criticism, for example, in Isaiah 56–59. Judah's economic and demographic situation was comparatively modest during the Persian period, leading in the texts of the Old Testament to repeated new formulations of hopes for salvation.[31]

II. Theological Characterizations

From a theological point of view the Old Testament tradition from the Persian period—viewing it very schematically—can be characterized in two ways: first it should be emphasized that no book of the Old Testament with origins in the monarchical period has survived in a form arising from before the Persian period. This means in turn that the traditional material of the Old Testament has been subjected redactionally to a certain redefinition and refinement, possibly including various processes of selection, and it is now shaped by certain basic theological decisions that were highly significant for Judaism in the Persian period and later, such as the move towards monotheism,[32] the acknowledgment of the law and the covenant, or marks of cultic identification such as the Sabbath and male circumcision.[33]

However, this tendency towards a certain uniformity in particular fundamental theological positions, especially as regards the doctrine of God, faced a second tendency that can be described as a broad diversification of positions within the now-orthodox spectrum of possibilities.[34] This was true especially of political theology. These positions can be broadly categorized within three strands.

Above all in the prophetic books we find, first of all, the idea that the current political experiences are to be interpreted as the onset of salvation, full of promise and irreversible. By means of the Persians, whose king, Cyrus, could even be called "messiah" in Isa 45:1, YHWH is in the process of realizing his all-encompassing saving will for Israel within a fundamentally peaceful world. This salvation, however, must be completed by Yʜᴡʜ himself. To that extent it is obvious that the tradents of the prophetic books who adopted this position had to continually observe and interpret current history in order to identify signs of the inbreaking of the expected salvation as well as historical elements that hindered it.[35]

Not completely different from this idea, but with another accent, was a second position that assumed that with the rule of the Persians the saving goal of Yʜᴡʜ's history with Israel and the world—to say it pointedly, in the sense of a "realized eschatology"[36]—has already been achieved. Of course, this goal still had to be brought to completion in various places, but in principle the turn to salvation could be regarded as accomplished. This position, again internally differentiated, can be seen above all in the Priestly document, in the fourth and fifth books of the Psalter (Psalms 107–150), in the non-eschatological Daniel stories in Daniel 1–6, in the book of Ezra, and in Chronicles. It is essentially nothing other than the Jewish reception of the official Persian imperial ideology: David and Solomon, in their respective roles as initiator and builder of the temple, were the "primitive" models for Cyrus and Darius.

A third option differed sharply from the two positions just described and emphatically denied the saving character of the political developments then current. Above all the texts of the "Deuteronomistic" tradition gave voice to this view, especially within the narrative books but also, for example, in the book of Jeremiah, which was correspondingly redacted. The present is still to be interpreted as ongoing judgment because Israel is still scattered in the diaspora, does not live united in its land, and has no king of its own. That Cyrus (Isa 45:1), or even Nebuchadnezzar (Jer 27:6; Daniel 1–4), could be a divinely ordained king is unthinkable for this position. The foreign rule of the Persians, while comparatively tolerant, remains unacceptable as such.

Within this position we can also observe some variety: of course, some ameliorations of the overall situation can take place during the period of judgment, but that has nothing to do with a turn to salvation; it was merely a matter of divine mercy, though still as a part of judgment. The expectation was that another decisive intervention by God in history will be required to turn aside judgment; it will bring with it the destruction of Israel's enemies and the final liberation of Israel and will go far beyond what the Persian period may have to offer in the way of salvific experiences. But this eschatological saving action of God depends on penance, awareness of sin, and repentance on the part of the people of God (cf. Ezra 9; Nehemiah 9), or even—theologically more radical—on an eschatological reshaping of the human: Deut 30:6 expects a "circumcision" of the human heart, Jer 32:40 the implantation of "the fear of God" in the heart, and Ezek 36:26 even the transplantation of a new heart in place of the old.[37]

The role of the Persians is differently accented in the three positions we have sketched: for the tradents of the prophetic books they are divine instruments in a gradual process of the realization of salvation. For the Priestly document, Chronicles, and positions related to them they are divinely legitimated representatives of the now-realized universal rule of God. For the adherents of the still active "Deuteronomistic" tradition, finally, they are signs of the judgment under which Israel stands.

Besides these writings, which primarily reflect problems in political theology, there are also other deeply reflective texts, especially in the realm of the so-called wisdom traditions, that continue the efforts of the Babylonian period to give closer attention to the *conditio humana*. They contain a post-monarchical anthropology that, after the loss of the kingdom, made human beings themselves the object of theological reflection. It has long been known that these anthropological forms of thought have parallels in far older Mesopotamian or Egyptian texts.[38] That they were not received sooner in Israel has little to do with their being unknown. Rather, these materials seem to have been taken up at a time when similar problematics appeared in the history of Israel's own experience.

It is also noteworthy that from the Persian period onward we can observe an explicit expansion of YHWH's authority in the sphere of the underworld.[39] The underworld, as archaeology and epigraphy have shown, was, in the nature of things, a religiously occupied space even in the monarchical period. But now it appears that this space—in the wake of the universalizing of God—was more and more explicitly assigned to the sphere of YHWH's power.

III. Spheres of Tradition

1. Cultic and Wisdom Traditions

a. The Priestly Document

Like the distinction between Isaiah 1–39 and Isaiah 40–66, the delimitation of the Priestly document in the Pentateuch as an originally independent source document is one of the most widely acknowledged achievements of biblical criticism.[40] It contains theologically programmatic texts such as Genesis 1; 9; 17; Exodus 6, and above all it is broadly present in the description of the tabernacle in Exodus 25–31 + 35–40. The reason for the success of the Priestly hypothesis lies in the long-familiar observations that remain as obvious as they were at the beginnings of historical biblical criticism: the doubling of material, whether placed in sequence as in Genesis 1–3 or interwoven as in Genesis 6–9, also the striking use "Elohim" as a divine name in the narrative presentation of Genesis 1–Exodus 6.[41] Add to this a different scribal-linguistic and theological-conceptual shaping that assures the identification of this writing. The enumerative and repetitive style of the Priestly document that was so thoroughly criticized by nineteenth-century exegesis must be seen as closely linked to the priestly interests: the cult, in order to be correctly performed, must be regulated down to the last detail. It must be made clear that in any arrangement the various performances correspond exactly to these orders. Therefore we find in the Priestly document great numbers of lists and "repetitions" that have much more to do with their theology than with "poor style."

The Priestly document—at any rate in the texts of Genesis through Leviticus—must be seen as the proper basic document of the Pentateuch. Its texts organize the course of the Pentateuch; the non-Priestly sections are inserted into it and are redactionally determined by it. This assessment is true also for the existing "Documentary Hypothesis": even in the JEPD model the latest source document, P, was considered the one that had been made the basis for the combination of the sources and therefore the best preserved. Its later date was apparent especially from a comparison with Deuteronomy: the cultic centralization demanded by the latter was accepted unquestioningly by the Priestly document as regards the sanctuary it expects for Israel; thus the Priestly document is not ancient, certainly not Mosaic, as was still largely assumed in the nineteenth century. At the earliest it was a product of the exile.

According to the convictions of the most recent Pentateuch research, the Priestly document is the basis for the Pentateuch not only in the techniques of redaction but also conceptually:[42] if it is true that the patriarchal and Moses-exodus themes were only combined by the Priestly document,[43] then it is the origin of one of the most important literary-historical syntheses in the Old Testament. This innovative potential of the Priestly document may also be the reason why it was created not as a continuation of the existing textual material but from the outset as a source document.[44]

As for its extent, its original end is probably in the Sinai pericope, though the particular point is variously identified.[45] This is indicated, on the one hand, by the thematic weight it accords to the cultic laws given at Sinai. On the other hand, we can also observe some striking literary *inclusio*s between creation and Sinai that construct a parallel between the creation of the world and the construction of the sanctuary and so point in the same direction:

Genesis 1:31a	Exodus 39:43a
God *saw* everything that he had made, and *indeed*, it was very good.	When Moses *saw* that they had done all the work *just as* Yhwh had commanded, he blessed them.
2:1 Thus the heavens and the earth *were finished*, and all their multitude.	39:32a In this way all the work of the tabernacle of the tent of meeting *was finished*.
2:2a And on the seventh day God *finished* the *work* that he had done.	40:33b So Moses *finished* the *work*.
2:3a So God *blessed* the seventh day . . .	39:43b [Moses] *blessed* them.

The traditional delimitation of the Priestly document in terms of the extent of the Pentateuch breaks down especially if one conducts an internal analysis of Deuteronomy 34.[46] In the traditional documentary model this theory was primarily based on the conviction that the construction of the Pentateuch must have been modeled on one of its sources and could not be purely redactional.

Within the Bible there is a competition especially between the merely two-dimensional temple projection in Ezekiel 40–48[47] and the Priestly document's depiction of the sanctuary in Exodus 25–40.[48] Because of these discrepancies the book of Ezekiel remained the object of theological dispute for a considerable time in early Judaism.

Besides the current scholarly majority that restricts the Priestly document to the arc between creation and Sinai, the contacts between Gen 1:28; 2:1 and Josh 18:1; 19:51 have occasionally led to the proposal that the Priestly document ended with the book of Joshua.[49] But the passages in question are not from the source itself; they serve the purpose of working the Priestly document into the sequence of the historical books.

The theology of the Priestly document can be derived in the first instance from what it says about the covenant, which gives us a view of its overall divisions. Contrary to Wellhausen's proposal to classify the Priestly document as a *liber quattuor foederum* and therefore give it the *siglum* Q, the Priestly document speaks explicitly of only two covenants, the one with Noah (Genesis 9) and the one with Abraham (Genesis 17), which formulate God's fundamental ordinance for the world and the Abrahamic peoples—Israel (Isaac/Jacob) as well as the Arabs (Ishmael) and the Edomites (Esau). Accordingly, the Priestly document is first of all divided into two major sections that can be called accordingly "the world cycle" and "the Abraham cycle." In Genesis 9 God places his bow in the clouds and guarantees endurance to creation. God here, therefore, having exercised violence once and for all against "all flesh" in the Flood story from the primeval history just narrated, renounces every kind of violence:[50] "And God said to Noah, 'I have *determined* to make an *end* (*qṣ*) of all flesh, for the earth is filled with violence because of them; now I am going to destroy them along with the earth" (Gen 6:13). This severe decree of the "end" that is "determined" did not originate with the Priestly document; it is taken from the prophecies of judgment in Amos and Ezekiel:

He said, "Amos, what do you see?" And I said, "A basket of summer fruit (*qyṣ*)." Then Yʜwʜ said to me, "The *end* (*qṣ*) has come upon my people Israel; I will never again pass them by." (Amos 8:2)

You, O mortal, thus says the Lord Yʜwʜ to the land of Israel: An *end*! The *end* (*qṣ*) has come upon the four corners of the land. Now the *end* (*qṣ*) is upon you, I will let loose my anger upon you; I will judge you according to your ways, I will punish you for all your abominations. (Ezek 7:2-3)

Evidently the Priestly document thus adopts the message of the prophets of judgment, but translates it to the Primeval History: yes, there was a divine determination that the "end" had come, but that was in the past, not in the future. In terms of content, then, the Priestly document also sets itself against Deuteronomy and its curse proclamations (Deuteronomy 28).[51]

The theological message of the Priestly document for Israel is shaped accordingly: as the covenant with Noah guarantees the eternal existence of the world, so the covenant with Abraham guarantees that God will always remain close to Israel. In neither case is there any condition (male circumcision is a symbol, not a condition of the covenant, and the promised punishment for neglect of the requirement of circumcision does not apply to Israel as a whole, but only to individuals).[52]

As Zimmerli in particular has shown,[53] the disqualification of Sinai events as a covenant, and the sole concentration on the making of the covenant with Abraham constitute a theological program for the Priestly document: God's promises of salvation (increase, land, closeness to God) are *not* conditioned in the Priestly document by Israel's obedience to the law, unlike the earlier promises envisioned in the Deuteronomistic shaping of the Sinai pericope. Rather, for the Priestly document "covenant" is a unilateral promise of salvation from the side of God. Certainly, individuals can fall away from this covenant (if, for example, they do not practice male circumcision), but not the collective entity of the Abrahamic peoples as a whole. This is shown in detail in the characteristic adaptation of the so-called covenant formula in Gen 17:7: "to be God to you and to your offspring after you." The second half of the formula found in Deuteronomistic theology ("that you will be my people") is omitted here, evidently on purpose, because whatever Abraham and his descendants may do or not do changes nothing about the unconditionally promised nearness of God.

If we compare the circle of the world with the Abrahamic circle in the Priestly document, it is striking that the Noachic covenant follows the judgment of the world (the Flood), while the Abrahamic covenant precedes the judgment on Israel, the national catastrophe. The intention behind this structure is evidently that God's change of heart in the Primeval History, which led to his offering the covenant to Noah, now benefits the Abraham circle from the beginning in the offering of the covenant to Abraham.

However, the overall structure of the Priestly document is not in two parts, as its covenant theology might lead us to expect. It is rather in three parts, as indicated by its doctrine of God: alongside the circle of the world and the Abrahamic circle, which are concentric in relation to one another, there is a third and inmost circle of people, that of Israel. Although the Priestly document pursues an "ecumenical" theology in its Abraham circle, linking Israelites, Arabs, and

Edomites,[54] it is still unmistakably clear that only Israel is given complete knowledge of God, and only Israel, through the gift of sacrificial worship, possesses the means to make possible a partial restoration of the "very good" order of creation in Genesis 1.[55] The three circles correspond to three modes of divine revelation: for the whole world God is "Elohim." In Genesis 1 (and later) the Priestly document uses the Hebrew generic "God" indeterminately, as a proper name, identifying the genre "God" with its sole content and thus proclaiming an inclusive monotheism.[56] To the patriarchs Abraham, Isaac, and Jacob, God presents himself as "El Shaddai," and his proper name for worship, namely "Yhwh," is revealed only to the Moses generation. This theory of the stages of revelation is at its clearest in the Priestly presentation of the call of Moses in Exod 6:2-3: "God also spoke to Moses and said to him: 'I am Yhwh. I appeared to Abraham, Isaac, and Jacob as "El Shaddai," but by my name "Yhwh" I did not make myself known to them.'" Overall, the Priestly document represents an entirely non-eschatological and pacifist (and in this sense altogether political) position, which in the author's time, the Persian period, was regarded as the divinely willed goal of history.

It is true that some scholars attribute to the Priestly document, contrary to its traditional, apolitical interpretation, the hope for a national restoration under Israel's own king,[57] because of the promises of a king found in Gen 17:6, 16; 35:11. But this perspective is remarkably undeveloped within the overall framework of the Priestly document. It seems more probable that these promises were regarded by the Priestly document as having been long since fulfilled in the history that followed and so were "historicized" from the outset.

The one God ("Elohim," who can be worshiped under various names, including "El Shaddai" in the Abrahamite world of the nations and "Yhwh" in Israel) rules over the whole world created by him, within which the nations, each in its own place, with its own language and cult, live together peacefully forever. Only Egypt is regarded with hostility in the Priestly document, as we can see from the plague cycle and the note in Exod 12:12. Probably this reflects the contemporary opinion of the Priestly document, before the incorporation of Egypt into the Persian empire under Cambyses in 525 B.C.E. The Priestly document, with its pacifist and pro-Persian attitude, is precisely *the* counter-concept to the Deuteronomistic strand of tradition,[58] which evaluates the Persian era as fundamentally deficient in terms of salvation: as long as Israel does not live united in its land as a sovereign nation under its own king, God cannot have consummated his history with his people. Therefore the present time is still considered a time of judgment, and in turn, this of course means that Israel is still in the status of sin, for from the Deuteronomistic perspective judgment is the punishment for sin.

The anti-Deuteronomistic orientation of the Priestly document can also be demonstrated exegetically. It can be read in its most elementary guise in the Priestly document's transformation of the Deuteronomistic theology of covenant: the disqualification of the Sinai events as covenant in the Priestly document is a direct critique of the covenant theology of the Deuteronomistic Sinai pericope. According to the Priestly document there is no connection between law and covenant, but only between promise and covenant. Therefore in Gen 17:7 the Priestly document uses only "half" of the covenant formula. Likewise, the "Deuteronomistic" echoes in Gen 17:9-14 do not point to a growth of the text,[59] but are instead to be interpreted as critical allusions. The Priestly document also differs from the Deuteronomistic tradition in its ideas about God and worship. God is fundamentally separate from the world; he does not reside in heaven, but is present to the world a-locally.[60] However, this is in order that he may, by means of the form of his presence, his "glory" (*kbwd*), at the same time "dwell among" the Israelites (Exod 25:8; 29:45-46).[61] The cult that serves him takes place without words—thus acknowledging the otherness of his holiness—in a "sanctuary of silence."[62]

In the contrast between the Priestly document and Deuteronomism we can perceive an elementary antagonism that, following Otto Plöger, has been summarily described as the conflict between "theocracy and eschatology."[63] This broad contrast between "theocracy and eschatology" has often been criticized, but one should not misunderstand the concepts as complementary categories into which the whole literature of the Persian period can be slotted. Rather, these are two fundamental perspectives within which individual texts or writings may be located with greater or lesser precision. The distinction between theocratic and eschatological stances may still be applied in the sense of a heuristic description of positions with appropriate further differentiation as long as the purpose is not to dichotomize them.

> Related to the perspective of cordiality toward the nations within the Priestly document are also the books of Jonah and Ruth. Jonah polemicizes against prophetic expectations of judgment on foreign empires—in the perspective of this book the power is Nineveh—and Ruth, in its conclusion in 4:18-22, whether original or secondary, traces the genealogy of David to a woman of Moab.

b. Theocratic Psalms

Theologically close to the Priestly document is a series of psalms in the last part of the Psalter.[64] They praise God as the creator and the true king of the world, who—without any earthly mediator such as a king—rules eternally over his creation. These psalms are unusually a-political. They neither criticize the foreign rule of the Persians nor develop ambitions for a new kingdom in Israel. Instead, for them God's rule is expressed concretely above all in that God provides elementary nourishment for his creation. The Persian empire is thus implicitly interpreted by these psalms as a God-endorsed organization of the world through which the Creator has, politically speaking, set the creation generally at peace, toward which he now turns his attention as its elementary caregiver and provider.

> Praise. Of David. I will extol you, my God and King, and bless your name forever and ever. . . . Your kingdom is an everlasting kingdom, and your dominion endures throughout all generations. . . . The eyes of all look to you, and you give them their food in due season. You open your hand, satisfying the desire of every living thing. (Ps 145:1, 13, 15-16)

> Happy are those whose help is the God of Jacob, whose hope is in YHWH their God, who made heaven and earth, the sea, and all that is in them; who keeps faith forever; who executes justice for the oppressed; who gives food to the hungry. YHWH sets the prisoners free; YHWH opens the eyes of the blind. YHWH lifts up those who are bowed down; YHWH loves the righteous. YHWH watches over the strangers; he upholds the orphan and the widow, but the way of the wicked he brings to ruin. YHWH will reign forever, your God, O Zion, for all generations. Hallelujah. (Ps 146:5-10)

> Sing to YHWH with thanksgiving; make melody to our God on the lyre. He covers the heavens with clouds, prepares rain for the earth, makes grass grow on the hills. He gives to the animals their food, and to the young ravens when they cry. (Ps 147:7-9)

These psalms speak implicitly against the Deuteronomistic and parts of the prophetic traditions that hope for a national restoration under a king of Israel's own. David appears in Psalm 145 as the exemplary pious person who acknowledges and praises God's universal royal rule. There is not a word about the yoke of the foreign Persian ruler or political ambitions for national restitution.

It is something of an accident that we can locate Psalm 20 in the Persian period, thanks to an Aramaic parallel text from the fifth century B.C.E. The text is especially remarkable as a transcultural reception of a pagan Phoenician original.[65] It is possible, though difficult to establish firmly, that other individual collections of several psalms were formed in the Persian period as "books" for guilds of singers; these could include the Psalms of Korah (Pss 42–48, 84–85, 87–88) and the Asaph Psalms (Pss 73–83),[66] or thematic groups such as the YHWH-is-King Psalms (Pss 93, 96–99), the pilgrim psalms (Pss 120–134), or the collections of psalms of David (Pss 3–41, among others).

That, in any case, in the Persian period we can still account only for loose partial collections of psalms and cannot yet reckon with a thoroughly redacted Psalter is illuminated rather clearly by the so-called "Elohistic Psalter," Psalms 42–83,[67] in which—as a consequence of the theological program of the Priestly document—the Tetragrammaton is consistently replaced by "Elohim." The fact that this measure was applied only to Psalms 42–83 but was used consistently in those psalms can only be explained by supposing that the psalms traditions were not at that time united without leaving any out in a *single* Psalter, but existed in a variety of collections.

c. Job

The book of Job is not only thematically but also theologically one of the most dramatic books of the Old Testament.[68] Its point cannot be discussed simply on the basis of individual texts viewed in isolation; but the place of each text in the development of the book as a whole must be kept in mind. It appears that the theology of the book of Job becomes visible precisely in the development of the problem throughout the parts of the book, which seem so disparate both formally and theologically. However one assesses the literary relationship between the frame and the dialogues and the prehistory of the material,[69] the frame and the dialogues in the book as we have it are meaningfully set in relation to the other. The differences complained of as a rule, namely the image of Job as a patient sufferer on the one hand (Job 1–2) and as a rebel on the other (Job 3–31), are at any rate accommodated within the framework of the book as a whole in the sense of a narrative progression.[70]

If we approach the book of Job in this way it is apparent that the central theme of the book is neither the suffering of the righteous nor the theodicy question. Rather, it discusses and addresses the problem of whether theology is possible at all. This theme is introduced in the prologue, with its heavenly scene that not only exposes the problem of Job but at the same time resolves it (for the readers): Job has to suffer because of a heavenly test. By means of this fundamental tension—the readers are in the know, the actors in the book are not—the book of Job formulates a radical critique of theology and even of revelation: neither Job's friends, with their orthodox theologies (Job 3–27; 32–37), nor God himself with his mighty speeches (Job 38–41)[71] uncovers Job's real situation. Thus in principle the book of Job represents a negative theology: one cannot speak of God; neither theology nor revelation is able to reflect with certainty what is actually the case. Talking about God is indeed impossible, but the book of Job sees speaking *to* God as the adequate possibility for relating oneself to God (Job 42:7).[72]

The book of Job is hard to date only because it takes place altogether in a fictive space. Even ancient and medieval interpretations do not suppose that Job was a historical figure; they recognize the paradigmatic character of the book. Essentially, one must rely on references to other Old Testament texts in order to place it within literary history.[73] The depiction of the catastrophe in Job 1:17 gives a certain absolute indicator, since it mentions the neo-Babylonian "Chaldeans," and so apparently alludes to the Babylonians' destruction of Jerusalem. Among the literary texts that are presupposed are, first of all and with some certainty, the Priestly document and the prophetic tradition as redacted by the Deuteronomists, because the book of Job argues vehemently against their theology of order: God is neither nonviolent (so the Priestly document) nor does he punish only the wicked and godless (so the Deuteronomistic strand of tradition). Instead, God can also, apparently without reason, turn against the pious and the righteous. But the book of Job also polemicizes against the piety of the Psalms:[74] its very structure, which has been described as a dramatized lament, reveals borrowings from the Psalter.[75] Added to these, however, are the striking and subversive receptions of statements from the Psalms in Job's laments. The reworking of Ps 8:4-5 in Job 7:17-18 is especially harsh (cf. also Ps 137:9//Job 16:12, and Ps 139:8-10//Job 23:9-10).

Psalm 8:4-5	Job 7:17
<u>What are human beings that</u> you are mindful of them, mortals, that you *care for them* (*pqd*)? Yet you have made them a little lower than God, and crowned them with glory and honor.	<u>What are human beings, that you</u> make so much of them, that you set your mind on them, *visit them* (*pqd*) every morning, test them every moment?

While Psalm 8 marvels that God embraces human beings at all and constantly cares for them, Job complains in chapter 7 about this same unceasing attention, now viewed negatively, and laments that God does not leave human beings alone but continually tests and watches them, even though he need not do so. Why, then, does God concern himself (*pqd*) with Job? If only he would leave him alone! What Psalm 8 praises has become a torture for Job 7—in Hebrew the term *pqd* can have both a positive meaning ("care for, show concern") and a negative one ("visit, haunt").

Further, is it possible that the book of Job was familiar with and adopted the thematically related poems *Ludlul bēl nēmeqi*[76] and the so-called "Babylonian theodicy"[77]—possibly in an Aramaic translation.[78] The book of Job seems like a structural combination of "Babylonian theodicy" (discussion with friends, cf. Job 3–27) and *Ludlul bēl nēmeqi* (petitioner's lament, divine response, cf. Job 3; 29–31; 38–41).[79] These parallels may also have inspired the setting of the book of Job in the Babylonian era.

Given its negative theology, it is hard to imagine that the book of Job is drawn simply from traditional material of the Jerusalem temple. On the other hand, however, it attests to such a high degree of scribal learning that is cannot have been created at a great distance from it.

2. Narrative Traditions

a. The Non-Priestly Primeval History

The non-Priestly components of the Primeval History (Genesis 1–11) are among the best-known texts of the Old Testament (Genesis 2–3: Paradise; Genesis 4: Cain and Abel; Genesis 6–9*: the Flood; Genesis 11*: the Tower of Babel). As regards their location within literary history they are likewise among the most difficult to place. The reason for the present uncertainty among scholars, who are at odds regarding nearly all the non-Priestly texts as to whether they should be placed before or after the Priestly document, is associated above all with the crisis of the Yahwist hypothesis, which remains so severe that the assumption of a Yahwist historical work can no longer be taken as a starting point for the analysis.[80]

In the most recent scholarship there is debate about an alternative suggestion—in addition to the fundamental location of all non-Priestly contributions only posterior to the Priestly writing[81]—namely, whether one should postulate an originally independent, non-Priestly primeval history extending from Genesis 2*–8,[82] whose thematic combination of creation and flood was oriented to the Atrahasis epic.[83] Or is it the case that the non-Priestly primeval history is better interpreted as a redactional extension of the patriarchal history that never existed independently?[84]

One's conclusion depends essentially on how one evaluates the Flood pericope.[85] Only if one can demonstrate that its non-Priestly components are pre-Priestly can there be any possibility of positing an independent primeval history made up of Genesis 2*–8 before or alongside the Priestly document. If we look at the non-Priestly prologue and epilogue to the Flood story in Gen 6:5-8; 8:20-22, we do get the impression that the Priestly document is presumed. This is indicated by the Priestly term for creation, *br'*, in Gen 6:6, the listing of the animals in Gen 6:7 in the diction of Genesis 1, the distinction between clean and unclean animals in accord with the Priestly sacrificial Torah in Leviticus 1–7, and the expression "pleasing odor" (*ryḥ ḥnnyḥwh*) of the sacrifice in 8:21, otherwise attested only in the Priestly document. There has been no dearth of attempts at a literary-critical "purification" of these two passages from allusions to the Priestly document, but we may question how much power of persuasion such a process can achieve.

Genesis 6:5-8	Genesis 8:20-22
YHWH saw that the wickedness of humankind was great in the earth, and that every inclination of the thoughts of their hearts was only evil <u>every day</u>. And YHWH was sorry that he had made humankind on the earth, and it grieved him **to his heart**. So YHWH said, "I will blot out from the earth the human beings I have created—people together with animals and creeping things and birds of the air, *for* (*ky*) I am sorry that I have made them." But Noah found favor in the sight of YHWH.	Then Noah built an altar to YHWH, and took of every clean animal and of every clean bird, and offered burnt offerings on the altar. And when YHWH smelled the pleasing odor, YHWH said **in his heart**, "I will never again curse the ground because of humankind, *for/although* (*ky*) the inclination of the human heart is evil from youth; nor will I ever again destroy every living creature as I have done. <u>Every day</u> that the earth endures, seedtime and harvest, cold and heat, summer and winter, day and night, shall not cease."

In terms of theology also the connection for the reader between the prologue and epilogue to the Flood is clearly inspired by the Priestly document: it offers an explanation in terms of the primeval history for God's definitive renunciation of violence against his creatures after the Flood. People remain "evil," but God has changed: the assertion of human wickedness results not in divine grief and regret, but on God's part it leads to a divinely guaranteed life for humanity. Both take place—to speak in boldly anthropomorphic terms—simultaneously "in the heart" of God (6:6; 8:21). Consequently the passage of time ("all days," 6:5; 8:22) is not determined by the wickedness of human beings, which is the same as before, but by God's guarantee of life. The Flood has, so to speak, transformed divine logic, as can be read from the different usages of Hebrew *ky*, which in 6:7 is causal but in 8:21 is used adversatively. The pacifistic and quite non-eschatological concept of God in 6:5-8 and 8:20-22 is thus substantively very close to the Priestly document, which, together with the terminological contacts, could point to dependence on the Priestly document. The absence of the non-Priestly description of the building and the leaving of the ark in Genesis 6–9 is also unfavorable to a different solution to the source problem in Genesis 6–9.

Accordingly, there is much to be said for the proposal that the non-Priestly material in Genesis 6–9 should be interpreted as a post-Priestly augmentation. In the other direction, we would thus have to take into account a non-Priestly Primeval History in Genesis 2–4 + 11(ff.), which in turn is supported by the fact that Genesis 2–4 does not point to the Flood. The etiological structure of the Cainite genealogy in Genesis 4 is apparently not yet aware of the depiction of the Flood that will follow. In addition, a previous connection to Genesis 4 (cf. v. 16) seems to have survived in Genesis 11:1-2:

> Then Cain went away from the presence of Yнwн, and settled in the land of Nod, *east* of Eden. (Gen 4:16)

> Now the whole earth had one language and the same words. And as they migrated from the *east,* they came upon a plain in the land of Shinar and settled there. (Gen 11:1-2)

Genesis 11 seems as yet unaware of the repopulation of the earth after the Flood according to the list of the nations in Genesis 10.

The late dating of the non-Priestly components of the Flood narrative does not mean in turn that Genesis 2–4 + 11 are especially ancient. In Genesis 2–3, for example, we can clearly see that the text, on the one hand, bears the marks of later wisdom teaching in its terminology and consciousness of certain problems.[86] On the other hand it is familiar with and works with the Deuteronomistic theology of history. Paradise is lost because of disobedience to a divine command; this presumes the Deuteronomistically interpreted history of Israel in (Exodus)–Joshua–2 Kings, through a universalistic interpretation.[87] But that Genesis 2–3 should in principle be placed before or at least alongside the Priestly

document and can scarcely be seen as a continuation of Genesis 1 is evident even
from the beginnings in Gen 2:5-9 of contradictions of the cosmogony in Genesis
1.[88] These are neither to be expected from a continuation text nor can they be
explained in those terms.

But in its theological position Genesis 2–3 stands isolated within the Old
Testament. It is the literary expression of the experience that adult human life
guided by the "knowledge of good and evil"—and utterly unable to step aside
from that guidance—necessarily moves away from God. The human being can
have only one of the two: immediate closeness to God in childlike simplic-
ity or self-determined adult life. In terms of experience we have only the latter, and Genesis 2–3 explains why that is so. Interestingly enough, Genesis
2–3 thus places itself against the tradition—visible, for example, in Ezekiel
28—of a primeval human being equipped with great wisdom who lost that
wisdom as a result of being driven out of the Garden of Eden: "Your heart
was proud because of your beauty; you corrupted your wisdom for the sake
of your splendor. I cast you to the ground; I exposed you before kings, to
feast their eyes on you" (Ezek 28:17). In Genesis 2–3 the expulsion from the
Garden of Eden involves not the loss but the acquisition of wisdom. What
human beings forever lose as a consequence is the ability to achieve "eternal
life," something that was open to them in the Garden (all that was forbidden
was the Tree of Knowledge, not the Tree of Life, cf. Gen 2:16-17). However,
the factual inclusion of the Tree of Life in the prohibition as described by the
woman (through the formulation "tree [i.e., collective] in the midst of the garden"), as well as her intensification of it, "nor shall you touch it"), shows that
the first human couple—in their effort to obey God's will in every case!—did
not grasp the possibility of eternal life. To that extent Genesis 2–3 not only
describes the situation after the so-called "Fall" ambivalently (human beings
now have knowledge of good and evil, but they are banished from the presence
of God), but also their previous state (human beings had the ability to achieve
eternal life, but *de facto* they did not perceive it and could not do so without
the ability to know).[89]

The theological-historical function of the non-Priestly primeval history can
be called a universalization and de-eschatologization of the Israel traditions
that follow. The main "Deuteronomistic" motif of the loss of the land because
of disobedience to God's command is universalized, having now been transferred from Israel and its land to the first human couple and the Garden of
Eden. In this way the Deuteronomistic theology of history is connected to and
grounded in the *conditio humana*. All the utopian projects in the Old Testament
that look to a return to the paradisiacal conditions of the primeval time are de-
eschatologized: against these, Genesis 2–3 (cf. especially 3:24) asserts with full
clarity that there is no retreat from earthly human existence. Still more: what
can be known about life—what is beneficial and what is harmful—is available
to human beings, because by reason of their "knowledge of good and evil" they
have become like God (Gen 3:22). The human being will not be fundamentally

changed, as Deuteronomy 30; Jeremiah 31; 32; or Ezekiel 36 anticipate with references to a "new heart" or a "new spirit"—either by their own efforts or by God's initiative. People will remain as they are: ambivalent. And therefore their lives will be ambivalent: distant from, not close to God, but to a degree responsible, not in the condition of a child.

b. Daniel Legends (Daniel 1–6*)
The book of Daniel, in its present form, is rightly regarded as one of the latest books of the Old Testament. It bears clear traces of the Maccabean period, as seen, for example, in the interpretation in Daniel 9 of the prophecy of the "seventy-year-long" destruction of Jerusalem in the book of Jeremiah, read as "seventy weeks of years," that is, seventy times seven years, apparently until the time of Antiochus IV and the Maccabean revolt against him (see below):

> . . . and the troops of the prince who is to come shall destroy the city and the sanctuary. Its end shall come with a flood, and to the end there shall be war. Desolations are decreed. He shall make a strong covenant with many for one week, and for half of the week he shall make sacrifice and offering cease; and in their place shall be an abomination that desolates, until the decreed end is poured out upon the desolator. (Dan 9:26-27)

But it is equally clear that this Maccabean book of Daniel has prior literary levels,[90] as suggested simply by the shifts in language (Daniel 2–7 are in Aramaic, Daniel 1 and 8–12 in Hebrew). From the world-historical visions in Daniel 2 and 7 we see that they were originally pre-Maccabean in orientation and reacted to the collapse of the Persian empire. In addition, the theological shaping of the Daniel legends in Daniel 1–6* clearly point to the Persian period itself.

This is apparent especially in the foreign rulers' confessions of the God of the Jews, the leitmotif that concludes each of the legends:

> The king said to Daniel, "Truly, your God is God of gods and Lord of kings and a revealer of mysteries, for you have been able to reveal this mystery!" (Dan 2:47)

> Nebuchadnezzar said, "Blessed be the God of Shadrach, Meshach, and Abednego, who has sent his angel and delivered his servants who trusted in him. They disobeyed the king's command and yielded up their bodies rather than serve and worship any god except their own God. Therefore I make a decree: Any people, nation, or language that utters blasphemy against the God of Shadrach, Meshach, and Abednego shall be torn limb from limb, and their houses laid in ruins; for there is no other god who is able to deliver in this way." (Dan 3:28-29)

> King Nebuchadnezzar to all peoples, nations, and languages that live throughout the earth: May you have abundant prosperity! The signs and

wonders that the Most High God has worked for me I am pleased to recount. How great are his signs, how mighty his wonders! His kingdom is an everlasting kingdom, and his sovereignty is from generation to generation." (Dan 3:31-33 [English 4:1-3])

Now I, Nebuchadnezzar, praise and extol and honor the King of heaven, for all his works are truth, and his ways are justice; and he is able to bring low those who walk in pride. (Dan 4:34 [English 4:37])

Then King Darius wrote to all peoples and nations of every language throughout the whole world: "May you have abundant prosperity! I make a decree, that in all my royal dominion people should tremble and fear before the God of Daniel: For he is the living God, enduring forever. His kingdom shall never be destroyed, and his dominion has no end. He delivers and rescues, he works signs and wonders in heaven and on earth; for he has saved Daniel from the power of the lions." So this Daniel prospered during the reign of Darius and the reign of Cyrus the Persian. (Dan 6:26-29 [English: 6:25-28])

In the Daniel legends Nebuchadnezzar and Darius appear as the rulers of foreign great powers who, after particular challenges or perils, acknowledge the power of the one God, the God of Israel. This somewhat fantastic notion ultimately links thematically to the interpretation of Cyrus as "messiah" in Isa 45:1 and unfolds still further the confessional motif that was beginning to develop there (cf. 45:4: "I surname you, though you do not know me" in contrast to the probably somewhat later statement in 45:3: "so that you may know that it is I, YHWH, the God of Israel, who call you by your name"). The thematic links to theocratic psalms such as Psalms 145; 146; 147 are also obvious.

The Daniel legends thus—like the older Priestly document or the later Chronicles—represent the theocratic position in the post-exilic history of the literature: God rules over his creation by means of the dominant empire at the time, which is responsible to him and that—at least this is the thinking of Daniel 1–6*—also acknowledges him as the sole God and ruler.

c. The Origins of the Major Historical Work Genesis–2 Kings

If we follow the most recent research on the Pentateuch we must accept that the great syntheses that created the present course of the narrative books from Genesis through 2 Kings emerge at a relatively late point in time, namely in the Persian period.[91] This is true especially of the combining of Genesis and Exodus (and the following books), which was probably undertaken in the wake of the Priestly document.[92] Whether the Priestly document found its way into this major historical presentation at a second stage or simultaneously with the combining of Genesis and Exodus (and following) is difficult to determine.

Especially for independent Genesis, this incorporation into the course of Genesis–2 Kings represented a major shift in meaning: the previously open theology of promise in Genesis now finds its fulfillment in the establishment of Israel as a people in Exodus 1 and the occupation of the land in Joshua, and is thus historicized. The result, in Genesis–2 Kings, is the development first of salvation history (Genesis–Joshua), and then the history of perdition (Judges–2 Kings), with the salvation history culminating in the gift of the land and the history of perdition ending with the loss of the land. The fact that Genesis–2 Kings as a whole ends as a theological zero-sum game indicates that this body did not come into being for itself. Nor should we attempt to discover the decisive insight into the future beyond the judgment in the last four verses in 2 Kgs 25:27-30.[93] Instead, the *corpus propheticum* continues, thematically speaking, the historical depiction and contains the corresponding perspectives on salvation.[94] Thus it is only here that the historical picture of the "twice broken line" originates, leading from the older history of salvation (from the patriarchs to the occupation of the land) through the history of perdition (monarchical period) to a new salvation history promised by the prophets, something that in the twentieth century—corresponding to the early dating of the traditional Yahwist and Elohist presentations of salvation history—was popularly seen as the background to the first writing prophets and their proclamation.[95]

The working together of Genesis and Exodus (and following) is signaled above all in three programmatic texts in Genesis 15, Exodus 3–4, and Joshua 24. It is true that the literary integrity of these texts is disputed, but there can be no doubt that in their present form they bear the principal burden of the redactional combination of Genesis and Exodus (and following), since they contain the most important relevant allusions forward and backward. Genesis 15 is the only text in the patriarchal history—apart from the framing text in Genesis 50—that contains, in vv. 13-16, an explicit allusion forward to the Exodus event.

Of course there are also certain other parallels between Genesis and Exodus, such as the Exodus prolepsis in Gen 12:10-20 (cf. the adoption of the keywords *šlḥ*, "send," and *ngʿ*, "strike," from Exodus 5–11), the texts about struggles with God in Gen 32:23-32//Exod 4:24-26, or the scenes at a well in Genesis 24//Exodus 2,[96] but these texts do not constitute explicit redactional bridges between the patriarchs and the exodus. Rather, it is altogether possible to see them as borrowings between separate literary textual entities. By contrast, within the framing of the Moses-exodus narrative, the primary function of the call of Moses in Exodus 3–4 is to provide a link with the patriarchal history; there is prominent reference back to the "God of your fathers, Abraham, Isaac, and Jacob."

For Genesis 15 as for Exodus 3–4 a good case can be made that they are post-Priestly in origin, either as a whole[97] or in any case as far as the relevant parts of these important texts are concerned.[98] Both in Genesis 15 and in Exodus 3–4 we find language that is markedly influenced by the Priestly document. In addition, Genesis 15 and Exodus 3–4 can each be understood as redactional *relecture* of the parallel Priestly texts of Genesis 17 and Exodus 6.

The joining of Genesis with Exodus (and following—as well as the inclusion of the Priestly document) is one of the most important steps in the formation of the Torah. What should be especially emphasized is the theological multidimensionality thus produced in what was previously only a tradition of Israel's origins. The pacifist, inclusive, autochthonous patriarchal tradition and the more aggressive, exclusive, allochtonous Moses-exodus tradition are linked together. As a result the previous theological characteristics of the separate traditions become aspects of a whole that may be more or less heavily accented in the interpretation.

Also of high literary-historical significance is the connection, now visible for the first time, between the historical books (Genesis–2 Kings) and the prophetic books (Isaiah–Zechariah/Malachi) in the sense of a thematic sequence. Here we can observe the attempt at an overall theological organization of the Old Testament tradition.

It is possible that the thematic and terminological ties between the closing chapter of Genesis–2 Kings (2 Kings 25) and the first chapter of Isaiah, which directly follows it in the canonical sequence, were deliberately shaped with regard to the now-established reading sequence of historical and prophetic books. Various statements in Isaiah 1 leave the impression of having been formulated as direct "answers" to problems raised by the description in 2 Kings 25. Isaiah 1:2-9, especially verse 7, looks back to a judgment and a fiery catastrophe like that reported in 2 Kgs 25:9; the description of Zion after the catastrophe as a "booth in a vineyard" or a "shelter in a cucumber field" (Isa 1:8) matches the depiction of the rural remnant in 2 Kgs 25:12 ("vinedressers and tillers of the soil"). The radical critique of sacrifice in Isa 1:10-15 can be read as an ongoing interpretation of the destruction of the temple and the removal of the cultic vessels in 2 Kgs 25:8-12, 13-21. Theologically, Isaiah 1 adopts a multitude of "covenant theology" motifs from Deuteronomy (and Leviticus 26),[99] and so accentuates the "Deuteronomistic" logic of 2 Kings 25.

d. Ezra–Nehemiah

Following Leopold Zunz,[100] twentieth-century German scholars in particular assumed that Ezra–Nehemiah, though themselves formed from different sources,[101] were from the outset the organic continuation of 1–2 Chronicles. Since the work of Sara Japhet this idea has been sharply criticized.[102] Today, however, it is not stated simply as an alternative but is more subtly regarded through the lens of redaction criticism.[103] It appears more and more persuasive that Ezra–Nehemiah are basically older than 1–2 Chronicles. One can speculate whether they may have functioned at one time as an older, pre-prophetic and "theocratic" continuation of the historical books Genesis–2 Kings before they were combined with 1–2 Chronicles.

In antiquity Ezra–Nehemiah were a single book, as indicated by the lack of final masorah at the end of Ezra. The combined Ezra–Nehemiah reports the restoration in Judah and thus in its own unique fashion blends the efforts of the priest Ezra and the rebuilding commissioner Nehemiah. The description of the return and the building of the temple in Ezra 1–6 is followed first by a section on Ezra's work in Jerusalem (Ezra 7–10). Nehemiah 1–7 reports the measures adopted by Nehemiah, while Nehemiah 8–10 links all that back to Ezra and his public reading of the law. Finally, Nehemiah 11–13 contains accounts of further instructions given by Nehemiah. Thus on the compositional level Ezra–Nehemiah suggests, apparently deliberately, the simultaneity of the appearance of Ezra and Nehemiah, even though historically that is impossible (see above). The idea behind this presentation seems to be the conception of a positive counterpart for the "Deuteronomistic" historical theology in the Former Prophets (Joshua–2 Kings). While in the latter disobedience to the law and rejection of the prophets leads to judgment, so Ezra–Nehemiah show the opposite: how observance of the law and respect for the prophets lead to prosperity.

Even in the opening passage, Ezra 1–6, it is made clear that the project of rebuilding the temple cannot succeed without prophetic support.[104] So it is only the second attempt that is successful: "So the elders of the Jews built and prospered, through the prophesying of the prophet Haggai and Zechariah son of Iddo. They finished their building by command of the God of Israel and by decree of Cyrus, Darius, and King Artaxerxes of Persia" (Ezra 6:14).

In the statement in Ezra 7:27 ("Blessed be YHWH, the God of our ancestors, who put such a thing as this into the heart of the king *to glorify* [*p'r*] *the house of YHWH in Jerusalem*") there is a clear echo of the idea that the promise of Isaiah 60 has thus reached its fulfillment:

> (7) All the flocks of Kedar shall be gathered to you [Zion], the rams of Nebaioth shall minister to you; they shall be acceptable on my altar, *and I will glorify* [*p'r*] *my glorious house.* . . . (9) For the coastlands shall wait for me, the ships of Tarshish first, to bring your children from far away, their silver and gold with them, for the name of YHWH your God, and for the Holy One of Israel, *because he has glorified* [*p'r*] *you.* . . . (13) The glory of Lebanon shall come to you, the cypress, the plane, and the pine, to beautify the place of my sanctuary; and I will *glorify* [*p'r*] where my feet rest. (Isa 60:7-13)

We can also observe elsewhere that Ezra–Nehemiah attempts to characterize Israel's history in the Persian period as the fulfillment of what was foreseen by the prophets.[105] Ezra–Nehemiah thus link substantively to the major presentation in Genesis–2 Kings and continue the history of perdition of the monarchical period with a complementary presentation of the restoration period that in turn is influenced by prophecy. Ezra–Nehemiah—at least in the form that was still independent of 1–2 Chronicles—thus stand on the threshold between the Deuteronomistic and the Chronistic images of history. The connection between law and well-being is shaped by "Deuteronomism," while the high estimation of Persian rule, which according to Ezra 1–6 gave the initiative for the rebuilding of the temple, is close to "Chronistic" theology. From this point of view the counter-concept to Ezra–Nehemiah is formulated by the complex of Haggai/Zechariah 1–8, which links the building of the temple to the expectation of the overthrow of the Persian empire and the reestablishment of the Davidic dynasty.[106]

3. Prophetic Traditions

a. Haggai/Zechariah

The books attributed to the prophets Haggai and Zechariah are the latest prophetic books of the Old Testament that can be traced to identifiable prophetic figures. Their historicity is adequately secured by the mentions of them external to their books, in Ezra 5:1; 6:14.[107] The books of Joel, Habakkuk, and Malachi were most likely composed later, but probably they should be viewed from the outset and as being completely the prophecy of scribal tradents.[108]

In the present form of the Old Testament, Haggai and Zechariah are regarded as the crucial promoters of the building of the temple because of the evidence that their redactors adapted them to one another, also on the basis of Ezra 5:1; 6:14, but strikingly enough they seem ignorant of any Persian initiative for that purpose.[109] Historically it seems that Haggai in particular approved of building the temple. The movements of resistance to the temple reconstruction, apparently arising out of all groups of those returning from exile and economically motivated, are opposed by the book of Haggai, which in contrast argues that only the restoration of the temple will make economic prosperity possible. Haggai thus pushes the "positive Deuteronomism" of Ezra–Nehemiah over against the "negative Deuteronomism" of Joshua–Kings.

The laying of the cornerstone for the temple is regarded by the book of Haggai as a crucial theological and epochal threshold that, after a shaking of heaven and earth (Hag 2:6) and the overthrow of the "thrones of the kingdoms" (Hag 2:22), that is, probably the throne of the Persian imperial ruler,[110] will bring with it the universal acknowledgment of the rule of YHWH by the nations and the restoration of the Davidic dynasty. But this cannot be promised without discussing competing prophetic statements in other parts of the Old Testament. Therefore Hag 2:21-23 takes up Jer 22:24-26, 30 and revokes these statements with reference to Zerubbabel.

Jeremiah 22:24, 30	Haggai 2:21-23
As I live, says YHWH, even if King Coniah [i.e., Jehoiachin], son of Jehoiakim of Judah were the <u>signet ring</u> on my right hand, even from there I would tear you off. . . . Thus says YHWH: Record this man as childless, a man who shall not succeed in his days; for none of his offspring shall succeed in sitting on the throne of David, and ruling again in Judah.	Speak to Zerubbabel, governor of Judah, saying . . . On that day, says YHWH of hosts, I will take you, O Zerubbabel my servant, son of Shealtiel, says YHWH, and make you like a <u>signet ring</u>; for I have chosen you, says YHWH of hosts.

Also from this political perspective of the restoration of the Davidic kingship through Zerubbabel, together with the expectation of the destruction of the Persian empire, the Haggai tradition is close to the Deuteronomistic strand. Historically Haggai's expectations as regards both the person of Zerubbabel and the fall of the Persian empire were not fulfilled. Nevertheless, his message was handed on as an image of hope for the future.

Closely adjusted to fit the prophecy of Haggai is Zechariah 1–8, especially in its system of dating and the thematic ties between Zechariah 7–8 and Haggai.[111] The conclusion suggested is that Haggai and Zechariah 1–8 were redacted in view of each other. The purpose of this redactional combination was apparently to have Zechariah 1–8 read as a continuation of the prophecy of Haggai. Haggai describes the earthly changes to follow the shaking of heaven and earth (2:6), while Zechariah 1–8 opens a view into the heavens: "The overthrow announced in Haggai 2:21-23 is seen by Zechariah, in seven visions in one night, as a sequence of events resulting from heavenly strategy. From there the riders swarm to inspect the situation on earth (Zech 1:7-15), and from there the chariots are launched in every direction of the compass (6:1-8) in order to cause the event beheld in the cycle to become reality."[112]

The "night visions," that is, dreams of Zechariah, originally had a broader theological horizon extending beyond the impending construction of the temple: they propose a vision of a completely restored Jerusalem as the center of YHWH's presence.[113] They are concentrically structured: I and VII: horses; II and VI: twofold foreign themes (horns + smiths//woman + banishment); III and V: Jerusalem as an unwalled but secure city, purification of the land from thieves and false swearing; IV (center): lampstands.

Zechariah I: 1:8-13, 14-15	II: 2:1-4	III: 2:5-9	IV: 4:1-6a, 10b-14	V: 5:1-4	VI: 5:5-11	VII: 6:1-8
Riders and horses	Horns and smiths	Man with measuring line	Lampstands	Flying scrolls	Woman in basket	Chariots and horses
Patrolling of the whole earth	Disempowerment of the world	Jerusalem as an open city	Presence of YHWH	Purification of the land	Eradication of idolatry	Mission to the whole world

The concrete orientation to the building of the temple is accomplished primarily by the subsequent continuations in Zech 6:9-15 and 7–8, which accommodate Zechariah to Haggai. As in Hag 2:21-23, we find in Zechariah 3–4 exalted expectations for Zerubbabel. The section in 4:6b-10a, which clearly interrupts its context, appears to point to problems (which cannot be more closely defined) in Zerubbabel's mission that make necessary a renewed reassurance, with promises of salvation apparently grounded in excerpts from Isa 40:3-4 and echoes of Isa 52:7, the framing texts of the basic layer of Deutero-Isaiah:

Zechariah 4:6b-10a	Isaiah 40:3
"This is the word of YHWH to Zerub-babel: Not by might, nor by power, but by my spirit, says YHWH of hosts. *What are you, O great mountain? Before Zerubbabel you shall become a plain*; and he shall bring out the top stone amid <u>shouts of 'Grace, grace to it!'</u>" Moreover, the word of YHWH came to me, saying, "The hands of Zerubbabel have laid the foundation of this house; his hands shall also complete it. Then you will know that YHWH of hosts has sent me to you. For whoever has despised the day of small things shall rejoice, and shall see the plummet in the hand of Zerubabbel."	A voice cries out: "In the wilderness prepare the way of YHWH, make straight in the desert a highway for our God. *Every valley shall be lifted up, and every mountain and hill be made low; the uneven ground shall become level, and the rough places a plain.*

	Isaiah 52:7
	<u>How beautiful upon the mountains are the feet of the messenger who announces peace, who brings good news, who announces salvation, who says to Zion,</u> "Your God reigns."

The books of Haggai and Zechariah represent the enormous expectations associated in Judah with the building of the temple. Their extensive perspectives on salvation, fulfilled neither in the immediate nor in the distant future, were probably only imaginable because the theological way had been prepared by the Deutero-Isaiah tradition. At any rate it is characteristic of the literary and theological history of prophecy in the Persian period that these projections were not rejected as false; instead, the delay in their realization was explained by constantly renewed interpretations.

It is likewise characteristic of the night visions of Zechariah that the dream, theologically discredited in Deuteronomy and the Deuteronomistic tradition, is once again regarded as a legitimate means of revelation. Thus a bit of "natural theology" is rehabilitated in the face of strict Deuteronomism. Likewise, within the framework of these visions the mediating figure of an interpreting angel (*angelus interpres*) stands out; this will be attested in other visions from this point forward (cf., e.g., Daniel 8–9) and constitutes an important (though not the sole) starting point for later intertestamental angelology.[114] The interpretive dialogues in the visions of the pre-exilic writing prophets (Amos 7–9; Isaiah 6; Jeremiah 1; 24, etc.) always took place directly between God and the prophet. In Zechariah 1–8, by contrast, in the wake of the establishment of monotheism, a greater distance to God in literary depiction makes its appearance.

The vision in Zech 5:5-11 reports the transportation to Babylon of a woman in a basket. Whether one may see in this a programmatic vision of the banishment of the goddess from Israel[115] is a matter of dispute.[116] The interpretation remains attractive, however, since on the one hand the woman seems to be endowed with divine attributes and on the other hand it would be quite expected that the Old Testament would formulate a literary reaction to the loss of the gender polarity in the religious symbolic system attested in the monarchical period ("YHWH and his Asherah").[117] In that case Zech 5:5-11—unlike Deuteronomy and the "Deuteronomistic" books of Kings (cf. Deut 16:21; 2 Kgs 21:3; 23:4, and frequently)—would not make the Asherah an object of loathing, but would transfer her to Babylon, where a legitimate place is allotted to her within the pagan cult of the gods (5:11).

b. Continuations of Deutero-Isaiah and Trito-Isaiah

The salvation announced by Deutero-Isaiah was originally seen as being realized in contemporary political experience. In the wake of the miraculous events (from Judah's point of view) of the time of Darius, which brought the beginning of the rebuilding of the temple and the first major waves of returnees, some of the interpretive texts in Isaiah 40–52 identified the figure of Cyrus with the "servant of God," quite clearly in the first Servant Song (42:1-4),[118] though anonymous in the continuation (42:5-7).

> Thus says God, YHWH, who created the heavens and stretched them out, who spread out the earth and what comes from it, who gives breath to the people upon it and spirit to those who walk in it: I am YHWH, I have called you in righteousness, I have taken you by the hand and kept you; I have given you as a covenant to the people, a light to the nations, to open the eyes that are blind, to bring out the prisoners from the dungeon, from the prison those who sit in darkness. (Isa 42:5-7)

This position is a Judahite reception of the Persian imperial ideology as we find it, for example, in Persian royal inscriptions: God (Ahuramazda to the Persians) rules the world through the Persian monarchs (cf. also Ezra 5:11-16).[119]

But after Darius the situation changed. The deplorable situation of Judah and Jerusalem, despite the rebuilding of the temple, was interpreted more as a "delay of the parousia," of the saving events foreseen in the Deutero-Isaiah tradition. The texts reflecting on this delay led to a development of Isaiah 40–52 to form the present salvation section of the whole book of Isaiah in chapters 40–66. The traditional distinction between chapters 40–55 ("Deutero-Isaiah") and 56–66 (Trito-Isaiah"), if understood in the sense of two originally independent literary core traditions, can no longer be sustained. It remains true that Isaiah 40–55 offers an unconditional prophecy of salvation, while from Isaiah 56 onward we again encounter words of warning that place conditions on the proclaimed and expected salvation. This challenge allows for the conclusion that the texts in Isaiah 56–66 react to experiences of delay that contradicted the Deutero-Isaianic prophecy of salvation with its application to the present. The salvation promised by Deutero-Isaiah did not appear, either to the extent or at the time (namely, the present) imagined in Isaiah 40–55. In the face of this sense of deficiency Isaiah 56–66 sought the reasons for the delay and found them in hindrances to salvation, namely the wrong attitude of the people of God. Accordingly, Isaiah 56–66 began to formulate warnings and accusations. However, contrary to the old "Trito-Isaiah" hypothesis, Isaiah 56–66 was not drawn from the previously oral proclamation of an independent prophet ("Trito-Isaiah"). Rather, these chapters are to be understood as the prophecy of scribal tradents that never existed except as texts for a book.[120] This was suggested earlier by Duhm, the "father" of the Trito-Isaiah hypothesis himself: "Certainly it is possible that Trito-Isaiah composed his writing simply as a continuation of that of Deutero-Isaiah."[121] By way of example, the scribal character of Isaiah 56–66 can be recognized in the adaptation of Isa 40:3 in Isa 57:14:

Isaiah 40:3	Isaiah 57:14
A voice cries out: "In the wilderness *prepare* the way of Yʜwʜ, make straight in the desert a <u>highway</u> (*mᵉsillah*) for our God."	It shall be said, "<u>Build up, build up</u> (*sollū, sollū*), *prepare* the way, remove every obstruction from my people's **way**."

Isaiah 40:3 calls for the building of a processional road for Yʜwʜ so that he can return to his sanctuary in Zion/Jerusalem. Isaiah 57:14 takes up this call, but reinterprets it in ethical terms: the unjust social and religious conditions among the people must be eliminated so that salvation may break through. In view of the scribal nature of Isaiah 56–66 the abrogation of a Torah text in Isa 56:1-7 is remarkable:[122] the exclusion of foreigners or eunuchs from the community can be set aside through prophetic authority.

Within Isaiah 56–66 a fundamental distinction can be drawn between chapters 56–59 + 63–66 on the one hand and chapters 60–62 on the other. Only chapters 56–59 are conceptually "Trito-Isaianic" in the sense of new conditions placed on the proclamations of salvation, while chapters 60–62, with their unconditional announcements of salvation for Zion, reveal an immediate connection to chapters 40–55. We may therefore suppose with good reason that chapters 60–62 are older than chapters 56–59 (as well as 63–66) and were originally connected to chapters 40–55*. These Zion texts are especially significant for the history of theology because they separate the "messianic" ideology from the Davidic dynasty (Isa 9:1-6), Nebuchadnezzar (Jer 27:6, 8), and Cyrus (Isa 45:1) and are now able to draw the portrait of the city of Jerusalem itself in messianic character:

Isaiah 60:1-12	Isaiah 9:1
Arise, **shine**, for your **light** has come, and the glory of Yʜwʜ *has risen upon you*. For <u>darkness</u> shall cover the earth, and <u>thick darkness</u> the peoples; but Yʜwʜ will *arise upon* you, and his glory will appear over you. Nations shall come to your **light**, and kings to the brightness *of your dawn*.	The people who walked in <u>darkness</u> have seen a great **light**; those who lived in a land of <u>deep darkness</u>—*on them* **light** *has shined*. **Jer 27:6** Now I have given all these lands into the hand of King Nebuchadnezzar of Babylon, my servant . . .

. . . Your gates shall always be open; day and night they shall not be shut, so that nations shall bring you their wealth, with their kings led in procession. For the <u>nation and kingdom</u> that <u>will not serve you</u> *shall perish; those nations shall be utterly laid waste.*	**Jeremiah 27:8** But <u>if any nation or kingdom will not</u> <u>serve</u> this king, Nebuchadnezzar of Babylon . . . then I *will punish that nation with the sword, with famine, and with pestilence . . . until I have completed its destruction by his hand.*

Apparently this perspective in Isaiah 60 gives a critique of both the local and the foreign kingship and separates the concept of a messiah from personalities. Jerusalem itself is to take on "messianic" qualities (cf. below). Lamentations 1:10 can thus refer to the temple as "Jerusalem's" sanctuary and thus place the city within the rightful succession of the Judahite kings.[123]

What is remarkable in all this is, on the one hand, that the light metaphors drawn from Isa 9:1 are theologized in Isaiah 60: YHWH himself is the light. On the other hand, the horizon of Isaiah 60 is more universal in scope: Zion-Jerusalem has a messianic quality not only for the people Israel but for all nations. Accordingly, the power of Zion-Jerusalem is drawn in the imperial "Babylonian" colors of Jeremiah 27.

Isaiah 63–66 should be conceptually distinguished from Isaiah 56–59 since here the hoped-for coming of the promised salvation is not made dependent on continual expansion, but is restricted to a group within Israel, the "devout," who, however, may also draw to themselves adherents from among the nations (see below).

c. Continuations of Jeremiah and Ezekiel

Events during the reign of Darius—the beginning of the rebuilding of the temple, a new wave of returnees, the suppression of uprisings in Babylon under pretenders to the throne—led to corresponding continuations not only in Deutero-Isaiah (Cyrus as the "servant of God") but also in the book of Jeremiah. Thus, for example, Nebuchadnezzar, who had been responsible for the destruction of Jerusalem, can be soberly reinterpreted as "my [i.e., God's] servant" in Jer 25:9; 27:6; 43:10 and seen as the precursor of Cyrus. A broader reflection on this set of experiences can be found in the two "seventy-year" prophecies in Jer 25:11 and 29:10, which reciprocally augment one another and now, after the "seventy-year" judgment on Jerusalem and Judah, expect salvation for Israel and an evil end for Babylon. The one is expressed literarily in Jeremiah 30–31, the other in Jeremiah 50–51.[124]

This whole land shall become a ruin and a waste, and these nations shall serve the king of Babylon seventy years. (Jer 25:11)

For thus says YHWH: Only when Babylon's seventy years are completed will I visit you, and I will fulfill to you my promise and bring you back to this place. (Jer 29:10)

Finally, we can distinguish two programmatic redactional perspectives in the books of Jeremiah and Ezekiel that on the basis of their political profile can be dated with absolute certainty to the Persian period. These are continuation texts traceable either to the Babylonian Golah, those deported in 597 B.C.E., or to the worldwide diaspora as the legitimate successor of the destroyed Israel of the monarchical period. They were created in stages. Basically, the diaspora-oriented texts appear to be correctives to the Golah-oriented program, but there are also positive statements about the diaspora in the prophets that appear to be older (cf., e.g., Jer 23:3). It is true that from time to time someone advocates the position that the Golah-oriented statements could have been created immediately after 597 B.C.E.,[125] but the way they establish such sharply opposing positions between the exiles and those remaining in the land could scarcely be explained in that epoch. Instead, these seem to be texts undergirding the theological legitimation of those returning from exile who wanted to see their leadership claims anchored in prophecy.

The discovery and normative description of these two redactional programs was essentially the work of Pohlmann.[126] The Golah-oriented perspective can be most clearly seen in Jeremiah 24, the vision of the good and bad figs:

> YHWH showed me two baskets of figs placed before the temple of YHWH. This was after King Nebuchadrezzar of Babylon had taken into exile from Jerusalem King Jeconiah son of Jehoiakim of Judah, together with the officials of Judah, the artisans, and the smiths, and had brought them to Babylon. One basket had very good figs, like first-ripe figs, but the other basket had very bad figs, so bad that they could not be eaten. And YHWH said to me, "What do you see, Jeremiah?" I said, "Figs, the good figs very good, and the bad figs very bad, so bad that they cannot be eaten." Then the word of YHWH came to me: Thus says YHWH, the God of Israel: Like these good figs, so I will regard as good the exiles from Judah, whom I have sent away from this place to the land of the Chaldeans. I will set my eyes upon them for good, and I will bring them back to this land. I will build them up, and not tear them down; I will plant them, and not pluck them up. I will give them a heart to know that I am YHWH; and they shall be my people and I will be their God, for they shall return to me with their whole heart. But thus says YHWH: Like the bad figs that are so bad they cannot be eaten, so will I treat King Zedekiah of Judah, his officials, the remnant of Jerusalem who remain in this land, and those who live in the land of Egypt. I will make them a horror, an evil thing, to all the kingdoms of the earth—a disgrace, a byword, a taunt, and a curse in all the places where I shall drive them. And I will send sword, famine, and pestilence upon them, until they are utterly destroyed from the land that I gave to them and their ancestors. (Jer 24:1-10)

Before Pohlmann[127] it was common to date these texts, because of their linguistic characteristics, as an insertion into the book of Jeremiah by the "Deuteronomistic" redaction.[128] But if we consider the thematic profile of Jeremiah 24, this interpretation is not at all plausible. In Jeremiah 24 the criterion for judgment or salvation is not obedience to the law but belonging to a particular group: the "good figs" are the members of the Jehoiachin Golah who were deported to Babylon in 597 B.C.E. YHWH's future plan for the salvation of Israel will be accomplished through them. The "bad figs" are those who remained in the land or fled to Egypt; they will be utterly rooted out of the land and scattered throughout the world.

The religio-political implications of this program are obvious: Jeremiah 24 is the prophetic legitimation of the proverbial "upper ten-thousand" deported in 597 B.C.E. (see 2 Kgs 24:14), who anchor their claims to hegemony in Jeremiah's preaching. It appears that we encounter here, for the first time in the theological history of ancient Israel, the concept that Israel as the unit of salvation is to be abandoned in favor of a distinction within Israel. In the Hellenistic period such a division, in terms of a separation of the wicked and the pious, will be altogether common, and the idea is previewed here in elementary terms.

However, there are traces of this throughout the book of Jeremiah, not merely in a single chapter but in the course of a redaction that extended over the entire Jeremiah tradition: Jeremiah 24, with its stylization as a vision, creates a clear link back to Jer 1:11-14, so that the whole proclamation of judgment from Jeremiah 1–24 is now applied to the "bad figs." In turn, from a redactional perspective the quotation of Jeremiah 24 in Jer 29:16—immediately before the proclamations of salvation in Jeremiah 30–33—makes it clear that only the "good figs" will experience the salvation here announced.[129]

Even though the "Golah-oriented" program is prominent and easy to grasp in the book of Jeremiah, it originated elsewhere. Instead, it seems to have been inspired and legitimated by the Ezekiel tradition, which from its earliest beginnings was at least implicitly marked by a "Golah orientation." The historical prophet Ezekiel himself was apparently one of those deported to Babylon in 597 B.C.E., and accordingly the words of his book are dated throughout in terms of that event.

But even beyond this implicit Golah orientation, the book of Ezekiel is explicitly reworked in the same terms. In complete correspondence to Jeremiah 24, we find in Ezekiel 11 the view that only the descendants of the first Golah will constitute the true Israel; they will receive a new heart and so will constitute God's people.

> . . . Then I fell down on my face, cried with a loud voice, and said, "Ah Lord YHWH! will you make a full end of the remnant of Israel?" Then the word of YHWH came to me: Mortal, your kinsfolk, your own kin, your fellow exiles, the whole house of Israel, all of them, are those

of whom the inhabitants of Jerusalem have said, "They have gone far
from YHWH; to us this land is given for a possession." Therefore say:
Thus says the Lord YHWH: Though I removed them far away among the
nations, and though I scattered them among the countries, yet I have
been a sanctuary to them for a little while in the countries where they
have gone. Therefore say: Thus says the Lord YHWH: I will gather you
from the peoples, and assemble you out of the countries where you have
been scattered, and I will give you the land of Israel. When they come
there, they will remove from it all its detestable things and all its abominations. I will give them one heart, and put a new spirit within them;
I will remove the heart of stone from their flesh and give them a heart
of flesh, so that they may follow my statutes and keep my ordinances
and obey them. Then they shall be my people, and I will be their God.
But as for those whose heart goes after their detestable things and their
abominations, I will bring their deeds upon their own heads, says the
Lord YHWH. (Ezek 11:13-21)

Just as in Jeremiah, so also in Ezekiel the promises of salvation have all been
redactionally narrowed in "Golah-oriented" fashion. This is made clear at the
beginning of the block of text in Ezekiel 33 with its prophecies of salvation:

Now the hand of YHWH had been upon me the evening before the fugitive came; but he had opened my mouth by the time the fugitive came
to me in the morning; so my mouth was opened, and I was no longer
unable to speak. The word of YHWH came to me: Mortal, the inhabitants of these waste places in the land of Israel keep saying, "Abraham
was only one man, yet he got possession of the land; but we are many;
the land is surely given us to possess." Therefore say to them, Thus says
the Lord YHWH: You eat flesh with the blood, and lift up your eyes to
your idols, and shed blood; shall you then possess the land? You depend
on your swords, you commit abominations, and each of you defiles his
neighbor's wife; shall you then possess the land? Say this to them, Thus
says the Lord YHWH: As I live, surely those who are in the waste places
shall fall by the sword; and those who are in the open field I will give to
the wild animals to be devoured; and those who are in strongholds and
in caves shall die by pestilence. I will make the land a desolation and
a waste, and its proud might shall come to an end; and the mountains
of Israel shall be so desolate that no one will pass through. Then they
shall know that I am YHWH, when I have made the land a desolation
and a waste because of all their abominations that they have committed. (Ezek 33:22-29)

However, this restrictive program in Jeremiah and Ezekiel was in turn subjected immediately to a reworking that removed this internal division within

Israel and asserted to the contrary that future salvation belonged not solely to the Babylonian Golah but to the entire worldwide diaspora. Accordingly, we may here speak of a "diaspora-oriented" redaction. Interestingly, this redaction appears to have been familiar with the horizons of the Golah-oriented theology enunciated throughout the books of Jeremiah and Ezekiel; accordingly it inserted its own point of view at literarily significant spots in each book. In Jeremiah there is a corresponding statement immediately before Jeremiah 24 (if we consider the position of Jer 23:7-8 according to the LXX, where these verses come at the very end of chapter 23):

> Therefore, the days are surely coming, says YHWH, when it shall no longer be said, "As YHWH lives who brought the people of Israel up out of the land of Egypt," but "As YHWH lives who brought out and led the offspring of the house of Israel out of the land of the north and out of all the lands where he had driven them." Then they shall live in their own land.

Likewise, the diaspora-oriented statement in Jer 29:14 counters the existing Golah-oriented restriction of the promise of salvation in Jer 29:16:

> . . . I will restore your fortunes and gather you from all the nations and all the places where I have driven you, says YHWH, and I will bring you back to the place from which I sent you into exile.

Finally, the story of the field in Jeremiah 32, a sign of future salvation, has been reinterpreted in a diaspora-oriented sense:

> See, I am going to gather them from all the lands to which I drove them in my anger and my wrath and in great indignation; I will bring them back to this place, and I will settle them in safety. (Jer 32:37)

We may suspect that a similar diaspora-oriented redaction, conscious of the overall content of the book, has been applied to Ezekiel. Here a correspondingly crucial statement is given in Ezek 39:25-29, immediately before the great vision of the building of the temple in Ezekiel 40–48:

> Therefore thus says the Lord YHWH: Now I will restore the fortunes of Jacob, and have mercy on the whole house of Israel; and I will be jealous for my holy name. They shall forget their shame, and all the treachery they have practiced against me, when they live securely in their land with no one to make them afraid, when I have brought them back from the peoples and gathered them from their enemies' lands, and through them have displayed my holiness in the sight of many nations. Then

they shall know that I am YHWH their God because I sent them into exile among the nations, and then gathered them into their own land. I will leave none of them behind; and I will never again hide my face from them, when I pour out my spirit upon the house of Israel, says the Lord YHWH.

d. The "Deuteronomistic" Theology of Repentance

Contrary to Noth's classic theory on the "Deuteronomistic historical work," which still regarded that composition as the work of "a man" writing shortly after 562 B.C.E.,[130] in the current highly diverse discussion of Deuteronomism there is broad agreement that the "Deuteronomistic" tradition goes back to a long-lived school of tradents and is marked by its use of scribal language, as can be demonstrated in late texts such as Daniel 9, the special material in the MT version of Jeremiah, or 4 Ezra.[131]

Within the framework of this recently acknowledged longevity of Deuteronomism, which has also demonstrated the necessity of distinguishing different "Deuteronomistic" positions within it,[132] it has become clear that the theme of "repentance," to which Hans Walter Wolff devoted an influential study on the "kerygma of the Deuteronomistic historical work,"[133] resting on Judg 2:11-12; 1 Sam 7:3; 12:14-15; 1 Kgs 8:46-53; 2 Kgs 17:13; 2 Kgs 23:25, is by no means part of the oldest components of the Deuteronomistic interpretive passages in the Former (as well as the Latter) Prophets.

Neither Jeremiah nor the first Deuteronomists were "preachers of repentance" in their own time. Rather, they became such only in the course of the later literary history of their traditions. Even in Deuteronomy itself the theme of repentance is anchored primarily in the prospects of salvation in Deut 4:30 and 30:2, 10, which even Wolff attributed to a "secondary hand" in the Deuteronomistic historical work.[134] Deuteronomy 4 is a post-Priestly chapter in Deuteronomy that clearly presupposes and makes use of Genesis 1.[135] Likewise, Deuteronomy 30, whose historical sequence of "judgment of the people Israel," "judgment against foreign peoples," and "salvation for the people Israel" conceptually anticipates the whole course of Isaiah 1–39, Ezekiel, Zephaniah, and Jeremiah (the LXX version), assumes a Persian-period state of theological-historical discussion.

Judgment against the people Israel	Deut 30:1-2: When all these things have happened to you, the blessings and the curses that I have set before you, if you call them to mind among all the nations where YHWH your God has driven you, *and return to YHWH your God* . . .
Judgment against foreign peoples	Deut 30:7: YHWH your God will put all these curses on your enemies and on the adversaries who took advantage of you.

Salvation for the people Israel	Deut 30:8-10: *Then you shall again obey* YHWH, observing all his commandments that I am commanding you today, and YHWH your God will make you abundantly prosperous in all your undertakings, in the fruit of your body, in the fruit of your livestock, and in the fruit of your soil. For YHWH will again take delight in prospering you, just as he delighted in prospering your ancestors, when you obey YHWH your God by observing his commandments and decrees that are written in this book of the law, *because you turn to* YHWH *your God* with all your heart and with all your soul.

Similarly, the prominent prophetic passages regarding repentance in Jer 3:1—4:2;[136] Zech 1:3; Mal 3:7 point to a Persian-period setting. This does not mean that "repentance" (or "turning back") only became a plausible concept in this period, but it does mean that the theme was first prominently developed at this time. Essentially, we may interpret the theme of repentance as a further possible reaction to the experience of the delay of the promised salvation. Unless Israel repents and turns back, God's salvation cannot be realized.

e. The Biblical Construction of Classical Prophecy

The pseudonymous work of the authors who added to the prophetic books, writing under the authority of the several prophets who gave their names to the books, was by no means an objectionable act from the point of view of the ancients: those who continued the prophetic books had neither the interest nor occasion to appear as individual figures in their own right. Instead, they apparently believed that they were offering the appropriate interpretation of the prophetic proclamation for their own time, which therefore deserved to be directly written into the text of the prophetic book in question and to circulate under the name of the specific prophet. Thus emerged the idea that the prophets had not only spoken for their own historical epochs but saw far into the future. This can be seen most clearly in the Isaiah tradition, which on the one hand asserts in its superscription in Isaiah 1:1 that Isaiah received the message during the reigns of the Judahite kings Uzziah, Jotham, Ahaz, and Hezekiah in the second half of the eighth century B.C.E., but on the other hand shows that the content of these oracles comprehends the whole history of the world from the time of Isaiah to the most distant future of a new heaven and a new earth (Isaiah 65–66). The biblical view of the prophets as those who saw into the future of world history thus arose essentially from the literary-historical processes of the ongoing writing of their books in stages over an extended period of time. Of course, the prophetic books still allow us to see that the historical prophets also made statements about the future—this is especially clear, for example, in the unfulfilled prophecies (cf. Jer 22:18-19)—and yet the world-historical horizon is the result of extensive redactional work on the various books.

Accompanying the temporal expansion of the prophetic message—especially in the book of Jeremiah, the prophet whose biblical proximity was closest to the catastrophe of Jerusalem—was substantively adjusted to the standard of the Torah.[137] In the Persian period the prophets were what they were thought to be for many centuries in the history of the interpretation of the Bible: those who interpreted the Mosaic Law and applied it to history.

4. Legal Traditions

a. The Holiness Code

Following August Klostermann, the complex in Leviticus 17–26 has been called "the Holiness Code" by scholars on the basis of the recurring refrain "you shall be holy, for I Yhwh your God am holy."[138] There is disagreement about the literary status of this corpus: was it an originally independent collection of laws, or a continuation of the Priestly document[139]—in negotiation with Deuteronomy[140]—or an integral component of the Priestly document,[141] or a redactional insertion in the course of the formation of the Pentateuch?[142] The hypotheses of continuation are especially appealing because we can clearly see in Leviticus 17–26 an accommodation between Deuteronomistic and Priestly lawgiving. It is not readily evident that the redactional horizon of the Pentateuch was in the foreground in any of this.[143]

This can be most readily grasped in the blessings portion of the Holiness Code in Leviticus 26. As Norbert Lohfink has made clear, Lev 26:9, 11-13 adopts central promises from Priestly texts such as Genesis 17, Exod 6:2-8, and 29:45-46, but conditions them by placing them in the concluding blessings/curses section of the Holiness Code, which is introduced by "*if* you follow my statutes and keep my commandments and observe them faithfully (Lev 26:3).[144] Thus their fulfillment is no longer promised unconditionally but is made dependent on obedience to the law, which amounts to a certain "deuteronomizing" of Priestly theology.

Genesis 17:6-7	Leviticus 26:3, 9-13
I will make you exceedingly **fruitful**; and I will make nations of you, and kings shall come from you. <u>I will establish my covenant between me and you, and your offspring after you</u> throughout their generations, for an everlasting covenant, <u>to be God to you and to your offspring after you.</u>	If you follow my statutes and keep my commandments and observe them faithfully, (9) I will look with favor upon you and make you **fruitful** and multiply you; <u>and I will maintain my covenant with you.</u> . . . . *I will place my dwelling in your midst*, and I shall not abhor you. And *I will walk among you*, <u>and will be your God</u>, **and you shall be my people. I am Yhwh your God who brought you out of the land of Egypt**, to be their slaves no more; I have broken the bars of your yoke and made you walk erect.

Exodus 6:4-7	
<u>I also established my covenant with them</u> . . . I will free you from the burdens of the Egyptians and deliver you from slavery to them. I will redeem you with an outstretched arm and with mighty acts of judgment. <u>I will take you as my people, and I will be your God.</u> You shall know that **I am** YHWH **your God, who has freed you from the burdens of the Egyptians.**	
Exodus 29:45-46	
I will dwell among the Israelites, <u>and I will be their God.</u> And they shall know that **I am** YHWH **their God, who brought them out of the land of Egypt** *that I might dwell among them;* I am YHWH their God.	

The now-complete covenant formula in Lev 26:11, "I will be your God, *and you shall be my people,*" also points in the same direction, contrary to the theological program of the Priestly document, amply illustrated by the examples in Gen 17:7; Exod 6:7; 29:46, all of which use only the first half of the formula. The Holiness Code reformulates the one-sidedness of the Priestly theology in a Deuteronomistic sense, so that now the statements in the Priestly document about salvation are no longer direct divine decrees but are mediated by the theology of the law.

From a politico-theological point of view it is worth noting that the Holiness Code explicitly anchors the office of the high priest in the Torah (Lev 17:16-26).[145]

b. The Book of Numbers

The book of Numbers—which is not really a book, but a literary stage of the Pentateuch—has repeatedly presented scholars with massive problems since it resists location within the source theory. Even though there are still attempts to discover the traditional sources in Numbers,[146] a number of recent studies tend to interpret broad sections of the book of Numbers as catchalls for laws that found no place in Exodus–Leviticus or Deuteronomy after those corpora had reached a certain stage of completeness.[147] One could regard Numbers as the forerunner of the halachic midrash literature; it seems to have developed as a kind of "rolling corpus" of various interpretations of Torah.

The very superscription of Numbers, after the "colophon" in Lev 27:34, points to the thus indicated "final-text" augmentative character of the book: "These are the commandments that YHWH gave to Moses for the people of Israel *on Mount Sinai* (Lev 27:34). YHWH spoke to Moses *in the wilderness of Sinai*, in the tent of meeting . . . (Num 1:1)." The laws in Numbers, according to Num 1:1, were not revealed on the mountain of God but in the wilderness of Sinai. They are thus no longer a direct component of the divine revelation on Mount Sinai, and yet they are connected to it by having been given in the wilderness near the mountain—in the sense of an augmentation.[148]

From a literary-historical point of view the theme of rebellion that is so broadly developed in Numbers appears to be a reaction to the theology of the "Deuteronomistically" interpreted Former Prophets (Joshua–2 Kings). In those books' presentation of the events, Israel's rebellion against God's commands led to national collapse and the loss of the land, whereas the book of Numbers asserts that Israel's foundational history was itself marked by backsliding and rebellion against God, which in turn led to judgment. However, it is noteworthy that the story of Israel's "murmuring" before the proclamation of the law at Mount Sinai had a much milder outcome than afterward. Thus from this perspective the giving of the law seems to represent a kind of turning point. Over long passages the book of Numbers reflects Israel's diaspora existence outside its land and emphasizes that the Pentateuchal laws are not only of vital significance for life in the land but have immediate relevance anywhere. As soon as they are received, they are binding on Israel.

c. The Formation of the Torah

The formation of the Torah, that is, the literary constitution and shaping of the boundaries of Genesis–Deuteronomy as a single entity, was one of the most important literary-historical events of the Persian period.[149] With it the substantive and historical core of the later Old Testament canon was complete. It is true that work was done on some parts of the Torah well into the Maccabean period, but this scarcely included the additional insertion of whole blocks of text and consisted mainly of individual retouchings (for example, in Genesis 5 and Numbers 22–24),[150] so that it should be regarded in its substance as belonging to the Persian era. This is indicated especially by the absence of clear contemporary reflections on the collapse of the Persian empire like those found very explicitly in the *corpus propheticum* in the form of pronouncements on the judgment of the world (e.g., in Isa 34:2-4 or Jer 25:27-31).[151] In addition, the material in Chronicles + Ezra–Nehemiah presupposes the written form of the Torah. Certainly the previous location of the corresponding texts in Chronicles and Ezra–Nehemiah in the Persian period has been called into question, and increasingly scholars contemplate a longer history of literary development for those texts. Nevertheless, even the older parts of the book of Ezra, in chapter 10, appear to refer back to fully developed written Torah texts such as Deut 7:1-6,[152] which would favor the traditional argument. Finally, we should mention the creation of the LXX, which as regards the books of the Pentateuch should be located around the middle of the third century B.C.E. and marks a *terminus ad quem*.[153]

For about twenty years it has been quite common to appeal to a theory about the reasons for the formation of the Torah that at first appeared very satisfying but has recently experienced increased critical opposition. Following Peter Frei and Erhard Blum, a "Persian imperial authorization" of the Torah was posited.[154] The assumption was that the formation of the Torah was inspired from without, namely by Persian imperial politics. There was no supervening imperial law in the Persian empire, but some functional equivalent of such a law existed, probably, in the form of local laws that were, however, authorized by the Persian administration and were thus elevated to the status of imperial law. That is: by the very fact that the component peoples of the Persian empire lived according to their own laws they were following Persian imperial law. It would then seem likely that for Persian-period Judah the Torah (and possibly some of its prior stages) took on this function. This thesis of a Persian-period imperial authorization of the Torah would also explain the substantive divergences within it and its theological compromise character:[155] external pressure was responsible for the combination, for example, of "Deuteronomistic" and "Priestly" theology in the Torah.

This idea of an imperial Persian authorization was widely accepted at first, but today it is viewed more critically.[156] In any case, two things can be said: first, there is still need of an explanation for why Genesis–Deuteronomy were separated from the larger sequence of narrative books. Second, the literary presentation especially in Ezra 7 makes it clear that the letter of authorization given to Ezra by the Persian king Artaxerxes, reproduced here, is meant to present the Torah as a document having Persian authority, whether that rests on historical facts or not.[157]

Be that as it may, the formation of the Torah is apparently recorded within the text of Genesis–Deuteronomy itself. Two textual elements are of special importance here.[158] First is the explicit definition in Deut 34:10-12 of the Torah as the "arch-prophecy" of Moses, establishing all later prophecy as only exposition of this "arch-prophecy," as is made clear especially by the substantive counterparts in Josh 1:7-8 and Mal 3:22-24. Adopting and building on already-existing tendencies, this orients the prophetic tradition to the Torah.[159] The reason for the catastrophe is—in accordance with the message of the prophets reformulated in terms of the Torah—nonobservance of Torah: cf. Jer 9:12; 16:11; 32:23; Hos 8:1; Amos 2:4, and elsewhere. Of course, not all mentions of the Torah in the prophetic books presuppose the prior formation of Genesis–Deuteronomy, but with this codification other, older "Torah" passages become signposts of the fixed form of the Pentateuch.

Deuteronomy 34:10 is striking also because the idea of the incomparable character of Moses represented here takes deliberate contradictions with the preceding text of Deuteronomy into account:

Deuteronomy 18:15	Deuteronomy 34:10
YHWH your God <u>will raise up</u> (*yqym*) for you *a prophet like me* from among your own people; you shall heed such a prophet.	*Never* since has there <u>arisen</u> (*qm*) *a prophet* in Israel *like Moses*, whom YHWH knew face to face.

The promise of a prophet "like Moses" in Deut 18:15 is directly abrogated in Deut 34:10. The reason is apparently that the chain of prophetic succession envisioned in Deut 18:15, beginning with Moses, has to be cut in order to make it clear that none of Moses' successors is comparible with him. Deuteronomy 34:10 means to separate Moses from the subsequent prophets, and this distinction between "Moses" and the "prophets" is an argument that is most easily explained in terms of canonical technique: Moses must be set apart from the "prophets" if the Torah is to be made qualitatively superior to the "prophets" (i.e., the prophetic books from Joshua to Malachi, the canonical section of the "Prophets"). In addition, in the statement that follows in Deut 34:11-12 predicates of God ("signs and wonders," "with a mighty hand," etc.) are applied to Moses with striking boldness. This process of "theologizing" Moses is most readily understood as an effort to give the Torah ("Moses") an authoritative status. "Moses" is therefore brought into close relationship with God so that the Torah may command a corresponding authority.

Second, we should point to the narrative thread describing the promise of the land as an oath to Abraham, Isaac, and Jacob that runs throughout the books of the Torah (Gen 50:24; Exod 32:13; 33:1; Num 32:11; Deut 34:4) but is not encountered thereafter and should accordingly be regarded as a theme peculiar to the Pentateuchal redaction.[160] The Pentateuchal horizon is also brought to the fore by the quotation of Gen 12:7 in Deut 34:4:

Deuteronomy 34:4	Genesis 12:7a
YHWH said to him, "This is the land of which I swore to Abraham, to Isaac, and to Jacob, saying, '*I will give it to your descendants*'(*zr'*); I have let you see it with your eyes, but you shall not cross over there."	Then YHWH appeared to Abram, and said, "*To your offspring* (*zr'*) *I will give* this land."

The motif of a sworn promise of the land (originally addressed to the exodus generation) seems to have been adopted from the Deuteronomistic parts of Deuteronomy (cf. 1:35; 6:18, 23; 7:13; 8:1; 10:11; 11:9, 21; 19:8; 26:3, 15; 28:11; 31:7, 20-21), while its transfer to the patriarchs in Genesis (in Deuteronomy itself, cf. 1:8; 6:10; 9:5; 30:20) is motivated by the Priestly document, which sees the covenant with Abraham as the basis for God's action in Israel. Theologically, the sworn promise of the land to Abraham, Isaac, and Jacob accentuates the diaspora character of the Torah, which appears in any case from the fact that its narrative ends with the entry of Israel into the Promised Land. The Torah is the foundational document of an "exilic" Israel, a people whose history begins outside its land and in the present time of the readers is also taking place in large part outside that land. Thus the Torah sounds its own "prophetic" note.

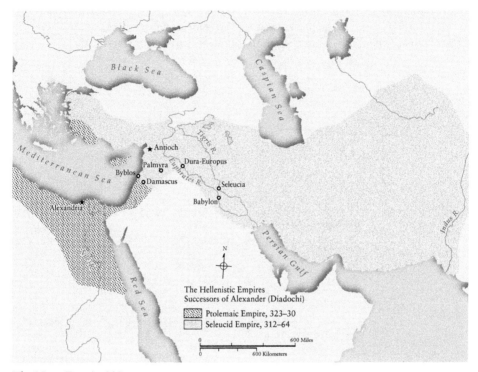

The Near East in 290 B.C.E.

Part F

The Literature of the Ptolemaic Period (Third Century B.C.E.)

I. Historical Backgrounds

After existing for about two hundred years, the Persian empire fell, in the last third of the fourth century, to the expansive efforts of the Macedonian Alexander. Particularly decisive were the defeats of the Persians at Issos (333 B.C.E.) and Gaugamela (331 B.C.E.), which happened not least because of the Macedonians' new strategic military techniques. But the massive empire that arose in the wake of Alexander the Great's conquests did not survive its founder. After his death in 323 B.C.E., bitter succession struggles flamed up among the so-called Diadochi.[1] After the battle at Gaza in 312 B.C.E., not far from Jerusalem, the Diadochi united in an agreement to try to maintain a certain *de facto* but fictional unity in the Alexandrian empire, but that had to be abandoned after the battle of Ipsos in 301 B.C.E.

In the third century B.C.E. the Levant first fell under the rule of the Ptolemaic empire, with its strongly centralist organization. Its center was in Egypt.[2] Josephus even reports a capture of Jerusalem by Ptolemy on the sabbath, though this is hard to evaluate.[3] It seems that during this period many Jews migrated to Alexandria, where they established important diaspora communities whose origins may extend back to the time of the city's founding.[4] As a number of documents that have survived in various conditions attest (cf. the so-called Zenon archive),[5] the Ptolemaic period seems to have been characterized by economic prosperity supported by a flourishing state capitalism and a comprehensive monetizing of the economy, although repeated military conflicts with the Seleucids, the Mesopotamian "brother"-empire, made political calm impossible. In the sequence of the so-called five kings of Syria the Ptolemies were able to retain the upper hand until, at the battle of Paneas in 198 B.C.E., the Levant fell under the hegemony of the Seleucids. In any case, the ability of Ptolemaic power to endure was not easily recognizable, even from an internal perspective. For example, the high priest Onias II at Jerusalem stopped paying tribute to the Ptolemies in the wake of the partial military successes of the Seleucids in the third

Syrian war (246–241 B.C.E.), which led to the rise of the rival Tobiad family.[6] The antagonism between the Oniads and the Tobiads, with shifting loyalties to the overlords of the moment, who in turn were dependent on the political participation of leading factions in Judah, together with inter-familial conflicts, marked the unfolding history of Judah into the Maccabean period.

From a cultural-historical point of view the most important factor in the period after Alexander was the successful expansion of Hellenism in the Near East. Following Johann Gustav Droysen, this has traditionally been understood to involve a melding of Greek and Near Eastern cultures, though current research is discerning cultural- and religious-historical distinctions.[7] In the wake of Alexander's conquests, the Greek language, in the form of Attic *koinē*, became the language of administration and thus enabled a comprehensive transfer of culture.[8] Hellenism represented a comprehensive intellectual force that affected religion, society, culture, and science.

Judaism had to contend with the new world culture, and this question rapidly became divisive: was the appropriate attitude one of assimilation or separation? Both options were apparently pursued, although the anti-Hellenistic voice seems to be more strongly represented in contemporary Old Testament literature. The encounter with Hellenism and its reception in Judaism transformed the latter deeply and unquestionably gave it a new identity.[9] A critical investigation also quickly reveals that—alongside the unquestioned Hellenization of culture and social life—explicit and reflexive pro-Hellenist positions seem to have been advocated in extraordinarily prominent fashion in Judaism during the third and second centuries B.C.E. As regards the major lines of Old Testament presentation of Hellenism, we find ourselves confronted, for example in the book of Daniel, with a phenomenon comparable to what we see in the Old Testament evaluation of the "Canaanite" cultic practices in the Former Prophets (Joshua–2 Kings). The Old Testament tends to take an orthodox stance and to demonize—or, as is possibly the case in Chronicles, to ignore—what can be perceived historically as having been a broad and well-established strand of religious and cultural reality at the time. Especially in the post-Old Testament period Jewish literary products were created that can be altogether characterized as genuinely "Hellenistic." Good examples include the Wisdom of Solomon, which was originally composed in Greek,[10] and the philosophical reformulation of Judaism in Philo's writings, though these received scarcely any recognition within Judaism.[11]

II. Theological Characterizations

From a theological point of view it appears that three factors were especially formative in this period: first, the collapse of the Persian empire followed rapidly by the fall of Alexander's empire in the last three decades of the fourth century B.C.E., which meant the loss of a worldwide political order. Second, there was the encounter with Hellenism, which created an urgent challenge to the question of Jewish identity.[12] Third and finally, there was the beginning of discussion regarding the relationship of the emerging biblical tradition to its crown, the Torah, formed in the late Persian period and bearing a more theocratic than eschatological accent.[13]

Prophetic tradents surveyed and commented on world history during the Ptolemaic period through clarifying insertions into the already-existing books.[14] These books experienced a clear shift in form in that the disastrous experiences of the collapses first of the Persian empire and only a generation later of that of Alexander were recorded literarily in the projection of a comprehensive judgment of the world. However, the prophetic interpretations of the contemporaneous events taking place during the Ptolemaic period were not made historically explicit. They appear as future prophecies from the lips of figures who, according to their biblical presentation, lived much earlier, and who are depicted in terms of this historical fiction. The bearers of the prophetic tradition saw themselves affirmed where they had interpreted the Persian period also as an ongoing situation of judgment.

The collapse of the Persian and Alexandrian empires brought decisive changes for those strands of Old Testament literature from the Persian period that had seen Persian rule as the realization of God's saving will. These positions were either eschatologized or retained their theocratic ideal despite actual political experience—in the sense that they formulated an extra-historical ideal image, motivated by the Torah understood accordingly. The process of eschatologization can probably be seen most clearly in the Daniel tradition.[15] The Persian-period Daniel legends in Daniel 1–6 were profoundly reinterpreted in the early diadochic period by the addition of Daniel 7 and some insertions in Daniel 2. The world empires succeed and replace one another, but the goal of history—in accordance with the experience that even a world empire like that of the Persians, once regarded as indestructible, can fall—is God's own rule over the world. The emperor worship initiated in the time of Alexander and Ptolemy I may also have been a catalyst for Daniel's perspective on the goal of a *divine* empire.[16] From a Jewish perspective this disqualified all the great powers as hybrids; nothing could be perceived as the goal of history but an empire ruled by God alone.

The Priestly document and Chronicles could be read and received after the Persian period entirely in the sense of sketching a primeval, mythical ideal condition. The political concept of the Priestly document, like the Daniel legends in Daniel 1–6*, reckoned with a goal of history corresponding to Persian rule. But on the one hand, it was fundamentally protected against needing changes as a result of historical developments, even those of such a revolutionary nature as the fall of the Persian empire, by its character as a "primeval document."[17] In addition, it could also be read in an "eschatologized" sense because of its integration into the context of Pentateuch and Former Prophets: here the Priestly document is only the capstone of a much great entity made up of Genesis–2 Kings, which in turn points forward to the *corpus propheticum*.[18]

Something similar is true of the historical work in Chronicles: it could be understood as describing a "mythical primeval time" that reviews the growth of the definitive institutions of the epoch of David and Solomon, the description of which occupies by far the most space in these books.

The wisdom traditions also continued to hold to a theocratic ideal in a broader sense. They distanced themselves from the world-political nervousness and, in critical dialogue with Hellenistic practical philosophies, exalted God's elementary provisions for food, clothing, and all that is necessary. In turn, the contemporary wisdom tradition fell into "theological" and "skeptical" strands. The "theological" strand is represented by Proverbs 1–9, which points to "fear of God" as the principle of theoretical and practical reason. The "skeptical" strand is found in Qoheleth, which is less enthusiastic about human ability to lead a successful life on the basis of right knowledge. But at the same time Qoheleth emphasizes that one can and should enjoy the life given by God, even though humans have no insight into the *ratio* of that life.

III. Spheres of Tradition

1. Wisdom Traditions

a. Proverbs 1–9
Even though the dating and literary genesis of Proverbs 1–9 are disputed and some recent studies tend to locate their origins in the Persian period,[19] the wisdom theology of Proverbs 1–9 can be easily understood against the background of the Isis theology that was powerfully propagated by the Ptolemies, and perhaps should even be placed in the Hellenistic era.[20] If it is older, in any case it found fertile ground for growth in the Hellenistic era.

The thematic profile of Proverbs 1–9 was shaped by three fundamental ideas. First, the framing in Prov 1:7 and 9:10 reveals that in Proverbs 1–9 Wisdom appears in a theologized form; it is understood in terms of fear of YHWH:

The *fear of* YHWH is the <u>beginning</u> of knowledge; fools despise wisdom and instruction. (Prov 1:7)

The *fear of* YHWH is the <u>beginning</u> of wisdom, and the knowledge of the Holy One is insight. (Prov 9:10)

Thus for Proverbs 1–9 Wisdom is not immediately or directly accessible; the way to her is through the fear of YHWH. It is possible that this process of the theologization of wisdom should be associated, in literary-sociological terms, with a stronger integration of and concern for wisdom literature at the temple, but such considerations must remain speculative.

Connected to the first theme is also the second: the idea of "personified" wisdom. In Proverbs 1–9 wisdom is no longer conceived as the ordering structural principle of the world that can be distinguished by empirical observation; instead, it (she) is an entity operating at a certain distance from the world. Wisdom, conceived as a woman, discourses and pleads her own case, just like her rival, Lady Folly:

Lady Wisdom	Lady Folly
And now, my children, listen to me: happy are those who keep my ways. Hear instruction and be wise, and do not neglect it. ... For whoever finds me finds life and obtains favor from YHWH. (Prov 8:32-33, 35)	Stolen water is sweet, and bread eaten in secret is pleasant. (Prov 9:17)

In fact, personified Wisdom was even present at the creation of the world. She knows the plan of creation.

> YHWH created me at the beginning of his work, the first of his acts of long ago. Ages ago I was set up, at the first, before the beginning of the earth. When there were no depths I was brought forth, when there were no springs abounding with water. Before the mountains had been shaped, before the hills, I was brought forth—when he had not yet made earth and fields, or the world's first bits of soil. When he established the heavens, I was there, when he drew a circle on the face of the deep, when he made firm the skies above, when he established the fountains of the deep, when he assigned to the sea its limit, so that the waters might not transgress his command, when he marked out the foundations of the earth, then I was beside him, like a master worker; and I was daily his delight, rejoicing before him always, rejoicing in his inhabited world and delighting in the human race. (Prov 8:22-31)

Third and finally, Proverbs 1–9 represents an optimistic position toward the practical and theoretical consequences of possessing wisdom:

> Happy are those who find wisdom, and those who get understanding, for her income is better than silver, and her revenue better than gold. She is more precious than jewels, and nothing you desire can compare with her. Long life is in her right hand; in her left hand are riches and honor. Her ways are ways of pleasantness, and all her paths are peace.

She is a tree of life to those who lay hold of her; those who hold her fast
are called happy. (Prov 3:13-18)

In comparison to the older wisdom teaching, in which an overarching idea of
order as such was more in the foreground, these statements emphasize the practical side of reward and punishment as consequences of human action. In terms of
the history of theology this position acts as a kind of "Deuteronomizing" of older
wisdom teaching, which, in view of the long endurance of the Deuteronomistic
tradition in the scribal circles, does not create any theoretical problems: it was still
able to influence various literary corpora well into the Hellenistic era.

It is difficult to say whether these three basic ideas belong together in terms
of their literary history, or whether they should be diachronically separated as
a process of steadily broadening theologization. In the composition as we now
have it, fear of YHWH is evidently regarded as the beginning of one's ascent, and
it is only from there that access to wisdom becomes possible at all.

This linkage of wisdom back to God's own self is made still more pointed in
the book of Sirach, where wisdom can be altogether concentrated on God: "All
wisdom is from the Lord, and with him it remains forever. . . . There is but one
who is wise, greatly to be feared, seated upon his throne—the Lord" (Sir 1:1, 8).

The close linkage of wisdom and fear of YHWH in Proverbs 1–9 results in
the framework of a theologized interpretation of wisdom that allows Prov 6:20-
22 to be perceived as, in fact, adopting a central Torah text, the *Shema Israel*
of Deut 6:4-9. The admonitions of Wisdom can thus be considered to have the
same attributes and attitudes as the words of Torah in Deut 6:4-9.

Proverbs 6:20-22	Deuteronomy 6:5-8
My child, keep your father's com-mandment, and do not forsake your mother's teaching. <u>Bind them upon</u> your **heart** always; *tie them around your neck*. **When you walk**, they will lead you; when you lie down, they will watch over you; and when you awake, they will talk with you.	You shall love YHWH your God with all your heart, and with all your soul, and with all your might. Keep these words that I am command-ing you today in your **heart**. Recite them to your children and talk about them when you are at home and **when you walk**, when you lie down and when you rise. <u>Bind them as a sign on your hand,</u> *fix them as an emblem on your forehead.*

With this association of wisdom and law Proverbs 6 is very similar to some
sayings in the Torah itself that are probably not much older:[21]

See, just as YHWH my God has charged me, I now teach you statutes
and ordinances for you to observe in the land that you are about to
enter and occupy.

> You must observe them diligently, for this will show your wisdom and discernment to the peoples, who, when they hear all these statutes, will say, "Surely this great nation is a wise and discerning people!" (Deut 4:5-6)

This strand of tradition will develop in Sirach 24 and Baruch 3 into an explicit identification between wisdom and written Torah (see below).

However, Proverbs 1–9 also reacts, especially in 1:20-33, to the "end of prophecy."[22] In its first discourse it presents Wisdom herself as a prophet—that is, the trustee of prophecy, which is now expiring—while on the other hand she moves, in many respects, into the position of God's own self, in that one's attitude toward her determines salvation or destruction.

> Wisdom cries out in the street; in the squares she raises her voice. At the busiest corner she cries out; at the entrance of the city gates she speaks: "How long, O simple ones, will you love being simple? How long will scoffers delight in their scoffing and fools hate knowledge? Give heed to my reproof; I will pour out my thoughts to you; I will make my words known to you. (Prov 1:20-23)

Wisdom universalizes political theology as formulated, for example, in Isa 11:1-5:[23] not only the future Davidic messiah, but all kings rule due to Wisdom's gift: "By me kings reign, and rulers decree what is just; by me rulers rule, and nobles, all who govern rightly" (Prov 8:15-16). Such a statement in itself fits well with the *pax Persica*. At the same time there is the hint of a Hellenistic background to this statement, since on the one hand there is an emphatic reference to a number of kings and rulers, and on the other hand the specific explication of this idea could point to some contrafactual experiences.

b. Job 28 and Job 32–37

Even though there is little agreement on the literary origins of the book of Job, it appears that the exclusion of the song of wisdom in Job 28 and the Elihu speeches in Job 32–37 from the earliest version is well supported and widely acknowledged. Both texts represent selections intended in some sense to reintroduce a moderate "orthodoxy" into the book of Job.[24] The song of wisdom in Job 28, which is connected to Job 27 as part of Job's speech, defends against the possible interpretation that Job altogether rejects wisdom and the fear of God in these dialogues. Instead, Job appears here—before he makes his "oath of purification" in Job 29–31—as the defender of a position that presents human beings in their finitude with the fear of God and ethical conduct as the way to wisdom, which in itself is hidden:

> Where then does wisdom come from? And where is the place of understanding? It is hidden from the eyes of all living, and concealed from the birds of the air.

Abaddon and Death say, "We have heard a rumor of it with our ears." God understands the way to it, and he knows its place. And he said to humankind, "Truly, the fear of YHWH, that is wisdom; and to depart from evil is understanding." (Job 28:20-23, 28)

The Elihu discourses as well, parts of which anticipate the divine discourses later in the book in their content, pursue a similar end. The fourth friend who appears here plays no role either before or after Job 32–37, and so it is not difficult to perceive him as a foreign body within the book. He adds nothing to the progression of the drama. Instead, his four monologues strive for an "orthodox" interpretation of Job's suffering. Elihu rejects both Job's assertion that he is righteous and the attempts of Job's friends to explain what has happened. His own interpretation of suffering as primarily God's method of instruction is, of course, altogether in the tradition of the speech of Eliphaz in Job 5, and thus is not so much "new" as adopted by him.

c. Qoheleth

The book of Qoheleth, probably composed in the second half of the third century B.C.E.,[25] is a writing that, on the one hand, is part of a discussion with non-Israelite partners,[26] but on the other hand is strongly influenced by dialogue with positions in early Jewish literature within the Old Testament.[27] Its literary form seems to have been particularly motivated by external influences: wisdom teachings as royal testaments are known to us from Egypt.[28] The form of the book recalls the discourse form of the so-called diatribes in Greek popular philosophy.[29] As to its content, a proximity between the book of Qoheleth and antique skepticism and the teachings of the Stoa and Epicureanism is often postulated. There can be no doubt that there are substantive points of agreement, probably traceable to corresponding cultural contacts, but on various points the position of the book of Qoheleth differs from the skepticism of Greek philosophy: what is constitutive of the latter is the assertion that understanding as such is impossible, and therefore it is necessary to withhold judgment. Qoheleth emphasizes the narrow limits of human understanding but by no means draws the conclusion that no judgments should be made. Instead, Qoheleth is able to adduce the achievements and limitations of human understanding as foundational elements for its practical philosophy: it is true that human beings cannot understand the world, but they can experience that eating, drinking, and joy in life are God's gifts accessible to human enjoyment.

He [God] has made everything suitable for its time; moreover he has put a sense of past and future into their minds, yet they cannot find out what God has done from the beginning to the end.
I know that there is nothing better for them than to be happy and enjoy themselves as long as they live; moreover, it is God's gift that all should eat and drink and take pleasure in all their toil. (Eccl 3:11-13)

From the perspective of Old Testament literary history the book of Qoheleth and its theology represent above all a discussion with the wisdom and prophetic traditions as well as the Torah.

In its discussion with contemporary wisdom teaching as attested especially in Proverbs 1–9, Qoheleth emphasizes the problems and limitations of human wisdom:[30] it can be an aid to a happy life, but not a guarantee. Above all, in view of death as our destiny, all are equal.

> Then I saw that wisdom excels folly as light excels darkness. The wise have eyes in their head, but fools walk in darkness. Yet I perceived that the same fate befalls all of them. Then I said to myself, "What happens to the fool will happen to me also; why then have I been so very wise?" And I said to myself that this also is vanity. For there is no enduring remembrance of the wise or of fools, seeing that in the days to come all will have been long forgotten. How can the wise die just like fools? (Eccl 2:13-16)

Proverbs 3:16-18 reaches a very different conclusion: "Long life is in her right hand; in her left hand are riches and honor. Her ways are ways of pleasantness, and all her paths are peace. She is a tree of life to those who lay hold of her; those who hold her fast are called happy."

It appears that this skeptical position on the part of Qoheleth receives and activates a potential latent within older wisdom teaching, reflected especially in its theologized sayings which display a highly critical self-understanding: "All our steps are ordered by YHWH; how then can we understand our own ways?" (Prov 20:24; cf. also Prov 16:1, 9; 19:21; 21:2, 30; 24:21-22). Because the human is mortal, his or her potential for understanding and action is limited. Qoheleth adopts a skeptical attitude toward theological programs that overestimate human possibilities.

Qoheleth also rejects wide-ranging hopes for a future eschatological intervention of God in world history. Against expectations of a "new heaven" and a "new earth," as in contemporary texts in the book of Isaiah, Qoheleth emphasizes that there is "nothing new":[31]

Ecclesiastes 1:9-11	Isaiah 65:17
What has been is what will be, and what has been done is what will be done; there is nothing <u>new</u> under the sun. Is there a thing of which it is said, "See, this is <u>new</u>"? It has already been, in the ages before us. *The people of long ago are not remembered, nor will there be any remembrance of people yet to come by those who come after them.*	For I am about to create <u>new</u> heavens and a <u>new</u> earth; *the former things shall not be remembered or come to mind.*

Qoheleth also expresses reserve toward a further fundamental conviction in Isaiah 56–66: for Qoheleth there is no theologically relevant distinction between the devout and the wicked. There may well be wise and foolish, righteous and unrighteous, but they are not separated by their fate, which is death:[32] "For the fate of humans and the fate of animals is the same; as one dies, so dies the other. They all have the same breath, and humans have no advantage over the animals; for all is vanity" (Eccl 3:19). In death all are alike; there is no compensation afterward, as one might hope on the basis of texts like Psalms 49 and 73 (cf. Eccl 9:1). Therefore, according to Qoheleth, human beings are directed to the elementary sustenance and ordering of life in creation. These things are not optimal, but neither are they bad; they are simply ambivalent. In this Qoheleth agrees with the theological approach of Genesis 1–11,[33] but also with some statements in the Psalms (cf. Psalm 104).

d. The "Messianic Psalter"

Comprehensive formational processes within the Psalter may also fall within the Hellenistic period. These—in much the same way as in the prophetic tradition—react to the collapse of the ordered world of the Persian period.[34] In particular, that context may explain the literary bracketing of Psalms 2–89 in Ps 2:1-2 and 89:51-52, which—possibly drawing a line of distinction against Ptolemaic ideologies of rule—establishes a "messianic Psalter" encompassing Psalms 2–89*.[35]

Psalm 2:1-2	Psalm 89:51-52
Why do the nations conspire, and the *peoples* plot in vain? The kings of the earth set themselves, and the rulers take counsel together, against YHWH and his anointed.	Remember, O Lord, how your servant is taunted; how I bear in my bosom the insults of the *peoples*, with which your enemies taunt, O YHWH, with which they taunted the footsteps of your anointed.

That this perspective is more recent than the Persian period is further suggested by the idea of the universal judgment of the peoples that is activated in Psalms 2–89* by this framing (cf. Ps 2:9). The formation of Psalms 2–89* politicizes the psalms placed within this context, in a receptional sense, as statements by the king. Interestingly enough, the collection of Psalms 2–89 thus revitalizes the original function of the individual songs of lament from the pre-exilic period as royal texts. Probably some passages, such as Pss 18:51; 20:7; 28:8-9; 84:9-10, had "messianic" perspectives redactionally introduced into them.[36]

Excursus: The Rise of Apocalypticism

"Apocalypticism" is usually understood as a collective term for an intellectual current, with the revelatory literature ("apocalyptic") that belongs to it, arising in the period between the third century B.C.E. and the third century C.E.[37] However, historically speaking it is an entity with sharp internal differentiations. Catalogue-style listings of crucial features that should be regarded as "apocalyptic" and those that should not[38] suggest a unity of form and content that cannot be demonstrated. The only possible solution is to establish a detailed picture of the late- and post-Old Testament literary and theological history of apocalyptic writings.[39] It is possible that then certain strands of "apocalyptic" tradition can be discerned. But we cannot speak of the existence of a consolidated "apocalypticism." There is a certain affinity among a series of texts previously viewed as apocalyptic in terms of the motif of the heavenly secret knowledge, which appears to play a decisive role, and on that basis the collective term "apocalypticism" can be partially justified (especially as regards 1 Enoch, Daniel, 4 Ezra, and 2 Baruch).

The discovery of the Qumran documents has played a crucial role in the discussion of the origins of apocalyptic literature.[40] These show on an empirical basis that it was not the biblical book of Daniel but the Enoch literature that represented the literary-historical starting point for the idea of the revelation of secret heavenly knowledge.

The much-discussed question whether apocalypticism is to be seen as derived from prophecy[41] or wisdom[42] should be abandoned. The first thing that ought to be discussed, or rather demonstrated, is whether prophecy and wisdom were still independent strands of tradition in the third and second centuries B.C.E. Evidently apocalyptic texts adopted important elements from both prophecy (perspectives on the future) and wisdom (righteousness).

The two-eons teaching, which has often been seen as a fundamental position in apocalypticism, can only be explicitly attested in texts whose dates of origin lie after 70 C.E. (especially 4 Ezra and 2 Baruch). Evidently it was the experience of the destruction of the Second Temple that completely destroyed hope in the perfectibility of the world. The promise of a new heaven and a new earth, found in the Old Testament solely in Isaiah 65, seems to be indebted primarily to a revocation of the theological program of the Torah and its anthropological orders of creation; there is no two-eon doctrine here as yet (God created the two eons from the beginning according, for example, to 4 Ezra 7:50; Isa 65:17-25 is about the future reshaping of heaven and earth).[43]

In terms of the history of theology the appearance of apocalyptic concepts should be seen within the context of a broad intellectual-historical development that can still be perceived and reconstructed in the Old Testament. The most important theological proposals of the pre-exilic period had as yet no overarching historical-theological shape (e.g., in the theology of the Jerusalem cult). Deuteronomistic theology then pushed through a covenant-theological interpretation of history, while consistently deterministic historical theologies are to be found first in the Maccabean period book of Daniel, simultaneous with some beginnings in the ordering of the ages of the world in the Pentateuch.[44] In tradition-historical terms they are apparently indebted to the fundamental theocratic understanding of God as the absolute ruler and guide of the world, which, under the influence of the collapse of the Persian empire, continued to be adopted in subsequent historical theologies.

2. Narrative Traditions

a. Chronicles

The books of Chronicles have often been treated by scholars in close connection with Ezra–Nehemiah, but (as discussed above) current exegesis regards them somewhat differently: while Ezra–Nehemiah were probably connected with 1–2 Chronicles as a "Chronistic historical work" at one time, the former were probably originally somewhat older than 1–2 Chronicles, even though all these writings stem from a similar theological milieu.

There is no consensus on the dating of Chronicles. In the past, because of their theocratic orientation, they were located in the Persian period. Since they seem to presume the completion of the Torah they were as a rule placed toward the end of the fourth century B.C.E.[45] There were also voices in favor of a dating in the third century B.C.E.[46] Certain technical military details could point in that direction: for example, catapults are first attested as siege machines in the latter period (2 Chr 26:14). More recently, Steins has suggested that Chronicles should not be dated earlier than the Maccabean period (though the image of David in Sirach 47 does not represent a definitive *terminus ante quem*).[47] He considers Chronicles to be a "phenomenon of the conclusion of the canon." The genre of Chronicles as "rewritten Bible" could favor this location; otherwise it is first attested in second-century B.C.E. texts. But against a later date is the complete absence of Hellenistic influences. To interpret this silence as an implicit anti-Hellenistic program may be a move suggested by such a late dating, but it seems an *ad hoc* argument that makes a virtue of necessity.

Probably we must make some fundamental redaction-critical distinctions. From the point of view of theological history it is attractive to locate the basic material of Chronicles in the late Persian period, but additions and adjustments to that basic material would have to have extended into the Maccabean era.[48] In terms of the structure and literary framework of the basic material, its intent was evidently to represent the cultic community in Jerusalem as the legitimate successor of monarchical-era Israel and Judah.[49]

In any case we must note that the question of the monarchy receives a peculiar accent in Chronicles. This is especially evident in the reformulations of the existing dynastic promise to David from 2 Samuel 7, as presented in 1 Chronicles 17.[50]

2 Samuel 7:12-17	1 Chronicles 17:11-15
When your days are fulfilled and you lie down with your ancestors, I will raise up your offspring after you, who shall come forth from your body, and I will establish his kingdom. . . . (16) but your house and your kingdom shall be made sure forever before me; your throne shall be established forever. (17) In accordance with all these words and with all this vision, Nathan spoke to David.	When your days are fulfilled to go to be with your ancestors, I will raise up your offspring after you, one of your own sons, and I will establish his kingdom. . . . (14) but I will confirm him in my house and in my kingdom forever, and his throne shall be established forever. (15) In accordance with all these words and all this vision, Nathan spoke to David.

Chronicles retains the promise of a dynasty to David, but profoundly reinterprets it. The kingdom in view is that of *God* (1 Chr 17:14), not David (2 Sam 7:16). Likewise, it is not David's throne (2 Sam 7:16), but the throne of those who come after him (1 Chr 17:14) that will be forever. In this the basic theocratic feature of Chronicles is quite clear: God is the true king; his earthly representatives are from the dynasty of David, though this is no longer restricted to Davidides, as indicated by the replacement of the biological term for descent, "who shall come forth from your body," with the expression "one of your own sons," which in Hebrew can also be understood functionally (as the king can also be traditionally regarded as God's "son"; cf. Ps 2:7). For Chronicles the Davidic dynasty ruled God's kingdom during the Judahite monarchy. After its fall, however, it was ultimately the Persians who inherited its legacy.[51]

The most important substantive difference between the Chronicler's historical work and its model in Genesis–2 Kings is seen in the overall structure of Chronicles: it summarizes the time before Saul in a genealogy (1 Chronicles 1–9) and, after the episodes surrounding Saul (1 Chronicles 10), devotes the longest and central space to the depiction of the reigns of David (1 Chronicles 11–29) and Solomon (2 Chronicles 1–9), painted in idealized tones.[52] That means, however, that from the point of view of the Chronicler neither the patriarchs nor the exodus, Sinai, the occupation of the land, or any other epoch in the classic history of Israel's salvation is the normative epoch of Israel's founding, but only the time of David and Solomon. The "genealogical vestibule" (1 Chronicles 1–9) functions merely as a pre-history.[53] Thus the

Chronicler's historical work, in contrast to its model, locates the central events of Israel's foundation much later, transferring it to the beginnings of the kingship: David and Solomon, as initiators of the cult, are Israel's founding figures. They are in some sense drawn on the model of the Persian kings Cyrus and Darius: as David prepared for the building of the first temple, the same is true of Cyrus, who issued the corresponding edict for the building of the second temple, and as the first temple was completed under Solomon, so the second temple was built under Darius.[54]

Chronicles thus represents a strongly autochthonous concept of Israel's origin, associating the time of the unified monarchy closely with that of the patriarchs, while the exodus and occupation of the land, though not ignored, retreat far into the background. Moses appears in Chronicles not as the leader of the exodus but as the lawgiver for Israel. The exodus itself is mentioned in Chronicles only six times (1 Chr 17:5, 21; 2 Chr 5:10; 6:5; 7:22; 20:10)—in the adaptation of 1 Kgs 8:21 in 2 Chr 6:11 it is, in fact, eliminated: YHWH's covenant, made with the ancestors in 1 Kgs 8:21 at the time when he led them out of the land of Egypt, is referred to in 2 Chr 6:11 simply as having been made with the Israelites.[55]

The emphasis on the epoch of David and Solomon is associated with a political perspective that holds essentially to a twelve-tribe ideal for Israel, including both north and south. It is, of course, striking that Chronicles altogether ignores the history of the cultically illegitimate Northern Kingdom, and yet it is clear that the Chronicler's Israel is more than Judah: apparently this work views Judah and Jerusalem as the center but advocates the addition of the north, that is, the Samaritans, to this center in order to reconstitute "Israel" as a cultic unit.

It is not only in its demotion of the exodus that the Chronicler's theology distances itself from Deuteronomism, which defines Israel as "Israel from Egypt." In its theology of sin it also sets some specifically different accents: for the Chronicler there is no historical accumulation of guilt. Instead, every generation is itself responsible to God and is likewise—when it falls away from God—punished in its own way. This individualized theology of sin reflects a Priestly background: the functioning of the cult of atonement depends on personal responsibility for sin.[56] The Chronicler's portrayal of sin, however, is not composed with moral undertones, but in terms of the theology of history: catastrophes are to be associated with sin, while times of prosperity witness to just and pious behavior. This is especially clear in the presentation of Manasseh in Chronicles. Manasseh reigned in Jerusalem for fifty-five years (2 Kgs 21:1), and therefore—contrary to the way he is portrayed in 2 Kings 21[57]—he must have been a pious man.

> Therefore YHWH brought against them the commanders of the army
> of the king of Assyria, who took Manasseh captive in manacles, bound

him with fetters, and brought him to Babylon. While he was in distress
he entreated the favor of YHWH his God and humbled himself greatly
before the God of his ancestors. He prayed to him, and God received
his entreaty, heard his plea, and restored him again to Jerusalem and
to his kingdom. Then Manasseh knew that YHWH indeed was God.
Afterward he built an outer wall for the city of David west of Gihon, in
the valley, reaching the entrance at the Fish Gate; he carried it around
Ophel, and raised it to a very great height. He also put commanders of
the army in all the fortified cities in Judah. He took away the foreign
gods and the idol from the house of YHWH, and all the altars that he
had built on the mountain of the house of YHWH and in Jerusalem,
and he threw them out of the city. He also restored the altar of YHWH
and offered on it sacrifices of well-being and of thanksgiving; and he
commanded Judah to serve YHWH the God of Israel. (2 Chr 33:11-16)

Correspondingly, the exile is traced to the sin of the last king of Judah, Zedekiah,
and his generation; their history is depicted in appropriately negative tones:

Zedekiah was twenty-one years old when he began to reign; he reigned
eleven years in Jerusalem. He did what was evil in the sight of YHWH
his God. He did not humble himself before the prophet Jeremiah who
spoke from the mouth of YHWH. He also rebelled against King Nebuchadnezzar, who had made him swear by God; he stiffened his neck and
hardened his heart against turning to YHWH, the God of Israel. All the
leading priests and the people also were exceedingly unfaithful, following all the abominations of the nations; and they polluted the house of
YHWH that he had consecrated in Jerusalem. (2 Chr 36:11-14)

It seems to have been above all these conceptual differences from Deuteronomism that caused Chronicles to be composed as a separate work and not as
a redactional layer of Genesis–2 Kings. Within the Old Testament the doubling
of Genesis–2 Kings and 1–2 Chronicles, and the uniqueness of 1–2 Chronicles
as a new edition of Genesis–2 Kings in the form of an external text, remained
the exception. From a hermeneutical point of view, however, it is of great significance because, through the canonization of both text and commentary—as
is also the case with the relationship between the Sinai pericope and Deuteronomy—the dynamics of interpretation becomes anchored within the Old Testament itself.

b. Development of the Balaam Pericope
As has often been noted, some very late entries seem to have become fixed within
the Balaam pericope in Numbers 22–24, which tells of the pagan seer Balaam
and his prophecies about Israel.[58] We find one such example in Num 24:23-24:

"Again he uttered his oracle, saying: 'Alas, who shall live when God does this? But ships shall come from Kittim and shall afflict Asshur and Eber; and he also shall perish forever.'" Those from Kittim are the Greeks (cf. Gen 10:4; in Dan 11:30 they are the Romans), while "Asshur" represents the Persians (the meaning of "Eber" remains unclear). The saying probably presupposes the fall of the Persian empire after the rise of Alexander the Great. Probably these insertions were motivated by the effort—catalyzed by the cultural contest with Hellenism—to see the decisive events in world history already anchored in the Torah through prophecy.

c. Hellenistic Elements in the Davidic Tradition

The David narratives contain a short passage in 2 Sam 23:13-17 that apparently retells an event that happened to Alexander the Great, as related by Arrian:[59]

> Towards the beginning of harvest three of the thirty chiefs went down to join David at the cave of Adullam, while a band of Philistines was encamped in the valley of Rephaim. David was then in the stronghold; and the garrison of the Philistines was then at Bethlehem. David said longingly, "O that someone would give me water to drink from the well of Bethlehem that is by the gate!" Then the three warriors broke through the camp of the Philistines, drew water from the well of Bethlehem that was by the gate, and brought it to David. But he would not drink of it; he poured it out to YHWH, for he said, "YHWH forbid that I should do this. Can I drink the blood of the men who went at the risk of their lives?" Therefore he would not drink it. The three warriors did these things.

The adoption of this episode into the David tradition shows that the Old Testament intends to depict its king, about whom it is able to relate a good deal that is rather unheroic, as fundamentally no less magnanimous than Alexander. The underlying motivation, the competition between Greek and Israelite culture, had probably already influenced the shape of the tragic tradition about Jephthah's daughter (Judg 1:29-40): Israel had its tragedies, just as Greece did.[60]

d. Esther

The book of Esther tells of the rescue of the Jews of the Persian empire from a persecution that was instigated by Haman, a confidant of the Persian king, but was foiled by the Jewish woman Esther and her uncle Mordechai. The Persian-era setting of the narrative, however, is novelistic and not to be associated with any historical situation. Moreover, the persecution of the Jews that is the focus of the book does not accord with Persian policy. Instead, the book was probably created in the Hellenistic diaspora.[61]

The book of Esther places the mythic primeval conflict between Israel and Amalek (Exod 17:8-16; Deut 25:17-19; 1 Samuel 15) into the history of the

Persian period by paralleling the antagonists, Haman and Mordechai, in terms of their heritage (Esther 3:1: Haman the Agagite; 2:5: Mordechai, son of Jair, son of Shimei, son of Kish) with the Amalekite King Agag and King Saul, the son of Kish. By means of the "Amalekization" of Haman the book of Esther establishes a clear critique with regard to the great powers, but it is not simply negative in its orientation. While Haman is a highly placed government official, the Persian king is able to take the Jewish Esther as his wife. In the end he has Haman and his sons executed and elevates Mordechai to Haman's position.

Within the Bible the book of Esther borrows especially from the Joseph story and the Daniel legends in Daniel 1–6.[62]

e. The Translation of the Torah into Greek
Even if this takes us outside the narrower compass of the literary history of the Hebrew Old Testament, we should mention in connection with the encounter between Judaism and Hellenism the translation of the books of the Torah into Greek. This probably began around the middle of the third century B.C.E., though distinctions should be made from book to book.[63] The so-called Septuagint is not simply a translation; it is the first synchronic interpretation, first of the Torah and then of the remaining books of the Old Testament as well. As such its influence was more important in many locales in antiquity, in the Middle Ages, and in the early modern period than that of the Hebrew original.

The Septuagint became necessary, on the one hand, because Jews in the diaspora, especially in Alexandria, were more and more dependent on Greek translations of their sacred Scriptures. On the other hand it probably exercised a reverse influence in turn on the literary history of the Hebrew Old Testament insofar as it represented an essential factor in the fixing of its textual scope. As soon as the writings of the Old Testament had been translated in a normative fashion, additions could no longer be made to the text in its original language.

The tendencies of the Septuagint as to its content cannot be summarized simply in terms of methodology, since each book was the work of a different translator, and we must likewise reckon with developments within the Greek versions of the text itself. However, some things are generally evident: besides a certain emphasis on eschatology, especially in regard to belief in the resurrection (cf., e.g., Psalm 1; Job 42) and messianism,[64] there is the adoption of Greek philosophical concepts, for example in the depiction of creation, which attempts to harmonize the terminology of Genesis 1 with Plato's *Timaeus*.[65] There is also the chronological extension of the time of the world's ordering through the lengthening of the generative age of the patriarchs in Genesis 5 and 11, in order to make some space in the prehistory for the mythical traditions of the Greeks,[66] and there is an avoidance of anthropomorphic language for God.[67] The Septuagint is one of the most important sources for the cultural contact of Judaism with Hellenism, a Judaism that attempts to demonstrate that its central tradition is compatible with the leading global culture.

3. Prophetic Traditions

a. Judgment-of-the-World Texts in the Corpus propheticum

The experience of the collapse of the two-hundred-year world rule of the Persians perhaps left its clearest literary evidence in the prophetic books. We can see in Isaiah, Jeremiah, and the Twelve Prophets how the idea of an all-encompassing cosmic judgment of the world was developed by means of a continuation of existing texts on judgment (of the nations).[68] Their character as continuations can be seen with particular clarity in Isa 34:2-4:

> **Isaiah 34:1**: Draw near, O nations, to hear; O peoples, give heed! Let the earth hear, and all that fills it; the world, and all that comes from it.

> **Isaiah 34:2-4**: *For YHWH is enraged against all the nations, and furious against all their hordes; he has doomed them, has given them over for slaughter. Their slain shall be cast out, and the stench of their corpses shall rise; the mountains shall flow with their blood. All the host of heaven shall rot away, and the skies roll up like a scroll. All their host shall wither like a leaf withering on a vine, or fruit withering on a fig tree.*

> **Isaiah 34:5-6**: When my sword has drunk its fill in the heavens, lo, it will descend upon Edom, upon the people I have doomed to judgment. YHWH has a sword; it is sated with blood, it is gorged with fat, with the blood of lambs and goats, with the fat of the kidneys of rams. For YHWH has a sacrifice in Bozrah, a great slaughter in the land of Edom.

The earlier text in Isa 34:1, 5-6 speaks of YHWH's judgment in Edom, to which all the peoples are summoned as witnesses. In verses 2-4 the same nations have a very different role. Here they are the ones being judged. In addition, in verse 5 the heavens seem still to be a stable entity, while in verses 2-4 they are rolled up "like a scroll."

In the book of Jeremiah also it is obvious that the statements about the judgment of the world are secondary expansions of existing texts. Thus we find the notion of a judgment of "all flesh" in the last two verses before the complex of sayings on the foreign nations in Jeremiah 46–51, which is thus reinterpreted as predicting a world judgment:

> Thus you [i.e., Jeremiah] shall say to him, "Thus says YHWH: I am going to break down what I have built, and pluck up what I have planted— that is, the whole land. And you, do you seek great things for yourself? Do not seek them; for I am going to bring disaster upon all flesh, says YHWH; but I will give you your life as a prize of war in every place to which you may go. (Jer 45:4-5)

The same process occurs in the addition to the cup oracle in Jeremiah 25, which also assumes a judgment of various nations but from v. 27 onward is interpreted as a "world judgment":

> Then you shall say to them, Thus says YHWH of hosts, the God of Israel: Drink, get drunk and vomit, fall and rise no more, because of the sword that I am sending among you. And if they refuse to accept the cup from your hand to drink, then you shall say to them: Thus says YHWH of hosts: You must drink! See, I am beginning to bring disaster on the city that is called by my name, and how can you possibly avoid punishment? You shall not go unpunished, for I am summoning a sword against all the inhabitants of the earth, says YHWH of hosts. You, therefore, shall prophesy against them all these words, and say to them: YHWH will roar from on high, and from his holy habitation utter his voice; he will roar mightily against his fold, and shout, like those who tread grapes, against all the inhabitants of the earth. The clamor will resound to the ends of the earth, for YHWH has an indictment against the nations; he is entering into judgment with all flesh, and the guilty he will put to the sword, says YHWH. (Jer 25:27-31)

Finally, we also find a number of insertions in the book of the Twelve Prophets that can be substantively linked to the corresponding texts in Isaiah and Jeremiah:

> Let the nations rouse themselves, and come up to the valley of Jehoshaphat; for there I will sit to judge all the neighboring nations. Put in the sickle, for the harvest is ripe. Go in, tread, for the wine press is full. The vats overflow, for their wickedness is great. Multitudes, multitudes, in the valley of decision! For the day of YHWH is near in the valley of decision. The sun and the moon are darkened, and the stars withdraw their shining. YHWH roars from Zion, and utters his voice from Jerusalem, and the heavens and the earth shake. But YHWH is a refuge for his people, a stronghold for the people of Israel. (Joel 4:12-16 [3:12-16])

> In that day they will come to you from Assyria to Egypt, and from Egypt to the River, from sea to sea and from mountain to mountain. But the earth will be desolate because of its inhabitants, for the fruit of their doings. (Mic 7:12-13)

> Therefore wait for me, says YHWH, for the day when I arise as a witness. For my decision is to gather nations, to assemble kingdoms, to pour out upon them my indignation, all the heat of my anger; for in the fire of my passion all the earth shall be consumed. (Zeph 3:8)

The idea behind these statements is that the world judgment is not a new and additional blow directed by God against the world; rather, these texts intend to show that God's previous judgmental blows are only parts and precursors of a comprehensive divine judgment of the world.

It is without question that this statement runs altogether contrary to the theology of theocratic positions such as those in the Priestly document, which in Genesis 9 had formulated an eternal guarantee for the existence of the world in the Noachic covenant. And in fact, within the framework of the world-judgment texts in the *corpus propheticum*, especially Isaiah 24–27, there are passages that openly oppose the theology of the Priestly document. This can be seen with particular clarity in Isa 24:4-6:

> The earth dries up and withers, the world languishes and withers; the heavens languish together with the earth. The earth lies polluted under its inhabitants; for they have transgressed laws, violated the statutes, broken the everlasting covenant. Therefore a curse devours the earth, and its inhabitants suffer for their guilt; therefore the inhabitants of the earth dwindled, and few people are left.

The eternal covenant that has been broken by humanity can scarcely be any other than the one with Noah in Genesis 9: the Old Testament is unaware of any other covenant with the whole human race. This is favored also by the theme of blood guilt, which plays an important role in the context of Isaiah 24–27. Thus Isa 24:4-6 states, contrary to anything imaginable in the Priestly document, that the Noachic covenant can also be broken. Therefore the world order envisioned by the Priestly document as irrevocable can also be overturned. Likewise in reference to Genesis 6–9, Isa 26:20-21 assumes that Israel, like Noah before it, will be rescued from the approaching judgment of the world:

> Come, my people, enter your chambers, and shut your doors behind you; hide yourselves for a little while until the wrath is past. For YHWH comes out from his place to punish the inhabitants of the earth for their iniquity; the earth will disclose the blood shed on it, and will no longer cover its slain.

b. The Formation of a Comprehensive Book of Isaiah (1–62)
Among scholars, following Bernhard Duhm, it is common to divide the book of Isaiah into three separate volumes (chs. 1–39, 40–55; 56–66) that are to the broadest possible degree independent of each other and are assigned to three different prophetic figures and epochs: chapters 1–39 contain the words of Isaiah ("proto-Isaiah"), the core of chapters 40–55 are traced to an anonymous person working during the Babylonian exile, who is given the artificial name "Deutero-Isaiah," and the fundamental text of chapters 56–66 is assigned to a third, likewise anonymous figure who is called "Trito-Isaiah."[69] This model was altogether in accord with classic research on the prophets and traced prophetic

literature essentially to prophetic figures who delivered their oracles orally.[70] Current research, in contrast, has discovered the phenomenon of scribal writing of prophetic traditions, and in many cases, with the aid of this concept, more convincing proposals can be made about the genesis of complex textual phenomena.

The models for the origins of the book of Isaiah as a whole currently being discussed can be divided into two major trajectories, assuming that the redactional creation of "Trito-Isaiah" (chs. 56–66) is certain,[71] and thus restricts the discussion to the determination of the relationship between Isaiah 1–39 and 40–55. According to the majority position in research the bases of Isaiah 1–39 and 40–55 go back to two different prophetic figures ("Isaiah" from the eighth century B.C.E. and "Deutero-Isaiah" from the sixth century B.C.E.). These bodies of tradition first stood alongside one another as separate literary entities and were only secondarily linked. Contrary to earlier scholarship, which interpreted the genesis of the larger book of Isaiah as something of an accident of bookmaking technology, it is today supposed that Isaiah 1–39 and 40–55 were literarily linked by means of a clear-cut and well-planned redactional process. The most important literary bridge-texts are found in Isaiah 35,[72] while insertions by the same hand can be seen in 11:11-16; 27:12-13; 51:1-11*; and 62:10-12 (the concluding text). Sometimes Isaiah 33 is also seen as an earlier bridging text.[73] The other strand of research links Isaiah 40–55 much more closely to Isaiah 1–39 by viewing chapters 40–55 as a deliberate continuation of Isaiah 1–39.[74] According to this view there never was an independent Deutero-Isaiah tradition or an individual prophet "Deutero-Isaiah." The prophecy in Isaiah 40–55 is regarded as a substantive development of the themes in Isaiah 1–39, and special emphasis is given, on the one hand, to the dependence of Isaiah 40 on Isaiah 6 (though this is restricted to vv. 6-8 of Isaiah 40), and on the other hand to the anonymity of Isaiah 40–55. However, the observed links between Isaiah 1–39 and 40–55 need not necessarily be evaluated in terms of a continuation model; these could also be literary references within a series of prophetic books.

Thus neither view disputes the basic differences between Isaiah 1–39 and 40–55, while support for the traditional three-book hypothesis has declined markedly. Whether it is to be reformulated as a two-book hypothesis depends on whether one argues for a tradition originally detached from Isaiah 1–39 behind Isaiah 40–55—either independently or as part of a combination with Jeremiah. In fact, this still seems to be the option most suited to explain the textual findings in Isaiah 40–55. Correspondingly, one must suppose that at some point in time the two parts, Isaiah 1–39 and Isaiah 40–55, were literarily combined.

If we follow Steck's suggestion, a corresponding "great Isaiah" redaction can be seen most prominently in the depiction of the preservation of Israel from the world judgment (Isa 34:2-4) in Isaiah 35.[75] This would first have linked the two major portions of the book, chapters 1–39 and 40–55, in literary fashion to form a great book of Isaiah containing chapters 1–62. Historically this was probably connected with political events in the early diadochic period, which offered a contemporary background for the theme of the judgment of the world thus evoked.

c. The Devout and the Wicked in Trito-Isaiah

The lament in Isa 63:7—64:11, which in the past was often regarded as a separate tradition from the exilic period, was more likely created as a continuation within its present context.[76] It may have emerged in the early Ptolemaic period, motivated by corresponding contemporary events (Ptolemy in Jerusalem 302/301 B.C.E.?),[77] as a further conclusion to the book of Isaiah, extending Isaiah 1–62. It documents the collapse of the "Trito-Isaianic" interpretive efforts in Isaiah 56–59 to make the advent of the promised salvation dependent on ever-expanding conditions. A related step of the highest importance for the history of theology was the breakup of the unity of the people of God, which has a kind of conceptual precursor in the Golah-oriented texts of Jeremiah and Ezekiel. The concluding texts in Isaiah 65–66, which were created still later as an answer to Isa 63:7—64:11, see salvation as only for the righteous, while the wicked will face judgment (Isa 65:1-15; cf. Isa 57:20-21). Thus, for example, the promise of a new heaven and a new earth in Isaiah 65:17-25, as the embedding in the context shows, is only for the servants of YHWH. It is formulated as a clear echo of the Deutero-Isaianic contrasting of the "old" and "new" exodus in Isa 43:16-21 ("do not remember the former things") and indicates that according to Isaiah 65, in contrast to Isaiah 43, it is no longer sufficient to reformulate "only" the salvation history of Israel. No, the order of creation as such must—in contrast to that of Genesis 1—be renewed.[78]

Isaiah 43:16-21	Isaiah 65:13-17
Thus says YHWH, who makes a way in the sea, a path in the mighty waters, who brings out chariot and horse, army and warrior. . . . *Do not remember the former things*, or consider the things of old. [See,] I am about to make a new thing; now it springs forth, do you not perceive it?	Therefore thus says the Lord YHWH: My servants shall eat, but you shall be hungry; my servants shall drink, but you shall be thirsty; my servants shall rejoice, but you shall be put to shame; my servants shall sing for gladness of heart, but you shall cry out for pain of heart, and shall wail for anguish of spirit. . . .
Genesis 1:1	
In the beginning God **created the heavens** and **the earth**.	For [see,] I am about to **create** new heavens and a new earth; *the former things shall not be remembered* or come to mind.

In this new creation there will no longer be need of a temple cult, which with its orientation to the cult of atonement presumes the fallenness of the previous creation. Accordingly, this creation can be declared to be a transformation of the Jerusalem temple itself into the temple of YHWH: "Thus says YHWH: Heaven is my throne and the earth is my footstool; what is the house that you would build for me, and what is my resting place?" (Isa 66:1).[79] The work of the pre-Hellenistic, largely undisputed entity of salvation called "Israel" prepares the way for the individualization of Jewish religion, something strengthened especially after the fall of Jerusalem in 70 B.C.E. In that form it also became an influential model for Christianity.

d. Return from the Diaspora and Restoration
   of the Davidic Kingdom in Jeremiah

A clearly accented theological program that can also be rather reliably dated is found in the Masoretic special material in Jer 33:14-26.[80] The fact that this longest addition to the Hebrew version of the book, which is some three thousand words shorter than the Greek version (which otherwise is quite literal), is missing from the Greek makes it very probable that Jer 33:14-26 entered into the book only at a time when the Greek translation was already complete. This means that the section cannot be older than the third century B.C.E. The scribal nature of the material makes it virtually impossible that this is an independent source text. Jeremiah 33:14-16 reinterprets Jer 23:5-6, and in the subsequent passages in the text we can also observe extensive textual borrowings.

Jeremiah 23:5-6	Jeremiah 33:14-16
The days are surely coming, says YHWH,	The days are surely coming, says YHWH, when I will fulfill the promise I made to the house of Israel and the house of Judah.
when I will raise up for David a righteous Branch, and he shall reign as king and deal wisely, and shall execute justice and righteousness in the land. (6) In his days Judah will be saved and Israel will live in safety. And this is the name by which he will be called: "YHWH is our righteousness."	(15) In those days and at that time I will cause a righteous Branch to spring up for David; and he shall execute justice and righteousness in the land. (16) In those days Judah will be saved and Jerusalem will live in safety. And this is the name by which she will be called: "YHWH is our righteousness."

At first glance Jer 33:14-16 may seem like a repetition of Jer 23:5-6, and in fact the two texts overlap over long stretches. But the particular task of 33:14-16 is above all to make it so that the extra passage, "I will fulfill the promise I made to the house of Israel and the house of Judah" in 33:14 causes the messianic promise of fulfillment to depend on the realization of this "promise." What that means we can read in Jer 29:10, where this "promise" is made explicit: "For thus says YHWH: Only when Babylon's seventy years are completed will I visit you, and I will fulfill to you my promise [LXX: my words] and bring you back to this place."

Thus Jer 33:14-16 reinterprets Jer 23:5-6 to mean that the coming of the messiah presupposes the return from the diaspora. The promised branch for David will only come when Israel lives united in its land. What is also striking about the position in Jer 33:14-16 is that the messiah is not conceived simply as a person, but instead—apparently adopting motifs from Isaiah 60–61—Zion is assigned the messianic title. The future title "YHWH is our righteousness" is clearly assigned in Jer 33:16 to a feminine entity. The reference is obviously to the city of Jerusalem, named immediately before this and imagined as a woman.

e. Deutero- and Trito-Zechariah

The Zechariah tradition was continued in Zechariah 9–14 with a number of elements that in the past were often distinguished, by analogy with the book of Isaiah, as Deutero- (Zechariah 9–11) and Trito-Zechariah (Zechariah 12–14). However, what we have in Zechariah 9–14—as is the case in Trito-Isaiah, at least—is not originally oral proclamation. This is prophecy produced and handed on by scribes.[81]

Linguistically, Zechariah 9–11 is distinguished from Zechariah 1–8 by its poetic form, while Zechariah 12–14 for the most part returns to prose. But above all, from Zechariah 9 onward the text reflects quite different historical conditions from those at the time of the building of the Second Temple. The temple has long since been built (Zech 11:13; 14:20-21). Zechariah 9:1–8 apparently reflects on the campaign of Alexander as far as Gaza after the fall of Tyre in the year 332 B.C.E.[82] Zechariah 9:13 even explicitly names the "sons of Yawan" (the "Ionians," that is, the Greeks), and reveals evidence of the Jewish resistance against campaigns of conquest, probably by the Ptolemies.[83]

The historical-theological positioning of Zechariah 9 is striking; apparently this chapter welcomes the actions of Alexander the Great—that is, to the extent that he puts an end to the foreign rule of the Persians. But Alexander is not celebrated as a new ruler. Instead, Zech 9:9-10—clearly adapting Isa 40:1-2; 11:1-5; and Ps 72:8—proposes the idea of a Davidic messiah with a far-flung dominion (corresponding to Israel's diaspora existence). Nevertheless, in his modest appearance he is in large part portrayed as an anti-Alexander:[84]

Rejoice greatly, O daughter Zion! Shout aloud, O daughter Jerusalem! Lo, your king comes to you; triumphant and victorious is he, humble and riding on a donkey, on a colt, the foal of a donkey. He will cut off the chariot from Ephraim and the war-horse from Jerusalem; and the battle bow shall be cut off, and he shall command peace to the nations; his dominion shall be from sea to sea, and from the River to the ends of the earth. (Zech 9:9-10)

This humble depiction of the messiah is explained, on the one hand, by use of traditional materials of older promises of rulers in the Old Testament, which almost without exception emphasize the subordination of the expected saving king to the power of Yнwн. On the other hand it is influenced by the overdrawn religious claims of Alexander's kingship and those of his third-century successors after him, especially the Ptolemies.[85]

f. The Redactional Alignment of the Books of Isaiah and the Twelve Prophets

As shown on the one hand by the non-adoption of the "prophetic" book of Daniel into the canon of the prophets, and on the other hand by the lack of any clear literary reflections on the Maccabean crisis, the prophetic books were essentially complete before the Maccabees (see below). Apparently this literary closure was deliberate. As evidenced in particular by the book of Isaiah and that of the Twelve Prophets, as well as the overall plan of the *corpus propheticum* they frame, prophecy was subjected to a process creating an intentional final form. This points to the effort at a certain harmonization of content among the prophetic books: how could the twelve minor prophets have predicted anything different from what Isaiah said? Was Isaiah not aware of everything the other prophets said? The tradents were evidently of the opinion that Old Testament prophecy was essentially one substantive unit. How can we know this?

First of all, it is clear that the four great prophetic books—if we join the ancient tradition in counting the book of the twelve "minor" prophets as one (cf. Sir 49:10)—are related to the epochs they describe as frame and center focus: Isaiah and the Twelve Prophets cover the whole spectrum of the prophetically attested history of Israel, from the Assyrians to the Persians, while Jeremiah and Ezekiel solely but extensively address the Babylonian era.

Isaiah 1–35: Assyria			Hosea, Amos, Micah: Assyria
Isaiah 36–39: Assyria/Babylon			
	Jeremiah: Babylon	Ezekiel: Babylon	Zephaniah, Obadiah: Babylon
Isaiah 40–66: Babylon/Persians			Haggai, Zechariah, Malachi: Persians

We can also observe in detail that the books of Isaiah and the Twelve Prophets were substantively and literarily harmonized with one another, apparently in succession.[86] If we select the most striking observations, we see that Isa 1:1 and Hos 1:1 begin with comparable superscriptions mentioning the same four Judahite kings. In addition, Isaiah 13 and Joel 2 correspond, as do Isa 66:18-24 and Zech 14:16-21, at the very end of the respective "complete books," to an extent that allows us to conclude there was intentional redactional shaping.

There seems to have been a deliberate final redactional shaping of the Twelve Prophets that resulted, in literary terms, in the exclusion and separation of the book of Malachi from the Zechariah tradition, to which it seems originally to have belonged.[87] This is indicated (in addition to the superscription system in Zech 9:1; 12:1, whose structure matches that of Mal 1:1, and numerous contacts within the content, such as the quotation of Zech 1:3 in Mal 3:7) by the fact that "Malachi" is not a name attested either biblically or in inscriptions. It appears to be an artificial name taken from Mal 3:1; it means "my messenger," and may have been coined in view of the promise at the end of the book that Elijah will return (Mal 3:22-24).[88] This reminiscence of Elijah, who according to 2 Kgs 2:11-12 did not die but was taken up to heaven, seems to reflect on the fact that prophecy, as a contemporary and active phenomenon, has come to an end, and that only once more—when Elijah returns—will a prophet directly sent by God arise. Until then, however, Israel must depend on the literary canon of the prophets.

g. The World Empires in Daniel 2 and 7

The Daniel legends in Daniel 1–6* were presented with an enormous challenge, like other theocratic concepts in the Persian period, as a result of the collapse of the political frame of reference for their theology. The tradents of the book of Daniel fulfilled their task by expanding the content of the vision in Daniel 2 into a four-part sequence of world empires, concluding the book in Daniel 7 with a corresponding vision.

	Daniel 2: Statue	Daniel 7: Four Beasts from the Sea
Babylonians	Head: gold	Lion with eagle's wings
Medes	Breast and arms: silver	Bear
Persians	Belly and legs: bronze	Leopard with bird's wings
Greeks	Feet: part iron, part clay	Beast with ten horns
Heavenly kingdom	Stone	Throne with an Ancient One, Son of Man

The goal of world history in this vision, however, is not the fourth kingdom, but the fifth, in which God will exercise direct rule over the world. This theocratic perspective on the end-time conveys the eschatological and theological positions in the Old Testament of the Persian period in the sense of a sequence, but it was probably catalyzed primarily by the disappointments in the political history of the third century B.C.E., which were altogether apt to destroy confidence in the great foreign powers once and for all: no salvation at all can be expected from them any longer.

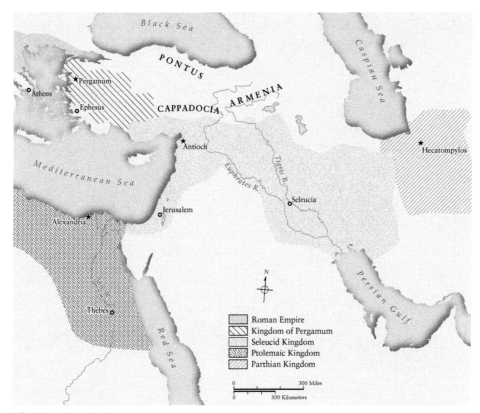

	Roman Empire
	Kingdom of Pergamum
	Seleucid Kingdom
	Ptolemaic Kingdom
	Parthian Kingdom

0   300 Miles
0   300 Kilometers

The Near East in 168 B.C.E.

Part G

The Literature of the Seleucid Period (Second Century B.C.E.)

I. Historical Backgrounds

With the victory of Antiochus III in the battle of Paneas in 198 B.C.E., rule over Syria-Palestine passed from the Ptolemies to the Seleucids. Antiochus III's rule was welcomed in Syria-Palestine—to judge, at any rate, by Josephus's account.[1] Apparently the political organization of his empire revived the active tolerance of subject peoples familiar from the time of the Persians. According to a decree reproduced by Josephus, he renewed the privileges of Jerusalem and its temple and ordered that "all members of the people were to live according to the laws of their ancestors."[2]

Barely a decade later, however, the Seleucids were under increasing pressure from the rising Roman power, which was able to dictate severe terms of tribute and the reduction of their fleet in the Peace of Apameia after the Seleucids lost the battle of Magnesia in 189 B.C.E. As a result, the Seleucids found it increasingly necessary to exploit the economies of their subject territories. From a biblical perspective, however, the major problem of this period was the extensive cultural Hellenization of the Seleucid empire. For Judah, of course, it is increasingly unclear whether this Hellenization, viewed historically, should be regarded as an imposition from without or—at least equally, if not primarily— traceable to movements within Judaism; the latter is the more prevalent opinion today.[3] The presentation in the books of the Maccabees of the motivation of the Seleucid kingdom seems to have been influenced above all by the book of Daniel, which viewed history, now approaching its end, as driven especially by the hostile great powers. In any case, the Hellenization seems to have had a profound effect on Jerusalem at the beginning of the second century B.C.E. A gymnasium was established; ". . . the priests were no longer intent upon their service at the altar. Despising the sanctuary and neglecting the sacrifices, they hurried to take part in the unlawful proceedings in the wrestling arena after the signal for the discus-throwing . . ." (2 Macc 4:14).

The books of Maccabees then report especially of the Seleucid king Antiochus IV Epiphanes that he issued religious edicts aiming at a prohibition of the practice of the Jewish religion (1 Macc 1:41-59; cf. 2 Macc 6:1-9):

> Then the king wrote to his whole kingdom that all should be one people, and that all should give up their particular customs. All the Gentiles accepted the command of the king. Many even from Israel gladly adopted his religion; they sacrificed to idols and profaned the sabbath. And the king sent letters by messengers to Jerusalem and the towns of Judah; he directed them to follow customs strange to the land, to forbid burnt offerings and sacrifices and drink offerings in the sanctuary, to profane sabbaths and festivals, to defile the sanctuary and the priests, to build altars and sacred precincts and shrines for idols, to sacrifice swine and other unclean animals, and to leave their sons uncircumcised. They were to make themselves abominable by everything unclean and profane, so that they would forget the law and change all the ordinances.
>
> He added, "And whoever does not obey the command of the king shall die." In such words he wrote to his whole kingdom. He appointed inspectors over all the people and commanded the towns of Judah to offer sacrifice, town by town. (1 Macc 1:41-51)

Here again doubts arise about whether, from a historical point of view, these measures were actually ordered by the Seleucid ruler—which would have been unusual—or whether they rest on the internal Jewish initiative of the high priest Menelaus, possibly with the sanction, perhaps even the programmatic participation of the king. Menelaus had bought his office, and under pressure he tried to suppress the Jewish religion so that he could maintain his position.[4] The climax of the religious crisis under Antiochus IV was the installation of the "abomination of desolation" (*šqqwṣ šmm*) in the Jerusalem temple. This probably refers to something placed on the altar to serve as the podium for a stone fetish for the worship of Olympian Zeus (2 Macc 6:2). The Olympian Zeus was regarded as a Hellenistic version of the Baal-shamem, the "lord of the heavens":[5]

> Now on the fifteenth [or 25th?] day of Chislev, in the one hundred forty-fifth year, they erected a desolating sacrilege on the altar of burnt offering. They also built altars in the surrounding towns of Judah, and offered incense at the doors of the houses and in the streets. The books of the law that they found they tore to pieces and burned with fire. Anyone found possessing the book of the covenant, or anyone who adhered to the law, was condemned to death by decree of the king.
>
> They kept using violence against Israel, against those who were found month after month in the towns. On the twenty-fifth day of the month they offered sacrifice on the altar that was on top of the altar of burnt offering. (1 Macc 1:54-59)

In the wake of these measures the so-called Maccabean revolt flared up; a national-religious orthodox group arose violently against the desecration of the temple and the prohibition of the Jewish religion. Because of their determination, but also because of the weakness of the Seleucid royal house, the rebels succeeded. They managed to capture Jerusalem, and worship in the temple could resume. With the assumption of the high priesthood in Jerusalem in 152 B.C.E. by Jonathan, an exponent of the Maccabean movement though he was not a Zadokite, the Maccabean revolt completed its transformation from a religious resistance movement to a political freedom struggle conscious of its power. As a result of the continuing weakness of the Seleucids, who were embroiled in their own internal quarrels and whose empire also reached its political nadir in the disastrous Parthian campaign of 129 B.C.E., it was possible for the Hasmoneans to establish a genuinely sovereign kingdom in Israel with a dynastic succession that endured until the capture of Jerusalem by the Romans in 64–63 B.C.E.

It appears that the movement of the Qumran Essenes separated itself from the Jerusalem temple as a result of the illegitimate occupation of the high priestly office by Jonathan, but also because of differences of opinion over the application of the lunar or solar calendar in cultic matters. This movement led to a separate existence near the Dead Sea until its collapse in the Jewish War of 68 C.E. It simulated the correct worship of the temple in order to be able to carry it out in Jerusalem when God intervened, as was expected in the near future.[6] The texts from Qumran, whose publication is now complete, give us a fascinating insight into the spiritual world of a particular group within the Judaism of the time. At the same time, however, we should keep in view that with the Qumran discoveries, the result of an archaeological accident, the state of the sources for pre-rabbinic Judaism has become rather unbalanced. Extrapolations and generalizations on the basis of Qumran are thus to be undertaken with the greatest caution on methodological grounds.

II. Theological Characterizations

The period of Seleucid rule in Syria-Palestine, like that of the Ptolemies, was shaped in particular by the now intensified encounter with Hellenism. Writings like Sirach at the beginning of the second century B.C.E. argue for the compatibility of Hellenistic culture and Jewish tradition, but they also emphasize that full knowledge is to be found only in the Torah. An accommodation between Wisdom and Torah is also found in the successful completion of the Psalter as a five-part "Torah of David" with a theological introduction pointing to the Torah in Psalm 1.[7]

The conflicts of the Maccabean period led, however, on the traditional and national-religious side to a sharpening of criticism and ultimately the rejection of Hellenism. These conflicts seem to have shaped the development of tradition to a considerable degree: the books of Maccabees and the book of Judith emphasize the necessity of violent resistance to Hellenism, while the book of Daniel, greatly expanded in the Maccabean period, fundamentally mythologized the religious crisis of the era and interpreted it as a sign of the end-times. Here the Maccabean revolt is nothing more than a "little help" (Dan 11:34) in God's great historical plan. The hope for the destruction of hostile nations entered into the Psalter (Ps 149) and the book of Sirach (Sirach 36). Somewhat later writings, such as Tobit and the traditions from Qumran that were specific to that group, go still farther in distancing themselves from the Maccabean and other this-worldly efforts to establish salvation on earth—probably because of the compromises the Maccabean movement made in power politics, especially in the wake of the religiously illegitimate seizure of the high-priestly office.

It is also important for ancient Israel's intellectual history that from an anthropological point of view this was the time when the first hopes of resurrection were formulated. In terms of religious history the expansion of YHWH's competence into the realm of death is much older, as the archaeology and epigraphy of burial customs show.[8] Yet it was probably the martyrdoms of the Maccabean period that first forced the theme of resurrection so much to the fore that its positive formulation found its way into the prophetic tradition, at least (Ezekiel 37;[9] Dan 12:2-3; perhaps also Isa 25:8; 26:19), though without remaining unchallenged (Qoh 3:19-22).[10] In Qumran the individual graves as well as some evidence (though very little) in the literature indicate that resurrection was part of the community's doctrine.[11]

III. Spheres of Tradition

1. Cultic and Wisdom Traditions

a. Theocratization and Re-eschatologization in the Psalter

The literary history of the Psalter has undergone various processes of reshaping; thus far we have mentioned, by way of example, only the construction of some Persian-period partial collections and a "messianic Psalter" composed of Psalms 2–89*.[12] The present form of the Psalter is due to a division into five parts, probably in analogy to the Torah, established by the four doxologies in Ps 41:14; 72:18-19; 89:53; 106:48.[13] This "Torah-shape" of the Psalter is also emphasized by the introduction (Psalm 1, cf. "Torah" in verse 2), and by Psalm 119.[14] In view of the considerable divergences in the arrangement of the Psalter in Qumran and the theological proximity of the overall frame of the Psalter in Psalms 1–2, 146–50 to contemporary non-Essene wisdom texts (the Book of Mysteries [1Q27; 4Q299-301]; 1Q/4QInstruction) this five-part division can scarcely be earlier than the second century B.C.E.[15] Corresponding to the thematic foci of the five books as well as the content of Psalms 41, 72, 89, and 106, each combined with a doxology, we can perceive behind the present division of the Psalter a picture of the history of Israel inspired by Chronicles, describing first the epochs of David (Pss 1–41) and Solomon (Pss 42–72), then the monarchical period (Pss 73–89) and the exile (Pss 90–106), culminating in a broad depiction of the restoration (Pss 107–150).

The Psalter, following the theological positions of the individual psalms linked together in Books 4 and 5,[16] develops the picture of a peaceful world under the governance of YHWH, who provides for its basic needs. The theocratic order of life thus described reveals no trace of national-political interests; where the perspectives are political they touch on social justice, the protection of foreigners, widows, and orphans. In cultural-historical terms this overall structure of the Psalter must be more recent than the proto-Psalter made up of Psalms 2–89*, which probably belongs to the Ptolemaic period. It is most likely that it can be understood in light of this *terminus a quo*, on the basis of the revival of the tolerant religious policies of the Persian period in the first decade of the second century B.C.E. under Antiochus III, who allowed and directed the Jews to live according to their "ancestral laws," if we may trust Josephus.

David: I	Solomon: II	Monarchical Period: III	Exile: IV	Restoration: V
(Pss 1–41)	(Pss 42–72)	(Pss 73–89)	(Pss 90–106)	(Pss 107–150)
Ps 41:14:	Ps 72:18-19:	Ps 89:53:	Ps 106:48:	Pss 146–150
Blessed be YHWH, *the God of Israel,*	Blessed be YHWH, *the God of Israel, who alone does wondrous things.* Blessed be his glorious name **forever;** *may his glory fill the whole earth.*	Blessed be YHWH	Blessed be YHWH, *the God of Israel,*	
from everlasting to everlasting.		forever.	from everlasting to everlasting. And let all the people say, "Amen."	
Amen and Amen.	Amen and Amen.	Amen and Amen.	*Praise* YHWH!	Ps 150:6: *Praise* YHWH!

Within the framework of the literary history of the Psalter, this concept may be seen as a transformation of the older monarchical perspectives in Psalms 2–89*: without a king of Israel's own, the traditional attributes and duties of the king are shifted to YHWH himself.[17] Probably the theocratic orientation was also derived from a preceding stage of redaction in which the "messianic Psalter" was theocratized, in a first stage, by the addition of Psalms 93–100.

The likely pre-Maccabean division of the Psalter into five parts, which already exhibit theocratic intent, received yet another new accentuation during the far-reaching upheavals of the Maccabean period. However, the literary interventions in the Psalter must have been relatively modest, as far as their extent is concerned. Even though there is no lack of older and newer attempts to date a significant number of psalms in the Maccabean or Hasmonean period (especially 74, 110, 149),[18] the fundamental problems of dating the Psalms remain, and skepticism toward such judgments seems required.

On the basis of its theological profile and its literary position in the Psalter, Psalm 149 is most likely to be located in the Maccabean period.[19]

> Let the faithful exult in glory; let them sing for joy on their couches. Let the high praises of God be in their throats and two-edged swords in their hands, to execute vengeance on the nations and punishment on the peoples, to bind their kings with fetters and their nobles with chains of iron, to execute on them the judgment decreed. This is glory for all his faithful ones. Praise YHWH! (Ps 149:5-9)

Psalm 149 in a sense again "re-eschatologizes" the theocratic finale of the Psalter and introduces the motif of the destruction of enemies before the closing echo of the Psalter in Psalm 150.

Whether we can see in Psalm 110 a literary legitimation of the Hasmonean claim to the high-priestly office is a matter of dispute.[20] Some scholars interpret the first letters of lines 2-5 (*š, m, ʻ, n*; "Šmʻon") as a concealed indication of the elevation of Simon to the office of high priest in 141 B.C.E. In any case, Psalm 110 could have been received in that sense in the Hasmonean period.

b. Sirach and the Wisdom of Solomon

The book of Sirach is a wisdom writing that may have been created around 180 B.C.E., as seen on the one hand from the prologue by the author's grandson, who translated the book into Greek, and on the other hand by the absence of any reflections on the Maccabean crisis.[21] Apart from a few suggestive glances, the book of Sirach is still uneschatological. But it does have some eschatological outlooks that, from a literary-critical point of view, may be secondary (Sirach 10; 36). These speak of the destruction of all foreign powers:

> Sovereignty passes from nation to nation on account of injustice and insolence and wealth. The Lord overthrows the thrones of rulers, and enthrones the lowly in their place. The Lord plucks up the roots of the nations, and plants the humble in their place. The Lord lays waste the lands of the nations, and destroys them to the foundations of the earth. He removes some of them and destroys them, and erases the memory of them from the earth. (Sir 10:8, 14-17)

Have mercy upon us, O God of all [= the universe], and put all the nations in fear of you. Lift up your hand against foreign nations and let them see your might. As you have used us to show your holiness to them, so use them to show your glory to us. Then they will know, as we have known, that there is no God but you, O Lord. (Sir 36:1-5)

The fundamental intent of the book of Sirach is to demonstrate that Jewish Torah devotion is superior to Hellenistic culture. The argumentative approach is not confrontational but integrative: the wisdom of the world, the plan of the world is to be learned by studying the Torah. The culminating statement of this position is found in Sir 24:1-8, 19-23, which identifies "wisdom" and "Torah":

Wisdom praises herself, and tells of her glory in the midst of her peo- ple. In the assembly of the Most High she opens her mouth, and in the presence of his hosts she tells of her glory: "I came forth from the mouth of the Most High, and covered the earth like a mist. I dwelt in the highest heavens, and my throne was in a pillar of cloud. Alone I compassed the vault of heaven and traversed the depths of the abyss. Over waves of the sea, over all the earth, and over every people and nation I have held sway. Among all these I sought a resting place; in whose territory should I abide? Then the Creator of all things gave me a command, and my Creator chose the place for my tent. He said, 'Make your dwelling in Jacob, and in Israel receive your inheritance.' Come to me, you who desire me, and eat your fill of my fruits. For the memory of me is sweeter than honey, and the possession of me sweeter than the honeycomb. Those who eat of me will hunger for more, and those who drink of me will thirst for more. Whoever obeys me will not be put to shame, and those who work with me will not sin." All this is the book of the covenant of the Most High God, the law that Moses commanded us as an inheritance for the congregations of Jacob.

In terms of the political theology of the book of Sirach in regard to Israel, it seems not to expect the return of a Davidic king, but it is not satisfied with the contemporary condition of foreign rule either. Instead, it apparently awaits a spirit-filled leadership for Israel like that under the judges in the pre-monarchical period. That seems to be the point, at any rate, of the striking passage in Sir 46:11-12 that promises the resurrection of the judges: "The judges also, with their respective names, whose hearts did not fall into idolatry and who did not turn away from the Lord—may their memory be blessed! May their bones send forth new life from where they lie, and may the names of those who have been honored live again in their children!"

The "Wisdom of Solomon," which, certainly, must have been created only toward the end of the first century B.C.E.,[22] has a similar interest to Sirach: defending the Jewish tradition against the offerings of pagan philosophy.

2. Prophetic Traditions

a. The Formation of the Nevi'im

The most important literary-historical development in the early Seleucid period was the combination of the Former Prophets (Joshua–2 Kings) with the Later Prophets (Isaiah–Malachi) to form the canonical section of Nevi'im, which simultaneously marks the end of prophecy. This left its mark in literary form in the *inclusio* between the first chapter (Joshua 1) and the last (Malachi 3):[23]

Malachi 3:22	Joshua 1:7-8, 13
	Only be strong and very courageous, being careful to act in accordance with all the law that **my servant Moses** commanded you; do not turn from it to the right hand or to the left, so that you may be successful wherever you go. This book of the <u>law</u> shall not depart out of your mouth; you shall meditate on it day and night, so that you may be careful to act in accordance with all that is written in it. For then you shall make your way prosperous, and then you shall be successful.
Remember <u>the law</u> of **my servant Moses**, the statutes and ordinances that I *commanded* him at Horeb for all Israel.	. . . *Remember* the word that **Moses the servant of** YHWH *commanded* you, saying, "YHWH your God is providing you a place of rest, and will give you this land."

The content of this *inclusio* is established by the memory of the Torah of Moses. Its thematic intent to establish the Torah as the normative part of the canon is quite evident (cf. Deut 34:10-12).

It is clear that the Nevi'im, as a collection, was closed at the beginning of the second century B.C.E., and in any event before the Maccabees, first of all from the observation that this textual corpus contains no clearly evident reflections on the Maccabean period. In the second place, the formation of the Nevi'im is already presumed by Sirach 44–50, and third, the observation that the Maccabean book of Daniel is classified among the Ketuvim, since it apparently could no longer find entry into the Nevi'im, is eloquent testimony to this dating.[24] We may suggest that the closing of the Nevi'im was motivated by the urging of Antiochus III that the Jews live according to their "ancestral laws," which posed the question of the textual definition of that tradition, a question that could be answered by "Moses and the prophets."

b. The Maccabean Book of Daniel

The book of Daniel, whose literary core consists of the theocratic legends in chapters 1–6* from the Persian period, was continued in the early Hellenistic period,[25] but its final and most profound reworking took place only in the Maccabean period. This is reflected primarily in redactions of the visions in Daniel 2 and 7 and in the addition of chapters 8–9, 10–12.[26] Since Daniel 8–12 is intimately familiar with current history up to the death of Antiochus IV, but his death is wrongly predicted in Dan 11:45 (Antiochus IV was supposed to die between the sea and Zion, but in fact he was killed while plundering a temple in the eastern part of the empire), we can locate the conclusion of the book of Daniel with great probability in the year 164 B.C.E.

The book of Daniel only became a properly prophetic book with its Maccabean-period expansions. It anticipates the fall of the current ruler and of all foreign powers and the deliverance of Israel in the near future; this will put an end to the time of judgment that has endured since the Babylonian era. The visions make it clear that the confused contemporary history of the world has long been modeled in heaven and can be discerned by the apocalyptic seer Daniel (with the aid of an interpreting angel).

The Maccabean interpretations can be easily recognized in Daniel 2 and 7 as expansions of an already existing text:

> After this I saw in the visions by night a fourth beast, terrifying and dreadful and exceedingly strong. It had great iron teeth and was devouring, breaking in pieces, and stamping what was left with its feet. It was different from all the beasts that preceded it, and it had ten horns. (Dan 7:7)

> *I was considering the horns, when another horn appeared, a little one coming up among them; to make room for it, three of the earlier horns were plucked up by the roots. There were eyes like human eyes in this horn, and a mouth speaking arrogantly.* (Dan 7:8)

In Daniel 8–12, by contrast, new blocks of text are introduced to depict the Maccabean religious crisis in similar terms to the announcements of judgment in Isaiah: what is happening in the Maccabean era is nothing but a further fulfillment of the prophecy of Isaiah. The other Old Testament writings also serve the book of Daniel as sources for historical knowledge. This is clearest in the great prediction of history in Daniel 9, where Daniel, placed in an exilic setting, asks how long Jerusalem will yet lie in ruins. He studies the passages in Scripture regarding the seventy years predicted by Jeremiah (Dan 9:2). Thus Daniel reads more than the book of Jeremiah. Then he formulates a prayer of penitence and finally receives an answer from the angel Gabriel: not seventy years, but seventy weeks of years, that is, 490 years, have been imposed as judgment on Jerusalem. But this is not simply a matter of an arbitrary extension of the time of judgment from seventy to 490 years; the lengthening is apparently derived exegetically from Lev 26:34-35 and 2 Chr 36:21, which explain that Israel's guilt will endure "until the land had made up for its sabbaths. All the days that it lay desolate it kept sabbath, to fulfill seventy years" (2 Chr 36:21). The sense of the biblical prediction of "seventy years," as explained by Gabriel, is that the seventy years to be made up for are *all and exclusively* sabbath years—not seventy regular years, which would restore only ten sabbath years. That is how Daniel 9 arrives at its extension of the time of judgment to 490 years, which in the historical scene as here projected would last precisely until the present time of the Maccabean-era author.

> Seventy weeks are decreed for your people and your holy city: to finish the transgression, to put an end to sin, and to atone for iniquity, to bring in everlasting righteousness, to seal both vision and prophet, and to anoint a most holy place.
>
> Know therefore and understand: from the time that the word went out to restore and rebuild Jerusalem until the time of an anointed prince, there shall be seven weeks (*539 B.C.E.: Cyrus, or 522 B.C.E.: Zerubbabel?*); and for sixty-two weeks it shall be built again with streets and moat, but in a troubled time. After the sixty-two weeks (*434 years*), an anointed one shall be cut off and shall have nothing (*175 B.C.E.: murder of the high priest Onias III?*), and the troops of the prince who is to come shall destroy the city and the sanctuary. Its end shall come with a flood, and to the end there shall be war. Desolations are decreed. He shall make a strong covenant with many for one week (*7 years*), and for half of the week (*3.5 years*) he shall make sacrifice and offering cease; and in their place shall be an abomination that desolates (*168 B.C.E.: desecration of the Temple at Jerusalem by Antiochus IV*), until the decreed end is poured out upon the desolator. (Dan 9:24-27)

The chronology presented in Daniel 9, which places the desecration of the Jerusalem temple at the midpoint of the last week of years before the expiration of the 490 years of judgment, shows how imminent the expectation of the Maccabean book of Daniel was: only three and a half years more would elapse until the 490 years were complete and salvation for Israel could arrive.

c. 1 Baruch

The deuterocanonical book of 1 Baruch may have been created around 164/163 B.C.E.[27] It projects its narrative back into the time of the catastrophe at Jerusalem under the Babylonians, preaching return to the law, which, like Sirach 24, it identifies with wisdom. However, the book of 1 Baruch presents no open attack on Hellenism. Instead, it argues for a higher value of the Torah in contrast to all pagan traditions. The assumed setting, as well as its theological profile, make it probable that it originated after the desecration of the temple by Antiochus IV.

3. Narrative Traditions

a. The Ages of the World in the Narrative Books
In Genesis–2 Kings there is an observable order of ages of the world that is essentially based on the genealogies in Genesis 5 and 11, the information on the length of the patriarchs' lives, the chronological bridging information in Gen 47:28; Exod 12:40-41; and 1 Kgs 6:1, as well as the chronological information in the books of Kings. These calculations of time vary, especially in Genesis 5 and 11 according to the different textual witnesses, but all these variants are dependent on particular intentions as to what should be said. According to the Masoretic account of time the exodus occurred in the year 2666, reckoned from creation. That represents two-thirds of four thousand years, which—if we take the information in 1 Kgs 6:1 to mean that Solomon's fourth year fell in 3146 *anno mundi*—apparently were fulfilled with the Maccabean reconsecration of the temple in 164 B.C.E.[28] Likewise, the correspondence of the 430-year existence of the first temple (from the fourth year of Solomon to Zedekiah) to the 430-year oppression of Israel in Egypt (Exod 12:40-41) seems to rest on chronological construction.

Thus it appears that as late as the Maccabean period the numbers in the Pentateuchal tradition were still being retouched in order to orient the ages of the world in the historical books in a somewhat "Danielic" direction, that is, within the meaning of the historical theology of Daniel 9: the rededication of the temple in 164 B.C.E. is a decisive threshold between epochs.

b. Maccabees, Tobit, Judith, Jubilees
The deuterocanonical books of Maccabees and the book of Judith were probably created in the second half of the second century B.C.E., the Hasmonean period. Tobit is somewhat more difficult to date, but it is certainly not pre-Hellenistic.[29]

The books of Maccabees were often regarded as documents of pro-Hasmonean court theology. However, it is clear that they convey a superior theocratic ideal that apparently presupposes the corruption of political power in the Maccabean movement and the usurpation of the high-priestly office and critiques them.[30]

The books of Judith and Tobit are comparable in that they describe existential threats from a foreign power in historicized form: in both cases Israel's antagonist is the Babylonian Nebuchadnezzar, represented as the king of Assyria, so that this figure seems to combine the Assyrians and the Babylonians. Thus, probably against the Daniel tradition, these books emphasize that godless foreign rulers had already appeared earlier in Israel's history and would probably reappear in future. They are not signs of a mythically shaped end-time, but are recurring elements in history. On the other hand, the book of Judith describes the resistance more in terms of the collective entity that is Israel, while Tobit concentrates on the individuals affected by events, in this case Tobit and Sarah.[31]

The book of Jubilees is often called "little Genesis," because it is essentially a retelling of Genesis 1 to Exodus 24 from the point of view of how the ancestors of Israel had been able to live without the law.[32] Jubilees resolves this problem by means of "heavenly tablets" shown to the patriarchs in Genesis, on the basis of which they were able to live in conformity to the law. This retelling is enclosed in a narrative frame in which an angel explains this to Moses on Sinai. The interest of Jubilees is clearly to make a statement that "Mosaicizes" the primeval and patriarchal history, which thus is incorporated into the Torah theology of the Moses narrative that begins with the exodus. Jubilees belongs to the genre of "rewritten Bible," which is represented within the Bible itself by the Chroniclers' historical work and is visible in other texts in Qumran.[33]

Part H

Becoming Scripture
and the Genesis of the Canon

The preceding presentation should already have made it clear that becoming Scripture and constructing a canon are not issues that—as the position of this section of the present book might suggest—belong exclusively to the conclusion of a literary history of the Old Testament. Rather, the Old Testament's literary history as a whole is determined by the process of scripturalization. Likewise, elementary stages of the "construction of the canon," such as the shaping of the Torah or the closing of the Nevi'im, are phenomena within the Old Testament itself.

If we can and must interpret the literary history of the Old Testament simultaneously in light of its becoming Scripture, this is connected with the fact that the Old Testament literature as it has been handed down now constitutes a cohesive whole that has undergone processes of "canonical" formation, including the redaction of the Pentateuch and the closing of the Nevi'im. But we should recall the fundamental problem that the writings of the Old Testament may be only a part of a perhaps more extensive literary corpus in ancient Israel. However, the associated processes of selection, which could be interpreted as a side effect of the scripturalization of the retained orthodox texts, can no longer be fully reconstructed, as the rejected texts only partially survived, for example in the canons of the Eastern churches.

I. Distinguishing "Scripture" from "Canon"

When reconstructing the Old Testament's process of scripturalization it is advisable to distinguish the concepts of "Scripture" and "canon."[1] The "canon" concept is in fact, from a historical point of view, an anachronism. As applied to the Bible it is attested only beginning in the fourth century C.E. In addition, the notion of a closed list of sacred writings whose textual limits are certain is a post-Old Testament phenomenon. As the biblical texts from Qumran show, in the first century B.C.E. and the first century C.E. the Old Testament was not yet fixed in writing, letter for letter.[2] The contents of the texts were indeed stable, but different scrolls still reveal repeated small deviations in the wording and spelling of the same biblical books.

1. Josephus and 4 Ezra 14

As a closed collection of writings, the Old Testament is first attested in witnesses from the late first century C.E., namely in Josephus and 4 Ezra 14. In an apologetic polemic, the Jewish historian Josephus characterizes the Old Testament tradition as follows:[3]

> For we have not an innumerable multitude of books among us, disagreeing from and contradicting one another [as the Greeks have], but only twenty-two books, which contain the records of all the past times [of Israel's history]; which are justly believed to be divine; and of them five belong to Moses, which contain his laws and the traditions of the origin of mankind till his death. This interval of time was little short of three thousand years; but as to the time from the death of Moses till the reign of Artaxerxes, king of Persia, who reigned after Xerxes, the prophets, who were after Moses, wrote down what was done in their times in thirteen books (Job, Joshua, Judges [+ Ruth], Samuel, Kings, Isaiah, Jeremiah [+ Lamentations], Ezekiel, the Twelve, Daniel, Chronicles, Ezra [+ Nehemiah], Esther). The remaining four books (Psalms, Proverbs, Qoheleth, Canticle) contain hymns to God, and precepts for the conduct of human life. It is true, our history hath been written since Artaxerxes very particularly, but hath not been esteemed of the like authority with the former by our forefathers, because there hath not been an exact succession of prophets since that time.[4]

Josephus is aware of a fixed number of biblical books (22), corresponding to the number of letters in the Hebrew alphabet and therefore indicating completeness and perfection. The categorization of the books is not entirely clear in his account; the lists included above in parentheses are only one possible interpretation among others. In addition, Josephus reveals a theory of prophetic authorship inasmuch as he connects the composition of the biblical books with an uninterrupted sequence of prophets from Moses to the time of Artaxerxes, under whom, according to the biblical witness, Ezra and Nehemiah appeared.

Likewise 4 Ezra, an apocalypse from the last decade of the first century C.E., proposes a canonical theory in its final chapter.[5] It describes the renewed composition of the biblical and other books after they had been burned in the destruction of Jerusalem. Ezra dictates them to a group of the learned, on the basis of divine inspiration:

> They sat forty days; they wrote during the daytime, and ate their bread at night. But as for me, I spoke in the daytime and was not silent at

night. So during the forty days, ninety-four books were written. And when the forty days were ended, the Most High spoke to me, saying, "Make public the twenty-four books that you wrote first, and let the worthy and the unworthy read them; but keep the seventy that were written last, in order to give them to the wise among your people. (4 Ezra 14:42-47)

The first twenty-four books are the Old Testament, accessible to all, while the seventy other books are to remain secret and apparently are the Old Testament "apocrypha," which include 4 Ezra itself. Here again the fixed number of Old Testament books (24) is clear; it differs from the number given by Josephus, but since this is not a theologically laden symbolic number like Josephus's twenty-two it probably represents an older tradition. Also evident is the motif of prophetic authorship of the biblical books, based on Ezra's dictation.

2. The Prologue to Sirach and "the Law and the Prophets"

It is nevertheless true that the comparatively solid ideas about an Old Testament "canon" in the first century C.E. (Josephus, 4 Ezra) contrast with some rather different concepts from the late Old Testament period. The Prologue to the Greek translation of the book of Sirach, written by the grandson of the book's author (ca. 132 B.C.E.), is of great significance for the history of the canon:

> Many great teachings have been given to us *through the Law and the Prophets* and the others [i.e., other writings] that followed them, and for these we should praise Israel for instruction and wisdom. . . . so my grandfather Jesus, who had devoted himself especially to the reading of *the Law and the Prophets* and the other books of our ancestors, and had acquired considerable proficiency in them, was himself also led to write something pertaining to instruction and wisdom, so that by becoming familiar also with his book those who love learning might make even greater progress in living *according to the law.* . . . Not only this book, but even *the Law itself, the Prophecies,* and the rest of the books differ not a little when read in the original. When I came to Egypt in the thirty-eighth year of the reign of Euergetes [132 B.C.E.] and stayed for some time, I found opportunity for no little instruction. It seemed highly necessary that I should myself devote some diligence and labor to the translation of this book. During that time I have applied my skill day and night to complete and publish the book for those living abroad who wished to gain learning and are disposed to live *according to the law.* (Sirach, Prologue)

Two elements of this testimony in particular should be emphasized. First, the introduction shows clearly that for the Prologue to Sirach the Old Testament consists essentially of two parts, the law and the prophets, but that besides these two parts there are also "other" books that—as the writer's grandfather's example shows—can be augmented further: "My grandfather Jesus . . . was himself also led to write something pertaining to instruction and wisdom." According to this prologue the textual material that belongs to the book is made up of "the law" and "the prophets," while the "other books" represent a category so open and so general that it can be further expanded.

But second, it is also evident that the "law" has an exalted authority among the biblical books, as the repeated and emphatic expressions about living according to the law show. As Chapman makes clear, however, "law" and "prophets" are always in close interaction.[6]

What the Sirach Prologue suggests (if we interpret the sequence of concepts "in the Law and the Prophets and the other [writings]" not in terms of the later three-part canon but in the text-immanent sense) can be confirmed by witnesses from Qumran and the New Testament. Around the turn of the age the Old Testament canon apparently consisted essentially of two parts, as the usage "Moses and the prophets" and similar phrases indicate:

1QS 1.1-3 [Rule of the Community]: in order to seek God [with all (one's) heart and with all (one's) soul; in order] to do what is good and just in his presence, as commanded by means of the hand of *Moses and his servants the prophets* . . .

1QS 8.15-16: This is the study of the law which he commanded through the hand of *Moses*, in order to act in compliance with all that has been revealed from age to age, and according to what *the prophets* have revealed through his holy spirit.

CD 5.21–6.2: And the land became desolate, for they spoke of rebellion against God's precepts through the hand of *Moses* and also of the *holy anointed ones*. They prophesied deceit in order to divert Israel from following God.

4QDibHam (4Q504) frag. 2.3.11-13: For [the curses of your covenant] have clung to us . . . which *Moses* wrote and your servants *the prophets* whom you sent.[7]

Luke 16:16: The *law and the prophets* were in effect until John came; since then the good news of the kingdom of God is proclaimed, and everyone tries to enter it by force.

Luke 16:29: Abraham replied, "They have *Moses and the prophets*; they should listen to them."

Luke 16:31: He said to him, "If they do not listen to *Moses and the prophets*, neither will they be convinced even if someone rises from the dead."

Luke 24:27: Then beginning with *Moses and all the prophets*, he inter-preted to them the things about himself in all the scriptures.

Acts 26:22: To this day I have had help from God, and so I stand here, testifying to both small and great, saying nothing but what *the prophets and Moses* said would take place.

Acts 28:23: After they had set a day to meet with him, they came to him at his lodgings in great numbers. From morning until evening he explained the matter to them, testifying to the kingdom of God and trying to convince them about Jesus both from the law of *Moses and from the prophets.*

Individual instances mention the Psalms explicitly alongside Moses and the prophets:

4QMMT*d* (4Q397): . . . that you must understand *the book of Moses [and the words of the] prophets and of David['s psalms].*

Luke 24:44: Then he said to them, "These are my words that I spoke to you while I was still with you—that everything written about me in *the law of Moses, the prophets, and the psalms* must be fulfilled."

But based on the note in the Psalms scroll, 11QPs[a] 27.11,[8] which interprets the Psalms as "prophecy" by David, one may suppose that in 4QMMT and Luke 24:22 the Psalms are not added alongside the prophets, but are simply empha-sized as one part thereof.

11QPs*a* 27.11: He [i.e., David] composed them all through the spirit of *prophecy* which had been given to him from before the Most High.

It appears that even in New Testament times the Old Testament was still perceived primarily as a two-part body of writing.[9] The three-part arrangement we know is not yet clearly evident, but we can perceive the unity of the books of the Old Testament as "law and prophets," which were regarded as "Scripture."

II. The Scripturalization of the Old Testament Literature within the Framework of Its History

1. The Biblical Presentation

As with nearly every topic in Old Testament scholarship, in regard to the ques-tion of scripturalization one must distinguish between a biblical and a histori-cal view of the matter.[10] The reason for the distinction is above all that the Old

Testament does not reason in historical-critical, but in resultative-historical terms. That is, it sees historical processes, as a rule, as simultaneous with their contemporary effects. In the Old Testament, interest in the past is structured in terms of function and myth; its narratives essentially attempt to deal with existential questions as questions of origin.

The same is true for the Old Testament's self-presentation as sacred Scripture. In the Bible, sacred Scripture is not pre-existent or something given at creation, but it does appear relatively early within the course of the narrative: it comes into being step by step from the book of Exodus onward (cf. Exod 17:14; 24:4; 34:27-28; Num 33:2; Deut 31:9). Hence the Old Testament is aware of the fact that Israel did not have a scripturally based religion from the beginning. The law was first given and written down under Moses; the patriarchs in Genesis were unaware of a law. However, as the Old Testament depicts it, the law of Moses was quickly forgotten and reappeared only during the reign of Josiah, in the course of renovations to the temple (2 Kings 22–23). As a result of the catastrophe that befell Judah and Jerusalem, it was again forgotten and was only reintroduced in Judah under Ezra. In short, one could say that Moses provided Israel with the Jewish scriptural religion, but it only came into effect under Ezra.[11]

2. Religious Texts, Normative Texts, Sacred Scripture, and Canon

This, in the most condensed form, is the Old Testament view of the matter. Historical reconstructions by Old Testament scholars are considerably different. They show that the religion of ancient Israel only developed into a "scriptural religion" or "religion of the book"—if we can for a moment make use of this category, which is so heavily burdened by the vicissitudes of the history of scholarship—little by little.[12]

The function of texts differed greatly in the course of the history of ancient Israel's religion. Ideally we would be able to distinguish between religious texts, normative texts, sacred Scripture, and a proper canon.[13] It does seem that these various functions of texts developed in succession, but on the other hand they certainly existed simultaneously alongside one another as well.

> There is a certain pressure toward a canon inherent in this development in that the texts of what became the Bible were probably used, without exception, in the curriculum for scribal education and were kept in the library of the Jerusalem temple. These two elements do not explain the existence of the canon, but they constitute influential factors: both the use of a text in the curriculum and its acceptance into a temple library reveal its dignity and simultaneously increase it.[14]

A religious text is understood to be one that is a regular element of the cult and is subordinated to it. An Old Testament example can be found in Ps 24:7-10.

This psalm still clearly reveals its rootedness in worship. Apparently it describes a procession—the entry of God into his sanctuary—accompanied by a cultic antiphonal song. Psalm 24's original function was within cultic religion and is fitted for its place there—basically, it is comparable to a cultic vessel.

A normative text adopts a critical and authoritative attitude with respect to the cult. This is where we may see the first crucial beginnings of transformation to a scriptural religion.[15] One Old Testament example of a normative text would be Deuteronomy, in the reception of the legend of the discovery of the book in 2 Kings 22–23. During renovations of the temple a book is found, and the high priest Hilkiah has it conveyed to King Josiah by the scribe Shaphan (2 Kgs 22:8-13). It is unimportant at this point whether the narrative reflects historical events or not.[16] What is crucial is that it accords the book thus discovered—in the perspective of the narrative this is a reference to Deuteronomy—a normative value. According to the narrative sequence in 2 Kings 22–23, this book brings about Josiah's cultic reform and determines its nature. The discovery legend indicates that this book claims for itself an extraordinary origin.[17] Its age, its authorship, and its source are thus concealed—entirely, of course, in the interest of sacralizing it so that it will have the authority necessary to make it superior to and authoritative for the cult.

The basic text of the Deuteronomy that is meant by the book discovered in the temple probably belongs to the seventh century B.C.E.[18] The legend of the discovery in 2 Kings 22–23, which of course reckons with a Mosaic origin of the book, is from a historical perspective scarcely anything more than a legitimation of a contemporary text as an authoritative document. However, in the seventh century B.C.E. one cannot yet speak of a "scriptural religion" in ancient Israel; at most there were the beginnings of such a religion. Deuteronomy is a document intended not to replace the cult but to reform it, namely by monopolizing and centralizing it. Nevertheless, this is the first time an institution, namely the centralized cult, is authorized by a text; previously texts were authorized by institutions.[19] All the same, Israel remained essentially a "cultic religion" and by no means mutated at that point into a "scriptural religion."[20]

The same is largely true for the whole period of the Second Temple (that is, from 515 B.C.E. to 70 C.E.). Though this is rightly seen as the period of the essential formation of the biblical books, it was also the most important epoch in Israel's history for the sacrificial cult: the daily sacrifices were the heart and center of religious actions. It is difficult to say what function was exercised by the writings of the Old Testament that then existed but were still in a state of literary development. If we consider the surrounding literary-sociological conditions, which can be reconstructed to some degree, we must probably conclude that the Old Testament writings were mainly read by those who wrote them, and it is likely that well into the Hellenistic period scarcely any of them circulated in more than one exemplar. Thus the Old Testament writings probably served in biblical times to legitimate those groups within the Jerusalem temple responsible for the production and care of the scriptures themselves. However, it would be inappropriate to conclude that these groups were homogeneous simply because they were all located in one geographical location. Against it is the internal diversity of the Bible, which is in large part owing to that same milieu.[21]

The concept of sacred Scripture is found in the Old Testament in only a few, relatively late passages. That, for example, the Torah itself can and should enjoy a form of cultic veneration is clear in Neh 8:5-8, a text whose conception, because of its affinity to synagogal worship, can scarcely be dated earlier than the third or second century B.C.E.:[22]

> And Ezra opened the book in the sight of all the people, for he was standing above all the people; and when he opened it, all the people stood up. Then Ezra blessed YHWH, the great God, and all the people answered, "Amen, Amen," lifting up their hands. Then they bowed their heads and worshiped YHWH with their faces to the ground. Also Jeshua, Bani, Sherebiah, Jamin, Akkub, Shabbethai, Hodiah, Maaseiah, Kelita, Azariah, Jozabad, Hanan, Pelaiah, the Levites, helped the people to understand the law, while the people remained in their places. So they read from the book, from the law of God, with interpretation. They gave the sense, so that the people understood the reading.

Only when Jerusalem was destroyed by the Romans in 70 C.E. did the daily sacrificial worship come to an abrupt and violent end, and only after 70 C.E. can we say that Judaism, now fundamentally shaped by the Pharisaic-Rabbinic approach, had been transformed into a scriptural religion. This process was readied by quite divergent elements such as the Maccabean crisis, the rise of the synagogue, the stylization of the Psalter as a literary sanctuary,[23] and other events, but it was only after 70 C.E. that the study of Scripture, at least in a functional sense, took the place of the temple cult: where one learns Torah, one needs no temple.[24]

It is only from this period on that one should speak of an Old Testament canon.[25] Before 70 C.E. there was an ensemble of authoritative writings known collectively as "the law and the prophets" or "Moses and the prophets,"[26] but there was no canon in the sense of a closed list of normative writings, set in their textual form and organized into three sections: Torah, Nevi'im, Kethubim (law, prophets, writings). Probably we should also hold in mind certain group-specific distinctions.[27]

The rise of scriptural religion is thus—from a historical point of view— a process that accompanied the whole course of the literary development of the Old Testament writings and only manifested itself completely in the construction of a canon after that literary development was fully completed. This processual emergence of scriptural religion is, to some extent, inverse to the comparably processual disappearance of traditional "cult religious" elements that the emerging scripture gradually absorbed and integrated.[28]

Both processes were doubly catalyzed by the two destructions of the temple, in 587 B.C.E. and 70 C.E.[29] The first of these aided the breakthrough of written prophecy by serving as its historical validation; the second led—beginning with the Psalter—to the construction of what became the third section of the canon, the "Writings," as the post-cultic hermeneutical complement to the law and the prophets.[30] It is possible that the "Writings" also served to establish a literary Jewish counter-canon over against Hellenistic-Roman culture.[31]

3. Literary and Canonical History of the Old Testament

So how do the literary and canonical histories of the Old Testament relate to one another? They are intimately connected[32] but not identical, as is evident even from the fact that the concluding of the Old Testament literature and the post-Old Testament closing of its canon are two historical processes finishing at different times. The canonical history interrogates the literary history, so to speak, regarding the elements of normativity and theologization, as well as the "thinking-together"[33] of their object, the Old Testament literature. Hence the literary history of the Old Testament should be reformulated from this perspective and augmented by its post-Old Testament canonical closing. We will not attempt to carry out this project again here from this particular angle,[34] but some remarks may serve to make the question of a canonical history of the Old Testament somewhat more concrete.

The special affinity of literary and canonical history in the case of the Old Testament has its internal grounding in the fact that the Old Testament literature, in its unique character as the religious and theological—or at least religiously and theologically *applied*—heritage of ancient Israel, maintains an internal discursive cohesion.[35] It is true that the Old Testament is a library, but it is also an entity that can be concisely characterized, and not only after the fact as a canonical unity, but also because of the coherence based in its inner-biblical exegesis.

The process of inner-biblical exegesis in the Old Testament has, in turn, certain implications. Its justification rests on the idea that religious or theological statements about God, as found in the Old Testament literature, can and must be brought into dialogue with one another. God—in the mirror of experiences with God—is constructed as a self-identical being. This happens (in light of the post-Old Testament history one must say is *still* happening) not in the sense of a philosophical principle, but instead according to the standard of ancient Near Eastern conceptions of kings. God is the sovereign who may appear as merciful or severe, just or arbitrary, but is described as the decisive power. Experiences with him are set in discursive relationship within the Old Testament to produce a complex image of possible and actual ways in which God works.

Of course, this basic idea of the inner-biblical discursivity of the Old Testament must be historically refined. Old Testament literary history clearly reveals that in nearly every realm of tradition there were at first somewhat disparate literary units that were neither originally linked together nor correlated with each other in terms of content. In Genesis we can reconstruct independent narratives and narrative complexes going back to time immemorial. The textual bases of Leviticus are ritual prescriptions that were not originally constructed for the literary context in which they now stand. In Joshua, Judges, Samuel, and Kings we find traditions that may originally have been independent. In the prophetic books the core of the tradition may not be "small units" (from a literary point of view), but in many cases they go back to collections that in the first instance have more to do with the prophet who gave his name to the book than with the broader Old Testament literature. The Psalms contain hymns and prayers that also had a certain degree of independence before they were inserted into the literary context of the Psalter. And the wisdom literature also goes back to older collections whose arrangement may have been endogenously motivated.

But when did the process of "thinking the canon together" begin? We can see from the Old Testament tradition that it must have been very early, even though at the outset the literary horizons were still narrow. This can perhaps be seen most clearly from the prophetic books: Amos, in its very earliest literary beginnings, was already adjusted to the book of Hosea,[36] while the book of Isaiah was from the outset influenced significantly by the Amos tradition.[37] It is possible that the prophetic tradition in particular conveyed in itself the claim that the word of God proclaimed by the prophets should not be understood as fragmented individual messages, but as a many-faceted and differentiated yet coherent whole.

That something similar can be seen even in the narrative tradition, especially the patriarchal narratives in Genesis, should not astonish us in light of the most important compositional elements of the promises:[38] these, too, are shaped as divine statements and hence directed toward an internal consistency. We may also see a special incentive in the conception of the law as divine ordinance in the redactions of the Book of the Covenant and Deuteronomy: the idea of a divine legislator and a body of law stemming directly from God—despite all the descriptive orientation of the law—contained in itself the idea of a codified will of God, which in turn developed, especially with the formation of the Torah, into a substantively determinative and normative crowning piece of the Old Testament tradition. For the initial stages of the shaping of particular legal doctrines in the Book of the Covenant, inspired by the social critique found in the prophetic tradition, it is noteworthy that at this point we can see, even in a comparatively early era in the literary history, a perspective encompassing several spheres of tradition. The divine law in the Book of the Covenant is rooted in the prophetic proclamation of the will of God. Deuteronomy, with its exaltation of God to the functional equivalent of the Assyrian great king and the associated claims to Israel's loyalty—couched in terms of a subversively applied "loyalty oath"—can certainly be regarded as the essential core of *normative literature as such* in the Old Testament.[39] This is confirmed, in its own way, by the discovery of "Deuteronomistically" revised books in the Old Testament in which we can see how a normative text like Deuteronomy was able to influence narrative tradition. This model is then in a sense repeated in the later influence of the Torah on the remaining parts of the Old Testament.

It should be noted, of course, that the priority of the Torah, perceivable above all in the history of its influence on the tradition outside the Torah itself, especially the prophets, is not as such a consistent "given" within the Old Testament.[40] Texts like Jer 30:18 or Isa 56:1-9 can be applied with prophetic authority against statements of the Torah such as Deut 13:17 or Deuteronomy 23, and can "abrogate" them. Apparently the authority of what later became the canonical sections of Torah and prophets was still seen as dynamic, and their scribal "thinking-together" was not a process that ran in only one direction.

The element of the unchangeableness of the letter, central for post-Old Testament canonical history, still played a very subordinate role within the Old Testament itself. The intellectual presupposition behind this idea is the prophetic inspiration of the biblical authors, as Josephus and Philo formulate it. By this means the biblical literature was excluded from the realm of the historical world into which it had to be reintroduced by the rise of historical criticism in the seventeenth and eighteenth centuries c.e.

Notes

Preface

1. Schmid 2007c.
2. Schmid 2004a.
3. Schmid 2004b.
4. Schmid 2006g.

Part A. Purpose, History, and Problems of a Literary History of the Old Testament

1. Köpf 2002.
2. Wellek and Warren 1949/1971, 276, emphasis added.
3. Wellek 1979.
4. Perkins 1992, 17.
5. Cf. Utzschneider 2002.
6. Cf. Jeremias 1996, 20–33; Steck 1996; 2001.
7. Steck 1992b; 1996; Blenkinsopp 2002.
8. Mohr 1988.
9. Cf. Schluchter 2006.
10. Cf. Blum 1995.
11. *TUAT* 2:138–48; cf. van der Toorn 2007, 176.
12. Contra Kratz 1997b; 2003b; 2003c.
13. Cf. Schmid 2007c.
14. Simon 1685; Lowth 1753; Herder 1782/83.
15. Hupfeld 1844, 12–13; cf. Kaiser 2005.
16. Meier 1856.
17. Ibid., vi.
18. Ibid., 24.
19. Fürst 1867–70.
20. Cassel 1872–73.
21. Wellhausen 1883; 6th ed. 1927; idem 1904.
22. Reuss 1881; on this cf. Vincent 1990.
23. Ibid., 21.
24. Ibid., xiii–xv.
25. Wildeboer 1893.
26. Ibid., 1; cf. 105.
27. Kautzsch 1897, iii.
28. Ibid., v–vi.
29. Gunkel 1906a; 1906b; cf. Klatt 1969, 166–92; Liwak 2004, ix–xxxi; Witte 2010; Schmid 2011c.

30. Gunkel 1913, 31. Cf. Blum 2006, 85.
31. Gunkel 1906b; 1963, 5.
32. Ibid., 26.
33. Ibid., 43.
34. Cf. Bertholet 1907.
35. Budde 1906.
36. Bewer 1922.
37. Hempel 1930.
38. Ibid., 11.
39. Lods 1950.
40. Ibid., 11.
41. Ibid.
42. Ibid., 13.
43. Ibid., 14.
44. Ibid., 305–23.
45. Koch 1964, 114.
46. Ebeling 1972, 26–27.
47. Jauss ^{2}1970, 144.
48. Staiger 1955.
49. Cf. Anderson ^{5}2006; Soggin 1968–69; Schmidt 1979.
50. Von Rad 1957–1960.
51. Keller 1958; cf. von Rad 1957, 7.
52. Weippert 1993, 73.
53. Gottwald 1985.
54. Fohrer 1989, 307 n. 2.
55. Kaiser 1991.
56. Ibid., 306.
57. Kaiser 2000b; cf. also Ruppert 1994, and Vriezen and van der Woude 2005.
58. Lemche 1996; Fritz 1996b; Dietrich 1997; Schoors 1998; Albertz 2001; Gerstenberger 2005; Haag 2003. For English translations, see Dietrich 1997 [ET = 2007].
59. Lemche 1996, 220.
60. Ibid., 217.
61. Schoors 176–77.
62. Dietrich 1997, 228.
63. Levin 2000.
64. Cf. Schmid 2011c. For recent comparable studies of the New Testament one may mention Koester 1971; 1980 (oddly enough appearing under the title "Introduction"); Vielhauer 1975; Strecker 1992; and Theissen 2007.
65. Cf. Weber 1907; Hallo 1975; Röllig 1978; Edzard, Röllig, and von Schuler 1987–1990; Knauf 1994, 221–25; Loprieno 1996; Burkard and Thissen 2003; Veldhuis 2003, 10; Quack 2005; Haas 2006, 16–17; Utzschneider 2006; Ehrlich 2011.
66. Rogerson 2001.
67. Schmid 1999a; 2011a, 269–84.
68. Von Rad 1957, 126.
69. Cf. Stolz 1997, 586.
70. Renz and Röllig 1995–2003; Smelik 1987.
71. *TUAT* 2:138–48.
72. *TUAT* 1:646–50; Knauf 1994, 129; cf. Dearman 1989.
73. *TUAT* 2/4: 555–56; Knauf 2001c.
74. Thompson and Zayadine 1974; Coote 1980; Knauf 1994, 127.
75. Schmid 1996a, 36 n. 164.
76. Keel 2007, 139–40.

77. Cf. Christensen 1998; Haran 1999; Vriezen and van der Woude 2005, 3–8; Na'aman 2006.

78. Keel 2007, 139.

79. Kratz 1997b; 2003b.

80. Jeremias 1994; Steck 1996.

81. *TUAT* 2:56–82.

82. Cf. Stolz 1997, 586.

83. Keel 2007, 783–84.

84. Tilly 2005.

85. For the various manuscripts cf. Swete ²1914, 201–14; Beckwith 1985; Brandt 2001; McDonald and Sanders 2002, 588; McDonald ³2007, 422, 451.

86. For the terminology see Gertz 2006a, 32.

87. Dahmen et al. 2000; Flint 2001; Fabry 2006; Tov 2006.

88. Blum 1991, 46.

89. Van der Woude 1992.

90. Tov 1992.

91. Van der Woude 1992, 161.

92. Van der Woude 1992, 63 n. 33.

93. Tov 1992; Stipp 1994; de Troyer 2005; Schenker 2006.

94. For the history of Israel see, e.g., Donner ³2000; Kinet 2001; for introduction see Zenger ⁵2004; Gertz 2006a; for theology see Kaiser 1993/1998/2003; Schreiner 1995; Rendtorff 1999/2001.

95. Eissfeldt 1926/1962, 112–13.

96. Albertz 1992.

97. Cf. the discussion in *JBT* 10 [1995] as well as Hermisson 2000.

98. Cf. Weippert 1988; Mazar 1992; Keel and Uehlinger ⁵2001; Zevit 2001; Stern 2001; Hartenstein 2003a; Vieweger 2003; Keel 2007.

99. Gertz 2006a.

100. Weippert 1990/1997, 1–24.

101. Von Rad 1957/1960.

102. Cf. Keller 1958, 308.

103. Cf. Smend 1982/1986; Gerstenberger 2001; Kratz 2002; for the history of scholarship cf. Schmid 2000b; for theologies outside Israel cf. Oeming et al. 2004.

104. Cf. Carr 2011. On the question of female authors cf. Schroer 2003.

105. Tigay 1985; Blenkinsopp 2006, 1-4; van der Toorn 2007; Schmid 2011a.

106. Cf. also Qoh 12:9-11; see Kaiser 2000b, 13–14; Höffken 1985.

107. Cf. Schniedewind 2004, 7–11; Wyrick 2004; Schmid 2007a; van der Toorn 2007, 27–49.

108. Cf. Knauf 1998.

109. Cf. Kirkpatrick 1988; Niditch 1996.

110. Finkelstein and Silberman 2002; and Schniedewind 2004.

111. Cf., e.g., Levin 2001; Gertz 2006a; Carr 2011.

112. Jamieson-Drake 1991; Niemann 1998.

113. Cf. Flint 2001.

114. Cf. Steck ¹⁴1999; Becker 2005b.

115. Though the oldest manuscripts of Daniel, 4QDan^{c,e}, are only half a century later than the conclusion of the book, and thus are fairly close to the first autographs; cf. Ulrich 2000, 171.

116. Cf. Carr 1996b; Van Seters 1999, 20–57.

117. Tigay 1985; Metso 1997.

118. Knauf 2005a.

119. Cf. Steck ¹⁴1999; Becker 2005b.

120. Weippert 1988; Mazar 1992; Keel and Uehlinger ⁵2001; Zevit 2001; Stern 2001; Hartenstein 2003a; Vieweger 2003; Köckert 2005; for discussion cf. Uehlinger 1995, 59–60; Schaper 2000, 18–22; Uehlinger 2001; Keel 2007, 152–53.

121. Renz and Röllig 1995–2003.

122. Gertz 2006a.

123. Cf. Lemche 2001; Diebner 1992/1993, and various earlier works.

124. Cf. Brettler 1999.

125. Cf. Dozeman, Schmid, and Schwartz 2011. Baden 2009 defends the traditional approach of the documentary hypothesis.

126. Blum 1984; 1990.

127. According to Blum in the framework of a "Deuteronomistic" and a "Priestly" layer of composition, a position followed, e.g., by Albertz 1992.

128. Cf. Gertz et al. 2002; Dozeman and Schmid 2006.

129. Gertz 2000a.

130. Niehr 1997; Uehlinger 1998b; 1998c; cf. Keel 2007, 305–6, 300, 478–82, who does not suggest an anthropomorphic cultic image of Yhwh but does propose an image of the Asherah in the first temple.

131. Cf. Schmid 2000a.

132. Cf. Kratz 2000a, 318.

133. Cf. Schmid 1996b; Steck 1996; Kratz 2003b; 2010; Becker 2004.

134. Von Rad 1957/1960.

135. Cf. Hertzberg 1936; Gelin 1959.

136. Marxsen 1956.

137. Zimmerli 1969.

138. E.g., Isaiah 56–66 (Steck 1991); Jeremiah 30–33 (Schmid 1996a; differently for Jeremiah 30–31, Stipp 2011a).

139. Cf. Wilson 1985; Hossfeld and Zenger 1993; 2000; Millard 1994; Zenger 1998; 2010; Hartenstein 2003b; 2010; Leuenberger 2004.

140. Cf., e.g., Krüger 1995; 1997; Scoralick 1995.

141. Gertz et al. 2002; Dozeman and Schmid 2006.

142. Weippert 1990/1997.

143. Levinson 2008; Schmid 2011a.

144. Cf. Knauf 1990; 2006; Young 1993; 2003; Saénz Badillos 1993; Emerton 2000; Hurvitz 2000; Schwartz 2005; Young/Rezetko 2008.

145. Young 2003, 277.

146. Kottsieper 2007.

147. Hurvitz 2000.

148. Knauf 2006, 338–39.

149. Joosten 1999.

150. Cf. Porten 1996.

151. Cf. Stegemann ⁹1999; Tov 2004; Ulrich 2010.

152. Welten 1981; Schmid 1996a, 35–43; Schmid 2006a.

153. Tov 2004, 74–79; Schmid 2006a.

154. Steck 1998; Korpel and Oesch 2000.

155. Niditch 1996; Ben Zvi 1997; Young 1998; 2005; Niemann 1998; van der Toorn 2007, 10–11; for the late period cf. Alexander 2003; Hezser 2001; for the question of media Frevel 2005.

156. Baines 1983; Haran 1988; Harris 1989; differently Lemaire 2001; Millard 1985; 1995; Hess 2002; 2006.

157. Wellhausen 1880/1965, 40.

158. Jamieson-Drake 1991.

159. Niemann 1998; cf. Lemaire 2004.

160. Cf. www.zeitah.net.

161. Schniedewind 2004, 167–72.

162. Cf. Lemaire 2002; 2007.

163. Wellhausen 1880/1965, 40.

164. Cf. *TUAT* 1:367–409.

165. *TUAT* 1:646–50.

166. *TUAT* 2:138–48.

167. Cf. Lohfink 1995; van der Toorn 2007, 146–47.

168. Van der Toorn 2007, 237–42; Lange 2007; cf. also Stemberger 1996.

169. Van der Toorn 2007, 16–20.

170. Klijn 1977; Beckwith 1988, 40–45; Sarna 1989; Schmid 1996a, 40–41 and n. 204; ben Zvi 1997; van der Kooij 1998.

171. Van der Toorn 2007, 237–40; Lange 2007.

172. Pedersén 1998; Michalowski 2003; Lange 2006; van der Toorn 2007, 240.

173. Wessetzky 1984.

174. Van der Toorn 2007, 241–42.

175. Schmid 2004a.

176. Avigad 1976; Keel 1995; many of the seal impressions assembled by Avigad are, however, fakes: cf. van der Toorn 2007, 84; for the problem as a whole cf. Uehlinger 2007a.

177. Van der Toorn 2007, 78–82.

178. Klostermann 1908; cf. Lemaire 1981; Delkurt 1991, 43–48; Jamieson-Drake 1991; Heaton 1994; Davies 1995; Schams 1998; Knauf 2004.

179. Knauf, 1994, 225–37; Volk 2000; Gesche 2001; Vegge 2006.

180. Van der Toorn 2007, 82–89.

181. *Y. Meg.* 73b; cf. van der Toorn 2007, 24.

182. Van der Toorn 2007, 89.

183. Duhm 1901, xviii–xix.

184. Donner 1980/1994.

185. Kratz 1997a.

186. Van Seters 2006, 398.

187. Ska 2005.

188. Cf. Schmid 2007f.

189. Jeremias 1988.

190. Steck 1985.

191. Schmid 1999c, 111.

192. Van der Toorn 2007, 14, 179.

193. Schmid 2011a.

194. Knox 1968.

195. Cf. Carr 2005; 2006; 2011; B. Schipper 2005.

196. Van der Toorn 2007, 194.

197. *TUAT* 1:621; cf. van der Toorn 2007, 12.

198. Wagner 1996; Blum 2006; Theissen 2007.

199. Pilhofer 1990.

200. Gertz 2006a, 337.

201. Kratz 1996.

202. Blum 1984.

203. Otto 1996d; 1999a.

204. *TUAT* 3/1:110–35.

205. *TUAT* 3/1:143–57.

206. Wettengel 2003.

207. Cf. Schmid 1996a.

208. Von Bormann 1983; Gumbrecht and Link-Heer 1985.

209. Japhet 2003.

210. Younger 2002; Weisberg 2002; cf. also Goldstein 2002; and Smith 1952.

211. Donner ³2000/2001; cf. Kuhrt 1994.

212. Münkler 2005, 87–88.

213. Rothenbusch 2000, 481–86; van der Toorn 2000; Horowitz et al. 2002; for ancient transportation and dissemination of information see Kolb 2000.

214. Cf. Sandmel 1962; Machinist 1991; Gordon 2005.
215. Steymans 1995a; 1995b; Otto 1996d; 1999a; cf. in a more detailed analysis Koch 2008.
216. Otto 2000b.
217. Cf. Van Seters 2003, which lacks the necessary diachronic differentiation; Levinson 2004.
218. Finkelstein and Silberman 2006.
219. Hurowitz 1992.
220. Blanco Wissmann 2008.
221. For the western reception of Iranian religion see Colpe 2003.
222. Koch 1991; Kratz 1991b.
223. Baumann 1996, 26–27.
224. Schwienhorst-Schönberger 1994 (^{2}1996); 2004; cf. Uehlinger 1997; Krüger 1999.
225. Cf. Johanning 1988; Lehmann 1994.
226. Cf. Oswald 2009.
227. Cf. Steck 1978/1982.
228. Cf. Albertz 1992; Kessler 2006.
229. Cf. also Japp 1980.
230. Cf. Applegate 1997; Rigger 1997; Redditt 2000.
231. On this cf. Fishbane 1985; Veijola 2000; Kratz et al. 2000b; Menn 2003; Schmid 2011a.
232. Cf. Fishbane 1985; O'Day 1999; Schmid 2000b; Tull 2000.
233. Krüger 2006; cf. also Schmid 2007f.
234. Dever 2001; on this problem cf. also Keel 2007, 153–54.

Part B. The Beginnings of Ancient Israel's Literature among the Syro-Palestinian City-States before the Advent of the Assyrians (Tenth–Eighth Centuries B.C.E.)

1. Keel 1993, 449–51, 457–60.
2. Weinstein 1981; Keel and Uehlinger ^{5}2001, 92–109.
3. Helck ^{2}1971, 224–46; Görg 1997, 70–71; Schipper 2003.
4. Münger 2003.
5. Fritz 1996a; Ehrlich 1996.
6. McKenzie 2003; Finkelstein and Silberman 2006; Dietrich 2006.
7. Keel 2007, 155
8. Cf. Knauf 1994, 121–25; Niemann 1998; Gertz 2004; Finkelstein and Silberman 2006; Kessler 2006, 80–81.
9. Holloway 1997.
10. Gertz 2004; Fischer 2005; Finkelstein and Silberman 2006.
11. *TUAT* supplementary volume, 176–78; Athas 2003; Keel 2007, 165–67.
12. Cf. Niemann 1993; Steiner 1998a; 1998b; Knauf 2000b; Finkelstein and Silberman 2002, 140–63; 2006; differently, e.g., Avishur and Heltzer 2000; there is an extensive discussion in Vaughn and Killebrew 2003; Keel 2007; Huber 2010.
13. Finkelstein 1996; Knauf 2000e.
14. Cf. in general Kleer 1996; cf. for Qohelet Reinert 2010.
15. Keel 2007, 236.
16. *TUAT* 1: 512–20.
17. Cf. Jamieson-Drake 1991; Niemann 1998; Finkelstein and Silberman 2006.
18. Veenhof 2001, 212–15; Stern 2001, 236–94.
19. Since Jamieson-Drake 1991.

20. Keel 2007, 155, 157; Keel himself describes Solomon's political establishment as "a kind of provincial copy of the Egyptian state" (336).

21. Kratz 2006c, 468: "From Prophets of Salvation to Prophets of Disaster"; 471: "From Secular Nation to the People of God"; 477: "From Divine Kingship to the Kingdom of God"; 474: "From Secular Law to Divine Law"; 479: "From Wise to Pious."

22. Hartenstein 1997; Schmid 2006c.

23. Cf. Brettler 1999.

24. Schmid 1968; Keel [4]1984; Assmann 1990a; Maul 1998.

25. Stola 1983b; 1988, 234–36.

26. Keel [4]1984; Bauks 2001.

27. *TUAT* 2: 556–57; 561–64.

28. Schmid 2003.

29. Stolz 1997, 587.

30. Broshi and Finkelstein 1992.

31. For the question of Samaria as capital or residence cf. Niemann 2005; for the archaeology see Tappy 1992/2001; Mazar 1992, 406–9.

32. But cf. Knauf 2006, 293–94.

33. Knauf 2004b; 2006; cf. the different explanation by Pakkala 2008.

34. Goulder 1982; Jeremias 1987.

35. Cf. *TUAT* 1:382; Uehlinger 1998; Becking 2001; Timm 2002.

36. Köckert 2006a.

37. Niemann 1993, 206ff..

38. Seybold 1986.

39. Cf. Stolz 1983a.

40. Zenger 1998; 1999; 2010.

41. Duhm [2]1922, xxvii.

42. Engnell 1943/[2]1967, 176 n. 2; Duhm [2]1922, xx–xxi .

43. Cf., with delimitations and arrangements that differ in detail, Spieckermann 1989, 211–12; Adam 2001; Janowski 2002a; 2003a; Saur 2004; Day 2004; Carr 2011, 386–402.

44. Day 2004, 228.

45. Keel 2007, 247–48.

46. But cf. Janowski 2003b, 103 n. 14.

47. Zwickel 1999; Keel 2007, 247–48, 286–330.

48. Cf. Keel 2002; 2007, 267–72; and the discussion of Rösel 2009.

49. Janowski 1995/1999; Keel 2007, 189–98, 267–72; Leuenberger 2011.

50. Steck 1972, 9; to the contrary Niehr 1990, 167–97.

51. Keel 2007, 111–13.

52. Keel 1993.

53. Kaiser 1993, 264 n. 3; 1994, 49–50; Hermisson [5]1996.

54. Preuss 1987; Lang 1990, 179; Dell 2004.

55. For the link between wisdom and the royal court cf. Keel 2007, 258–59.

56. Cf. Köhlmoos 2003, 487; Keel 2007, 261.

57. Scoralick 1995; Krüger 1995/1997.

58. Krüger 1995/1997.

59. Perdue 1977; Ernst 1994, 1–8.

60. Assmann 2000, 64–66.

61. Janowski 1994/1999.

62. See the discussions in Huber 2010; and Dozeman, Schmid, and Schwartz 2011.

63. Schmid 199c; Kratz 2000a; Gertz 2000a; 2000b; 2002b; 2006a; Witte et al. 2006.

64. On the state of the text itself cf. Tov 1997, 288.

65. Knauf 2000c.

66. Cf. with various delimitations Blum 1984; de Pury 1991; 2001; Macchi and Römer 2001.

67. Blum 1984, 164–67; 343–44 n. 11.

68. Cf., very critically, Köckert 2003b.

69. Blum 1984.

70. Kratz 2000a, 263–79; Otto 2001b.

71. Donner ³2001, 405 with nn. 23-24; 407 n. 35.

72. Cf. Köckert 1998; 2003a; 2006a; also Beck 1999.

73. Grabbe 2007.

74. On 2 Kings 11* see Levin 1982.

75. Keel 2007, 156–57.

76. Cf. Hardmeier 1990; Kratz 2000a, 164; Parker 2000; Dijkstra 2005; Grabbe 2007; Adam 2007; Köhlmoos 2007; Blanco Wissmann 2008; for the synchronism of the "synchronistic history" cf. *TUAT* n.s. 2:42–44.

77. Na'aman 1999b, 12–13.

78. Galil 1996; 2004.

79. De Vos 2003.

80. Rost 1926/1965; cf. Seiler 1998; to the contrary de Pury and Römer 2000; Kratz 2000a; Rudnig 2006; Adam 2007.

81. For the whole question cf. Dietrich and Naumann 1995; Keel 2007, 152–53, 158–59.

82. Cf. Adam 2007,

83. Van Seters 1981; 1983; 2000; cf. the critique in Keel 2007, 160–61.

84. Dietrich 1997; 2006; Kratz 2000a.

85. Dietrich 1997, 259–73; 2006, 27–28.

86. Kratz 2000a, 190–91; cf. also Fischer 2004, 316; Rudnig 2006, 330–31.

87. So Kratz 2000a; Rudnig 2006.

88. Finkelstein and Silberman 2006.

89. Pisano 2005.

90. Finkelstein and Silberman 2006, 50–54.

91. Finkelstein and Silberman 2006, 38–39.

92. Keel 2007, 159.

Part C. The Literature of the Assyrian Period (Eighth–Seventh Centuries B.C.E.)

1. Tadmor 1994.

2. Cf. Spieckermann 1982; Knauf 1994, 132–41.

3. Kessler 2006, 114–26.

4. Münkler 2005, 88.

5. Fuchs 1994, 457; Becking 1992.

6. Na'aman 1990.

7. Otto 1980, 64–76; Fischer 2005, 281 with n. 23; Steiner 2007; cf., however, Knauf 2006, 293–94; Na'aman 2009.

8. Knauf 2003; cf. Keel 2007, 463.

9. *TUAT* 1: 388-91; *TUAT* n.s. 2: 71-72.

10. Mazar 1992, 427–34.

11. Grabbe 2003.

12. Cf. Steiner 2007.

13. Knauf 2005b; Steymans 2006, 344–49; Keel 2007, 471–74.

14. Schmid 1997.

15. Cf. Keel and Uehlinger ⁵2001; Morrow 2005, 209–10.

16. Van der Toorn 2007, 240–41, 356.

17. Schipper 1999, 236–39; Vanderhooft 1999, 69–81.

18. Sass 1990; Steiner 2007.

19. Na'aman 1991; but cf. de Vos 2003.

20. Uehlinger 1995; Keel 2007, 545–55; see the discussion in Gieselmann 1994; Schmid 2006b, 42 n. 90; Noll 2007, 330–31; cf. also the alternative interpretation in Knauf 2005b, 184–88 of Deuteronomy 12 as a text not of cultic centralization but rather of cultic legitimation.

21. Knauf 1994, 80.

22. Cf. Smend 1982; Gerstenberger 2001; Kratz 2002.

23. Oeming et al. 2004.

24. Cf. Spieckermann 1992; for Psalm 48 also Körting 2006b, 177.

25. Keel 2007, 447.

26. Wanke 1966; cf. for Psalm 46 also Uehlinger and Grandy 2005; Körting 2006b, 186.

27. Knauf 2005b; cf. Keel 2007, 733–39.

28. Jeremias 1987; Kratz 2003a.

29. Pongratz-Leisten 1994.

30. Jeremias 1987.

31. Arneth 2000.

32. Hossfeld and Zenger 2000, 308 (English 205); Janowski 2002a; 2003a; Morrow 2005.

33. Cf., correspondingly, for Psalm 2, Otto 2003; dissenting in detail Hartenstein 2004.

34. Cf. Hossfeld and Zenger 2000, 319–20 (English 212–13).

35. Otto 1998c, 123: "all law, in Babylon and in the entire ancient Near East, was the king's law."

36. Assmann 1992, 65.

37. Knauf 200d.

38. Differently Emmendörffer 1998, 162–73.

39. Finkelstein and Silberman 2006, 157–58.

40. Meinhold 1991.

41. See Scherer 1999; Fox 1996.

42. Clifford 1999, 3, 7.

43. Whybray 1965; McKane 1970.

44. Wilson 1987; Ernst 1994, 68–79.

45. Hausmann 1995, 237–43.

46. Römheld 1999; B. Schipper 2004; 2005.

47. *TUAT* 3: 222-50.

48. Otto 1987/1996c.

49. But cf. Hutzli 2007, 238–45.

50. Levinson 1995; Steymans 1995a; 1995b; Otto 1997b; 1999a.

51. Weinfeld 1972, 244–319.

52. Steck 1967; Römer 2005; Person 2007.

53. Thus Thiel 1973; 1981.

54. Cf. especially, contrary to the classical position of Noth 1943, the more differentiated approaches of Weippert 1972; Lemaire 1986; Halpern and Vanderhooft 1991.

55. Wellhausen ³1899, 298; cf. Schmid 2006b; Stipp 2011b.

56. Wellhausen ³1899, 295.

57. Cross 1973; cf., e.g., Nelson 1981; 2005; Halpern and Vanderhooft 1991; Knoppers 1994; Eynikel 1996; Sweeney 2001; Römer 2005; Stipp 2011b.

58. Noth 1943; cf. the overview in Preuss 1993; Dietrich 1999.

59. Wellhausen ³1899, 298; Moenikes 1992, 335–36; Geoghegan 2003; 2006; but cf. Becking 2007, 12–18.

60. Schmid 1997.

61. Vanoni 1985; Schmid 2004b; 2006b; differently Aurelius 2003b, 45–47.

62. Cf. below, D.III.2.b.

63. Blanco Wissmann 2008.

64. Kratz 2000a; Fischer 2004; Dietrich 2006.

65. Guillaume 2004, 5–74; cf. the discussion in Richter 2009: 82–85.

66. Cf. Guillaume 2004, 75–78.

67. Cf. Waltisberg 1999; Neef 2002.

68. Guillaume 2004, 69–70.

69. Knauf 1992, 49–50; Na'aman 1997.

70. Knauf 1988b.

71. Reade 1979, 329–44; Guillaume 2004, 71, 74.

72. Schmid 1999c; Gertz 2000b; 2002a; Otto 2000b.

73. See below, E.III.1.a.

74. Cf. Otto 2000b, and on the whole motif of an abandoned child the material in Redford 1967.

75. Galter 2006.

76. *TUAT* supplementary volume, 56.

77. Schmid 1999c, 238–41.

78. Differently Oswald 2009.

79. Van Seters 1990; cf. Younger 1990; Arnold 2002, 346–47; Römer 2005, 105.

80. Redford 1987; 1992, 408–69; Finkelstein and Silberman 2002, 78–82.

81. Zenger 1994; Becker 2005a.

82. Cf. Knauf 1988b; Albertz 1992, 218–19; Särkiö 1998; 2000; Schmid 199c, 140–41; Blanco Wissmann 2001.

83. Cf. Finkelstein and Silberman 2002, 61–85; Becker 2005a.

84. Redford 1992, 412; Assmann 1996, 314–15.

85. Knauf 1988b, 124–41; de Moor 1996; Donner ³2000; cf. Drenkhahn 1980, 64–65.

86. *TGI*, 40–41; *ANET*, 259.

87. Hendel 2001; Gertz 2006a, 92–94; Na'aman 2011.

88. Zenger 1994; Smend 1995; Otto 2006.

89. Wellhausen 1883/⁶1927, 332–33 n. 1.

90. Cf. the discussions in Carr 1996b, 203–4; Kratz 2000a, 279.

91. De Pury 2000, 178–81; 2007.

92. Blum 1998.

93. But cf. Jericke 1997.

94. Stern 2001, 236–67.

95. Knauf 1994, 236.

96. Nissinen 2004.

97. *TUAT* 2: 83–93; *TUAT* 2: 56–82.

98. Cf., e.g., Nissinen 1998.

99. Jeremias 1994; Steck 1996.

100. Cf. Becker 2006.

101. Nissinen et al. 2003.

102. Parpola 1997, lxvii–lxxi.

103. Van der Toorn 2004.

104. Jeremias 1983; 1995; 1996; Wöhrle 2006; Rudnig-Zelt 2006; Vielhauer 2007.

105. Kratz 1997b; 2003b.

106. Van der Toorn 2007, 179.

107. Jeremias 1996.

108. Crüsemann 2002.

109. Jeremias 1983; cf. Vielhauer 2007, differently Rudnig-Zelt 2006.

110. Vielhauer 2007, 127–58 posits a scribal origin for Hosea 1–3 within the framework of the book, designating Hos 2:4-15 as its literary core.

111. Rudnig-Zelt 2006.

112. Ambraseys 2005, 330–34.

113. Blum 1994.

114. Jeremias 1995; Gertz 2003; differently Becker 2001.

115. Kratz 2003c.

116. Cf. Schmidt 1965.

117. Cf. below, III.3.c.

118. For the interpretive character of Isaiah 28–32 cf. Kratz 2010b.

119. Cf. Köckert, Becker, and Barthel 2003.

120. Cf. Becker 1997 on the one side of the pendulum, Stipp 2003 on the other. Cf. the detailed discussions in Hartenstein 2011; Schmid 2011d.

121. Cf. Becker 1997.

122. Hartenstein 1997.

123. Thus Becker 1997.

124. Schmid 2006c.

125. Steck 2003.

126. Blum 1996; 1997; Hardmeier 2007; Williamson 2004.

127. Barth 1977; see below.

128. Cf. Keel 2007, 463.

129. Blum 1992/1993; 1997; cf. Keel 2007, 374–75. This in turn had been expanded to include Jerusalem; see Blum 1994.

130. Jeremias 1995.

131. Barth 1977; Becker 1997 is critical.

132. For this problem cf. Perlitt 1989/1994.

133. Morrow 1995; Levinson 1997; Otto 1999a, c.

134. Cf. Otto 2000a.

135. Halbe 1975, 319–505.

136. Otto 1988; 1998b; 1991; Schwienhorst-Schönberger 1990; Osumi 1991; Rothenbusch 2000; Kratz 2000a, 145–50; Albertz 2003; for the history of the concept of "theologizing" cf. Albertz 2003b, 187 n. 1.

137. Alt 1934.

138. On this cf. Assmann 2000, 178–89; Lohfink 1995, 366; Houtman 1997, 18; Rothenbusch 2000, 408–73.

139. Assmann 2000, 179.

140. Rothenbusch 2000, 410 and n. 61.

141. Otto 2004, 105.

142. Assmann 2006, 321.

143. Cf. Otto 1999d.

144. Frymer-Kenski 2003, 979.

145. Assmann et al. 1998.

146. For the social-historical backgrounds cf. Kessler 1992; 2006.

147. Kratz 2000a, 147–48; cf. Albertz 2003b, 193.

148. Cf. Dearman 1988, 58–59.

149. Cf. Levinson 2004, 297 n. 41.

150. Morrow 1995; Levinson 1997; Otto 1999a; 1999c; Kratz 2000a; differently Van Seters 1996; 2003 (on which see Levinson 2004).

151. Cf. Schmid 2004b.

152. Levinson 1997.

153. De Wette 1805.

154. See C.I above.

155. Otto 1997b; 1999a.

156. Cf. the "battle over Deuteronomy" in the 1920s (Hölscher 1922; Baumgartner 1929); more recently Kaiser 1992, 90–99; Clements 1996; Sacchi 1999, 114; Kratz 2000a, 118–38; Kratz 2010a; Aurelius 2003a; Noll 2007, 331–32; Pakkala 2009 locate the origin of Deuteronomy in the exilic or post-exilic period. Cf. the further discussion in MacDonald 2010 and Pakkala 2011.

157. Otto 1999a, 57–90.

158. Cf. Rüterswörden 2002; Pakkala 2006a; also Morrow 2005; Steymans 2006, 332 n. 5.

159. Otto 1997b; 1999a; cf. Keel 2007, 578.
160. Maul 1997, 122; Otto 1999a, 350–51; cf. Keel 2007, 555–56.
161. Moran 1963; Olyan 1996; cf. Rüterswörden 2006.
162. Cf. Exod 21:2, 7 with Deut 15:12; see Köckert 2004.
163. Kratz 2000b; 2006.
164. Höffken 1984; Jeremias/Hartenstein 1999, 113 n. 135; Kratz 2000a, 130–33; Pakkala 1999, 73–84; Keel 2007, 583–84; cf. earlier Bade 1910.
165. Veijola 1992a; 1992b; van Oorschot 2002, 125; Aurelius 2003a.
166. Weinfeld 1972, 244–319; Brekelmans 1979; Braulik 1996/1997; 2003.
167. Zobel 1992.
168. Otto 1998a.
169. Levinson 1997.
170. Knauf 2000a.

Part D. The Literature of the Babylonian Period (Sixth Century B.C.E.)

1. Cf. Na'aman 1991.
2. For the traditional, but problematic assumption of a "power vacuum" cf. Keel 2007, 512–17.
3. Cf. Noth 1971.
4. Keel 2007, 613.
5. Keel 2007, 775.
6. But cf. Pakkala 2006b.
7. Knauf 2000f; Barstad 2003; somewhat differently Lipshits 2003b; Stern 2004; weighing all these Keel 2007, 614–19, 773–75.
8. Schmid 1997.
9. Cf. Oswald 1998, 132–33; contrary Keel 2007, 778–79.
10. Stipp 2000; Albertz 2001, 82 n. 153; cf. Keel 2007, 776–83.
11. For the restoration of an independent province of Yehud in the Persian period see Keel 2007, 967–92.
12. Barkay 1993.
13. Pohlmann 1996, 13–18; Becking 1998; Joannès and Lemaire 2999; Pearce 2006; cf. Zadok 1979.
14. See Beaulieu 1989; Kratz 2004a; Keel 2007, 848–49.
15. Keel 2007, 849–50.
16. Kratz 2000b.
17. White 1980, 183, 192 nn. 22-23.
18. *RTAT* 255–56.
19. Lambert 1967.
20. Falkenstein 1965, esp. 68–69.
21. Arnold 1994.
22. Cf., e.g., the Erra Epic (*TUAT* 3: 781–801) or the Adad-Guppi inscription (*TUAT* 2: 479–85); Rudnig 2007, 276.
23. For Herodotus 3.159 cf. Schmid 1996a, 253.
24. Van der Toorn 2007, 193–94.
25. Veenhof 2001, 264–65; Blanco Wissmann 2007, 220.
26. Schmid 2006c; Keel 2007, 799–800.
27. Stolz 1996; Oeming and Schmid 2003; Zenger 2003; Lemaire 2007; Keel 2007.
28. Mach 1992; Koch 1994; Stuckenbruck 2004.

29. *TUAT* 3: 565-602.
30. See below, E.III.1.a.
31. Japhet 1991; Willi-Plein 1999; Keel 2007, 779, 785; however, Knauf 2006 argues that Jer 41:5 refers to Bethel and not to Jerusalem.
32. Keel 2007, 786–800.
33. Fitzgerald 1972; 1975; Schmitt 1985; 1991; Steck 1989/1992c; Wischnowsky 2001; Maier 2003; Keel 2007, 787–90.
34. Cf. Emmendörffer 1998; Keel 2007, 800–32; for the problems of dating see Keel 2007, 831.
35. Krüger 1994/1997.
36. For Psalm 137 cf. Krüger 2001; Keel 2007, 833–35.
37. Keel 2007, 946.
38. Cf. Marttila 2006.
39. Cf. Hartenstein 2010.
40. *TUAT* 1: 388-91.
41. Cf. Schipper 1999, 215–16.
42. *TUAT* 1: 391–92.
43. Hardmeier 1990; cf. also Keel 1994, 91; 2007, 741–53.
44. Hardmeier 1990, 287ff.; cf. Albertz 2001, 215.
45. Vanoni 1985.
46. Vanoni 1985.
47. Aurelius 2003b, 45–47.
48. Cf. Schmid 1996a, 226; 2006d.
49. Römer 2005, 143.
50. Römer 2005, 144–45.
51. Veijola 1975; differently Pietsch 2003; Römer 2005, 97.
52. Römer 2005, 143.
53. Guillaume 2004.
54. Schmid 2004b, 209–10.
55. Cf. Blum 2002.
56. Cf. Gertz 2001.
57. Cf. Brettler 1989; Becking 2007, 88–122.
58. Cf., e.g., Donner 1976; for Kratz 2000a, 281–86, who proposes to define the Joseph story as a continuation of the patriarchal narratives, cf. Schmid 2002.
59. Wellhausen ³1899, 52.
60. Whybray 1968.
61. Cf. especially Donner 1976.
62. Meinhold 1975; Römer 1992.
63. Beyerle 2000.
64. Von Rad 1953/1958; 1954/1974.
65. On 47:31 cf. Levin 1993, 307–8.
66. *TUAT* supplementary volume, 147-65; Wettengel 2008.
67. Blum 1984.
68. Cf. Albertz 2001; Otto 2007, 187–89.
69. Gertz 2000a.
70. Von Rad 1938/1958, 12.
71. Rendtorff 1977; Blum 1984; Köckert 1988.
72. Alt 1929/1959.
73. Cf., somewhat differently, Otto 2007, 188.
74. Cf. Blum 1990, 214 n. 35, correcting Blum 1984.
75. Von Rad 1957, 171 (English 167).
76. Blum 1984, 300; Carr 1996b, 178.
77. Knoppers 2006, 268; Carter 1999, 235–36.

78. For Gen 12:1-3: Ska 1997; for Gen 46:2-4: Gertz 2000b, 273–77, 382–83.
79. Cf. Crüsemann 1981, 29; Ska 1997, 369–70; Schmid 1999c, 168.
80. Kratz 2000a, 239.
81. Cf. de Pury 1991; Schmid 1999c; Gertz 2000b; Kratz 2000a.
82. Schmid 2001.
83. For the classical model Schmidt 1983, or with new approaches Oswald 1998; Gertz 2001.
84. Pfeiffer 2005, 260–68; with far-ranging conclusions regarding the religious-historical origins of YHWH in the North instead of the South cf. also Köckert 2001; to the contrary Keel 2007, 200–2; Leuenberger 2011.
85. Cf. Oswald 1998; differently Levin 1985b.
86. Levin 1985b, 185; Oswald 1998, 104–5.
87. Levin 1985; Pohlmann 1989; Biddle 1990; Schmid 1996a; Kratz 2003b.
88. Keel 2007, 672–76.
89. Fitzgerald 1972; but cf. Wischnowsky 2001, 42–45.
90. Huwyler 1997.
91. Job 2006.
92. Thiel 1973; 1981.
93. Keel 2007, 676–728.
94. Pohlmann 1996, 33–36; cf. Rudnig 2000, 345.
95. Rudnig 2000; Keel 2007, 890–900.
96. Maier 1997.
97. Hermisson 1999.
98. Albertz 1990.
99. Kratz 199a; differently Albertz 2003c.
100. Keel 2007, 862–64.
101. Keel 2007, 857–61.
102. *TUAT* 1: 408-9; English translation by Irving Finkel.
103. Schmid 1996a, 229–49.
104. Cf. Albani 2000; 2003; Lemaire 2007, 105–8.
105. Cf. Macchi 2009.
106. Kratz 1991; reservedly Leene 1996.
107. Differently Ehring 2007, 262–67.
108. *TUAT* 2: 561-64.
109. Hossfeld 1982; Köckert 2007.
110. Alt 1934.
111. Otto 1999b, 626.
112. Cf. Veijola 1992a; 1992b; differently Pakkala 1999, 73–84.
113. Moran 1963; Olyan 1996; Rüterswörden 2006.
114. Otto 1999b, 627.
115. Uehlinger 1998b, c.
116. See Köckert 2002, 22.
117. Schmid 2004b.
118. Otto 1994; 1999b, 627.
119. Otto 1999c, 695.
120. Cf. Schmid 2004b.

Part E. The Literature of the Persian Period
(Fifth–Fourth Centuries B.C.E.)

1. Cf. Stolper 1985; see also Zadok 1979; Pearce 2006.
2. Beyerle 2000.

3. Cf., e.g., Grabbe 1991; Kratz 2004a, 111–18; Keel 2007, 1077–78.

4. Römer 1991; 2004.

5. Albertz 1992, 469; 2000.

6. Cf. Wellhausen 61927, 28: "From the exile returned not the nation, but a religious sect"; Smend 1882.

7. Blum 1995; Kratz 1998; Bringmann 2005, 7–11.

8. Schäfer 1983, 11–12; Donner 32000/2001, 474–75.

9. Cf. Neusner et al. 1987; Edelman 1995; Deines 2001; Neusner and Avery-Peck 2001, Cohen 2001 proposed to speak of "Jewishness."

10. Brettler 1999; Becking 2007, 10.

11. Beaulieu 1989; Albani 2003; Schaudig 2003.

12. See the "Cyrus cylinder," *TUAT* 1: 408-9; cf. also the "Nabonidus Chronicle," *TUAT* n.s. 2: 40-41.

13. "Polemic Poem," *TGI* 66-69.

14. Cf. Schmid 1996a, 252–53.

15. Cf. Na'aman 2000; Kratz 2004a, 105–6.

16. Dequeker 1993; 1997.

17. For this problem cf. Bedford 2001; Lux 2005, 158 n. 44, and, with a new suggested dating, under Artaxerxes I, Edelman 2005.

18. For the provincial status of Judah cf. Keel 2007, 967–92.

19. Lemaire 1996; cf. Kratz 2004a, 93–106.

20. Cf. Kratz 1991b, 140 n. 254.

21. *TUAT* 1: 419-50.

22. Kinet 2001, 195; Knauf 2006, 301–2.

23. Keel 2007, 835–38.

24. Hjelm 2004.

25. Oded 1979.

26. Hjelm 2004, 29–30; Knoppers 2006, 279; Keel 2007, 1123; and especially Magen 2007.

27. Knoppers 2006.

28. Keel 2007, 1067–80.

29. Ussishkin 2005; 2006; Noll 2007, 332 n. 63; cf. Bodi 2002; Keel 2007, 951–54.

30. Cf. Kessler 2006, 144–45; Keel 2007, 1074–75.

31. Carter 1999; Schmid and Steck 2005.

32. Stolz 1996; Oeming and Schmid 2003; Zenger 2003; Keel 2007, with summary on 1270–82; Schmid 2011b.

33. Grünwaldt 1992.

34. Grabbe 2000.

35. Cf. Schmid and Steck 2005.

36. Dodd 1935.

37. Krüger 1997; Leene 2000; Köckert 2004, 69–72.

38. E.g., Spieckermann 1998/2001.

39. Eberhardt 2007.

40. Cf. Koch 1987; Pola 1995; Otto 1997c; 2007, 179–80, 289–93; Zenger 1997b. Berner 2010 thinks differently, but without a sufficient analysis of the Priestly document. A convenient survey of current discussions is offered by Shectman and Baden 2009.

41. De Pury 2002.

42. Cf. Dozeman, Schmid, and Schwartz 2011.

43. Schmid 1999c; Gertz 2000b; Gertz et al. 2002b; Schmid and Dozeman 2006.

44. Cf. Levin 1993b, 437 n. 6, who places special value on the Priestly aspect of the cultic centralization, which demanded a "literary-historical break" with the existing tradition.

45. Pola 1995; Otto 1997c; Zenger 1997b; Kratz 2000a.

46. Perlitt 1988; differently again Frevel 2000.

47. Rudnig 2000; Keel 2007, 890–900.

48. Keel 2007, 912–29; for the relationship to the Second Temple, see 1030.
49. Blenkinsopp 1976; Lohfink 1978/1988; Knauf 2000a; Oswald 2009.
50. Rütersworden 1988; differently Keel 1977.
51. Otto 2007, 190.
52. Cf. Stipp 2005.
53. Zimmerli 1960/1963.
54. De Pury 2000.
55. For the sacrifices see Eberhart 2002; Keel 2007, 1036–41.
56. De Pury 2002; Schmid 2003.
57. Blum 1995; Gross 1987/1999.
58. Cf. Steck 1991a, 17–18 n. 19; Schmid 1999c, 256 n. 476 (with bibliography); Knauf 2000a.
59. Seebass 1997, 111–12.
60. Schmid 2006c.
61. Cf. Janowski 1987/1993; Rudnig 2007, 278.
62. Knohl 1995.
63. Plöger 1962; cf. Steck 1968; Dörrfuss 1994.
64. Kratz 1992; Leuenberger 2004.
65. Vleeming and Wesselius 1982; van der Toorn 2007, 134.
66. If these were not collected earlier, so Weber 2000.
67. Zenger ^{5}2004, 365; Süssenbach 2004.
68. Spieckermann 2001b; Oeming and Schmid 2001; Newsom 2007; Krüger et al. 2007; Schmid 2010.
69. Van Oorschot 2007; cf. Alt 1937; Wahl 1992.
70. Cf. Schmid 2001, 13–17.
71. Cf. Keel 1978.
72. Cf. Oeming 2000a; differently Kottsieper 2004.
73. Schmid 2007d.
74. Jeremias 1992, 313–25.
75. Westermann 1977, 27–39.
76. *TUAT* 3: 110–35.
77. *TUAT* 3: 143–57.
78. Spieckermann 1998/2001, 118; Uehlinger 2007b, 145, cf. 161 n. 183.
79. Albertz 1981/2003, 110 n. 12.
80. Cf. Gertz et al. 2002; Dozeman and Schmid 2006.
81. Blenkinsopp 1992; 1995; Schüle 2006; Arneth 2006.
82. Cf. Witte 1998; Baumgart 1999.
83. *TUAT* III, 612–45.
84. Kratz 2000a; cf. also the earlier discussion between Rendtorff 1961/1975 and Steck 1971/1982 within the framework of the J-hypothesis.
85. Cf., on one side, Kratz 2000a; Bosshard-Nepustil 2005; Arneth 2006; and on the other side Witte 1998; Gertz 2006b.
86. Schmid 2002.
87. Otto 1996b.
88. Contra Otto 1996b; Arneth 2006.
89. Cf. Spieckermann 2000; Schmid 2002.
90. Cf. Steck 1980/1982; Kratz 1991b.
91. Schmid 1999c, 241–301; Kratz 2000a, 314–31; Römer and Schmid 2007.
92. Gertz et al. 2002; Dozeman and Schmid 2006.
93. Cf. correctly Begg 1986; Becking 1990; J. Schipper 2005; differently, e.g., Zenger 1968; Levenson 1984.
94. Cf. Clements 2007; Schmid 2006a; cf. Keel 2007, 843.
95. Cf. Koch 1984a.

96. Cf. Carr 1996b; 2001.
97. Schmid 1999c.
98. Gertz 2000b; 2002b.
99. Becker 1997, 185.
100. Zunz 1892/²1992; cf. Pohlmann 1991.
101. Wright 2004; Pakkala 2004; Keel 2007, 959–60.
102. Japhet 1968; 1999; cf. Willi 1972.
103. Kratz 2000a, 14–98.
104. Cf. Krüger 1988.
105. McConville 1986.
106. Lux 2005.
107. Wolff 1985; Willi-Plein 1998; Meyers 2000.
108. Witte 2006; Bosshard and Kratz 1990; Steck 1991; for Joel see the material in Bergler 1988; cf. Jeremias 2007, 1–55.
109. Lux 2005, 158.
110. Lux 2005, 164–65.
111. Cf. Meyers and Meyers 1987, xlix; Meyers 2000.
112. Lux 2002, 198.
113. Keel 2007, 1010–26.
114. Koch 1994; Stuckenbruck 2004.
115. Uehlinger 1994.
116. Körting 2006a.
117. Cf. *TUAT* 2: 556–57, 561–64.
118. Cf. Kratz 1991a.
119. Koch 1984b; Wiesehöfer 1999.
120. Steck 1991b; differently Koenen 1990.
121. Duhm 1892/1968, 390.
122. Donner 1985/1994.
123. Cf. Keel 2007, 794.
124. Schmid 1996a, 220–53.
125. Seitz 1989.
126. Pohlmann 1978; 1989; 1996.
127. Pohlmann 1978.
128. Cf. Thiel 1973, 253–61.
129. Schmid 1996a, 253–69.
130. Noth 1943, 110.
131. Steck 1967; Römer 2005; Witte et al. 2006; Otto 2006c; Person 2007.
132. Römer 2005; Witte et al. 2006.
133. Wolff 1961/1964; cf. also Wolff 1951/1964.
134. Wolff 1961, 182, 184.
135. Schmid 1999c, 164–65 n. 660.
136. Schmid 1996a, 277–94.
137. Maier 2002; Otto 2006b; Achenbach 2007; for Maier cf. 265–66 n. 26.
138. Klostermann 1877.
139. Elliger 1966.
140. Nihan 2007, 616–17.
141. Blum 1990.
142. Otto 2000a.
143. So Nihan 2007, 617, against Otto 2000a.
144. Lohfink 1973/1988.
145. Cf. Otto 2007, 202.
146. L. Schmidt 1998; 2004; 2005.

147. Römer 2007; cf. Achenbach 2003 (and cf. the critique of Römer 2007, 436); Otto 2007, 202.
148. Römer 2007, 428.
149. Schmid 1999c, 290–91; 2006e; Crüsemann ³2005; Keel 2007, 1081.
150. Schmid 1999c, 21–22.
151. See below, F.III.3.a.
152. Pakkala 2004.
153. Siegert 2001, 42.
154. Frei ²1996; cf. *TUAT* supplementary volume, 194-97; Blum 1990, 342ff.
155. On this cf. Knauf 1998; Knohl 2003.
156. Watts 2001.
157. Schmid 2006e.
158. Cf. Schmid 2007b; 2011a, 159–84.
159. Cf. Maier 2002; Otto 2006b; Achenbach 2007.
160. Römer 1990, 566; Schmid 1999c, 296–99.

Part F. The Literature of the Ptolemaic Period (Third Century B.C.E.)

1. Schäfer 1983, 24–25; Maier 1990, 146–47.
2. Schäfer 1983, 29–34; Hölbl 1994.
3. *Ant.* 12.1.1 §5; *Contra Ap.* 1.22 §208-11; Schäfer 1983, 27.
4. Josephus, *Bell.* 2.487.
5. *TUAT* n.s. 1: 314-17.
6. Donner ³2000/2001, 479; Keel 2007, 1156–58.
7. Droysen 1836–1843/1952–1953; Gehrke 1990, 1–3, 129–31; Maier 1990, 291–92; Keel 2007, 1127–28.
8. Haag 2003, 104–5; for pre-Hellenistic contacts see Stern 2001, 217–28; Hagedorn 2005; Keel 2007 1126–27.
9. Hengel ³1988.
10. Kepper 1999.
11. Veltri 2003.
12. Hengel ³1988; Collins ²2000; 2005; Collins and Sterling 2001; Haag 2003; see the sketch of the history of scholarship in Collins 2005, 1–20.
13. Schmid 2007b.
14. Steck 1991a; 1996.
15. Steck 1980/1982; Kratz 1991a.
16. Seibert 1991.
17. Lohfink 1978/1988; Knauf 2000a.
18. Schmid 2006a.
19. Maier 1995, 67; Baumann 1996, 272; Müller 2000, 312.
20. Hengel ³1988, 275, 285–88; cf. Fox 2000, 6.
21. Krüger 2003b.
22. Baumann 1996, 197–99, 289.
23. Baumann 1996, 91–103, 301.
24. Knauf 1988a, 67; cf. Clines 2004; Greenstein 2003, each with suggestions for literary rearrangement.
25. Schwienhorst-Schönberger 1994/²1996; differently Seow 1997, who argues for composition in the Persian period.
26. Schwienhorst-Schönberger 1994/²1996; 2004; Uehlinger 1997.

27. Krüger 1997; 1999.
28. Wilke 2006.
29. Schwienhorst-Schönberger 2004.
30. Krüger 1999.
31. Krüger 1996/1997.
32. Zimmer 1999; Janowski 2001, 37–40.
33. Cf., e.g., Spieckermann 2000; Schmid 2002.
34. Zenger 2002; [5]2004, 365; differently Rösel 1999, 214–15.
35. Cf. Levin 1993a, 380; Steck 1991a, 108–9, 158; Zenger 2002.
36. Rösel 1999, 220.
37. Cf. Koch 1982/1996; Müller 1991; Beyerle 1998; Hahn 1998.
38. Cf. Vielhauer [6]1997.
39. Cf. Steck 1981.
40. Stegemann [2]1989; cf. Bachmann 2009.
41. Von der Osten-Sacken 1969; cf. Gese 1973/1974.
42. Von Rad 1960.
43. Cf. Steck 1997.
44. Schmid 2000a.
45. Japhet 2002, 52–54.
46. Welten 1972; Mathys 2000b.
47. Steins 1995.
48. Cf. Kratz 2000a, 97–98.
49. Cf. Noth 1943, 174; Willi 2007.
50. Cf. Schenker 2006.
51. Kratz 1991b, 173–77; Mathias 2005.
52. Finkelstein and Silberman 2006, 197–200.
53. Keel 2007, 1089–1112.
54. Kratz 1991b, 161ff.
55. Steins 1995, 451–54.
56. Schmid 1999b.
57. Schmid 1997.
58. Schmitt 1994, 184–87.
59. Gnuse 1998; Mathys 2002.
60. Römer 1998.
61. Zenger [5]2004, 307–8; Macchi 2005.
62. Zenger [5]2004, 308–9; cf. Beyerle 2000.
63. Siegert 2001, 42; Tilly 2005; Keel 2007, 1141–43.
64. Knibb 2006.
65. Rösel 1994.
66. Rösel 1994.
67. Siegert 2001, 243–62; Tilly 2005, 74–80; Rösel 2006.
68. Cf. Steck 1985, 53–54; Schmid 1996a, 305–9.
69. Duhm 1892.
70. Schmid 1996b; Becker 2004.
71. Steck 1991b.
72. Steck 1985.
73. Berges 1998.
74. Albertz 1990.
75. Steck 1985.
76. Steck 1991b, 217–42; Goldenstein 2001.
77. Cf. Steck 1991.
78. Steck 1997; Schmid 2011a, 185–205.

79. Schmid 2006c.
80. Goldman 1992; Schmid 1996a, 56–66; 2011, 207–221.
81. Boda and Floyd 2003; Gärtner 2006.
82. Mathys 2000b, 53.
83. Schäfer 1983, 27.
84. Knauf 1994, 177; Kunz 1998.
85. Cf. Hölbl 1997.
86. Bosshard-Nepustil 1997; Steck 1991a; with differences Gärtner 2006.
87. Bosshard and Kratz 1990; Steck 1991.
88. Cf. Mathys 2000a; van der Toorn 2007, 252–55.50. See below, F.III.3.a.

Part G. The Literature of the Seleucid Period (Second Century B.C.E.)

1. Gauger 2007.
2. *Ant.* 12.143.
3. Bringmann 1983; 2005; Haag 2003; cf. previously Bickerman 1937.
4. Haag 2003, 69, 71–73; cf. the critic in Keel 2007, 1186–93.
5. Haag 2003, 71; differently Keel 2000; 2007, 1193–1201, who identifies the "abomination of desolation" with the sacrifice of swine on the altar.
6. Stegemann [9]1999.
7. Kratz 1996.
8. Janowski 2001/2003; 2006; Eberhardt 2007.
9. Bartelmus 1985.
10. Cf. Janowski 2001/2003, 37–38.
11. Lichtenberger 2001.
12. See above, E.3.1.b.; F.3.1.d.
13. Kratz 1996.
14. Zenger [5]2004, 365.
15. Lange 1998; Leuenberger 2005.
16. See above, E.3.1.b.
17. Leuenberger 2004.
18. Cf. Duhm [2]1922; Diebner 1986; Treves 1988; Wilson 1990; Oeming 2000b.
19. Zenger 1997a; 1997c; Steck 1991, 161.
20. Donner 1994.
21. Marböck 1992; 1995.
22. Kepper 1999.
23. Steck 1992a, 18–19.
24. Differently Koch 1995.
25. Steck 1982; Kratz 1991b.
26. Kratz 2004b.
27. Steck 1993; 1998.
28. Schmid 1999c, 19–22; cf., however, Carr 2011, 171 n. 28.
29. Kaiser 2000a, 19, 23, 36, 44.
30. Haag 2003, 152–67; critically Keel 2007, 1185–86.
31. Haag 2003, 167–84.
32. Berger 1981; Schelbert 1988; Segal 2007.
33. Nickelsburg 1984; Tov 1998; Hofmann 2000.

Part H. Becoming Scripture and the Genesis of the Canon

1. Barton 1986.
2. Maier 1988; Fabry 1998; Stegemann ⁹1999.
3. Cf. Höffken 2001; Mason 2002.
4. Josephus, *Contra Apionem* 1.8.
5. Cf. Macholz 1990.
6. Chapman 2000.
7. All Qumran texts from García Martínez 1994.
8. Cf. Kleer 1996; Ulrich 2003a, 11–12; Leuenberger 2005; cf. van Oorshot 2000, 45.
9. Barton 1986; Ulrich 2003b; van der Toorn 2007, 248.
10. Steck 1992a; Hengel 1992/1994; Assmann 1999; VanderKam 2000; Ulrich 2003a; Schaper 2009.
11. Cf. Gertz 2002.
12. Rüpke 2005.
13. Cf. also Ulrich 1992, 269–76; Lange 2004, 57–58.
14. Van der Toorn 2007, 233–67.
15. Crüsemann 1987.
16. Cf. Schmid 2006b, 42 n. 90; Keel 2007, 545–55.
17. Speyer 1970.
18. See above, C.III.4.b.
19. Carr 1996a, 30 with n. 24; cf. Crüsemann 1987; Assmann 1999.
20. For these categories cf. Rüpke 2005.
21. See above, A.II.3.
22. Gunneweg 1987, 112.
23. Zenger 2010.
24. Schreiner 1999.
25. Barton 1986, 57.
26. With variations; see above.
27. Carr 1996a; but cf. Lange 2004, 60–62.
28. Van der Toorn 1997.
29. Hahn 2002.
30. Trebolle Barrera 2002.
31. Lang 1997; de Pury 2003; cf. Steinberg 2005.
32. Cf. Sæbø 1988.
33. Sæbø 1988.
34. Cf. van Oorshot 2000.
35. Janowski 2004.
36. Jeremias 1995; 1996.
37. Blum 1996; 1997.
38. Blum 1984.
39. Cf. Crüsemann 1987.
40. Cf. Chapman 2000.

Bibliography

Achenbach, Reinhard. 2003. *Die Vollendung der Tora: Studien zur Redaktionsgeschichte des Numeribuches im Kontext von Hexateuch und Pentateuch.* Beihefte zur Zeitschrift für altorientalische und biblische Rechtsgeschichte (BZABR) 3. Wiesbaden: Harrassowitz.

———. 2007. "The Pentateuch, the Prophets, and the Torah in the Fifth and Fourth Centuries B.C.E.," 253–85 in Oded Lipschits et al., eds., *Judah and the Judeans in the Fourth Century B.C.E.* Winona Lake, IN: Eisenbrauns.

Adam, Klaus-Peter. 2001. *Der königliche Held: Die Entsprechung von kämpfendem Gott und kämpfendem König in Psalm 18.* WMANT 91. Neukirchen-Vluyn: Neukirchener Verlag.

———. 2007. *Saul und David in der judäischen Geschichtsschreibung: Studien zu 1 Samuel 16–2 Samuel 5.* FAT 51. Tübingen: Mohr Siebeck.

Albani, Matthias. 2000. *Der eine Gott und die himmlischen Heerscharen: Zur Begründung des Monotheismus bei Deuterojesaja im Horizont der Astralisierung des Gottesverständnisses im Alten Orient.* Arbeiten zur Bibel und ihrer Geschichte (ABG) 1. Leipzig: Evangelische Verlagsanstalt.

———. 2003. "Deuterojesajas Monotheismus und der babylonische Religionskonflikt unter Nabonid," 171–201 in Manfred Oeming and Konrad Schmid, eds., *Der eine Gott und die Götter: Polytheismus und Monotheismus im antiken Israel.* ATANT 82. Zürich: Theologischer Verlag.

Albertz, Rainer. 1990. "Das Deuterojesaja-Buch als Fortschreibung der Jesaja-Prophetie," 1–12 in Erhard Blum et al., eds., *Die Hebräische Bibel und ihre zweifache Nachgeschichte. FS Rolf Rendtorff.* Neukirchen-Vluyn: Neukirchener Verlag.

———. 1992. *Religionsgeschichte Israels in alttestamentlicher Zeit.* GAT 8/1, 2. Göttingen: Vandenhoeck & Ruprecht.

———. 2000. "Die verhinderte Restauration," 1–12 in Erhard Blum, ed., *Mincha. FS Rolf Rendtorff.* Neukirchen-Vluyn: Neukirchener Verlag.

———. "2003a. Der sozialgeschichtliche Hintergrund des Hiobbuches und der 'Babylonischen Theodizee'" (1981), 107–34 in idem, *Geschichte und Theologie: Studien zur Exegese des Alten Testaments und zur Religionsgeschichte Israels.* BZAW 326. Berlin and New York: de Gruyter.

———. 2003b. "Die Theologisierung des Rechts im Alten Israel," 187–207 in idem, *Geschichte und Theologie.*

———. 2003c. "Darius in Place of Cyrus. The First Edition of Deutero-Isaiah (Isaiah 40.1–52.12)." *JSOT* 27: 371–83.

————. 2001. *Die Exilszeit: 6. Jahrhundert v. Chr.* Biblische Enzyklopädie 7. Stuttgart: Kohlhammer. English: *Israel in Exile: The History and Literature of the Sixth Century B.C.E.* Translated by David Green. Leiden and Boston: Brill, 2004.

Alexander, Philip S. 2003. "Literacy among Jews in Second Temple Palestine: Reflections on the Evidence from Qumran," 3–25 in Martin F. J. Baasten and Willem Theodor van Peursen, eds., *Hamlet on a Hill: Semitic and Greek Studies Presented to Professor Takamitsu Muraoka on the Occasion of His Sixty-Fifth Birthday.* Leuven and Dudley, MA: Peeters.

Alt, Albrecht. 1934. *Die Ursprünge des israelitischen Rechts.* Leipzig: S. Hirzel.

————. 1937. "Zur Vorgeschichte des Buches Hiob." *ZAW* 14: 265–68.

————. 1966. "Der Gott der Väter" (1929), 1–78 in idem, *Kleine Schriften zur Geschichte des Volkes Israel I.* Munich: Beck. English: *Essays on Old Testament History and Religion.* Translated by R. A. Wilson. Oxford: Blackwell, 1959.

Ambraseys, Nicolas. 2005. "Historical Earthquakes in Jerusalem—A Methodological Discussion." *Journal of Seismology* 9: 329–40.

Anderson, Bernhard W. ⁵2006. *Understanding the Old Testament.* Englewood Cliffs, NJ: Prentice-Hall.

Applegate, John. 1997. "Jeremiah and the Seventy Years in the Hebrew Bible," 91–110 in Adrian H. W. Curtis and Thomas Römer, eds., *The Book of Jeremiah and Its Reception, Le livre de Jérémie et sa réception.* BETL 128. Leuven: Leuven University Press.

Arneth, Martin. 2000. *"Sonne der Gerechtigkeit": Studien zur Solarisierung der Jahwe-Religion im Lichte von Psalm 72.* BZABR 1. Wiesbaden: Harrassowitz.

————. 2001. "Die antiassyrische Reform Josias von Juda. Überlegungen zur Komposition und Intention von 2 Reg 23, 4-15." *Zeitschrift für altorientalische und biblische Rechtsgeschichte* (ZABR) 7: 189–216.

————. 2006. *Durch Adams Fall ist ganz verderbt. . . : Studien zur Entstehung der alttestamentlichen Urgeschichte.* FRLANT 217. Göttingen: Vandenhoeck & Ruprecht.

Arnold, Bill T. 1994. "The Weidner Chronicle and the Idea of History in Israel and Mesopotamia," 129–48 in A. R. Millard et al., eds., *Faith, Tradition and History: Old Testament Historiography in Its Near Eastern Context.* Winona Lake, IN: Eisenbrauns.

————. 2002. "What Has Nebuchadnezzar to Do with David? On the Neo-Babylonian Period and Early Israel," 330–55 in Mark W. Chavalas and K. Lawson Younger, Jr., eds., *Mesopotamia and the Bible: Comparative Explorations.* Grand Rapids: Baker Academic.

Assmann, Jan. 1990a. *Ma'at: Gerechtigkeit und Unsterblichkeit im Alten Ägypten.* Munich: Beck.

————. 1990b. "Weisheit, Schrift und Literatur im Alten Ägypten," 475–500 in idem, ed., *Weisheit: Archäologie der literarischen Kommunikation III.* Munich: Fink.

————. 1992. *Politische Theologie zwischen Ägypten und Israel.* Munich: Carl Friedrich von Siemens Stiftung.

————. 1993. "Zur Geschichte des Herzens im Alten Ägypten," 81–113 in idem, ed., *Die Erfindung des inneren Menschen: Studien zur religiösen Anthropologie.* Gütersloh: Mohn.

————. 1997. *Mose der Ägypter.* Munich: Beck, 1998. English: *Moses the Egyptian: The*

Memory of Egypt in Western Monotheism. Cambridge, MA: Harvard University Press.

———. 1999. *Fünf Stufen auf dem Wege zum Kanon: Tradition und Schriftkultur im frühen Judentum und seiner Umwelt*. MTV 1. Münster: Lit.

———. 2000. *Herrschaft und Heil: Politische Theologie in Ägypten, Israel und Europa*. Munich and Vienna: Carl Hanser.

———. 2003. *Ägypten: Eine Sinngeschichte*. Munich and Vienna: Carl Hanser, 1996. English: *The Mind of Egypt: History and Meaning in the Time of the Pharaohs*. Translated by Andrew Jenkins. Cambridge, MA: Harvard University Press.

———. 2006. "Gottesbilder—Menschenbilder: anthropologische Konsequenzen des Monotheismus," 313–29 in Reinhard Gregor Kratz and Hermann Spieckermann, eds., *Götterbilder, Gottesbilder, Weltbilder: Polytheismus und Monotheismus in der Welt der Antike*. Vol. 2: *Griechenland und Rom, Judentum, Christentum und Islam*. FAT II/18. Tübingen: Mohr Siebeck.

———, Bernd Janowski, and Michael Welker, eds. 1998. *Gerechtigkeit: Richten und Retten in der abendländischen Tradition und ihren altorientalischen Ursprüngen*. Munich: Fink.

Athas, George. 2003. *The Tel Dan Inscription: A Reappraisal and a New Interpretation*. JSOTSup 360. Sheffield: Sheffield Academic Press.

Aurelius, Erik. 2003a. "Der Ursprung des Ersten Gebots." *ZTK* 100: 1–21.

———. 2003b. *Zukunft jenseits des Gerichts: Eine redaktionsgeschichtliche Studie zum Enneateuch*. BZAW 319. Berlin and New York: de Gruyter.

Avigad, Nahman. 1976. *Bullae and Seals from Post-Exilic Judean Archives*. Jerusalem: Hebrew University.

Avishur, Yitshaq, and Michael Heltzer. 2000. *Studies on the Royal Administration in Ancient Israel in Light of Epigraphic Sources*. Tel Aviv: Archaeological Center.

Bachmann, Veronika. 2009. *Die Welt im Ausnahmezustand: Eine Untersuchung zu Aussagegehalt und Theologie des Wächterbuches* (1Hen 1–36). BZAW 409. Berlin and New York: de Gruyter.

Bade, William F. 1910. "Der Monojahwismus des Deuteronomiums." *ZAW* 30: 81–90.

Baden, Joel. 2009. *J, E, and the Redaction of the Pentateuch*. FAT 68. Tübingen: Mohr Siebeck.

Baines, John. 1983. "Literacy and Ancient Egyptian Society." *Man* 18: 572–99.

Barkay, Gabriel. 1993. "The Redefining of Archaeological Periods. Does the Date 588/586 B.C. Indeed Mark the End of Iron Age Culture?" 106–9 in Avraham Biran and Joseph Aviram, eds., *Biblical Archaeology Today 1990: Proceedings of the Second International Congress on Biblical Archaeology, Jerusalem, June–July 1990*. Jerusalem: Israel Exploration Society.

Barstad, Hans M. 2003. "After the 'Myth of the Empty Land': Major Challenges in the Study of Neo-Babylonian Judah," 3–20 in Oded Lipschits and Joseph Blenkinsopp, eds., *Judah and the Judeans in the Neo-Babylonian Period*. Winona Lake, IN: Eisenbrauns.

Bartelmus, Rüdiger. 1985. "Ez 37,1-14, die Verbform wᵉqatal und die Anfänge der Auferstehungshoffnung." *ZAW* 97: 366–89.

Barth, Hermann. 1977. *Die Jesaja-Worte in der Josiazeit*. WMANT 48. Neukirchen-Vluyn: Neukirchener Verlag.

Barton, John. 1986. *Oracles of God: Perceptions of Ancient Prophecy in Israel after the Exile*. London: Darton, Longman, and Todd.

Bauks, Michaela. 2001. "'Chaos' als Metapher für die Gefährdung der Weltordnung," 431–64 in Bernd Janowski and Beate Ego, eds., *Das biblische Weltbild und seine altorientalischen Kontexte*. FAT 32. Tübingen: Mohr Siebeck.

Baumann, Gerlinde. 1996. *Die Weisheitsgestalt in Proverbien 1–9: Traditionsgeschichtliche und theologische Studien*. FAT 16. Tübingen: Mohr.

Baumgart, Norbert C. 1999. *Die Umkehr des Schöpfergottes. Zu Komposition und religionsgeschichtlichem Hintergrund von Gen 5–9*. Herders Biblische Studien (HBS) 22. Freiburg and New York: Herder.

Beaulieu, Paul-Alain. 1989. *The Reign of Nabonidus, King of Babylon (556–539 B.C.)*. Yale Near Eastern Researches (YNER) 10. New Haven: Yale University Press.

Beck, Martin. 1999. *Elia und die Monolatrie: Ein Beitrag zur religionsgeschichtlichen Rückfrage nach dem vorschriftprophetischen Jahwe-Glauben*. BZAW 281. Berlin and New York: de Gruyter.

Becker, Uwe. 1997. *Jesaja—von der Botschaft zum Buch*. FRLANT 178. Göttingen: Vandenhoeck & Ruprecht.

———. 2001. "Der Prophet als Fürbitter: Zum literarhistorischen Ort der Amos-Visionen." *VT* 51: 141–65.

———. 2004. "Die Wiederentdeckung des Prophetenbuches. Tendenzen und Aufgaben der gegenwärtigen Prophetenforschung." *BTZ* 21: 30–60.

———. 2005a. "Das Exodus-Credo. Historischer Haftpunkt und Geschichte einer alttestamentlichen Glaubensformel," 81–100 in idem and Jürgen van Oorschot, eds., *Das Alte Testament—ein Geschichtsbuch?! Geschichtsschreibung und Geschichtsüberlieferung im antiken Israel*. ABG 17. Leipzig: Evangelische Verlagsanstalt.

———. 2005b. *Exegese des Alten Testaments: Ein Methoden- und Arbeitsbuch*. Uni-Taschenbücher (UTB) 2664. Tübingen: Mohr Siebeck.

———. 2006. "Die Entstehung der Schriftprophetie," 3–20 in Rüdiger Lux and Ernst-Joachim Waschke, eds., *Die unwiderstehliche Wahrheit: Studien zur alttestamentlichen Prophetie. FS A. Meinhold*. ABG 23. Leipzig: Evangelische Verlagsanstalt.

Becking, Bob. 1990. "Jehoiachin's Amnesty, Salvation for Israel? Notes on II Kings 25,27-30," 283–93 in Christianus Brekelmans and Johan Lust, eds., *Pentateuchal and Deuteronomistic Studies: Papers Read at the XIIIth IOSOT Congress Leuven 1989*. BETL 94. Leuven: Leuven University Press.

———. 1992. *The Fall of Samaria: An Historical and Archaeological Study*. SHANE 2. Leiden and New York: Brill.

———. 1998. "Babylonisches Exil." *Religion in Geschichte und Gegenwart*, 4th ed. (*RGG*) 1: 1044–45.

———. 2001. "The Gods in Whom They Trusted . . . Assyrian Evidence for Iconic Polytheism in Ancient Israel?" 159–63 in idem et al., eds., *Only One God? Monotheism in Ancient Israel and the Veneration of the Goddess Asherah*. Sheffield: Sheffield Academic Press.

———. 2007. *From David to Gedaliah: The Book of Kings as Story and History*. OBO 228. Fribourg: Universitätsverlag; Göttingen: Vandenhoeck & Ruprecht.

Beckwith, Roger T. 1985. *The Old Testament Canon of the New Testament Church and Its Background in Early Judaism*. Grand Rapids: Eerdmans.

———. 1988. "Formation of the Hebrew Bible," 39–86 in Martin J. Mulder, ed., *Mikra: Text, Translation, Reading and Interpretation of the Hebrew Bible in Ancient Judaism and Early Christianity*. CRINT II/1. Assen: van Gorcum; Philadelphia: Fortress Press.

Bedford, Peter Ross. 2001. *Temple Restoration in Early Achaemenid Judah.* JSJSup 65. Leiden and Boston: Brill.

Begg, Christopher T. 1986. "The Significance of Jehoiachin's Release: A New Proposal." *JSOT* 36: 49–56.

Ben Zvi, Ehud. 1997. "The Urban Center of Jerusalem and the Development of the Hebrew Bible," 194–209 in Walter E. Aufrecht et al., eds., *Urbanism in Antiquity: From Mesopotamia to Crete.* JSOTSup 244. Sheffield: Sheffield Academic Press.

———. 1998. "Looking at the Primary (Hi)story and the Prophetic Books as Literary/ Theological Units within the Frame of the Early Second Temple: Some Considerations." *SJOT*: 26–43.

Berger, Klaus. 1981. *Das Buch der Jubiläen.* JSHRZ II/3. Gütersloh: Mohn.

Berges, Ulrich. 1998. *Das Buch Jesaja: Komposition und Endgestalt.* HBS 16. Freiburg and New York: Herder.

Bergler, Siegfried. 1988. *Joel als Schriftinterpret.* BEATAJ 16. Frankfurt and New York: Peter Lang.

Berner, Christoph. *Die Exoduserzählung: Das literarische Werden einer Ursprungslegende Israels.* FAT 73. Tübingen: Mohr Siebeck.

Bertholet, Alfred. 1907. "H. Gunkels 'Israelitische Literatur.'" *TRu* 10: 143–53.

Bewer, Julius A. 1922. *The Literature of the Old Testament in Its Historical Development.* New York: Columbia University Press.

Beyerle, Stefan. 1998. "Die Wiederentdeckung der Apokalyptik in den Schriften Altisraels und des Frühjudentums." *VF* 43: 34–59.

———. 2000. "Joseph und Daniel: zwei 'Väter' am Hofe eines fremden Königs," 1–18 in Axel Graupner et al., eds., *Verbindungslinien. FS Werner H. Schmidt.* Neukirchen-Vluyn: Neukirchener Verlag.

Biddle, Mark E. 1990. *A Redaction History of Jer 2:4–4:2.* ATANT 77. Zürich: Theologischer Verlag.

Bickerman, Elias J. 1937. *Der Gott der Makkabäer.* Berlin: Schocken.

Birch, Bruce C., et al., eds. 1999. *A Theological Introduction to the Old Testament.* Nashville: Abingdon.

Blau, Ludwig. 1902. *Studien zum althebräischen Buchwesen und zur biblischen Litteraturgeschichte.* Budapest: Trübner.

Blanco Wissmann, Felipe. 2001. "Sargon, Mose und die Gegner Salomos. Zur Frage vorneuassyrischer Ursprünge der Mose-Erzählung." *BN* 110: 42–54.

———. 2008. *"Er tat das Rechte . . .": Beurteilungskriterien und Deuteronomismus in 1Kön 12–2Kön 25.* ATANT 93. Zürich: Theologischer Verlag.

Blenkinsopp, Joseph. 1976. "The Structure of P." *CBQ* 38: 275–92.

———. 1992. *The Pentateuch: An Introduction to the First Five Books of the Bible.* ABRL. New York: Doubleday.

———. 1995. "J, P, and J in Genesis 1:1–11:26: An Alternative Hypothesis," 1–15 in Astrid B. Beck et al., eds., *Fortunate the Eyes That See. FS David Noel Freedman.* Grand Rapids: Eerdmans.

———. 2002. "The Formation of the Hebrew Bible Canon: Isaiah as a Test Case," 53–67 in Lee Martin McDonald and James A. Sanders, eds., *The Canon Debate.* Peabody, MA: Hendrickson.

———. 2006. *Opening the Sealed Book: Interpretation of the Book of Isaiah in Late Antiquity.* Grand Rapids: Eerdmans.

Blum, Erhard. 1984. *Die Komposition der Vätergeschichte*. WMANT 57. Neukirchen-Vluyn: Neukirchener Verlag.

———. 1990. *Studien zur Komposition des Pentateuch*. BZAW 189. Berlin and New York: de Gruyter.

———. 1991. "Gibt es die Endgestalt des Pentateuch?" 46–57 in John A. Emerton, ed., *Congress Volume Leuven 1989*. VTSup 43. Leiden and Boston: Brill.

———. 1992/1993. "Jesaja und der *dbr* des Amos. Unzeitgemässe Überlegungen zu Jes 5,25; 9,7-20; 10,1-4." *DBAT* 28: 75–95.

———. 1994. "'Amos' in Jerusalem. Beobachtungen zu Am 6,1-7." *Henoch* 16: 23–47.

———. 1995. "Volk oder Kultgemeinde? Zum Bild des nachexilischen Judentums in der alttestamentlichen Wissenschaft." *Kirche und Israel* 10: 24–42.

———. 1997. "Jesajas prophetisches Testament." *ZAW* 108 (1996): 547–68; *ZAW* 109: 12–29.

———. 1998. "Abraham." *RGG* 1: 70–74.

———. 2002. "Die literarische Verbindung von Erzvätern und Exodus. Ein Gespräch mit neueren Endredaktionshypothesen," 119–56 in Jan Christian Gertz, Konrad Schmid, and Markus Witte, eds., *Abschied vom Jahwisten: Die Komposition des Hexateuch in der jüngsten Diskussion*. BZAW 315. Berlin and New York: de Gruyter.

———. 2006. "'Formgeschichte': ein irreführender Begriff?" 85–96 in Helmut Utzschneider and Erhard Blum, eds., *Lesarten der Bibel: Untersuchungen zu einer Theorie der Exegese des Alten Testaments*. Stuttgart: Kohlhammer.

Boda, Mark J., and Michael H. Floyd. 2003. *Bringing Out the Treasure: Inner Biblical Allusion in Zechariah 9–14*. JSOTSup 370. Sheffield: Sheffield Academic Press.

Bodi, Daniel. 2002. *Jérusalem à l'époque perse: "levons-nous et bâtissons" (Néhémie 2, 18)*. Paris: Geuthner.

Bormann, Alexander von. 1983. "Zum Umgang mit dem Epochenbegriff," 178–94 in Thomas Cramer, ed., *Literatur und Sprache im historischen Prozess: Vorträge des Deutschen Germanistentages Aachen 1982*. Tübingen: Niemeyer.

Bosshard, Erich, and Reinhard G. Kratz. 1990. "Maleachi im Zwölfprophetenbuch." *BN* 52: 27–46.

Bosshard-Nepustil, Erich. 1987. "Beobachtungen zum Zwölfprophetenbuch." *BN* 40: 30– 62.

———. 1997. *Rezeptionen von Jesaja 1–39 im Zwölfprophetenbuch: Untersuchungen zur literarischen Verbindung von Prophetenbüchern in babylonischer und persischer Zeit*. OBO 154. Fribourg: Universitätsverlag; Göttingen: Vandenhoeck & Ruprecht.

———. 2005. *Vor uns die Sintflut: Studien zu Text, Kontexten und Rezeption der Fluterzählung Genesis 6–9*. BWANT 165. Stuttgart: Kohlhammer.

Brandt, Peter. 2001. *Endgestalten des Kanons: Das Arrangement der Schriften Israels in der jüdischen und christlichen Bibel*. BBB 131. Berlin: Philo.

Braulik, Georg. 2003. "Die sieben Säulen der Weisheit im Buch Deuteronomium," 13–43 in Irmtraud Fischer, Ursula Rapp, and Johannes Schiller, eds., *Auf den Spuren der schriftgelehrten Weisen. FS Johannes Marböck*. BZAW 331. Berlin and New York: de Gruyter.

Brekelmans, Christianus H. W. 1979. "Wisdom Influence in Deuteronomy," 28–38 in Maurice Gilbert, ed., *La Sagesse de l'Ancien Testament*. BETL 51. Leuven: Leuven University Press; Peeters.

Brettler, Marc Zvi. 1989. "Ideology, History and Theology in 2 Kings XVII 7-23." *VT* 39: 268–82.

———. 1999. "Judaism in the Hebrew Bible? The Transition from Ancient Israelite Religion to Judaism." *CBQ* 61: 429–47.

Bringmann, Klaus. 1983. *Hellenistische Reform und Religionsverfolgung*. Göttingen: Vandenhoeck & Ruprecht.

———. 2005. *Geschichte der Juden im Altertum: Vom babylonischen Exil bis zur arabischen Eroberung*. Stuttgart: Klett-Cotta.

Broshi, Magen, and Israel Finkelstein. 1992. "The Population of Palestine in Iron Age II." *BASOR* 287: 47–60.

Budde, Karl. 1906. *Geschichte der althebräischen Litteratur*. Leipzig: C. F. Amelang.

Burkard, Günter, and Heinz J. Thissen. 2003. *Einführung in die altägyptische Literaturgeschichte 1: Altes und Mittleres Reich*. Einführungen und Quellentexte zur Ägyptologie 1. Münster: Lit.

Campenhausen, Hans von. 1968. *Die Entstehung der christlichen Bibel*. BHT 39. Tübingen: Mohr Siebeck.

Carr, David M. 1996a. "Canonization in the Context of Community: An Outline of the Formation of the Tanakh and the Christian Bible," 22–64 in Richard D. Weis and David M. Carr, eds., *A Gift of God in Due Season: Essays on Scripture and Community in Honor of James A. Sanders*. JSOTSup 225. Sheffield: Sheffield Academic Press.

———. 1996b. *Reading the Fractures of Genesis: Historical and Literary Approaches*. Louisville: Westminster John Knox.

———. 2001. "Genesis in Relation to the Moses Story. Diachronic and Synchronic Perspectives," 273–95 in André Wénin, ed., *Studies in the Book of Genesis: Literature, Redaction and History*. BETL 155. Leuven: University Press.

———. 2005. *Writing on the Tablet of the Heart: Origins of Scripture and Literature*. Oxford and New York: Oxford University Press.

———. 2006. "Mündlich-schriftliche Bildung und der Ursprung antiker Literaturen," 183–98 in Helmut Utzschneider and Erhard Blum, eds., *Lesarten der Bibel: Untersuchungen zu einer Theorie der Exegese des Alten Testaments*. Stuttgart: Kohlhammer.

———. 2011. *The Formation of the Hebrew Bible: A New Reconstruction*. Oxford and New York: Oxford University Press.

Carter, Charles E. 1999. *The Emergence of Yehud in the Persian Period: A Social and Demographic Study*. JSOTSup 294. Sheffield: Sheffield Academic Press.

Cassel, David. 1872, 1873. *Geschichte der jüdischen Literatur*. 2 vols. Berlin: Gerschel.

Chapman, Stephen B. 2000. *The Law and the Prophets: A Study in Old Testament Canon Formation*. FAT 27. Tübingen: Mohr Siebeck.

Christensen, Duane. 1998. "The Lost Books of the Bible." *Bible Review* 14: 24–31.

Clements, Ronald E. 1996. "The Deuteronomic Law of Centralisation and the Catastrophe of 587 B.C.," 5–25 in John Barton and David J. Reimer, eds., *After the Exile: Essays in Honour of Rex Mason*. Macon, GA: Mercer University Press.

———. 2007. "A Royal Privilege: Dining in the Presence of the Great King (2 Kings 25.27-30)," 49–66 in Robert Rezetko et al., eds., *Reflection and Refraction. FS A. Graeme Auld*. VTSup 113. Leiden and Boston: Brill.

Clifford, Richard J. 1999. *Proverbs: A Commentary*. OTL. Louisville: Westminster John Knox.

Clines, David J. A. 2004. "Putting Elihu in His Place. A Proposal for the Relocation of Job 32–37." *JSOT* 29: 243–53.

Cohen, Shaye J. D. 2001. *The Beginnings of Jewishness: Boundaries, Varieties, Uncertainties*. Berkeley: University of California Press.

Collins, John J. ²2000. *Between Athens and Jerusalem: Jewish Identity in the Hellenistic Diaspora*. Grand Rapids: Eerdmans; Livonia, MI: Dove Booksellers.

———. 2005. *Jewish Cult and Hellenistic Culture: Essays on the Jewish Encounter with Hellenism and Roman Rule*. JSJSup 100. Leiden and Boston: Brill.

———, and Gregory E. Sterling, eds. 2001. *Hellenism in the Land of Israel*. Notre Dame, IN: Notre Dame University Press.

Colpe, Carsten. 2003. *Iranier, Aramäer, Hebräer, Hellenen. Iranische Religionen und ihre Westbeziehungen: Einzelstudien und Versuch einer Zusammenschau*. WUNT 154. Tübingen: Mohr Siebeck.

Coote, Robert B. 1980. "The Tell Siran Bottle Inscription." *BASOR* 240: 93.

Creelman, Harlan. 1917. *An Introduction to the Old Testament Chronologically Arranged*. New York: Macmillan.

Cross, Frank Moore. 1973. "The Themes of the Book of Kings and the Structure of the Deuteronomistic History," 274–89 in idem, *Canaanite Myth and Hebrew Epic: Essays in the History of the Religion of Israel*. Cambridge, MA: Harvard University Press.

Crüsemann, Frank. 1981. "Die Eigenständigkeit der Urgeschichte. Ein Beitrag zur Diskussion um den 'Jahwisten,'" 11–29 in Jörg Jeremias and Lothar Perlitt, eds., *Die Botschaft und die Boten, FS Hans Walter Wolff*. Neukirchen-Vluyn: Neukirchener Verlag.

———. 1987. "Das 'portative Vaterland,'" 63–79 in Aleida Assmann and Jan Assmann, eds., *Kanon und Zensur*. Munich: Fink.

———. 1996. *Die Tora: Theologie und Sozialgeschichte des alttestamentlichen Gesetzes*. 3d ed. Munich: Kaiser, 1992. English: *The Torah: Theology and Social History of Old Testament Law*. Translated by Allan W. Mahnke. Minneapolis: Fortress Press.

———. 2002. "'*th*—'Jetzt.' Hosea 4–11 als Anfang der Schriftprophetie," 13–31 in Erich Zenger, ed., *"Wort Jhwhs, das geschah . . ." (Hos 1,1): Studien zum Zwölfprophetenbuch*. HBS 35. Freiburg et al.: Herder.

Dahmen, Ulrich, Armin Lange, and Hermann Lichtenberger, eds. 2000. *Die Textfunde vom Toten Meer und der Text der Hebräischen Bibel*. Neukirchen-Vluyn: Neukirchener Verlag.

Davies, Graham I. 1995. "Were There Schools in Ancient Israel?" 199–211 in John Day, Robert P. Gordon, and H. G. M. Williamson, eds., *Wisdom in Ancient Israel. FS John A. Emerton*. New York and Cambridge: Cambridge University Press.

Day, John. 2004. "How Many Pre-Exilic Psalms Are There?" 225–50 in idem, ed., *In Search of Pre-Exilic Israel: Proceedings of the Oxford Old Testament Seminar*. JSOTSup 406. London and New York: T & T Clark.

Dearman, John Andrew. 1988. *Property Rights in the Eighth-Century Prophets: The Conflict and Its Background*. SBLDS 106. Atlanta: Scholars Press.

———, ed. 1989. *Studies in the Mesha Inscription and Moab*. Atlanta: Scholars Press.

Deines, Roland. 2001. "The Pharisees Between 'Judaisms' and 'Common Judaism,'" 443–504 in D. A. Carson et al., eds., *Justification and Variegated Nomism. 1: The Complexities of Second Temple Judaism*. WUNT 2d ser. 140. Tübingen: Mohr Siebeck.

Delkurt, Holger. 1991. "Grundprobleme alttestamentlicher Weisheit." *VF* 36: 38–71.

Dell, Katharine J. 2004. "How Much Wisdom Literature Has Its Roots in the Pre-Exilic Period" 251–71 in John Day, ed., *In Search of Pre-Exilic Israel: Proceedings of the Oxford Old Testament Seminar*. JSOTSup 406. London and New York: T & T Clark.

Dequeker, Luc. 1993. "Darius the Persian and the Reconstruction of the Jewish Temple in Jerusalem (Esr 4,23)," 67–92 in Jan Quaegebeur, ed., *Ritual and Sacrifice in the Ancient Near East*, OLA 55. Leuven: Peeters.

———. 1997. "Nehemia and the Restoration of the Temple after Exile," 547–67 in Marc Vervenne and Johan Lust, eds., *Deuteronomy and Deuteronomic Literature. FS C. H. W. Brekelmans*. BETL 133. Leuven: University Press; Peeters.

Dever, William G. 2001. *What Did the Biblical Writers Know and When Did They Know It?* Grand Rapids: Eerdmans.

Diebner, Bernd J. 1986. "Psalm 1 als 'Motto' der Sammlung des kanonischen Psalters." *DBAT* 23: 7–45.

———. 1992/1993. "The 'Old Testament'—Anti-Hellenistic Literature? Grundsätzliches ausgehend von Gedanken Niels Peter Lemches oder: Das Grosse Verschweigen . . ." *DBAT* 28: 10–40.

Dietrich, Walter. 1997. *Die frühe Königszeit in Israel: 10. Jahrhundert v. Chr.* Biblische Enzyklopädie 3. Stuttgart: Kohlhammer. English: *The Early Monarchy in Israel: the Tenth Century B.C.E.* Translated by Joachim Vette. Atlanta: SBL, 2007.

———. 1999. "Deuteronomistisches Geschichtswerk." *RGG* 2: 688–92.

———. 2006. *David: Der Herrscher mit der Harfe*. Biblische Gestalten (BG) 14. Leipzig: Evangelische Verlagsanstalt.

———, and Thomas Naumann. 1995. *Die Samuelbücher*. EdF 287. Darmstadt: Wissenschaftliche Buchgesellschaft.

Dijkstra, Meindert. 2005. "'As for the Other Events . . .' Annals and Chronicles in Israel and in the Ancient Near East," 14–44 in Robert P. Gordon and Johannes C. de Moor, eds., *The Old Testament in Its World: Papers Read at the Winter Meeting, January 2003*. OTS 52. Leiden and New York: Brill.

Dodd, Charles Harold. 1935. *The Parables of the Kingdom*. London: Nisbet.

Donner, Herbert. 1976. *Die literarische Gestalt der alttestamentlichen Josephsgeschichte*. SHAW. Philosophisch-Historische Klasse 2. Heidelberg: Winter.

———. 1985. "Jesaja XVI 1–7: Ein Abrogationsfall innerhalb des Kanons—Implikationen und Konsequenzen," 81–95 in John A. Emerton, ed., *Congress Volume Salamanca*. VTSup 36. Leiden: Brill = idem, *Aufsätze zum Alten Testament aus vier Jahrzehnten*, 165–79. BZAW 224. Berlin and New York: de Gruyter, 1994.

———. 1994a. "Der Redaktor. Überlegungen zum vorkritischen Umgang mit der Heiligen Schrift." *Henoch* 2 (1980): 1–30 = idem, *Aufsätze zum Alten Testament aus vier Jahrzehnten*, 259–85. BZAW 224. Berlin and New York: de Gruyter.

———. 1994b. "Der verlässliche Prophet. Betrachtungen zu I Makk 14,41ff und zu Ps 110," 213–23 in idem, *Aufsätze zum Alten Testament aus vier Jahrzehnten*. BZAW 224. Berlin and New York: de Gruyter.

———. ³2000, 2001. *Geschichte des Volkes Israel und seiner Nachbarn in Grundzügen*. GAT 4/1, 2. Göttingen: Vandenhoeck & Ruprecht.

Dörrfuss, Ernst Michael. 1994. *Mose in den Chronikbüchern: Garant theokratischer Zukunftserwartung*. BZAW 219. Berlin and New York: de Gruyter.

Dozeman, Thomas B., and Konrad Schmid, eds. 2006. *A Farewell to the Yahwist? The*

Composition of the Pentateuch in Recent European Interpretation. SBLSymS 34. Atlanta: SBL.

———, Konrad Schmid, and Baruch J. Schwartz, eds. 2011. *The Pentateuch: International Perspectives on Current Research.* FAT 78. Tübingen: Mohr Siebeck.

Drenkhahn, Rosemarie. 1980. *Die Elephantine-Stele des Sethnacht und ihr historischer Hintergrund.* ÄgAbh 36. Wiesbaden: Harrassowitz.

Driver, Godfrey R. 1948. *Semitic Writing: From Pictograph to Alphabet.* Oxford: Oxford University Press.

Droysen, Johann Gustav. 1952, 1953. *Geschichte des Hellenismus.* Hamburg: Perthes, 1836–1843. Edited by Erich Bayer. Basel: B. Schwabe.

Duhm, Bernhard. 1901. *Das Buch Jeremia.* KHC 11. Tübingen and Leipzig: Mohr (Siebeck).

———. 1902. *Das Buch Jesaia übersetzt und erklärt.* HKAT 3/1. Göttingen: Vandenhoeck & Ruprecht.

———. ^{2}1922. *Die Psalmen.* HAT 14. Freiburg et al.: Herder.

Ebeling, Gerhard. 1972. *Studium der Theologie: Eine enzyklopädische Orientierung.* UTB 446. Tübingen: Mohr. English: *The Study of Theology.* Translated by Duane A. Priebe. Philadelphia: Fortress Press, 1976.

Eberhardt, Gönke. 2007. *JHWH und die Unterwelt: Spuren einer Kompetenzausweitung JHWHs im Alten Testament.* FAT II/23. Tübingen: Mohr (Siebeck).

Eberhart, Christian. 2002. *Studien zur Bedeutung der Opfer im Alten Testament: Die Signifikanz von Blut- und Verbrennungsriten im kultischen Rahmen.* WMANT 94. Neukirchen-Vluyn: Neukirchener Verlag.

Edelman, Diana V., ed. 1995. *The Triumph of Elohim: From Yahwisms to Judaisms.* CBET 13. Kampen: Kok Pharos.

———. 2005. *The Origins of the "Second" Temple Period: Persian Imperial Policy and the Rebuilding of Yehud.* London: Equinox.

Edzard, Dietz Otto, Wolfgang Röllig, and Einar von Schuler. 1987–1990. "Literatur." *RlA* 7: 35–75.

Ehring, Christina. 2007. *Die Rückkehr JHWHs: Traditions- und religionsgeschichtliche Untersuchungen zu Jesaja 40, 1-11, Jesaja 52, 7-10 und verwandten Texten.* WMANT 116. Neukirchen-Vluyn: Neukirchener Verlag.

Ehrlich, Carl S. 1996. *The Philistines in Transition: A History from ca. 1000–730 B.C.E.* SHANE 10. Leiden and New York: Brill.

———, ed. 2011. *From an Antique Land: An Introduction to Ancient Near Eastern Literature.* Lanham: Rowland & Littlefield.

Eissfeldt, Otto. 1962. "Israelitisch-jüdische Religionsgeschichte und alttestamentliche Theologie" [1926], 105–14 in idem, *Kleine Schriften* 1. Tübingen: Mohr.

———. ^{3}1964. *Einleitung in das Alte Testament unter Einschluss der Apokryphen und Pseudepigraphen.* Tübingen: Mohr (Siebeck).

Elliger, Karl. 1966. *Leviticus.* HAT 1/4. Tübingen: Mohr.

Emerton, John A. 2000. "The Hebrew Language," 171–99 in Andrew D. H. Mayes, ed., *Text and Context: Essays by Members of the Society for Old Testament Study.* Oxford and New York: Oxford University Press.

Emmendörffer, Michael. 1998. *Der ferne Gott: Eine Untersuchung der alttestamentlichen Volksklagelieder vor dem Hintergrund der mesopotamischen Literatur.* FAT 21. Tübingen: Mohr (Siebeck).

Engnell, Ivan. ²1967. *Studies in Divine Kingship in the Ancient Near East,* 2nd ed. Oxford: Blackwell.

Ernst, Alexander B. 1994. *Weisheitliche Kultkritik: Zu Theologie und Ethik des Sprüchebuchs und der Prophetie des 8. Jahrhunderts.* BibS(N) 23. Neukirchen-Vluyn: Neukirchener Verlag.

Eynikel, Erik. 1996. *The Reform of King Josiah and the Composition of the Deuteronomistic History.* OTS 33. Leiden and New York: Brill.

Fabry, Heinz-Josef. 1998. "Qumran," 230–59. *Neues Bibel-Lexikon 3.* Zürich and Düsseldorf: Benziger.

———. 2006. "Die Handschriften vom Toten Meer und ihre Bedeutung für den Text der Hebräischen Bibel," 11–29 in Ulrich Dahmen, Hartmut Stegemann, and Günter Stemberger, eds., *Qumran, Bibelwissenschaften, Antike Judaistik.* Paderborn: Bonifatius.

Falkenstein, Adam. 1965. "Fluch über Akkade." *ZA* 57: 43–124.

Finkelstein, Israel. 1996. "The Archaeology of the United Monarchy. An Alternative View." *Levant* 28: 177–87.

———, and Neil Asher Silberman. 2001. *The Bible Unearthed.* New York et al.: Free Press.

———, and Neil Asher Silberman. 2006. *David and Solomon: In Search of the Bible's Sacred Kings and the Roots of the Western Tradition in Israel.* New York: Free Press.

Fischer, Alexander Achilles. 2004. *Von Hebron nach Jerusalem: Eine redaktionsgeschichtliche Studie zur Erzählung von König David in II Sam 1–5.* BZAW 335. Berlin and New York: de Gruyter.

———. 2005. "Die literarische Entstehung des Grossreiches Davids und ihr geschichtlicher Hintergrund. Zur Darstellung der Kriegs-Chronik in 2Sam 8,1-14(15)," 101–28 in Uwe Becker and Jürgen van Oorschot, eds., *Das Alte Testament—ein Geschichtsbuch?! Geschichtsschreibung und Geschichtsüberlieferung im antiken Israel.* ABG 17. Leipzig: Evangelische Verlagsanstalt.

Fishbane, Michael A. 1985. *Biblical Interpretation in Ancient Israel.* Oxford and New York: Oxford University Press.

Fitzgerald, Aloysius. 1972. "The Mythological Background for the Presentation of Jerusalem as a Queen and False Worship as Adultery in the OT." *CBQ* 34: 403–16.

———. 1975. "BTLWT and BT as Titles for Capital Cities." *CBQ* 37: 167–83.

Flint, Peter W., ed. 2001. *The Bible at Qumran: Text, Shape, and Interpretation.* Grand Rapids: Eerdmans.

Fohrer, Georg. 1989. *Erzähler und Propheten im Alten Testament: Geschichte der israelitischen und frühjüdischen Literatur.* UTB 1547. Heidelberg: Quelle & Meyer.

Fox, Michael V. 1996. "The Social Location of the Book of Proverbs," 227–39 in idem, ed., *Texts, Temples, and Traditions: A Tribute to Menahem Haran.* Winona Lake, IN: Eisenbrauns.

———. 2000. *Proverbs 1–9.* AB 18A. New York: Doubleday.

Frei, Peter, and Klaus Koch. ²1996. *Reichsidee und Reichsorganisation im Perserreich.* OBO 337. Fribourg: Universitätsverlag; Göttingen: Vandenhoeck & Ruprecht.

Frevel, Christian. 2000. *Mit Blick auf das Land die Schöpfung erinnern: Zum Ende der Priestergrundschrift.* HBS 23. Freiburg and New York: Herder.

———, ed. 2005. *Medien im antiken Palästina: Materielle Kommunikation und Medialität als Thema der Palästinaarchäologie.* FAT II/10. Tübingen: Mohr (Siebeck).

Fritz, Volkmar. 1996a. "Philister und Israel." *TRE* 26: 518–23.

———. 1996b. *Die Entstehung Israels im 12. und 11. Jh. v. Chr.* Biblische Enzyklopädie 2. Stuttgart: Kohlhammer.

Frymer-Kenski, Tikvah. 2003. "Israel," 975–1046 in Raymond Westbrook, ed., *A History of Ancient Near Eastern Law* 2. Handbook of Oriental Studies. I/72. Leiden and Boston: Brill.

Fuchs, Andreas. 1994. *Die Inschriften Sargons II. aus Khorsabad.* Göttingen: Cuvillier.

Fürst, Julius. 1867, 1870. *Geschichte der biblischen Literatur und des jüdisch-hellenistischen Schriftthums.* Leipzig: Tauchnitz.

Galil, Gershon. 1996. *The Chronology of the Kings of Israel and Judah.* Studies in the History and Culture of the Ancient Near East (SHCANE) 9. Leiden and New York: Brill.

———. 2004. "The Chronological Framework of the Deuteronomistic History." *Bib* 85: 413–21.

Galter, Hannes D. 2006. "Sargon der Zweite. Über die Wiederinszenierung von Geschichte," 279–302 in Robert Rollinger and Brigitte Truschnegg, eds., *Altertum und Mittelmeerraum: Die antike Welt diesseits und jenseits der Levante. FS P. W. Haider.* Stuttgart: F. Steiner.

García Martínez, Florentino. ²1994, 1996. *The Dead Sea Scrolls Translated.* Trans. Wilfrid G. E. Watson. Leiden: Brill; Grand Rapids: Eerdmans.

Gärtner, Judith. 2006. *Jesaja 66 und Sacharja 14 als Summe der Prophetie: Eine traditions- und redaktionsgeschichtliche Studie zum Abschluss des Jesaja- und Zwölfprophetenbuches.* WMANT 114. Neukirchen-Vluyn: Neukirchener Verlag.

Gauger, Jörg D. 2007. "Antiochos III und Artaxerxes. Der Fremdherrscher als Wohltäter." *JSJ* 38: 196–225.

Gehrke, Hans-Joachim. 1990. *Geschichte des Hellenismus.* Munich: Oldenbourg.

Gelin, Albert. 1959. "La question des 'relectures' bibliques à l'intérieur d'une tradition vivante," 303–15 in *Sacra Pagina. Miscellanea Biblica: Congressus Internationalis Catholici de re biblica.* BETL 12/13, Vol. 1. Gembloux: Duculot.

Geoghegan, Jeffrey C. 2003. "'Until This Day' and the Preexilic Redaction of the Deuteronomistic History." *JBL* 122: 201–27.

———. 2006. *The Time, Place and Purpose of the Deuteronomistic History: The Evidence of "Until This Day."* BJS 347. Providence RI: Brown Judaic Studies.

Gerstenberger, Erhard S. 2001. *Theologien im Alten Testament: Pluralität und Synkretismus alttestamentlichen Gottesglaubens.* Stuttgart: Kohlhammer. English: *Theologies in the Old Testament.* Translated by John Bowden. Minneapolis: Fortress Press, 2002.

———. 2005. *Israel in der Perserzeit. 5. und 4. Jahrhundert v. Chr.* Biblische Enzyklopädie 8. Stuttgart: Kohlhammer.

Gertz, Jan Christian. 2000a. "Die Stellung des kleinen geschichtlichen Credos in der Redaktionsgeschichte von Deuteronomium und Pentateuch," 30–45 in Reinhard G. Kratz and Hermann Spieckermann, eds., *Liebe und Gebot: Studien zum Deuteronomium. FS Lothar Perlitt.* FRLANT 190. Göttingen: Vandenhoeck & Ruprecht.

———. 2000b. *Tradition und Redaktion in der Exoduserzählung.* FRLANT 189. Göttingen: Vandenhoeck & Ruprecht.

———. 2001. "Beobachtungen zu Komposition und Redaktion in Exodus 32–34," 88–106 in Matthias Köckert and Erhard Blum, eds., *Gottes Volk am Sinai.*

Veröffentlichungen der Wissenschaftlichen Gesellschaft für Theologie (VWGT) 18. Gütersloh: Kaiser; Gütersloher Verlagshaus.

———. 2002. "Mose und die Ursprünge der jüdischen Religion." *ZTK* 99: 3–20.

———. 2003. "Die unbedingte Gerichtsankündigung des Amos," 153–70 in Franz Sedlmeier, ed., *Gottes Wege suchend: Beiträge zum Verständnis der Bibel und ihrer Botschaft. FS Rudolf Mosis.* Würzburg: Echter Verlag.

———. 2004. "Konstruierte Erinnerung. Alttestamentliche Historiographie im Spiegel von Archäologie und literarhistorischer Kritik am Fallbeispiel des salomonischen Königtums." *BTZ* 21: 3–29.

———, ed. 2006a. *Grundinformation Altes Testament: Eine Einführung in Literatur, Religion und Geschichte des Alten Testaments.* UTB 2745. Göttingen: Vandenhoeck & Ruprecht.

———. 2006b. "Beobachtungen zum literarischen Charakter und zum geistesgeschichtlichen Ort der nichtpriesterschriftlichen Sintfluterzählung," 41–57 in Martin Beck and Ulrike Schorn, eds., *Auf dem Weg zur Endgestalt von Genesis bis II Regum. FS Hans-Christoph Schmitt.* BZAW 370. Berlin and New York: de Gruyter.

———, Konrad Schmid, and Markus Witte, eds. 2002. *Abschied vom Jahwisten: Die Komposition des Hexateuch in der jüngsten Diskussion.* BZAW 215. Berlin and New York: de Gruyter.

Gesche, Petra. 2001. *Schulunterricht in Babylonien im ersten Jahrtausend v. Chr.* AOAT 275. Münster: Ugarit-Verlag.

Gese, Hartmut. 1974. "Anfang und Ende der Apokalyptic, dargestellt am Sacharjabuch." *ZTK* 70 (1973): 20–49 = idem, *Vom Sinai zum Zion: Alttestamentliche Beiträge zur biblischen Theologie*, 202–30. BevT 64. Munich: Kaiser.

Gieselmann, Bernd. 1994. "Die sogenannte josianische Reform in der gegenwärtigen Forschung." *ZAW* 106: 223–42.

Glessmer, Uwe. 1993. "Liste der biblischen Texte aus Qumran." *RdQ* 62: 153–92

Gnuse, Robert. 1998. "Spilt Water—Tales of David (2 Sam 23:13-17) and Alexander (Arrian, Anabasis of Alexander 6.26.1-3)." *SJOT* 12: 233–48.

Goldstein, Johannes. 2001. *Das Gebet der Gottesknechte: Jesaja 63,7–64,11 im Jesajabuch.* WMANT 92. Neukirchen-Vluyn: Neukirchener Verlag.

Goldman, Yohanan. 1992. *Prophétie et royauté au retour de l'exil: Les origines littéraires de la forme massorétique du livre de Jérémie.* OBO 118. Fribourg: Universitätsverlag; Göttingen: Vandenhoeck & Ruprecht.

Goldstein, Jonathan. 2002. *Peoples of an Almighty God: Competing Religions in the Ancient World.* ABRL. New York: Doubleday.

Gordon, Robert P. 2005. "'Comparativism' and the God of Israel," 45–67 in idem and Johannes C. de Moor, eds., *The Old Testament in Its World: Papers Read at the Winter Meeting, January 2003.* OTS 52. Leiden and Boston: Brill.

Görg, Manfred. 1997. *Die Beziehungen zwischen dem alten Israel und Ägypten: Von den Anfängen bis zum Exil.* Darmstadt: Wissenschaftliche Buchgesellschaft.

Gottwald, Norman K. 1985. *The Hebrew Bible: A Socio-Literary Introduction.* Minneapolis: Fortress Press.

Goulder, Michael. 1982. *The Psalms of the Sons of Korah.* JSOTSup 20. Sheffield: JSOT Press.

Grabbe, Lester L. 1991. "Reconstructing History from the Book of Ezra," 98–106 in Philip R. Davies, ed., *Second Temple Studies 1: Persian Period.* JSOTSup 177. Sheffield: JSOT Press.

———. 2000. *Judaic Religion in the Second Temple Period: Belief and Practice from the Exile to Yavneh*. London and New York: Routledge.

———, ed. 2003. *"Like a Bird in a Cage": The Invasion of Sennacherib in 701 BCE*. JSOTSup 363/European Seminar in Historical Methodology (ESHM) 4. Sheffield: Sheffield Academic Press; London and New York: T & T Clark/Continuum.

———. 2007. "Mighty Oaks from (Genetically Manipulated?) Acorns Grow: The Chronicle of the Kings of Judah as a Source of the Deuteronomistic History," 155–73 in Robert Rezetko et al., eds., *Reflection and Refraction. FS A. Graeme Auld*. VTSup 113. Leiden and Boston: Brill.

Greenstein, Edward L. 2003. "The Poem of Wisdom in Job 28 in Its Conceptual and Literary Contexts," 253–80 in Ellen van Wolde, ed., *Job 28: Cognition in Context*. Leiden: Brill.

Gross, Walter. 1987. "Israels Hoffnung auf die Erneuerung des Staates," 87–122 in Josef Schreiner, ed., *Unterwegs zur Kirche: Alttestamentliche Konzeptionen*. QD 110. Freiburg: Herder = idem, *Studien zur Priesterschrift und alttestamentlichen Gottesbildern*, 65–96. SBAB 30. Stuttgart: Katholisches Bibelwerk, 1999.

———. 2009. *Richter*. Herders Theologischer Kommentar zum Alten Testament. Freiburg et al.: Herder.

Grünwaldt, Klaus. 1992. *Exil und Identität: Beschneidung, Passa und Sabbat in der Priesterschrift*. BBB 85. Frankfurt: Hain.

Guillaume, Philippe. 2004. *Waiting for Josiah: The Judges*. JSOTSup 385. London: T & T Clark.

Gumbrecht, Hans-Ulrich, and Ursula Link-Heer, eds. 1985. *Epochenschwellen und Epochenstrukturen im Diskurs der Literatur- und Sprachhistorie*. Suhrkamp Taschenbuch Wissenschaft (stw) 486. Frankfurt: Suhrkamp.

Gunkel, Hermann. 1906a. "Die Grundprobleme der israelitischen Literaturgeschichte." OLZ 27: 1797–1800, 1861–66.

———. 1906b. "Die israelitische Literatur," 51–102 in Paul Hinneberg, ed., *Die Kultur der Gegenwart: Ihre Entwicklung und ihre Ziele*. Berlin: Teubner. Reprints Leipzig: Teubner, 1925; Darmstadt: Wissenschaftliche Buchgesellschaft, 1963.

———. 1913. *Reden und Aufsätze*. Göttingen: Vandenhoeck & Ruprecht.

Gunneweg, Antonius H. J. 1987. *Nehemia*. KAT. Gütersloh: Gerd Mohn.

Haag, Ernst. 2003. *Das hellenistische Zeitalter: Israel und die Bibel im 4. bis 1. Jahrhundert v. Chr*. Biblische Enzyklopädie 9. Stuttgart: Kohlhammer.

Haas, Volkert. 2006. *Die hethitische Literatur: Texte, Stilistik, Motive*. Berlin and New York: de Gruyter.

Hagedorn, Anselm C. 2005. "'Who Would Invite a Stranger from Abroad?' The Presence of Greeks in Palestine in Old Testament Times," 68–93 in Robert P. Gordon and Johannes C. de Moor, eds., *The Old Testament in Its World: Papers Read at the Winter Meeting, January 2003*. OTS 52. Leiden and New York: Brill.

Hahn, Ferdinand. 1998. *Frühjüdische und urchristliche Apokalyptik: Eine Einführung*. Biblisch-theologische Studien (BTSt) 36. Neukirchen-Vluyn: Neukirchener Verlag.

Hahn, Johannes, ed. 2002. *Zerstörungen des Jerusalemer Tempels: Geschehen—Wahrnehmung—Bewältigung*. WUNT 147. Tübingen: Mohr (Siebeck).

Halbe, Jörn. 1975. *Das Privilegrecht Jahwes Ex 34,10-26: Gestalt und Wesen, Herkunft und Wirken in vordeuteronomischer Zeit*. FRLANT 114. Göttingen: Vandenhoeck & Ruprecht.

Hallo, William W. 1976. "Toward a History of Sumerian Literature," 123–57 in

Sumeriological Studies in Honor of Thorkild Jacobsen. Assyriological Studies 20. Chicago: University of Chicago Press.

Halpern, Baruch, and David S. Vanderhooft. 1991. "The Editions of Kings in the 7th–6th Centuries B.C.E." *HUCA* 62: 179–244.

Haran, Menahem. 1985. "Book Size and the Device of Catch-Lines in the Biblical Canon." *JJS* 36: 1-11.

———. 1988. "On the Diffusion of Literacy and Schools in Ancient Israel," 81–95 in John A. Emerton, ed., *Congress Volume Jerusalem 1986*, VTSup 40. Leiden: Brill.

———. 1999. "The Books of the Chronicles 'of the Kings of Judah' and 'of the Kings of Israel': What Sort of Books Were They?" *VT* 49: 156–64.

Hardmeier, Christof. 1990. *Prophetie im Streit vor dem Untergang Judas: Erzählkommunikative Studien zur Entstehungssituation der Jesaja- und Jeremiaerzählungen in II Reg 18–20 und Jer 37–40*. BZAW 187. Berlin and New York: de Gruyter.

———. (in press.) "Geschichtsdivinatorik und Zukunftsheuristik im schriftprophetischen Diskurs (Jesaja 9,7–10,27). Eine exegetische sowie geschichts- und religionsphilosophisch reflektierte Studie zu den Jesajadiskursen in Jesaja 1–11," in Frank Bezner and Karl-Joachim Hölkeskamp, eds., *Diesseits von Geschichte und Gedächtnis: Vormoderne (Re-)konstruktion von Vergangenheit als kulturwissenshaftliche Herausforderung*. Cologne and Weimar.

Harris, William V. 1989. *Ancient Literacy*. Cambridge, MA: Harvard University Press.

Hartenstein, Friedhelm. 1997. *Die Unzugänglichkeit Gottes im Heiligtum: Jesaja 6 und der Wohnort JHWHs in der Jerusalemer Kulttradition*. WMANT 75. Neukirchen-Vluyn: Neukirchener Verlag.

———. 2003. "Religionsgeschichte Israels—ein Überblick über die Forschung seit 1990." *VF* 48: 2–28.

———. 2004. "'Der im Himmel thront, lacht' (Ps 2,4). Psalm 2 im Wandel religions- und theologiegschichtlicher Kontexte," 148–88 in Dieter Sänger, ed., *Gottessohn und Menschensohn: Exegetische Studien zu zwei Paradigmen biblischer Intertextualität*. BTSt 67. Neukirchen-Vluyn: Neukirchener Verlag.

———. 2010. "'Schaffe mir Recht, JHWH!' (Psalm 7,9): Zum theologischen und anthropologischen Profil der Teilkomposition Psalm 3–14," 229–58 in Erich Zenger, ed., *The Composition of the Book of Psalms*. BETL 238. Leuven: Peeters.

———. 2011. *Das Archiv des verborgenen Gottes: Studien zur Unheilsprophetie Jesajas und zur Zionstheologie der Psalmen in assyrischer Zeit*. BTSt 74. Neukirchen-Vluyn: Neukirchener.

———, and Bernd Janowski. 2003. "Psalmen/Psalter I.–III." *RGG* 6: 1762–77.

Hausmann, Jutta. 1995. *Studien zum Menschenbild der älteren Weisheit*. FAT 7. Tübingen: Mohr (Siebeck).

Heaton, Eric William. 1994. *The School Tradition of the Old Testament*. Oxford and New York: Oxford University Press.

Helck, Wolfgang. 1971. *Die Beziehungen Ägyptens zu Vorderasien im 3. und 2. Jahrtausend v. Chr.*, 2nd ed. Ägyptologische Abhandlungen (ÄA) 5. Wiesbaden: Harrassowitz.

Hempel, Johannes. 1930. *Die althebräische Literatur und ihr hellenistisch-jüdisches Nachleben*. Wildpark-Potsdam: Akademische Verlagsgesellschaft Athenaion.

Hendel, Ron. 2001. "The Exodus in Biblical Memory." *JBL* 120: 601–22.

Hengel, Martin. 1974. *Judentum und Hellenismus*. WUNT 10. Tübingen: Mohr, ³1988.

English: *Judaism and Hellenism: Studies in their Encounter in Palestine During the Early Hellenistic Period*. Translated by John Bowden. London: SCM; Philadelphia: Fortress Press.

———. 1992. "Die Septuaginta als 'christliche Schriftensammlung,' ihre Vorgeschichte und das Problem ihres Kanons," 34–127 in Wolfhart Pannenberg and Theodor Schneider, eds., *Verbindliches Zeugnis I: Kanon, Schrift, Tradition*. Dialog der Kirchen 7. Freiburg: Herder; Göttingen: Vandenhoeck & Ruprecht = idem and Anna Maria Schwemer, eds., *Die Septuaginta zwischen Judentum und Christentum*, 182–284. WUNT 72. Tübingen: Mohr (Siebeck), 1994.

Herder, Johann Gottfried. 1890. *Vom Geist der Ebräischen Poesie (1782–83)*. 2 vols. Gotha: Perthes.

Hermisson, Hans-Jürgen. 1996. "Weisheit," 200–26 in Hans Jochen Boecker et al., *Altes Testament*, 5th ed. Neukirchen-Vluyn: Neukirchener Verlag.

———. 1999. "Deuterojesaja." *RGG* 2: 684–88.

———. 2000. *Alttestamentliche Theologie und Religionsgeschichte Israels*. Forum Theologische Literaturzeitung (FTL) Series 1. Leipzig: Evangelische Verlagsanstalt.

Hertzberg, Hans Wilhelm. 1936. "Nachgeschichte alttestamentlicher Texte innerhalb des Alten Testaments," 110–21 in Paul Volz et al., eds., *Werden und Wesen des Alten Testaments*. BZAW 66. Berlin: de Gruyter = idem, *Beiträge zur Traditionsgeschichte und Theologie des Alten Testaments*, 69–80. Göttingen: Vandenhoeck & Ruprecht, 1962.

Hess, Richard S. 2002. "Literacy in Iron Age Israel," 82–102 in V. Phillips Long et al., eds., *Windows into Old Testament History: Evidence, Argument, and the Crisis of "Biblical Israel."* Grand Rapids: Eerdmans.

———. 2006. "Writing about Writing: Abecedaries and Evidence for Literacy in Ancient Israel." *VT* 56: 342–46.

Hezser, Catherine. 2001. *Jewish Literacy in Roman Palestine*. TSAJ 81. Tübingen: Mohr.

Hjelm, Ingrid. 2004. "What Do Samaritans and Jews Have in Common?" Recent Trends in Samaritan Studies." *Currents in Biblical Research (CBR)* 3: 9–59.

Höffken, Peter. 1984. "Eine Bemerkung zum religionsgeschichtlichen Hintergrund von Dtn 6,4." *BZ* 28: 88–93.

———. 1985. "Das EGO des Weisen. Subjektivierungsprozesse in der Weisheitsliteratur." *TZ* 41: 121–34.

———. 2001. "Zum Kanonbewusstsein des Josephus Flavius in Contra Apionem und in der Antiquitates." *JSJ* 32: 159–77.

Hofmann, N. J. 2000. "Die 'nacherzählte' Bibel. Erwägungen zum sogenannten 'Rewritten-Bible-Phänomen.'" *Salesianum* 62: 3–17.

Hölbl, Günther. 1994. *Geschichte des Ptolemäerreiches: Politik, Ideologie und religiöse Kultur von Alexander dem Grossen bis zur römischen Eroberung*. Darmstadt: Wissenschaftliche Buchgesellschaft. English: *A History of the Ptolemaic Empire*. Translated by Tina Saavedra. London and New York: Routledge, 2001.

———. 1997. "Zur Legitimation der Ptolemäer als Pharaonen," 21–34 in Rolf Gundlach and Christine Raedler, eds., *Selbstverständnis und Realität: Akten des Symposiums zur Ägyptischen Königsideologie in Mainz, 15.–17.6.1995*. Ägypten und Altes Testament (ÄAT) 36 = *Beiträge zur (alt)ägyptischen Königsideologie* I. Wiesbaden: Harrassowitz.

Holloway, Steven W. 1997. "Assyria and Babylonia in the Tenth Century BCE," 202–16 in Lowell K. Handy, ed., *The Age of Solomon: Scholarship at the Turn of the Millennium*. SHCANE 11. Leiden and New York: Brill.

Hölscher, Gustav. 1922. "Komposition und Ursprung des Deuteronomiums." *ZAW* 40: 161–255.

Horowitz, Wayne, Takayoshi Oshima, and Seth Sanders. 2002. "A Bibliographical List of Cuneiform Inscriptions from Canaan, Palestine/Philistia, and the Land of Israel." *JAOS* 122: 753–66.

Hossfeld, Frank-Lothar. 1982. *Der Dekalog: Seine späte Fassung, die originale Komposition und seine Vorstufen*. OBO 35. Fribourg: Universitätsverlag; Göttingen: Vandenhoeck & Ruprecht.

———, and Erich Zenger. 1993. *Ps 1–50*. NEB. Würzburg: Echter Verlag.

———, and Erich Zenger. 2000. *Psalmen 51–100*. HTKAT. Freiburg et al.: Herder. English: *Psalms 2: A Commentary on Psalms 51–100*. Translated by Linda M. Maloney. Hermeneia. Minneapolis: Fortress Press, 2005.

Houtman, Cornelis. 1997. *Das Bundesbuch: Ein Kommentar*. DMOA 24. Leiden and New York: Brill.

Huber, Michael 2010. *Gab es ein davidisch-salomonisches Großreich? Forschungsgeschichte und neuere Argumentationen aus der Sicht der Archäologie*. SBB 63. Stuttgart: Katholisches Bibelwerk.

Hupfeld, Hermann. 1844. *Ueber Begriff und Methode der sogenannten biblischen Einleitung nebst einer Uebersicht ihrer Geschichte und Literatur*. Marburg: N. G. Elwert.

Hurowitz, Victor. 1992. *I Have Built You an Exalted House: Temple Building in the Bible in Light of Mesopotamian and Northwest Semitic Writings*. JSOTSup 115/ASORMS 5. Sheffield: JSOT Press.

Hurvitz, Avi. 2000. "Can Biblical Texts Be Dated Linguistically? Chronological Perspectives in the Historical Study of Biblical Hebrew," 143–60 in André Lemaire and Magne Sæbø, eds., *Congress Volume Oslo 1998*. VTSup 80. Leiden and Boston: Brill.

Hutzli, Jürg. 2007. *Die Erzählung von Hanna und Samuel: Textkritische und literarische Analyse von 1. Samuel 1–2 unter Berücksichtigung des Kontextes*. ATANT 89. Zürich: Theologischer Verlag.

Huwyler, Beat. 1997. *Jeremia und die Völker: Untersuchungen zu den Völkersprüchen in Jeremia 46–49*. FAT 20. Tübingen: Mohr (Siebeck).

Jamieson-Drake, David W. 1991. *Scribes and Schools in Monarchic Judah: A Socio-Archaeological Approach*. JSOTSup 109/SWBA 9. Sheffield: Almond Press.

Janowski, Bernd. 1987. "'Ich will in eurer Mitte wohnen.' Struktur und Genese der exilischen Schekina-Theologie," 165–93 in Ingo Baldermann et al., eds., *Der eine Gott der beiden Testamente*. Jahrbuch für Biblische Theologie 2. Neukirchen-Vluyn: Neukirchener Verlag = idem, *Gottes Gegenwart in Israel: Beiträge zur Theologie des Alten Testaments*, 119–47. Neukirchen-Vluyn: Neukirchener Verlag, 1993.

———. 1994. "Die Tat kehrt zum Täter zurück. Offene Fragen im Umkreis des 'Tun-Ergehen-Zusammenhangs,'" *ZTK* 91: 247–71 = idem, *Die rettende Gerechtigkeit: Beiträge zur Theologie des Alten Testaments 2*, 167–91. Neukirchen-Vluyn: Neukirchener Verlag, 1999.

———. 1995. "JHWH und der Sonnengott. Aspekte der Solarisierung JHWHs in vorexilischer Zeit," 214–41 in Joachim Mehlhausen, ed., *Pluralismus und Identität*. Gütersloh: Kaiser = idem, *Die rettende Gerechtigkeit*, 192–219.

———. 2002a. "Die Frucht der Gerechtigkeit. Psalm 72 und die judäische

Königsideologie," 94–134 in Eckart Otto and Erich Zenger, eds., *"Mein Sohn bist du" (Ps 2,7): Studien zu den Königspsalmen*. SBS 192. Stuttgart: Katholisches Bibelwerk.

———. 2002b. "Die heilige Wohnung des Höchsten. Kosmologische Implikationen der Jerusalemer Tempeltheologie," 24–68 in Othmar Keel and Erich Zenger, eds., *Gottesstadt und Gottesgarten: Zu Geschichte und Theologie des Jerusalemer Tempels*. QD 191. Freiburg et al.: Herder.

———. 2001. "Die Toten loben JHWH nicht. Psalm 88 und das alttestamentliche Todesverständnis," 3–45 in Friedrich Avemarie and Hermann Lichtenberger, eds., *Auferstehung—Resurrection: The Fourth Durham-Tübingen Research Symposium: Resurrection, Transfiguration and Exaltation in Old Testament, Ancient Judaism, and Early Christianity* (Tübingen, September 1999). WUNT 135. Tübingen: Mohr (Siebeck). = idem, *Der Gott des Lebens: Beiträge zur Theologie des Alten Testaments* 3, 201–43. Neukirchen-Vluyn: Neukirchener Verlag, 2003.

———. 2003a. "Der andere König. Psalm 72 als Magna Charta der judäischen Königsideologie," 97–112 in Marlis Gielen and Joachim Kügler, eds., *Liebe, Macht und Religion: Interdisziplinäre Studien zu Grunddimensionen menschlicher Existenz*. FS Helmut Merklein. Stuttgart: Katholisches Bibelwerk.

———. 2003b. *Konfliktgespräche mit Gott: Eine Anthropologie der Psalmen*. Neukirchen-Vluyn: Neukirchener Verlag.

———. 2004. "Kanon und Sinnbildung. Perspektiven des Alten Testaments," 15–36 in Friedhelm Hartenstein et al., eds., *Schriftprophetie*. FS Jörg Jeremias. Neukirchen-Vluyn: Neukirchener Verlag.

———. 2006. "Sehnsucht nach Unsterblichkeit. Zur Jenseitshoffnung in der weisheitlichen Literatur." *BK* 61: 34–39.

Japhet, Sara. 1968. "The Supposed Common Authorship of Chronicles and Ezra–Nehemia Investigated Anew." *VT* 18: 332–72.

———. 1991. "The Temple in the Restoration Period: Reality and Ideology." *USQR* 34: 195–251.

———. 1999. "Chronikbücher." *RGG* 2: 344–48.

———. 2002. *1 Chronik*. HTKAT. Freiburg et al.: Herder.

———. 2003. "Periodization: Between History and Ideology. The Neo-Babylonian Period in Biblical Historiography," 75–89 in Oded Lipschits and Joseph Blenkinsopp, eds., *Judah and Judeans in the Neo-Babylonian Period*. Winona Lake, IN: Eisenbrauns.

Japp, Uwe. 1980. *Beziehungssinn: Ein Konzept der Literaturgeschichte*. Frankfurt: Europäische Verlagsanstalt.

Jauss, Hans Robert. ²1970. *Literaturgeschichte als Provokation*. Frankfurt: Suhrkamp.

Jeremias, Jörg. 1987. *Der Prophet Hosea*. ATD 24/1. Göttingen: Vandenhoeck & Ruprecht.

———. 1987. *Das Königtum Gottes in den Psalmen: Israels Begegnung mit dem kanaanäischen Mythos in den Jahwe-König-Psalmen*. FRLANT 141. Göttingen: Vandenhoeck & Ruprecht.

———. 1988. "Amos 3–6. Beobachtungen zur Entstehungsgeschichte eines Prophetenbuches." *ZAW* 100 Sup.: 123–38.

———. 1992. "Umkehrung von Heilstraditionen im Alten Testament," 309–20 in Jutta Hausmann and Hans-Jürgen Zobel, eds., *Alttestamentlicher Glaube und Biblische Theologie*. FS Horst Dietrich Preuss. Stuttgart: Kohlhammer.

————. 1994. "Das Proprium der alttestamentlichen Prophetie." *TLZ* 119: 485–94.

————. 1995. *Der Prophet Amos.* ATD 24/2. Göttingen: Vandenhoeck & Ruprecht.

————. 1996. *Hosea und Amos: Studien zu den Anfängen des Dodekapropheton.* FAT 13. Tübingen: Mohr (Siebeck).

————. 2007. *Die Propheten Joel, Abadja, Jona, Micha.* ATD 24/3. Göttingen: Vandenhoeck & Ruprecht.

————, and Friedhelm Hartenstein. 1999. "'JHWH und seine Aschera.' 'Offizielle Religion' und 'Volksreligion' zur Zeit der klassischen Propheten," 79–138 in Bernd Janowski and Matthias Köckert, eds., *Religionsgeschichte Israels: Formale und materiale Aspekte.* VWGT 15. Gütersloh: Kaiser.

Jericke, Detlef. 1997. "Die Geburt Isaaks—Gen 21,1-8." *BN* 88: 31–37.

Joannès, Francis, and André Lemaire. 1999. "Trois tablettes cunéiformes à onomastique ouest-sémitique (collection Sh. Moussaïëff)." *Transeuphratene* 17: 17–34.

Job, John B. 2006. *Jeremiah's Kings: A Study of the Monarchy in Jeremiah.* Aldershot: Ashgate.

Johanning, Klaus. 1988. *Der Bibel-Babel-Streit: Eine forschungsgeschichtliche Studie.* Europäische Hochschulschriften (EHS) Series 23:Theology, 343. Frankfurt et al.: Peter Lang.

Joosten, Jan. 1999. "Pseudo-Classicisms in Late Biblical Hebrew, in Ben Sira, and in Qumran Hebrew," 146–59 in Takamitsu Muraoka and John F. Elwolde, eds., *Sirach, Scrolls, and Sages: Proceedings of a Second International Symposium on the Hebrew of the Dead Sea Scrolls, Ben Sira, and Mishnah, Held at Leiden University, 15–17 December 1997.* STDJ 33. Leiden and Boston: Brill.

Kaiser, Otto. 1991. "Literaturgeschichte, Biblische I." *TRE* 21: 306–37.

————. 1991, 1994. *Grundriss der Einleitung in die kanonischen und deuterokanonischen Schriften des Alten Testaments.* Vol. 1: *Die erzählenden Werke.* Vol. 3: *Die poetischen und weisheitlichen Werke.* Gütersloh: Gerd Mohn.

————. 2000a. *Die alttestamentlichen Apokryphen: Eine Einleitung in Grundzügen.* Gütersloh: Kaiser; Gütersloher Verlagshaus. English: *The Old Testament Apocrypha: an Introduction.* Peabody, MA: Hendrickson, 2004.

————. 2000b. *Studien zur Literaturgeschichte des Alten Testaments.* Forschung zur Bibel (FzB) 90. Würzburg: Echter Verlag.

————. 1993, 1998, 2003. *Der Gott des Alten Testaments: Wesen und Wirken: Theologie des Alten Testaments.* Part 1: *Grundlegung.* UTB 1747. Part 2: *Jahwe, der Gott Israels, Schöpfer der Welt und des Menschen.* UTB 2024. Part 3: *Jahwes Gerechtigkeit.* UTB 2392. Göttingen: Vandenhoeck & Ruprecht.

————. 2005. *Zwischen Reaktion und Revolution: Hermann Hupfeld (1796–1866)—ein deutsches Professorenleben.* Abhandlungen der Akademie der Wissenschaften in Göttingen (AAWG) III/268. Göttingen: Vandenhoeck & Ruprecht.

Kautzsch, Emil. 1897. *Abriss der Geschichte des alttestamentlichen Schrifttums nebst Zeittafeln zur Geschichte der Israeliten und anderen Beigaben zur Erklärung des alten Testaments.* Freiburg and Leipzig: Mohr. English: *An Outline of the History of the Literature of the Old Testament: With Chronological Tables for the History of the Israelites and Other Aids to the Explanation of the Old Testament.* Translated by John Taylor. London: Williams & Norgate, 1898.

————. 1907. Review of Karl Budde, 1906. *Geschichte der althebräischen Litteratur, Theologische Studien und Kritiken* 80: 472–81.

Keel, Othmar. 1977. "Der Bogen als Herrschaftssymbol. Einige unveröffentlichte

Skarabäen aus Israel und Ägypten zum Thema 'Jagd und Krieg,'" *ZDPV* 93: 141–77.

———. 1978. *Jahwes Entgegnung an Ijob: Eine Deutung von Ijob 38–41 vor dem Hintergrund zeitgenössischer Bildkunst.* FRLANT 121. Göttingen: Vandenhoeck & Ruprecht.

———. ⁴1984. *Die Welt der altorientalischen Bildsymbolik und das Alte Testament: Am Beispiel der Psalmen.* Neukirchen-Vluyn: Neukirchener Verlag. English: *The Symbolism of the Biblical World: Ancient Near Eastern Iconography and the Book of Psalms.* Translated by Timothy J. Hallett. New York: Seabury, 1978.

———. 1993. "Fern von Jerusalem. Frühe Jerusalemer Kulttraditionen und ihre Träger und Trägerinnen," 439–502 in Ferdinand Hahn et al., eds., *Zion: Ort der Begegnung. FS Laurentius Klein.* BBB 90. Bodenheim: Athenäum Hain Hanstein.

———. 1994. "Sturmgott—Sonnengott—Einziger. Ein neuer Versuch, die Entstehung des judäischen Monotheismus historisch zu verstehen." *BK* 49: 82–92.

———. 1995. *Corpus der Stempelsiegel-Amulette aus Palästina, Israel: Einleitung.* OBO Series Archaeologica 10. Fribourg: Universitätsverlag; Göttingen: Vandenhoeck & Ruprecht.

———. 2000. "Die kultischen Massnahmen Antiochus' IV. Religionsverfolgung und/ oder Reformversuch? Eine Skizze," 87–121 in idem and Urs Staub, *Hellenismus und Judentum: Vier Studien zu Daniel 7 und zur Religionsnot unter Antiochus IV.* OBO 178. Fribourg: Universitätsverlag; Göttingen: Vandenhoeck & Ruprecht.

———. 2002. "Der salomonische Tempelweihspruch. Beobachtungen zum religionsgeschichtlichen Kontext des Ersten Jerusalemer Tempels," 9–23 in idem and Erich Zenger, eds., *Gottesstadt und Gottesgarten: Zur Geschichte und Theologie des Jerusalemer Tempels.* QD 191. Freiburg: Herder.

———. 2007. *Die Geschichte Jerusalems und die Entstehung des Monotheismus.* 2 vols. Orte und Landschaften der Bibel VI/1. Göttingen: Vandenhoeck & Ruprecht.

———, and Christoph Uehlinger. ⁵2001. *Göttinen, Götter und Gottessymbole: Neue Erkentnisse zur Religionsgeschichte Kanaans und Israels aufgrund bislang unerschlossener ikonographischer Quellen.* QD 134. Freiburg et al.: Herder. English: *Gods, Goddesses, and Images of God in Ancient Israel.* Translated by Allan W. Mahnke. Minneapolis: Fortress Press, 1996.

Keller, Carl-A. 1958. "Review of Gerhard von Rad, *Theologie des Alten Testaments I.*" *TZ* 14: 306–9.

Kepper, Martina. 1999. *Hellenistische Bildung im Buch der Weisheit.* BZAW 280. Berlin and New York: de Gruyter.

Kessler, Rainer. 1992. *Staat und Gesellschaft im vorexilischen Juda: Vom 8. Jahrhundert bis zum Exil.* VTSup 47. Leiden and New York: Brill.

———. 2006. *Sozialgeschichte des alten Israel: Eine Einführung.* Darmstadt: Wissenschaftliche Buchgesellschaft. English: *The Social History of Ancient Israel: An Introduction.* Translated by Linda M. Maloney. Minneapolis: Fortress Press, 2008.

Kinet, Dirk. 2001. *Geschichte Israels.* NEB Supplementary Volume 2. Würzburg: Echter Verlag.

Kirkpatrick, Patricia G. 1988. *The Old Testament and Folklore Study.* JSOTSup 62. Sheffield: JSOT Press.

Klatt, Werner. 1969. *Hermann Gunkel: Zu seiner Theologie der Religionsgeschichte und zur Entstehung der formgeschichtlichen Methode.* FRLANT 100. Göttingen: Vandenhoeck & Ruprecht.

Kleer, Martin. 1996. *"Der liebliche Sänger der Psalmen Israels": Untersuchungen zu David als Richter und Beter der Psalmen.* BBB 108. Bodenheim: Philo.

Klijn, A. F. J. 1977. "A Library of Scriptures in Jerusalem," 265–72 in Kurt Treu, ed., *Studie Codicologica.* TU 124. Berlin: Akademie-Verlag.

Klostermann, August. 1893. "Ezechiel und das Heiligkeitsgesetz." *Zeitschrift für die gesammte lutherische Theologie und Kirche* 38 (1877): 401–45. Reprinted in idem, *Der Pentateuch: Beiträge zu seinem Verständnis und seiner Entstehungsgeschichte,* 368–418. Leipzig: Böhme.

———. 1908. "Schulwesen im Alten Israel," 193–232 in G. Nathanael Bonwetsch, ed., *Theologische Studien: Theodor Zahn zum 10. Oktober 1908.* Leipzig: A. Deichert.

Knauf, Ernst Axel. 1988a. "Hiobs Heimat." *WO* 19: 65–83.

———. 1988b. *Midian: Untersuchungen zur Geschichte Palästinas und Nordarabiens am Ende des 2. Jt. v. Chr.* Abhandlungen des Deutschen Palästinavereins 0173-1904. Wiesbaden: Harrassowitz.

———. 1990. "War 'Biblisch-Hebräisch' eine Sprache? Empirische Gesichtspunkte zur linguistischen Annäherung an die Sprache der althebräischen Literatur." *ZAH* 3: 11–23.

———. 1992. "The Cultural Impact of Secondary State Formation: The Cases of the Edomites and the Moabites," 47–54 in Piotr Bienkowski, ed., *Early Edom and Moab.* Sheffield Archaeological Monographs 7. Sheffield: J. R. Collis.

———. 1994. *Die Umwelt des Alten Testaments.* Neuer Stuttgarter Kommentar. Altes Testament (NSK.AT) 29. Stuttgart: Katholisches Bibelwerk.

———. 1998. "Audiatur et altera pars. Zur Logik der Pentateuch-Redaktion." *BK* 53: 118–26.

———. 2000a. "Die Priesterschrift und die Geschichten der Deuteronomisten," 101–18 in Thomas Römer, ed., *The Future of the Deuteronomistic History.* BETL 147. Leuven: Leuven University Press.

———. 2000b. "Jerusalem in the Late Bronze and Early Iron Periods. A Proposal." *Tel Aviv* 27: 73–89.

———. 2000c. "Kinneret und Naftali," 219–33 in André Lemaire and Magne Sæbø, eds., *Congress Volume Oslo 1998.* VTSup 80. Leiden and Boston: Brill.

———. 2000d. "Psalm LX und Psalm CVIII." *VT* 50: 55–65.

———. 2000e. "The 'Low Chronology' and How Not to Deal with It." *BN* 101: 56–63.

———. 2000f. "Wie kann ich singen im fremden Land? Die 'babylonische Gefangenschaft' Israels." *BK* 55: 132–39.

———. 2001a. "Israel II. Geschichte." *RGG* 4: 284–93.

———. 20001b. "Israel und seine Nachbarn in Syrien-Palästina." *RGG* 4: 313–14.

———. 2001c. "Hezekiah or Manasseh? A Reconsideration of the Siloam Tunnel and Inscription." *Tel Aviv* 28: 281–87.

———. 2003. "Sennacherib at the Berezina," 141–49 in Lester L. Grabbe, ed., *"Like a Bird in a Cage": The Invasion of Sennacherib in 701 BCE.* JSOTSup 363/ESHM 4. Sheffield: Sheffield Academic Press; London and New York: T & T Clark/ Continuum.

———. 2004a. "Les milieux producteurs de la Bible hebraïque," 49–60 in Thomas Römer et al., eds., *Introduction à l'Ancien Testament.* Le Monde de la Bible 49. Geneva: Labor et Fides.

———. 2004b. Review of Klaus Koenen, *Bethel: Geschichte, Kult und Theologie.* OBO

192. (Fribourg: Universitätsverlag; Göttingen: Vandenhoeck & Ruprecht, 2003), in *RBL* 10, http://www.bookreviews.org/pdf/3813_3765.pdf.

———. 2005a. "Der Text als Artefakt," 51–66 in John Barton et al., eds., *Das Alte Testament und die Kunst*. Altes Testament und Moderne 15. Münster: Lit.

———. 2005b. "The Glorious Days of Manasseh," 164–88 in Lester L. Grabbe, ed., *Good Kings and Bad Kings*. Library of Hebrew Bible/Old Testament Studies (LHBOTS) 393/EHSM 5. London and New York: T & T Clark International.

———. 2006. "Bethel. The Israelite Impact on Judean Language and Literature," 291–349 in Oded Lipschits and Manfred Oeming, eds., *Judah and the Judeans in the Persian Period*. Winona Lake, IN: Eisenbrauns.

Knibb, Michael A., ed. 2006. *The Septuagint and Messianism*. BETL 195. Leuven: Leuven University Press; Dudley, MA: Peeters.

Knohl, Israel. 1995. *The Sanctuary of Silence: The Priestly Torah and the Holiness School*. Minneapolis: Fortress Press.

———. 2003. *The Divine Symphony: The Bible's Many Voices*. Philadelphia: Jewish Publication Society.

Knoppers, Gary N. 1993, 1994. *Two Nations under God: The Deuteronomistic History of Solomon and the Dual Monarchies*. 2 vols. HSM 52/53. Atlanta: Scholars Press.

———. 2005. "Revisiting the Samarian Question in the Persian Period," 265–89 in Oded Lipschits and Manfred Oeming, eds., *Judah and the Judeans in the Persian Period* Winona Lake, IN: Eisenbrauns.

Knox, B. M. W. 1968. "Silent Reading in Antiquity." *GRBS* 9: 421–35.

Koch, Christoph. 2008. *Vertrag, Treueid und Bund: Studien zur Rezeption des altorientalischen Vertragsrechts im Deuteronomium und zur Ausbildung der Bundestheologie im Alten Testament*. BZAW 383. Berlin and New York: de Gruyter.

Koch, Klaus. ⁵1989. *Was ist Formgeschichte? Methoden der Bibelexegese*. Neukirchen-Vluyn: Neukirchener Verlag, 1964.

———. 1982. "Einleitung," 1–29 in idem and Johann Michael Schmidt, eds., *Apokalyptik*. Wege der Forschung (WdF) 365. Darmstadt: Wissenschaftliche Buchgesellschaft. = idem, *Vor der Wende der Zeiten: Beiträge zur apokalyptischen Literatur*. Gesammelte Aufsätze 3, 109–33. Neukirchen-Vluyn: Neukirchener Verlag, 1996.

———. 1984a. "Geschichte/Geschichtsschreibung/Geschichtsphilosophie II. Altes Testament." *TRE* 12: 569–86.

———. 1984b. "Weltordnung und Reichsidee im alten Iran," 45–119 in idem and Peter Frei, *Reichsidee und Reichsorganisation im Perserreich*. OBO 55. Fribourg: Universitätsverlag; Göttingen: Vandenhoeck & Ruprecht.

———. 1987. "P—kein Redaktor! Erinnerung an zwei Eckdaten der Quellenscheidung." *VT* 37: 446–67.

———. 1991. "Weltgeschichte und Gottesreich im Danielbuch und die iranischen Parallelen," 189–205 in Rüdiger Liwak and Siegfried Wagner, eds., *Prophetie und geschichtliche Wirklichkeit im alten Israel. FS Siegfried Hermann*. Stuttgart et al: Kohlhammer.

———. 1994. "Monotheismus und Angelologie," 565–81 in Walter Dietrich and Martin A. Klopfenstein, eds., *Ein Gott allein? Jahweverehrung und biblischer Monotheismus im Kontext der israelitischen und altorientalischen Religionsgeschichte*. OBO 139. Fribourg: Universitätsverlag; Göttingen: Vandenhoeck & Ruprecht.

———. 1995. "Ist Daniel auch unter den Profeten," 1–15 in idem, *Die Reiche der*

Welt und der kommende Menschensohn: Studien zum Danielbuch: Gesammelte Aufsätze 2. Neukirchen-Vluyn: Neukirchener Verlag.

———. 1999. "Esra/Esrabücher I. II." *RGG* 2: 1581–86.

Köckert, Matthias. 1988. *Vätergott und Väterverheissungen: Eine Auseinandersetzung mit Albrecht Alt und seinen Erben.* FRLANT 142. Göttingen: Vandenhoeck & Ruprecht.

———. 1998. "Von einem zum einzigen Gott. Zur Diskussion der Religionsgeschichte Israels." *BTZ* 15: 137–75.

———. 2001. "Die Theophanie des Wettergottes Jahwe in Psalm 18," 209–26 in Thomas Richter et al., eds., *Kulturgeschichten: Altorientalische Studien für Volkert Haas zum 65. Geburtstag.* Saarbrücken: SDV Saarbrücker Druckerei und Verlag.

———. 2002. "Wie kam das Gesetz an den Sinai?" 13–27 in Christoph Bultmann et al., eds., *Vergegenwärtigung des Alten Testaments. FS Rudolf Smend.* Göttingen: Vandenhoeck & Ruprecht.

———. 2003a. "Elia. Literarische und religionsgeschichtliche Probleme in 1Kön 17–18," 111–44 in Manfred Oeming and Konrad Schmid, eds., *Der eine Gott und die Götter: Polytheismus und Monotheismus im antiken Israel.* ATANT 82. Zürich: Theologischer Verlag.

———. 2003b. "War Jakobs Gegner in Gen 32,23-33 ein Dämon?" 160–81 in Armin Lange et al., eds., *Die Dämonen: Die Dämonologie der israelitisch-jüdischen und frühchristlichen Literatur im Kontext ihrer Umwelt. = Demons: The Demonology of Israelite-Jewish and Early Christian Literature in Context of Their Environment.* Tübingen: Mohr (Siebeck).

———. 2004. *Leben in Gottes Gegenwart: Studien zum Verständnis des Gesetzes im Alten Testament.* FAT 43. Tübingen: Mohr (Siebeck).

———. 2005. "Wandlungen Gottes im antiken Israel." *BTZ* 22: 3–36.

———. 2006a. "'Gibt es keinen Gott in Israel?' Zum literarischen, historischen und religionsgeschichtlichen Ort von IIReg 1," 253–71 in Martin Beck and Ulrike Schorn, eds., *Auf dem Weg zur Endgestalt von Gen–II Reg. FS Hans-Christoph Schmitt.* BZAW 370. Berlin and New York: de Gruyter.

———. 2006b. "Die Geschichte der Abrahamüberlieferung," 103–27 in André Lemaire, ed., *Congress Volume Leiden 2004.* VTSup 109. Leiden and Boston: Brill.

———. 2007. *Die Zehn Gebote.* Munich: Beck.

———, Uwe Becker, and Jörg Barthel. 2003. "Das Problem des historischen Jesaja," 105–35 in Irmtraud Fischer et al., eds., *Prophetie in Israel: Beiträge des Symposiums "Das Alte Testament und die Kultur der Moderne" anlässlich des 100. Geburtstags Gerhard von Rads (1901–1971).* Altes Testament und Moderne 11. Münster: Lit.

Koenen, Klaus. 1990. *Ethik und Eschatologie im Tritojesajabuch: Eine literarkritische und redaktionsgeschichtliche Studie.* WMANT 62. Neukirchen-Vluyn: Neukirchener Verlag.

———. 2003. *Bethel: Geschichte, Kult und Theologie.* OBO 192. Fribourg: Universitätsverlag; Göttingen: Vandenhoeck & Ruprecht.

Koester, Helmut. 1971. "The Intention and Scope of Trajectories," 269–79 in James M. Robinson and Helmut Koester, *Trajectories through Early Christianity.* Philadelphia: Fortress Press.

———. 1995–2000. *Einführung in das Neue Testament im Rahmen der Religionsgeschichte und Kulturgeschichte der hellenistischen und römischen Zeit.* English: *Introduction to the New Testament.* Berlin and New York: de Gruyter.

Köhlmoos, Melanie. 2007. "Weisheit/Weisheitsliteratur II." *TRE* 35 (2003): 486–97.

———. "'Die übrige Geschichte.' Das 'Rahmenwerk' als Grunderzählung der Königebücher," 216–31 in Sylke Lubs et al., eds., *Behutsames Lesen: Alttestamentliche Exegese im interdisziplinären Methodendiskurs. FS Christoph Hardmeier.* ABG 28. Leipzig: Evangelische Verlagsanstalt.

Kolb, Anne. 2000. *Transport und Nachrichtentransfer im römischen Reich.* Klio n.s. 2. Berlin: Akademie Verlag.

Kooij, Arie van der. 1998. "Canonization of Hebrew Books Kept in the Temple of Jerusalem," 17–40 in idem and Karel van der Toorn, eds., *Canonization and Decanonization: Papers Presented to the International Conference of the Leiden Institute for the Study of Religions (LISOR) Held at Leiden 9–10 January 1997.* SHR 82. Leiden and Boston: Brill.

Köpf, U. 2002. "Literaturgeschichte/Literaturgeschichtsschreibung." *RGG* 5: 403–5.

Korpel, Marjo C. A., and Josef M. Oesch, eds. 2000. *Delimitation Criticism: A New Tool in Biblical Scholarship.* Assen: Van Gorcum.

Körting, Corinna. 2006a. "Sach 5,5-11—Die Unrechtmässigkeit wird an ihren Ort verwiesen." *Bib* 87: 477–92.

———. 2006b. *Zion in den Psalmen.* FAT 48. Tübingen: Mohr (Siebeck).

Kottsieper, Ingo. 2004. "'Thema verfehlt!' Zur Kritik Gottes an den drei Freunden in Hi 42,7-9," 775–85 in Markus Witte, ed., *Gott und Mensch im Dialog. FS Otto Kaiser* BZAW 345/II. Berlin and New York: de Gruyter.

———. 2007. "'And They Did Not Care to Speak Yehudit': On Linguistic Change in Judah During the Late Persian Era," 95–124 in Oded Lipshits et al., eds., *Judah and the Judeans in the Fourth Century* B.C.E. Winona Lake, IN: Eisenbrauns.

Kratz, Reinhard G. 1991a. *Kyros im Deuterojesaja-Buch: Redaktionsgeschichtliche Untersuchungen zu Entstehung und Theologie von Jes 40–55.* FAT 1. Tübingen: Mohr (Siebeck).

———. 1991b. *Translatio imperii: Untersuchungen zu den aramäischen Danielerzählungen und ihrem theologiegeschichtlichen Umfeld.* WMANT 63. Neukirchen-Vluyn: Neukirchener Verlag.

———. 1992. "Die Gnade des täglichen Brots. Späte Psalmen auf dem Weg zum Vaterunser." *ZTK* 89: 1–40.

———. 1996. "Die Tora Davids. Ps 1 und die doxologische Fünfteilung des Psalters." *ZTK* 93: 1–34.

———. 1997a. "Redaktionsgeschichte I. Altes Testament." *TRE* 28: 367–78.

———. 1997b. "Die Redaktion der Prophetenbücher," 9–27 in idem and Thomas Krüger, eds., *Rezeption und Auslegung im Alten Testament und in seinem Umfeld.* OBO 153. Fribourg: Universitätsverlag; Göttingen: Vandenhoeck & Ruprecht.

———. 1998. "Die Entstehung des Judentums." *ZTK* 95: 167–84.

———. 2000a. *Die Komposition der erzählenden Bücher des Alten Testaments.* UTB 2137. Göttingen: Vandenhoeck & Ruprecht. English Translation: *The Composition of the Narrative Books of the Old Testament.* London: T&T Clark, 2005.

———. 2000b. "Israel als Staat und als Volk." *ZTK* 97: 1–17.

———. 2002. "Noch einmal: Theologie im Alten Testament," 310–26 in Christoph Bultmann et al., eds., *Vergegenwärtigung des Alten Testaments: Beiträge zur biblischen Hermeneutik.* Göttingen: Vandenhoeck & Ruprecht.

———. 2003a. "Der Mythos vom Königtum Gottes in Kanaan und Israel." *ZTK* 100: 147–62.

————. 2003b. *Die Propheten Israels.* Beck'sche Reihe 2326. Munich: Beck Wissen.

————. 2003c. "Die Worte des Amos von Tekoa," 54–89 in Matthias Köckert and Martti Nissinen, eds., *Propheten in Mari, Assyrien und Israel.* FRLANT 201. Göttingen: Vandenhoeck & Ruprecht.

————. 2004a. *Das Judentum im Zeitalter des Zweiten Tempels.* FAT 42. Tübingen: Mohr (Siebeck).

————. 2004b. "Die Visionen des Daniel," 227–44 in idem, *Das Judentum im Zeitalter des Zweiten Tempels.* FAT 42. Tübingen: Mohr (Siebeck).

————. 2006a. "Israel in the Book of Isaiah." *JSOT* 31: 103–28.

————. 2006b. "Mose und die Propheten. Zur Interpretation von 4QMMT C," 151–76 in Florentino García Martínez et al., eds., *From 4QMMT to Resurrection: Mélanges qumraniens en hommage à Émile Puech.* STDJ 61. Leiden and Boston: Brill.

————. 2006c. "The Growth of the Old Testament," 459–88 in John W. Rogerson and Judith M. Lieu, eds., *The Oxford Handbook of Biblical Studies.* Oxford: Oxford University Press.

————. 2010a. "The Idea of Cultic Centralization and Its Supposed Ancient Near Eastern Analogies." 121–44 in: Reinhard Gregor Kratz and Hermann Spieckermann, eds, *One God — One Cult — One Nation.* BZAW 405. Berlin and New York: de Gruyter.

————. 2010b. "Rewriting Isaiah: The Case of Isaiah 28-31," 245–66 in John Day, ed., *Prophecy and the Prophets in Ancient Israel, Proceedings of the Oxford Old Testament Seminar,* New York: T & T Clark.

————. 2011. *Prophetenstudien: Kleine Schriften II.* FAT 74. Tübingen: Mohr (Siebeck).

————, Thomas Krüger, and Konrad Schmid, eds. 2000b. *Schriftauslegung in der Schrift.* FS Odil Hannes Steck. BZAW 300. Berlin and New York: de Gruyter.

————, and Hermann Spieckermann, eds. 2000. *Liebe und Gebot: Studien zum Deuteronomium. FS Lothar Perlitt.* FRLANT 190. Göttingen: Vandenhoeck & Ruprecht.

Krüger, Thomas. 1988. "Esra 1–6: Struktur und Konzept." *BN* 41: 65–75.

————. 1997. "Psalm 90 und die 'Vergänglichkeit des Menschen,'" *Bib* 75 (1994): 191–219 = idem, *Kritische Weisheit: Studien zur weisheitlichen Traditionskritik im Alten Testament,* 67–89. Zürich: Pano Verlag.

————. 1995. "Komposition und Diskussion in Proverbia 10." *ZTK* 89: 413–33 = idem, *Kritische Weisheit* (1997), 194–214.

————. 1996. "Dekonstruktion und Rekonstruktion prophetischer Eschatologie im Qohelet-Buch," 107–29 in Anja A. Diesel et al., eds., *"Jedes Ding hat seine Zeit . . .": Studien zur israelitischen und altorientalischen Weisheit. FS Diethelm Michel.* BZAW 241. Berlin and New York: de Gruyter = idem, *Kritische Weisheit* (1997), 151–72.

————. 1997. "Die Rezeption der Tora im Buch Kohelet," 173–93 in Ludger Schwienhorst-Schönberger, ed., *Das Buch Kohelet: Studien zur Struktur, Geschichte, Rezeption und Theologie.* BZAW 254. Berlin and New York: de Gruyter.

————. 1999. "Le livre de Qohélet dans le contexte de la littérature juive des IIIe et IIe siècles avant Jésus-Christ." *RTP* 131: 135–62 = Martin Rose, ed., *Situer Qohéleth: Regards croisés sur une livre biblique,* 47–74. Neuchâtel: Secrétariat de l'Université, 1999.

————. 2000. *Kohelet (Prediger).* BKAT 19 (Extra Volume). Neukirchen-Vluyn: Neukirchener Verlag. English: *Qoheleth: A Commentary.* Translated by O. C. Dean. Hermeneia. Minneapolis: Fortress Press, 2004.

————. 2001. "'An den Strömen von Babylon . . .' Erwägungen zu Zeitbezug und Sachverhalt in Psalm 137," 79–84 in Rüdiger Bartelmus and Norbert Nebes, eds., *Sachverhalt und Zeitbezug: Semitistische und alttestamentliche Studien: Adolf Denz zum 65. Geburtstag*. Wiesbaden: Harrassowitz.

————. 2003a. "Erkenntnisbindung im Weisheitsspruch. Überlegungen im Anschluss an Gerhard von Rad," 53–66 in David J. A. Clines, Hermann Lichtenberger, and Hans-Peter Müller, eds., *Weisheit in Israel*. Altes Testament und Moderne 12. Münster: Lit.

————. 2003b. "Gesetz und Weisheit im Pentateuch," 1–12 in Irmtraud Fischer, Ursula Rapp, and Johannes Schiller, eds., *Auf den Spuren der schriftgelehrten Weisen. FS Johannes Marböck*. BZAW 331. Berlin and New York: de Gruyter.

————. 2006. "Überlegungen zur Bedeutung der Traditionsgeschichte für das Verständnis alttestamentlicher Texte und zur Weiterentwicklung der traditionsgeschichtlichen Methode," 233–45 in Helmut Utzschneider and Erhard Blum, eds., *Lesarten der Bibel: Untersuchungen zu einer Theorie der Exegese des Alten Testaments*. Stuttgart: Kohlhammer.

————, Manfred Oeming, Konrad Schmid, and Christoph Uehlinger, eds. 2007. *Das Buch Hiob und seine Interpretationen: Beiträge des Hiob-Symposiums auf dem Monte Verita vom 14.–19. August 2005*. ATANT 88. Zürich: Theologischer Verlag.

Kuhrt, Amélie. 1995. *The Ancient Near East c. 3000–330 BC*. 2 vols. London and New York: Routledge.

Kunz, Andreas. 1998. *Ablehnung des Krieges: Untersuchungen zu Sacharja 9 und 10*. HBS 17. Freiburg and New York: Herder.

Lambert, Wilfred G. 1967. "Enmeduranki and Related Matters." *JCS* 21: 126–38.

Lang, Bernhard. 1990. "Klugheit als Ethos und Weisheit als Beruf: Zur Lebenslehre im Alten Testament," 177–92 in Aleida Assmann, ed., *Weisheit: Archäologie der literarischen Kommunikation III*. Munich: Fink1990.

————. 1997. "The 'Writings': A Hellenistic Literary Canon in the Hebrew Bible," 41–65 in Arie van der Kooij and Karel van der Toorn, eds., *Canonization and Decanonization: Papers Presented to the International Conference of the Leiden Institute for the Study of Religion (LISOR), held at Leiden 9–10 January 1997*. SHR 82. Leiden and Boston: Brill.

Lange, Armin. 1998. "Die Endgestalt des protomasoretischen Psalters und die Toraweisheit. Zur Bedeutung der nichtessenischen Weisheitstexte aus Qumran für die Auslegung des protomasoretischen Psalters," 101–36 in Erich Zenger, ed., *Der Psalter in Judentum und Christentum*. HBS 18. Freiburg: Herder.

————. 2004. "From Literature to Scripture: The Unite and Plurality of the Hebrew Scriptures in Light of the Qumran Library," 51–107 in Christine Helmer and Christof Landmesser, eds., *One Scripture or Many? Canon from Biblical, Theological, and Philosophical Perspectives*. Oxford: Oxford University Press.

————. 2006. "The Qumran Dead Sea Scrolls—Library or Manuscript Corpus?" 177–93 in Florentino García Martínez et al., eds., *From 4QMMT to Resurrection: Mélanges qumraniens en hommage à Émile Puech*. STDJ 61. Leiden and Boston: Brill.

————. 2007. "2 Maccabees 2:13-15: Library or Canon?" 155–67 in Géza G. Xeravits and József Zsengellér, eds., *The Books of the Maccabees: History, Theology, Ideology: Papers of the Second International Conference on the Deuterocanonical Books, Pápa, Hungary, 9–11 June, 2005*. JSJSup 118. Leiden and Boston: Brill.

Leene, Henk. 1996. "Auf der Suche nach einem redaktionskritischen Modell für Jesaja 40–55." *TLZ* 121: 803–18.

———. 2000. "Ezekiel and Jeremiah. Promises of Inner Renewal in Diachronic Perspective," 150–75 in Johannes C. de Moor and Harry F. van Rooy, eds., *Past, Present, Future: The Deuteronomistic History and the Prophets*. OTS 44. Leiden and Boston: Brill.

Lehman, Reinhard G. 1994. *Friedrich Delitzsch und der Babel-Bibel-Streit*. OBO 133. Fribourg: Universitätsverlag; Göttingen: Vandenhoeck & Ruprecht.

Leiman, Sid Z. ²1991. *The Canonization of Hebrew Scripture: The Talmudic and Midrashic Evidence*. New Haven: Connecticut Academy of Arts.

Lemaire, André. 1981. *Les écoles et la formation de la Bible dans l'ancien Israël*. OBO 39. Fribourg: Universitätsverlag; Göttingen: Vandenhoeck & Ruprecht.

———. 1986. "Vers l'histoire de la rédaction des livres des Rois." *ZAW* 98: 221–36.

———. 1996. "Zorobabel et la Judée à la lumière de l'épigraphie." *RB* 103: 48–57.

———. 2001. "Schools and Literacy in Ancient Israel and Early Judaism," 207–17 in Leo G. Perdue, ed., *The Blackwell Companion to the Hebrew Bible*. Oxford, UK and Malden, MA: Blackwell.

———. 2002. "Das achämenidische Juda und seine Nachbarn im Lichte der Epigraphie," 210–30 in Reinhard G. Kratz, ed., *Religion und Religionskontakte im Zeitalter der Achämeniden*. VWGT 22. Gütersloh: Kaiser, Gütersloher Verlagshaus.

———. 2007. "Administration in Fourth-Century B.C.E. Judah in Light of Epigraphy and Numismatics," 53–74 in Oded Lipshits et al., eds., *Judah and the Judeans in the Fourth Century B.C.E.* Winona Lake, IN: Eisenbrauns.

———. 2004. "Hebrew and West Semitic Inscriptions and Pre-Exilic Israel," 366–85 in John Day, ed., *In Search of Pre-Exilic Israel: Proceedings of the Oxford Old Testament Seminar*. JSOTSup 406. London and New York: T & T Clark.

———. 2007. *The Birth of Monotheism: The Rise and Disappearance of Yahwism*. Washington, DC: Biblical Archaeology Society.

Lemche, Niels Peter. 1998. *Die Vorgeschichte Israels: Von den Anfängen bis zum Ausgang des 13. Jahrhunderts v. Chr.* Biblische Enzyklopädie 1. Stuttgart: Kohlhammer, 1996. English: *Prelude to Israel's Past: Background and Beginnings of Israelite History and Identity*. Translated by E. F. Maniscalco. Peabody, MA: Hendrickson.

———. 2001. "The Old Testament—a Hellenistic Book?" 287–318 in Lester L. Grabbe, ed., *Did Moses Speak Attic? Jewish Historiography and Scripture in the Hellenistic Period*. JSOTSup 317. Sheffield: Sheffield Academic Press.

Leuenberger, Martin. 2004. *Konzeptionen des Königtums Gottes im Psalter*. ATANT 83. Zürich: Theologischer Verlag.

———. 2005. "Aufbau und Pragmatik des 11QPsᵃ-Psalters." *RevQ* 22: 165–211.

———. 2011. *Gott in Bewegung: Religions- und theologiegeschichtliche Beiträge zu Gottesvorstellungen im alten Israel*. FAT 76, Tübingen: Mohr (Siebeck).

Levenson, Jon D. 1984. "The Last Four Verses in Kings." *JBL* 103: 353–61.

Levin, Christoph. 1982. *Der Sturz der Königin Atalja: Ein Kapitel zur Geschichte Judas im 9. Jahrhundert v. Chr.* SBS 105. Stuttgart: Katholisches Bibelwerk.

———. 1985a. *Die Verheissung des neuen Bundes in ihrem theologiegeschichtlichen Zusammenhang ausgelegt*. FRLANT 137. Göttingen: Vandenhoeck & Ruprecht.

———. 1985b. "Der Dekalog am Sinai." *VT* 35: 165–91.

———. 1993a. "Das Gebetbuch der Gerechten. Literargeschichtliche Beobachtungen am Psalter." *ZTK* 90: 355–81.

———. 1993b. *Der Jahwist.* FRLANT 157. Göttingen: Vandenhoeck & Ruprecht.

———. 2000. "Das vorstaatliche Israel." *ZTK* 97: 385–403.

———. 2005. *Das Alte Testament.* Munich: Beck, 2001. English: *The Old Testament: A Brief Introduction.* Translated by Margaret Kohl. Princeton: Princeton University Press.

Levinson, Bernard M. 1995. "'But You Shall Surely Kill Him!' The Text-Critical and Neo-Assyrian Evidence for MT Deuteronomy 13:10," in Georg Braulik, ed., *Bundesdokument und Gesetz: Studien zum Deuteronomium.* Herders Biblische Studien 4. Freiburg et al.: Herder.

———. 1997. *Deuteronomy and the Hermeneutics of Legal Innovation.* Oxford and New York: Oxford University Press.

———. 2004. "Is the Covenant Code an Exilic Composition? A Response to John Van Seters," 272–325 in John Day, ed., *In Search of Pre-Exilic Israel: Proceedings of the Oxford Old Testament Seminar.* JSOTSup 406. London and New York: T & T Clark.

———. 2008. *Legal Revision and Religious Renewal in Ancient Israel.* Cambridge: Cambridge University Press.

Lichtenberger, Hermann. 2001. "Auferstehung in den Qumranfunden," 79–91 in Friedrich Avemarie and Hermann Lichtenberger, eds., *Auferstehung—Resurrection: The Fourth Durham-Tübingen Research Symposium. Resurrection, Transfiguration and Exaltation in the Old Testament, Ancient Judaism and Early Christianity* (Tübingen, September 1999). WUNT 135. Tübingen: Mohr (Siebeck).

Lipschits, Oded, and Joseph Blenkinsopp, eds. 2003a. *Judah and Judeans in the Neo-Babylonian Period.* Winona Lake, IN: Eisenbrauns.

———. 2003b. "Demographic Changes in Judah between the Seventh and the Fifth Centuries B.C.E.," 323–76 in idem and Joseph Blenkinsopp, eds., *Judah and Judeans in the Neo-Babylonian Period.* Winona Lake, IN: Eisenbrauns.

Liwak, Rüdiger, ed. 2004. *Hermann Gunkel zur israelitischen Literatur und Literaturgeschichte.* Theologische Studien-Texte 6. Waltrop: Spenner.

Lods, Adolphe. 1950. *Histoire de la littérature heebraïque et juive depuis les origines jusqu'à la ruine de l'état juif (135 après J.-C.).* Paris: Payot.

Lohfink, Norbert. 1973. "Die Abänderung der Theologie des priesterlichen Geschichtswerks im Segen des Heiligkeitsgesetzes. Zu Lev. 26,9.11-13," 129–36 in Hartmut Gese and Hans Peter Rüger, eds., *Wort und Geschichte. FS Karl Elliger.* AOAT 18. Kevelaer: Butzon & Bercker; Neukirchen-Vluyn: Neukirchener Verlag, 1973 = idem, *Studien zum Pentateuch,* 157–68. SBAB 4. Stuttgart: Katholisches Bibelwerk, 1988.

———. 1988. "Die Priesterschrift und die Geschichte," 183–225 in John A. Emerton, ed., *Congress Volume Göttingen 1977.* VTSup 29. Leiden: Brill, 1978 = idem, *Studien zum Pentateuch,* 213–53. SBAB 4. Stuttgart: Katholisches Bibelwerk. English: "The Priestly Narrative and History. In Memory of Peter Charlier," 136–72 in idem, *Theology of the Pentateuch: Themes of the Priestly Narrative and Deuteronomy.* Translated by Linda M. Maloney. Minneapolis: Fortress Press, 1994.

———. 1995. "Gab es eine deuteronomistische Bewegung?" 313–82 in Walter Gross, ed., *Jeremia und die "deuteronomistische Bewegung."* BBB 98. Weinheim: Beltz Athenäum = idem, *Studien zum Deuteronomium und zur deuteronomistischen Literatur III,* 65–142. SBAB 20. Stuttgart: Katholisches Bibelwerk, 1995.

Loprieno, Antonio, ed. 1996. *Ancient Egyptian Literature: History and Forms*. Probleme der Ägyptologie 10. Leiden and New York: Brill.

Lowth, Robert. 1847. *De sacra poesia Hebraeorum*. Oxford: Clascudonna,1753. English: *Lectures on the Sacred Poetry of the Hebrews translated from the Latin of Robert Lowth by G. Gregory; to which are added the principal notes of Professor Michaelis and notes by the translator and others*. London: S. Chadwick.

Lux, Rüdiger. 2002. "Das Zweiprophetenbuch. Beobachtungen zu Aufbau und Struktur von Haggai und Sacharja 1–8," 191–217 in Erich Zenger, ed., *"Wort Jhwhs, das geschah . . ." (Hos 1,1): Studien zum Zwölfprophetenbuch*. HBS 35. Freiburg: Herder.

———. 2005. "Der Zweite Tempel von Jerusalem—ein persisches oder prophetisches Projekt?" 145–72 in Uwe Becker and Jürgen van Oorschot, eds., *Das Alte Testament—ein Geschichtsbuch? Geschichtsschreibung oder Geschichtsüberlieferung im antiken Israel*. ABG 17. Leipzig: Evangelische Verlagsanstalt.

Macchi, Jean-Daniel. 2005. "Le livre d'Esther: regard hellénistique sur le pouvoir et le monde perses." *Transeu* 30: 97–135.

———. 2009. "'Ne ressassez plus les choses d'autrefois.' Esaïe 43,16-21, un surprenant regard deutéro-ésaïen sur le passé." *ZAW* 121: 225–241.

———, and Thomas Römer, eds. 2001. *Jacob: Commentaire à plusieurs voix de/Ein mehrstimmiger Kommentar zu/A plural commentary of Gen. 25–36. Mélanges offerts à Albert de Pury*. Le Monde de la Bible 44. Geneva: Labor et Fides.

MacDonald, Nathan. 2010. "Issues in the Dating of Deuteronomy: A Response to Juha Pakkala." *ZAW* 122: 431–435.

Machinist, Peter. 1991. "The Question of Distinctiveness in Ancient Israel. An Essay," 192–212 in Mordechai Cogan and Israel Eph'al, eds., *Ah, Assyria . . . : Studies in Assyrian History and Ancient Near Eastern Historiography. FS Hayim Tadmor*. ScrHier 33. Jerusalem: Magnes Press; Hebrew University.

Mach, Michael. 1992. *Entwicklungsstadien des jüdischen Engelglaubens in vorrabinischer Zeit*. TSAJ 34. Tübingen: Mohr (Siebeck).

Macholz, Christian. 1990. "Die Entstehung des hebräischen Bibelkanons nach 4Esra 14," 379–91 in Erhard Blum et al., eds., *Die hebräische Bibel und ihre zweifache Nachgeschichte. FS Rolf Rendtorff*. Neukirchen-Vluyn: Neukirchener Verlag.

Magen, Yitzhak. 2007. "The Dating of the First Phase of the Samaritan Temple on Mount Gerizim in Light of the Archaeological Evidence," 157–211 in Oded Lipschits et al., eds., *Judah and the Judeans in the Fourth Century B.C.E.* Winona Lake, IN: Eisenbrauns.

Maier, Christl. 1995. *Die "fremde Frau" in Proverbien 1–9: Eine exegetische und sozialgeschichtliche Studie*. OBO 144. Fribourg: Universitätsverlag; Göttingen: Vandenhoeck & Ruprecht.

———. 2002. *Jeremia als Lehrer der Tora: Soziale Gebote des Deuteronomiums in Fortschreibungen des Jeremiabuches*. FRLANT 196. Göttingen: Vandenhoeck & Ruprecht.

———. 2003. "Tochter Zion im Jeremiabuch. Eine literarische Personifikation mit altorientalischem Hintergrund," 157–67 in Irmtraud Fischer et al., eds., *Prophetie in Israel*. Altes Testament und Moderne 11. Münster: Lit.

Maier, Johann. 1988. "Zur Frage des biblischen Kanons im Frühjudentum im Licht der Qumranfunde." *JBTh* 3: 135–46.

———. 1990. *Zwischen den Testamenten: Geschichte und Religion in der Zeit des zwei-ten Tempels.* NEB Supplementary Volume 3. Würzburg: Echter Verlag.

———. 1995. *Die Qumran-Essener: Die Texte vom Toten Meer I.* UTB 1862: Munich: Reinhardt.

———. 1997. *Die Tempelrolle vom Toten Meer und das "Neue Jerusalem."* 11Q19 und 11Q20, 1Q32, 2Q24, 4Q554-555, 5Q15 und 11Q18: *Übersetzung und Erläuterung, mit Grundrissen der Tempelhofanlage und Skizzen zur Stadtplanung.* UTB 829. Munich and Basel: Reinhardt.

Marböck, Johannes. 1992. "Jesus Sirach (Buch)." *Neues Bibel-Lexikon* 2. Zürich and Düsseldorf: Benziger, 338–41.

———. 1995. *Gottes Weisheit unter uns: Zur Theologie des Buches Sirach.* Edited by Irmtraud Fischer. HBS 6. Freiburg and New York: Herder.

Marttila, Marko. 2006. *Collective Reinterpretation in the Psalms.* FAT II/13. Tübingen: Mohr (Siebeck).

Marxsen, Willi. 1956; [2]1959. *Der Evangelist Markus: Studien zur Redaktionsgeschichte des Evangeliums.* FRLANT 49. Göttingen: Vandenhoeck & Ruprecht.

Mason, Steve. 2002. "Josephus and his Twenty-Two Book Canon," 110–27 in Lee Martin McDonald and James A. Sanders, eds., *The Canon Debate: On the Origins and Formation of the Bible.* Peabody, MA: Hendrickson.

Mathias, Dietmar. 2005. "Der König auf dem Thron JHWHs. Überlegungen zur chro-nistischen Geschichtsdarstellung," 173–202 in Uwe Becker and Jürgen van Oor-schot, eds., *Das Alte Testament—ein Geschichtsbuch? Geschichtsschreibung oder Geschichtsüberlieferung im antiken Israel.* ABG 17. Leipzig: Evangelische Verlagsanstalt.

Mathys, Hans-Peter. 2000a. "Anmerkungen zu Mal 3,22-24," 30–40 in idem, *Vom Anfang und vom Ende: Fünf alttestamentliche Studien.* BEATAJ 47. Frankfurt: Peter Lang.

———. 2000b. "Chronikbücher und hellenistischer Zeitgeist," in idem, *Vom Anfang und vom Ende,* 41–155.

———. 2002. "Das Alte Testament—ein hellenistisches Buch," 278–93 in Ulrich Hübner and Ernst Axel Knauf, eds., *Kein Land für sich allein: Studien zum Kulturkontakt in Kanaan, Israel/Palästina und Ebirnâri für Manfred Weippert zum 65. Geburts-tag.* OBO 186. Fribourg: Universitätsverlag; Göttingen: Vandenhoeck & Ruprecht.

Matthews, Isaac A. 1923. *Old Testament Life and Literature.* New York: MacMillan.

Maul, Stefan. 1997. "Die altorientalische Hauptstadt—Abbild und Nabel der Welt," 109–24 in Gernot Wilhelm, ed., *Die orientalische Stadt: Kontinuität, Wandel, Bruch.* Colloquien der Deutschen Orient-Gesellschaft 1. Saarbrücken: SDV Saar-brücker Druckerei und Verlag.

———. 1998. "Der assyrische König—Hüter der Weltordnung," 65–77 in Jan Assmann et al., eds., *Gerechtigkeit: Richten und Retten in der abendländischen Tradition und ihren altorientalischen Ursprüngen.* Munich: Fink.

Mazar, Amihay. 1992. *Archaeology of the Land of the Bible 10000–586 B.C.E.* New York: Doubleday.

McConville, J. Gordon. 1986. "Ezra–Nehemiah and the Fulfilment of Prophecy." *VT* 36: 205–24.

McDonald, Lee Martin, and James A. Sanders, eds. 2002. *The Canon Debate: On the Origins and Formation of the Bible.* Peabody, MA: Hendrickson.

———. [3]2007. *The Biblical Canon: Its Origin, Transmission, and Authority.* Peabody, MA: Hendrickson.

McKane, William. 1970. *Proverbs: A New Approach*. OTL. London: Student Christian Movement Press; Philadelphia: Westminster.

McKenzie, Steven L. 2000. *King David: A Biography*. Oxford and New York: Oxford University Press. German translation by Christian Wiese: *König David: Eine Biographie*. Berlin and New York: de Gruyter, 2002.

Meier, Ernst Heinrich. 1856. *Geschichte der poetischen National-Literatur der Hebräer*. Leipzig: W. Engelmann.

Meinhold, Arndt. 1975. "Die Gattung der Josephsgeschichte und des Estherbuches: Diasporanovelle I." *ZAW* 87: 306–24.

———. 1919. *Die Sprüche*. I: *Sprüche Kapitel 1–15*. ZBKAT 16.1. II: *Sprüche Kapitel 16–31*. ZBKAT 16.2. Zürich: Theologischer Verlag.

Meinhold, Johannes. 1919. *Einführung in das Alte Testament: Geschichte, Literatur und Religion Israels*. Giessen: Töpelmann.

Menn, Esther. 2003. "Inner-Biblical Exegesis in the Tanak," 55–79 in Alan J. Hauser and Duane F. Watson, eds., *A History of Biblical Interpretation*. Grand Rapids: Eerdmans.

Metso, Sarianna. 1997. *The Textual Development of the Qumran Community Rule*. STDJ 21. Leiden and New York: Brill.

Meyers, Carol L. 2000. "Haggai/Haggaibuch." *RGG* 3: 1374–76.

———, and Eric M. Meyers. 1987. *Haggai, Zechariah 1–8*. AB 25B. Garden City, NY: Doubleday.

Michalowski, Piotr. 2003. "The Libraries of Babel. Text, Authority, and Tradition in Ancient Mesopotamia," 105–29 in Gillis J. Dorleijn and Herman L. J. Vanstiphout, eds., *Cultural Repertoires: Structure, Functions and Dynamics*. Groningen Studies in Cultural Change 3. Leuven and Dudley, MA: Peeters.

Millard, Alan R. 1985. "An Assessment of the Evidence for Writing in Ancient Israel," 301–12 in Janet Amitai, ed., *Biblical Archaeology Today: Proceedings of the International Congress on Biblical Archaeology, Jerusalem April 1984*. Jerusalem: Israel Exploration Society.

———. 1995. "The Knowledge of Writing in Iron Age Palestine." *TynBul* 46: 207–17.

Millard, Matthias. 1994. *Die Komposition des Psalters*. Tübingen: Mohr (Siebeck).

Miller, James M., and John H. Hayes. 1986. *A History of Ancient Israel and Judah*. Philadelphia: Westminster.

Moenikes, Ansgar. 1992. "Zur Redaktionsgeschichte des sogenannten Deuteronomistischen Geschichtswerks." *ZAW* 104: 333–48.

Mohr, Hubert. 1988. "Die 'Ecole des Annales,'" *Handbuch religionswissenschaftlicher Grundbegriffe* 1 (Stuttgart: Kohlhammer): 263–72.

Moor, Johannes C. de. 1996. "Egypt, Ugarit and Exodus," 213–47 in Nick Wyatt et al., eds., *Ugarit, Religion and Culture: Proceedings of the International Colloquium on Ugarit, Religion, and Culture, Edinburgh, July 1994*. FS John C. L. Gibson. Münster: Ugarit-Verlag.

Moran, William L. 1963. "The Ancient Near Eastern Background of the Love of God in Deuteronomy." *CBQ* 25: 77–87.

Morrow, William S. 1995. *Scribing the Center: Organization and Redaction in Deuteronomy 14:1–17:13*. SBLMS 49. Atlanta: Scholars Press.

———. 2005. "Cuneiform Literacy and Deuteronomic Composition." *BibOr* 62: 204–13.

Müller, Achim. 2000. *Proverbien 1–9: Der Weisheit neue Kleider*. BZAW 291. Berlin and New York: de Gruyter.

Müller, Karlheinz. 1991. *Studien zur frühjüdischen Apokalyptik.* SBAB 11. Stuttgart: Katholisches Bibelwerk.

Münger, Stefan. 2003. "Egyptian Stamp-Seal Amulets and their Implications for the Chronology of the Early Iron Age." *Tel Aviv* 30: 66–82.

Münkler, Herfried. 2005. *Imperien: Die Logik der Weltherrschaft—vom Alten Rom bis zu den Vereinigten Staaten.* Berlin: Rowohlt. English: *Empires: the Logic of World Domination from Ancient Rome to the United States.* Translated by Patrick Camiller. Cambridge, UK, and Malden, MA: Polity, 2007.

Na'aman, Nadav. 1990. "The Historical Background to the Conquest of Samaria (720 B.C.)." *Bib* 71: 206–25.

———. 1991. "The Kingdom of Judah under Josiah." *Tel Aviv* 18: 3–71.

———. 1997. "King Mesha and the Foundation of the Moabite Monarchy." *IEJ* 47: 83–92.

———. 1999a "No Anthropomorphic Graven Image." *UF* 31: 391–415.

———. 1999b. "The Contribution of Royal Inscriptions for a Re-Evaluation of the Book of Kings as a Historical Source." *JSOT* 82: 3–17.

———. 2000. "Royal Vassals or Governors? On the Status of Sheshbazzar and Zerubbabel in the Persian Empire." *Henoch* 22: 35–44.

———. 2006. "The Temple Library of Jerusalem and the Composition of the Book of Kings," 129–52 in André Lemaire, ed., *Congress Volume Leuven 2004.* VTSup 109. Leiden and Boston: Brill.

———. 2011. "The Exodus Story: Between Historical Memory and Historiographical Composition." *Journal of Ancient Near Eastern Religions* 11: 39–69.

Neef, Heinz-Dieter. 2002. *Deboraerzählung und Deboralied: Studien zu Jdc 4,1–5,31.* BTS 49. Neukirchen-Vluyn: Neukirchener Verlag.

Nelson, Richard D. 1981. *The Double Redaction of the Deuteronomistic History.* JSOTSup 18. Sheffield: JSOT Press.

———. 2005. "The Double Redaction of the Deuteronomistic History. The Case is Still Compelling." *JSOT* 29: 319–37.

Neusner, Jacob et al., eds. 1987. *Judaisms and Their Messiahs at the Turn of the Christian Era.* Cambridge and New York: Cambridge University Press.

———, and Alan J. Avery-Peck. 2001. *Judaism in Late Antiquity. Part 5: The Judaism of Qumran: A Systemic Reading of the Dead Sea Scrolls.* Vol. 2: *World View, Comparing Judaisms.* HO 1, vol. 57. Leiden and New York: Brill.

Newsom, Carol A. 2007. "Re-considering Job." *CBR* 15: 155–82.

Nickelsburg, George W. E. 1984. "The Bible Rewritten and Expanded," 89–156 in Michael E. Stone, ed., *Jewish Writings of the Second Temple Period: Apocrypha, Pseudepigrapha, Qumran Sectarian Writings, Philo, Josephus.* CRINT II/2. Assen: Van Gorcum; Philadelphia: Fortress Press.

Niditch, Susan. 1996. *Oral World and Written Word: Ancient Israelite Literature.* Louisville: Westminster John Knox.

Niehr, Herbert. 1990. *Der höchste Gott.* BZAW 190. Berlin and New York: de Gruyter.

———. 1997. "In Search of Yhwh's Cult Statue in the First Temple," 73–95 in Karel van der Toorn, ed., *The Image and the Book.* CBET 21. Leuven: Peeters.

Niemann, Hermann Michael. 1993. *Herrschaft, Königtum und Staat: Skizzen zur soziokulturellen Entwicklung im monarchischen Israel.* FAT 6. Tübingen: Mohr.

———. 1998. "Kein Ende des Büchermachens in Israel und Juda (Koh 12,12)—wann begann es?" *BK* 53: 127–34.

———. 2007. "Royal Samaria—Capital or Residence? or: The Foundation of the City of Samaria by Sargon II," 184–207 in Lester L. Grabbe, ed., *Ahab Agonistes: The Rise and Fall of the Omri Dynasty*. Library of Hebrew Bible 421/ESHM 5. London and New York: T & T Clark.

Nihan, Christoph. 2007. *From Priestly Torah to Pentateuch: A Study in the Composition of the Book of Leviticus*. FAT II/25. Tübingen: Mohr (Siebeck).

Nissinen, Martti. 1998. "Prophecy against the King in Neo-Assyrian Sources," 157–70 in Klaus-Dietrich Schunck and Matthias Augustin, eds., *"Lasset uns Brücken bauen . . .": Collected Communications to the XVth Congress of the International Organization for the Study of the Old Testament, Cambridge 1995*. BEAT 42. Frankfurt and New York: Peter Lang.

———. 2004. "What is Prophecy? An Ancient Near Eastern Perspective," 16–37 in John Kaltner and Louis Stulman, eds., *Inspired Speech: Prophecy in the Ancient Near East. FS Herbert B. Huffmon*. JSOTSup 378. Edinburgh: T & T Clark.

———, Choon Leong Seow, and Robert K. Ritner. 2003. *Prophets and Prophecy in the Ancient Near East*. SBLWAW 12. Atlanta: Scholars Press.

Nogalski, James M. 1993. *Literary Precursors to the Book of the Twelve*. BZAW 217. Berlin and New York: de Gruyter.

Noll, K. L. 2007. "Deuteronomistic History or Deuteronomic Debate? (A Thought Experiment)." *JSOT* 31: 311–45.

Noth, Martin. 1943. *Überlieferungsgeschichtliche Studien*. Halle: M. Niemeyer. English: *The Deuteronomistic History*. Sheffield: JSOT Press, 1981, 2001.

———. 1971. "Die Einnahme von Jerusalem im Jahre 597 v. Chr.," 111–32 in idem, *Aufsätze zur biblischen Landes- und Altertumskunde*. Vol. 1: *Archäologische, exegetische und topographische Untersuchungen zur Geschichte Israels*. Neukirchen-Vluyn: Neukirchener Verlag.

Noyes, Carleton Eldredge. 1924. *The Genius of Israel: A Reading of Hebrew Scriptures Prior to the Exile*. Boston: Houghton Miffin.

O'Day, Gail. 1999. "Intertextuality," 546–48 in J. H. Hayes, ed., *Dictionary of Biblical Interpretation*. 2 vols. Nashville: Abingdon.

Oesch, Josef M. 1979. *Petucha und Setuma: Untersuchungen zu einer überlieferten Gliederung im hebräischen Text des Alten Testaments*. OBO 27: Fribourg: Universitätsverlag.

Oded, Bustenay. 1979. *Mass Deportations and Deportees in the Neo-Assyrian Empire*. Wiesbaden: Reichert.

Oeming, Manfred. 2000a. "'Ihr habt nicht recht von mir geredet wie mein Knecht Hiob'—Gottes Schlusswort als Schlüssel zur Interpretation des Hiobbuchs und als kritische Anfrage an die moderne Theologie." *EvT* 60: 103–16.

———. 2000b. *Das Buch der Psalmen: Psalm 1–41*. NSKAT 13/1. Stuttgart: Katholisches Bibelwerk.

———, and Konrad Schmid. 2001. *Hiobs Weg: Stationen von Menschen im Leid*. BTS 45. Neukirchen-Vluyn: Neukirchener Verlag.

———, and Konrad Schmid, eds. 2003. *Der eine Gott und die Götter: Polytheismus und Monotheismus im antiken Israel*. ATANT 82. Zürich: Theologischer Verlag.

———, Konrad Schmid, and Andreas Schüle, eds. 2004. *Theologie in Israel und in den Nachbarkulturen*. ATM 9. Münster: Lit.

Olyan, Saul M. 1996. "Honor, Shame, and Covenantal Relations in Ancient Israel and Its Environment." *JBL* 115: 201–18.

Oorschot, Jürgen van. 2000. "Altes Testament," 29–56 in Udo Tworuschka, ed., *Heilige Schriften: Eine Einführung*. Darmstadt: Wissenschaftliche Buchgesellschaft.

———. 2002. "'Höre Israel . . . !' (Dtn 6,4f). Der eine und einzige Gott Israels im Widerstreit," 113–35 in idem and Manfred Krebernik, eds., *Polytheismus und Monotheismus in den Religionen des Vorderen Orients*. AOAT 298. Münster: Ugarit-Verlag.

———. 2007. "Die Entstehung des Hiobbuches," 165–84 in Thomas Krüger et al., eds., *Das Buch Hiob und seine Interpretationen: Beiträge zum Hiob-Symposium auf dem Monte Verità von 14.–19. August 2005*. ATANT 88. Zürich: Theologischer Verlag.

Osten-Sacken, Peter von der. 1969. *Die Apokalyptik in ihrem Verhältnis zu Prophetie und Weisheit*. Munich: Kaiser.

Osumi, Yuichi. 1991. *Die Kompositionsgeschichte des Bundesbuches Exodus 20,22b–23,33*. OBO 105. Fribourg: Universitätsverlag; Göttingen: Vandenhoeck & Ruprecht.

Oswald, Wolfgang. 1998. *Israel am Gottesberg: Eine Untersuchung zur Literargeschichte der vorderen Sinaiperikope Ex 19–24 und deren historischem Hintergrund*. OBO 159. Fribourg: Universitätsverlag; Göttingen: Vandenhoeck & Ruprecht.

———. 2009. *Staatstheorie im Alten Israel: Der politische Diskurs im Pentateuch und in den Geschichtsbüchern des Alten Testaments*. Stuttgart: Kohlhammer.

Otto, Eckart. 1980. *Jerusalem—die Geschichte der Heiligen Stadt*. Kohlhammer Urban-Taschenbücher (UB) 308. Stuttgart et al.: Kohlhammer.

———. 1988. *Wandel der Rechtsbegründungen in der Gesellschaftsgeschichte des antiken Israel: Eine Rechtsgeschichte des "Bundesbuches": Ex XX 22–XXIII 13*. StudBib 3. Leiden and New York: Brill.

———. 1991. *Körperverletzungen in den Keilschriftrechten und im Alten Testament: Studien zum Rechtstransfer im Alten Orient*. AOAT 226. Kevelaer: Butzon & Bercker; Neukirchen-Vluyn: Neukirchener Verlag.

———. 1994. "Von der Gerichtsordnung zum Verfassungsentwurf. Deuteronomische Gestaltung und deuteronomistische Interpretation im 'Ämtergesetz' Dtn 16,18–18,22," 142–55 in Ingo Kottsieper et al., eds., *"Wer ist wie du, Herr, unter den Göttern": Studien zur Theologie und Religionsgeschichte Israels. FS Otto Kaiser*. Göttingen: Vandenhoeck & Ruprecht.

———. 1996a. "Die nachpriesterschriftliche Pentateuchredaktion im Buch Exodus," 61–111 in Marc Vervenne, ed., *Studies in the Book of Exodus: Redaction—Reception—Interpretation*. BETL 126. Leuven: Leuven University Press; Peeters.

———. 1996b. "Die Paradieserzählung Gen 2–3: Eine nachpriesterschriftliche Lehrerzählung in ihrem religionshistorischen Kontext," 167–92 in Anja A. Diesel et al., eds., *"Jedes Ding hat seine Zeit . . .": Studien zur israelitischen und altorientalischen Weisheit. FS Diethelm Michel*. BZAW 241. Berlin and New York: de Gruyter.

———. 1996c. "Sozial- und rechtshistorische Aspekte in der Ausdifferenzierung eines altisraelitischen Ethos aus dem Recht" (1987), 94–111 in idem, *Kontinuum und Proprium: Studien zur Sozial- und Rechtsgeschichte des Alten Orients und des Alten Testaments*. Orientalia Biblica et Christiana 8. Wiesbaden: Harrassowitz.

———. 1996d. "Treueid und Gesetz. Die Ursprünge des Deuteronomiums im Horizont neuassyrischen Vertragsrechts." *ZABR* 2: 1–52.

———. 1997a. "Recht/Rechtstheologie/Rechtsphilosophie I." *TRE* 28: 197–209.

———. 1997b. "Das Deuteronomium als archimedischer Punkt der Pentateuchkritik. Auf dem Wege zu einer Neubegründung der de Wette'schen Hypothese," 321–39 in Marc Vervenne and Johan Lust, eds., *Deuteronomy and Deuteronomic Literature. FS C. H. W. Brekelmans*. BETL 133. Leuven: Peeters.

———. 1997c. "Forschungen zur Priesterschrift." *TRu* 62: 1–50.

———. 1998a. "'Das Deuteronomium krönt die Arbeit der Propheten.' Gesetz und Prophetie im Deuteronomium," 277–309 in Friedrich Diedrich and Bernd Willmes, eds., *Ich bewirke das Heil und erschaffe das Unheil (Jesaja 45,7): Studien zur Botschaft der Propheten. FS Lothar Ruppert*. fzb 88. Würzburg: Echter Verlag.

———. 1998b. "Bundesbuch." *RGG* 1: 1876–77.

———. 1998c. "'Um Gerechtigkeit im Land sichtbar werden zu lassen . . . .' Zur Vermittlung von Recht und Gerechtigkeit im Alten Orient, in der Hebräischen Bibel und in der Moderne," 107–45 in Joachim Mehlhausen, ed., *Recht—Macht—Gerechtigkeit*. VWGT 14. Gütersloh: Gütersloher Verlagshaus Kaiser.

———. 1999a. *Das Deuteronomium: Politische Theologie und Rechtsreform in Juda und Assyrien*. BZAW 284. Berlin and New York: de Gruyter.

———. 1999b. "Dekalog." *RGG* 2: 625–28.

———. 1999c. "Deuteronomium." *RGG* 2: 693–96.

———. 1999d. "Exkarnation ins Recht und Kanonsbildung in der Hebräischen Bibel. Zu einem Vorschlag von Jan Assmann." *ZABR* 5: 99–110.

———. 2000a. "Heiligkeitsgesetz." *RGG* 3: 1570–71.

———. 2000b. "Mose und das Gesetz. Die Mose-Figur als Gegenentwurf Politischer Theologie zur neuassyrischen Königsideologie im 7. Jh. v. Chr.," 43–83 in idem, ed., *Mose: Ägypten und das Alte Testament*. SBS 189. Stuttgart: Katholisches Bibelwerk.

———. 2001a. "Israel und Mesopotamien." *RGG* 4: 308–9.

———. 2001b. "Jakob I. Altes Testament." *RGG* 4: 352–54.

———. 2003. "Psalm 2 in neuassyrischer Zeit. Assyrische Motive in der judäischen Königstheologie," 335–49 in Klaus Kiesow and Thomas Meurer, eds., *Textarbeit: Studien zu Texten und ihrer Rezeption aus dem Alten Testament und der Umwelt Israels. FS Peter Weimar*. AOAT 294. Münster: Ugarit-Verlag.

———. 2004. "Recht und Ethos in der ost- und westmediterranen Antike: Entwurf eines Gesamtbildes," 91–109 in Markus Witte, ed., *Gott und Mensch im Dialog. FS Otto Kaiser*. BZAW 345/1. Berlin and New York: de Gruyter.

———. 2006. *Mose: Geschichte und Legende*. Munich: Beck.

———. 2007. *Das Gesetz des Mose*. Darmstadt: Wissenschaftliche Buchgesellschaft.

Pakkala, Juha. 1999. *Intolerant Monolatry in the Deuteronomistic History*. Suomen Eksegeettisen Seuran julkaisuja (SESJ) 76. Helsinki: Finnish Exegetical Society; Göttingen: Vandenhoeck & Ruprecht.

———. 2004. *Ezra the Scribe: The Development of Ezra 7–10 and Nehemia 8*. BZAW 347. Berlin and New York: de Gruyter.

———. 2006a. "Der literar- und religionsgeschichtliche Ort von Deuteronomium 13," 125–36 in Markus Witte, Konrad Schmid, Doris Prechel, and Jan Christian Gertz, eds., *Die deuteronomistischen Geschichtswerke: Redaktions- und religionsgeschichtliche Perspektiven zur "Deuteronomismus"-Diskussion in Tora und Vorderen Propheten*. BZAW 365. Berlin and New York: de Gruyter.

———. 2006b. "Zedekiah's Fate and the Dynastic Succession." *JBL* 125: 443–52.

———. 2008. "Jeroboam Without Bulls." *ZAW* 120: 501–25.

———. 2009. "The Date of the Oldest Edition of Deuteronomy." *ZAW* 121: 388–401.

———. 2011. "The Dating of Deuteronomy: A Response to Nathan MacDonald." *ZAW* 123: 431–36.

Parker, Simon B. 2000. "Did the Authors of the Books of Kings Make Use of Royal Inscriptions?" *VT* 50: 357–78.

Parpola, Simo. 1997. *Assyrian Prophecies*. SAA IX. Helsinki: Helsinki University Press.

Pearce, Laurie E. 2006. "New Evidence for Judeans in Babylonia," 399–411 in Oded Lipschits and Manfred Oeming, eds., *Judah and the Judeans in the Persian Period*. Winona Lake, IN: Eisenbrauns.

Pedersén, Olof. 1998. *Archives and Libraries in the Ancient Near East 1500–300 B.C.* Bethesda, MD: CDL Press.

Perdue, Leo G. 1977. *Wisdom and Cult: A Critical Analysis of the Views of the Cult in the Wisdom Literature of Israel and the Ancient Near East*. SBLDS 30. Missoula: Scholars Press.

Perkins, David. 1992. *Is Literary History Possible?* Baltimore and London: Johns Hopkins University Press.

Perlitt, Lothar. 1988. "Priesterschrift im Deuteronomium?" *ZAW* 100 Suppl.: 65–87.

———. 1994. "Jesaja und die Deuteronomisten" (1989), 157–71 in idem, *Deuteronomium-Studien*. FAT 8. Tübingen: Mohr (Siebeck).

Person, Raymond F. 2007. "The Deuteronomic History and the Books of Chronicles: Contemporary Competing Historiographies," 315–36 in Robert Rezetko et al., eds., *Reflection and Refraction. FS A. Graeme Auld*. VTSup 113. Leiden and Boston: Brill.

Pfeiffer, Henrik. 2005. *Jahwes Kommen vom Süden: Jdc 5; Hab 3; Dtn 33 und Ps 68 in ihrem literatur- und theologiegeschichtlichen Umfeld*. FRLANT 211. Göttingen: Vandenhoeck & Ruprecht.

Pietsch, Michael. 2003. *"Dieser ist der Spross Davids . . .": Studien zur Rezeptionsgeschichte der Nathanverheissung im alttestamentlichen, zwischentestamentlichen und neutestamentlichen Schrifttum*. WMANT 100. Neukirchen-Vluyn: Neukirchener Verlag.

Pilhofer, Peter. 1990. *Presbyteron Kreitton: Der Altersbeweis der jüdischen und christlichen Apologeten und seine Vorgeschichte*. WUNT II/39. Tübingen: Mohr.

Pisano, Stephen. 2005. "Alcune osservazioni sul racconto di Davide e Golia. Confronto fra TM e LXX." *Annali di Scienze Religiose* (Milan) 10: 129–37.

Plöger, Otto. ²1962. *Theokratie und Eschatologie*. WMANT 2. Neukirchen-Vluyn: Neukirchener Verlag. English: *Theocracy and Eschatology*. Translated by S. Rudman. Oxford: Blackwell; Richmond: John Knox, 1968.

Pohlmann, Karl-Friedrich. 1978. *Studien zum Jeremiabuch: Ein Beitrag zur Frage nach der Entstehung des Jeremiabuches*. FRLANT 118. Göttingen: Vandenhoeck & Ruprecht.

———. 1989. *Die Ferne Gottes: Studien zum Jeremiabuch. Beiträge zu den "Konfessionen" im Jeremiabuch und ein Versuch zur Frage nach den Anfängen der Jeremiatradition*. BZAW 179. Berlin and New York: de Gruyter.

———. 1991. "Zur Frage von Korrespondenzen und Divergenzen zwischen den Chronikbüchern und dem Esra/Nehemia-Buch," 314–30 in John A. Emerton, ed., *Congress Volume Leuven 1989*. VTSup 43. Leiden: Brill.

———. 1996. *Das Buch des Propheten Hesekiel (Ezechiel) Kapitel 1–19*. ATD 22/1. Göttingen: Vandenhoeck & Ruprecht.

Pola, Thomas. 1995. *Die ursprüngliche Priesterschrift: Beobachtungen zur Literarkritik und Traditionsgeschichte von* P^g. WMANT 70. Neukirchen-Vluyn: Neukirchener Verlag.

Pongratz-Leisten, Beate. 1994. *Ina šulmi irub: Die kulttopographische und ideologische Programmatik der akitu-Prozession in Babylonien und Assyrien im 1. Jahrtausend vor Christus*. Mainz: von Zabern.

Porten, Bezalel. 1996. *The Elephantine Papyri in English: Three Millennia of Cross-cultural Continuity and Change*. Documenta et Monumenta Orientis Antiqui (DMOA) 22. Leiden and New York: Brill.

Preuss, Horst-Dietrich. 1987. *Einführung in die alttestamentliche Weisheitsliteratur*. UB 383. Stuttgart et al.: Kohlhammer.

———. 1993. "Zum deuteronomistischen Geschichtswerk." *TRu* 58: 229–64, 341–95.

Pury, Albert de. 1991. "Le cycle de Jacob comme légende autonome des origines d'Israël," 78–96 in John A. Emerton, ed., *Congress Volume Leuven 1989*. VTSup 43. Leiden: Brill.

———. 2000. "Abraham. The Priestly Writer's 'Ecumenical' Ancestor," 163–81 in Steven L. McKenzie et al., eds., *Rethinking the Foundations: Historiography in the Ancient World and in the Bible. FS John Van Seters*. BZAW 294. Berlin and New York: de Gruyter.

———. 2001. "Situer le cycle de Jacob. Quelques réflexions, vingt-cinq ans plus tard," 213–41 in André Wénin, ed., *Studies in the Book of Genesis: Literature, Redaction and History*. BETL 155. Leuven: Leuven University Press; Sterling, VA: Peeters.

———. 2002. "Gottesname, Gottesbezeichnung und Gottesbegriff. Elohim als Indiz zur Entstehungsgeschichte des Pentateuch," 25–47 in Jan Christian Gertz et al., eds., *Abschied vom Jahwisten: Die Komposition des Hexateuch in den jüngsten Diskussion*. BZAW 315. Berlin and New York: de Gruyter.

———. 2003. "Zwischen Sophokles und Ijob. Die Schriften (Ketubim): ein jüdischer Literatur-Kanon." *Welt und Umwelt der Bibel* 28/8: 24–27.

———. 2007. "P^g as the Absolute Beginning," 99–128 in Thomas Römer and Konrad Schmid, eds., *Les dernières rédactions du Pentateuque, de l'Hexateuque et de l'Ennéateuque*. BETL 203. Leuven and Dudley, MA: Leuven University Press; Peeters.

———, and Thomas Römer, eds. 2000. *Die sogenannte Thronfolgegeschichte Davids: Neue Einsichten und Anfragen*. OBO 176. Fribourg: Universitätsverlag; Göttingen: Vandenhoeck & Ruprecht.

Quack, Joachim Friedrich. 2005. *Einführung in die altägyptische Literaturgeschichte III: Die demotische und gräkoägyptische Literatur*. Einführungen und Quellentexte zur Ägyptologie 3. Münster: Lit.

Rad, Gerhard von. 1938. "Das formgeschichtliche Problem des Hexateuch," 9–86 in idem, *Gesammelte Studien zum Alten Testament*. TB 8. Munich: Kaiser, 1958. English: *The Problem of the Hexateuch, and Other Essays*. Edinburgh and London: Oliver & Boyd; New York: McGraw-Hill, 1966.

———. 1953. "Josephsgeschichte und ältere Chokma," 272–80 in idem, *Gesammelte Studien zum Alten Testament*. TB 8. Munich: Kaiser, 1958.

———. 1957; 1960. *Theologie des Alten Testaments*. 2 vols. Munich: Kaiser. English: *Old Testament Theology*. Translated by D. M. G. Stalker. OTL. Louisville et al.: Westminster John Knox, 2001.

———. 1954. "Die Josephsgeschichte," 22–41 in idem, *Gottes Wirken in Israel*. Neukirchen-Vluyn: Neukirchener Verlag, 1974. English: *God at Work in Israel*. Translated by John H. Marks. Nashville: Abingdon, 1980.

Reade, Julian. 1979. "Ideology and Propaganda in Assyrian Art," 329–44 in Mogens Trolle Larsen, ed., *Power and Propaganda: A Symposium on Ancient Empires*. Mesopotamia 7. Copenhagen: Akademisk Forlag.

Redditt, Paul L. 2000. "Daniel 9: Its Structure and Meaning." *CBQ* 62: 236–49.

Redford, Donald B. 1992. *Egypt, Canaan, and Israel in Ancient Times*. Princeton: Princeton University Press.

Rendtorff, Rolf. 1961. "Genesis 8,21 und die Urgeschichte des Jahwisten." *KD* 7: 69–78 = idem, *Gesammelte Studien zum Alten Testament*, 188–97. TB 57. Munich: Kaiser, 1975.

———. 1977. *Das überlieferungsgeschichtliche Problem des Pentateuch*. BZAW 147. Berlin and New York: de Gruyter. English: *The Problem of the Process of Transmission in the Pentateuch*. Translated by John J. Scullion. Sheffield: JSOT Press, 1990.

———. 1999; 2001. *Theologie des alten Testaments: Ein kanonischer Entwurf*. Vol. 1: *Kanonische Grundlegung*. Vol. 2: *Thematische Entfaltung*. Neukirchen-Vluyn: Neukirchener Verlag. English: *The Canonical Hebrew Bible: A Theology of the Old Testament*. Translated by David E. Orton. Leiden: Deo Publications, 2005.

Reinert, Andreas. 2010. *Die Salomofiktion: Studien zu Struktur und Komposition des Koheletbuches*. WMANT 126. Neukirchen-Vluyn: Neukirchener.

Renz, Johannes, and Wolfgang Röllig. 1995–2003. *Handbuch der althebräischen Epigraphik*. 3 vols. Darmstadt: Wissenschaftliche Buchgesellschaft.

Reuss, Eduard. 1881. *Die Geschichte der Heiligen Schriften des Alten Testaments*. Braunschweig: C. A. Schwetschke.

Rigger, Hansjörg. 1997. *Siebzig Siebener: Die "Jahrwochenprophetie" in Dan 9*. TThSt 57. Trier: Paulinus-Verlag.

Rogerson, John W. 2001. "Die Bibel lesen wie jedes andere Buch? Auseinandersetzungen um die Autorität der Bibel vom 18. Jahrhundert an bis heute," 211–34 in Stephen Chapman et al., eds., *Biblischer Text und theologische Theoriebildung*. BTS 44 Neukirchen-Vluyn: Neukirchener Verlag.

Röllig, Wolfgang, ed. 1978. *Altorientalische Literaturen*. Neues Handbuch der Literaturwissenschaft 1. Wiesbaden: Akademische Verlagsgesellschaft Athenaion.

Römer, Thomas C. 1990. *Israels Väter: Untersuchungen zur Väterthematik im Deuteronomium und in der deuteronomistischen Literatur*. OBO 99. Fribourg: Universitätsverlag; Göttingen: Vandenhoeck & Ruprecht.

———. 1991. "Exode et Anti-Exode. La nostalgie de l'Egypte dans les traditions du désert," 155–72 in idem, ed., *Lectio difficilior probabilior? L'exégèse comme expérience de décloisonnement*. FS Françoise Smyth-Florentin. DBAT Beihefte 12. Heidelberg: Wiss.-theol. Seminar.

———. 1992. "Joseph approche: source du cycle, corpus, unité," 73–85 in Olivier Abel and Françoise Smyth-Florentin, eds., *Le livre de traverse de l'exégèse biblique à l'anthropologie*. Paris: Cerf.

———. 1998. "Why Would the Deuteronomists Tell about the Sacrifice of Jephthah's Daughter?" *JSOT* 77: 27–38.

———. 2004. "Le jugement de Dieu dans les traditions du séjour d'Israël dans le désert," 63–80 in Eberhard Bons, ed., *Le jugement dans l'un et l'autre Testament. I: Mélanges offerts à Raymond Kuntzmann*. LD 197. Paris: Cerf.

———. 2005. *The So-Called Deuteronomistic History: A Sociological Historical and Literary Introduction*. London and New York: T & T Clark.

———. 2007. "Israel's Sojourn in the Wilderness and the Construction of the Book of

Numbers," 419–45 in Robert Rezetko et al., eds., *Reflection and Refraction. FS A. Graeme Auld.* VTSup 113. Leiden and Boston: Brill.

———, and Konrad Schmid, eds. 2007. *Les dernières rédactions du Pentateuque, de l'Hexateuque et de l'Ennéateuque.* BETL 203. Leuven and Dudley, MA: Leuven University Press; Peeters.

Römheld, Diethard. 1989. *Wege der Weisheit: Die Lehren Amenemopes und Proverbien 22,17–24,22.* BZAW 184. Berlin and New York: de Gruyter.

Rösel, Christoph. 1999. *Die messianische Redaktion des Psalters: Studien zu Entstehung und Theologie der Sammlung Psalm 2–89*.* Calwer theologische Monographien (CTM), Series A, Bibelwissenschaft, vol. 19. Stuttgart: Kohlhammer.

Rösel, Martin. 1994. *Übersetzung als Vollendung der Auslegung: Studien zur Genesis–Septuaginta.* BZAW 223. Berlin and New York: de Gruyter.

———. 2006. "Towards a 'Theology of the Septuagint,'" 239–52 in Wolfgang Kraus and R. Glenn Wooden, eds., *Septuagint Research: Issues and Challenges in the Study of the Greek Jewish Scriptures.* SBLSCS 53. Atlanta: Society of Biblical Literature.

———. 2009. "Salomo und die Sonne. Zur Rekonstruktion des Tempelweihspruchs I Reg 8,12f." *ZAW* 121/3: 402–17.

Rost, Leonhard. 1965. *Die Überlieferung von der Thronnachfolge Davids.* BWANT Series III, 6. Stuttgart: Kohlhammer, 1926 = idem, *Das kleine Credo und andere Studien zum Alten Testament,* 119–253. Heidelberg: Quelle & Meyer.

Rothenbusch, Ralf. 2000. *Die kasuistische Rechtssammlung im "Bundesbuch" (Ex 21,2-11.18–22,16) und ihr literarischer Kontext im Licht altorientalischer Parallelen.* AOAT 259. Münster: Ugarit-Verlag.

Rudnig, Thilo Alexander. 2000. *Heilig und Profan: Redaktionskritische Studien zu Ez 40–48.* BZAW 287. Berlin and New York: de Gruyter.

———. 2006. *Davids Thron: Redaktionskritische Studien zur Geschichte von der Thronnachfolge Davids.* BZAW 358. Berlin and New York: de Gruyter.

———. 2007. "'Ist denn Jahwe nicht auf dem Zion?' (Jer 8,19)." *ZTK* 104: 267–86.

Rudnig-Zelt, Susanne. 2006. *Hoseastudien: Redaktionskritische Untersuchungen zur Genese des Hoseabuches.* FRLANT 213. Göttingen: Vandenhoeck & Ruprecht.

Rüpke, Jörg. 2005. "Heilige Schriften und Buchreligionen. Überlegungen zu Begriffen und Methoden," 189–202, 248–49 in Christoph Bultmann et al., eds., *Heilige Schriften: Ursprung, Geltung und Gebrauch.* Münster: Aschendorff.

Ruppert, Lothar. 1994. *Studien zur Literaturgeschichte des Alten Testaments.* SBAB 18. Stuttgart: Katholisches Bibelwerk.

Rüterswörden, Udo. 1988. "Der Bogen in Genesis 9. Militär-historische und traditionsgeschichtliche Erwägungen zu einem biblischen Symbol." *UF* 20: 247–63.

———. 2002. "Dtn 13 in der neueren Deuteronomiumsforschung," 185–203 in André Lemaire, ed., *Congress Volume Basel 2001.* VTSup 92. Leiden and Boston: Brill.

———. 2006. "Die Liebe zu Gott im Deuteronomium," 229–38 in Markus Witte, Konrad Schmid, Doris Prechel, and Jan Christian Gertz, eds., *Die deuteronomistischen Geschichtswerke: Redaktions- und religionsgeschichtliche Perspektiven zur "Deuteronomismus"-Diskussion in Tora und Vorderen Propheten.* BZAW 365. Berlin and New York: de Gruyter.

Sæbø, Magne. 1988. "Vom 'Zusammen-Denken' zum Kanon." *Jahrbuch für Biblische Theologie (JBTh)* 3: 115–33.

Sacchi, Paolo. 1999. *The History of the Second Temple Period.* JSOTSup 285. Sheffield: Sheffield Academic Press.

Saénz Badillos, Ángel. 1993. *A History of the Hebrew Language*. Translated by John Elwolde. Cambridge and New York: Cambridge University Press.

Sandmel, Samuel. 1962. "Parallelomania." *JBL* 81: 1–13.

Särkiö, Pekka. 1998. *Exodus und Salomo: Erwägungen zur verdeckten Salomokritik anhand von Ex 1–2, 5, 14 und 32*. SESJ 71. Göttingen: Vandenhoeck & Ruprecht.

———. 2000. "Concealed Criticism of King Solomon in Exodus." *BN* 102: 74–83.

Sarna, Nahum M. 1971. "*The Order of the Books*," in Chares Berlin, ed., *Studies in Jewish Bibliography, History and Literature in Honor of I. Edward Kiev*. New York: KTAV, 407–413.

———. 1989. *Ancient Libraries and the Ordering of the Biblical Books: A Lecture Presented at the Library of Congress, March 6, 1989*. The Center for the Book Viewpoint Series 25. Washington, DC: Library of Congress.

Sass, Benjamin. 1990. "Arabs and Greeks in Late First Temple Jerusalem." *PEQ* 122: 59–61.

Saur, Markus. 2004. *Die Königspsalmen: Studien zu ihrer Entstehung und Theologie*. BZAW 340. Berlin and New York: de Gruyter.

Schäfer, Peter. 1983. *Geschichte der Juden in der Antike: Die Juden Palästinas von Alexander dem Grossen bis zur arabischen Eroberung*. Stuttgart: Katholisches Bibelwerk; Neukirchen-Vluyn: Neukirchener Verlag. English: *The History of the Jews in Antiquity: the Jews of Palestine from Alexander the Great to the Arab Conquest*. Translated by David Chowcat. Luxembourg: Harwood Academic Publishers, 1995.

Schams, Christine. 1998. *Jewish Scribes in the Second-Temple Period*. JSOTSup 291. Sheffield: Sheffield Academic Press.

Schaper, Joachim. 2000. *Priester und Leviten im achämenidischen Juda: Studien zur Kult- und Sozialgeschichte Israels in persischer Zeit*. FAT 31. Tübingen: Mohr (Siebeck).

———. 2009. *Die Textualisierung der Religion*. FAT 62. Tübingen: Mohr (Siebeck).

Schaudig, Hanspeter. 2003. "Nabonid, der 'Archäologe auf dem Königsthron.' Zum Geschichtsbild der ausgehenden neubabylonischen Reiches," 447–97 in Gebhard J. Selz, ed., *Festschrift für Burkhart Kienast: Zu seinem 70. Geburtstage dargebracht von Freunden, Schülern und Kollegen*. AOAT 274. Münster: Ugarit-Verlag.

Schelbert, Georg. 1988. "Jubiläenbuch." *TRE* 17: 285–89.

Schenker, Adrian. 2006. "Die Verheissung Natans in 2Sam 7 in der Septuaginta. Wie erklären sich die Differenzen zwischen Massoretischem Text und LXX, und was bedeuten sie für die messianische Würde des davidischen Hauses in der LXX?" 177–92 in Michael A. Knibb, ed., *The Septuagint and Messianism*. BETL 195. Leuven: Leuven University Press; Peeters.

Scherer, Andreas. 1999. *Das weise Wort und seine Wirkung: Eine Untersuchung zu Komposition und Redaktion von Proverbia 10,1–22,16*. WMANT 83. Neukirchen-Vluyn: Neukirchener Verlag.

Schipper, Bernd Ulrich. 1999. *Israel und Ägypten in der Königszeit: Die kulturellen Kontakte von Salomo bis zum Fall Jerusalems*. OBO 170. Fribourg: Universitätsverlag; Göttingen: Vandenhoeck & Ruprecht.

———. 2003. "Vermächtnis und Verwirklichung. Das Nachwirken der ramessidischen Aussenpolitik im Palästina der frühen Eisenzeit," 241–75 in Rolf Gundlach and Ursula Rössler-Köhler, eds., *Das Königtum der Ramessidenzeit: Voraussetzung, Verwirklichung, Vermächtnis. Akten des 3. Symposiums zur ägyptischen Königsideologie, Bonn, 7.–9.6.2001*. ÄAT 36. Wiesbaden: Harrassowitz.

————. 2004. "Israels Weisheit im Kontext des Alten Orients." *BK* 59: 188–94.

————. 2005. "Die Lehre des Amenemope und Prov 22,17–24,22. Eine Neubestimmung des literarischen Verhältnisses." *ZAW* 117: 53–72, 232–48.

Schipper, Jeremy. 2005. "'Significant Resonances' with Mephibosheth in 2 Kings 25:27-30: A Response to D. F. Murray." *JBL* 124: 521–29.

Schluchter, Wolfgang. 2006. *Grundlegungen der Soziologie: Eine Theoriegeschichte in systematischer Absicht*. Vol. 1. Tübingen: Mohr (Siebeck).

Schmid, Hans Heinrich. 1968. *Gerechtigkeit als Weltordnung: Hintergrund und Geschichte des alttestamentlichen Gerechtigkeitsbegriffs*. BHT 40. Tübingen: Mohr (Siebeck).

Schmid, Konrad. 1996a. *Buchgestalten des Jeremiabuches: Untersuchungen zur Redaktions- und Rezeptionsgeschichte von Jer 30–33 im Kontext des Buches*. WMANT 72. Neukirchen-Vluyn: Neukirchener Verlag.

————. 1996b. "Klassische und nachklassische Deutungen der alttestamentlichen Prophetie." *Zeitschrift für Neuere Theologiegeschichte* 3: 225–50.

————. 1997. "Manasse und der Untergang Judas: 'Golaorientierte' Theologie in den Königsbüchern?" *Bib* 78: 87– 99.

————. 1999a. "Ausgelegte Schrift als Schrift. Innerbiblische Schriftauslegung und die Frage nach der theologischen Qualität biblischer Texte," 115–29 in Reiner Anselm, Stephan Schleissing, and Klaus Tanner, eds., *Die Kunst des Auslegens: Zur Hermeneutik des Christentums in der Kultur der Gegenwart*. Frankfurt and New York: Peter Lang.

————. 1999b. "Biblische Geschichte zwischen Historie und Fiktion." *Zeitschrift* 48: 122–25.

————. 1999c. *Erzväter und Exodus: Untersuchungen zur doppelten Begründung der Ursprünge Israels innerhalb der Geschichtsbücher des Alten Testaments*. WMANT 81. Neukirchen-Vluyn: Neukirchener Verlag. English Translation: *Genesis and the Moses Story: Israel's Dual Origins in the Hebrew Bible*. Siphrut 3. Winona Lake, IN: Eisenbrauns, 2010.

————. 1999d. "Kollektivschuld? Der Gedanke übergreifender Schuldzusammenhänge im Alten Testament und im Alten Orient." *ZABR* 5: 193–222.

————. 2000a. "Der Geschichtsbezug des christlichen Glaubens," 71–90 in Wilfried Härle, Heinz Schmidt, and Michael Welker, eds., *Das ist christlich: Nachdenken über das Wesen des Christentums*. Gütersloh: Kaiser.

————. 2000b. "Innerbiblische Schriftauslegung. Aspekte der Forschungsgeschichte," 1–22 in Reinhard G. Kratz, Thomas Krüger, and Konrad Schmid, eds., *Schriftauslegung in der Schrift*. FS Odil Hannes Steck. BZAW 300. Berlin and New York: de Gruyter.

————. 2001. "Israel am Sinai. Etappen der Forschungsgeschichte zu Ex 32–34 in seinen Kontexten," 9–40 in Erhard Blum and Matthias Köcker, eds., *Gottes Volk am Sinai: Untersuchungen zu Ex 32–34 und Dtn 9–10*. VWGT 18. Gütersloh: Kaiser, Gütersloher Verlagshaus.

————. 2002. "Die Unteilbarkeit der Weisheit. Überlegungen zur sogenannten Paradieserzählung und ihrer theologischen Tendenz." *ZAW* 114: 21–39.

————. 2003. "Differenzierungen und Konzeptualisierungen der Einheit Gottes in der Religions- und Literaturgeschichte Israels. Methodische, religionsgeschichtliche und exegetische Aspekte zur neueren Diskussion um den sogenannten 'Monotheismus' im antiken Israel," 11–38 in Manfred Oeming and Konrad Schmid, eds.,

Der eine Gott und die Götter: Polytheismus und Monotheismus im antiken Israel. ATANT 82. Zürich: Theologischer Verlag.

———. 2004a. "Schreiber/Schreiberausbildung in Israel." *RGG* 7: 1001–2.

———. 2004b. "Das Deuteronomium innerhalb der 'deuteronomistischen Geschichts-werke' in Gen–2Kön," 193–211 in Eckart Otto and Reinhard Achenbach, eds., *Das Deuteronomium zwischen Pentateuch und deuteronomistischem Geschichtswerk.* FRLANT 206. Göttingen: Vandenhoeck & Ruprecht.

———. 2006a. "Buchtechnische und sachliche Prolegomena zur Enneateuchfrage," 1–14 in Martin Beck and Ulrike Schorn, eds., *Auf dem Weg zur Endgestalt von Gen–II Reg. FS Hans-Christoph Schmitt.* BZAW 370. Berlin and New York: de Gruyter.

———. 2006b. "Hatte Wellhausen recht? Das Problem der literarhistorischen Anfänge des Deuteronomismus in den Königebüchern," 19–43 in Markus Witte, Konrad Schmid, Doris Prechel, and Jan Christian Gertz, eds., *Die deuteronomistischen Geschichtswerke: Redaktions- und religionsgeschichtliche Perspektiven zur "Deuteronomismus"-Diskussion in Tora und Vorderen Propheten.* BZAW 365. Berlin and New York: de Gruyter.

———. 2006c. "Himmelsgott, Weltgott und Schöpfer. 'Gott' und der 'Himmel' in der Literatur der Zeit des Zweiten Tempels," 111–48 in Dorothea Sattler and Samuel Vollenweider, eds., *Der Himmel.* Neukirchen-Vluyn: Neukirchener Verlag.

———. 2006d. "L'accession de Nabuchodonosor à l'hégémonie mondiale et la fin de la dynastie davidique. Exégèse intra-biblique et construction de l'histoire universelle dans le livre de Jérémie." *ETR* 81: 211–27.

———. 2006e. "Persische Reichsautorisation und Tora." *TRu* 71: 494–506.

———. 2006f. "Gibt es 'Reste hebräischen Heidentums' im Alten Testament? Methodi-sche Überlegungen anhand von Dtn 32,8f und Ps 82," 105–20 in Andreas Wagner, ed., *Primäre und sekundäre Religion als Kategorie der Religionsgeschichte des Alten Testaments.* BZAW 364. Berlin and New York: de Gruyter.

———. 2007a. "Authorship." *Encyclopedia of the Bible and Its Reception.* Berlin and New York: de Gruyter.

———. 2007b. "Der Pentateuchredaktor. Beobachtungen zum theologischen Profil des Toraschlusses in Dtn 34," 183–97 in Thomas Römer and Konrad Schmid, eds., *Les dernières rédactions du Pentateuque, de l'Hexateuque et de l'Ennéateuque.* BETL 203. Leuven and Dudley, MA: Leuven University Press; Peeters.

———. 2007c. "Methodische Probleme und historische Entwürfe einer Literaturge-schichte des Alten Testaments," 340–66 in Sylke Lubs et al., eds., *Behutsames Lesen: Alttestamentliche Exegese im interdisziplinären Methodendiskurs. FS Christof Hardmeier.* ABG 28. Leipzig: Evangelische Verlagsanstalt.

———. 2007d. "Innerbiblische Schriftdiskussion im Hiobbuch," 241–61 in Thomas Krüger et al., eds., *Das Buch Hiob und seine Interpretationen: Beiträge zum Hiob-Symposium auf dem Monte Verità vom 14.–19. August 2005.* ATANT 88. Zürich: Theologischer Verlag.

———. 2008. *Literaturgeschichte des Alten Testaments*: Eine Einführung. Darmstadt: Wissenschaftliche Buchgesellschaft.

———. 2010. *Hiob als biblisches und antikes Buch: Intellektuelle und historische Kon-texte seiner Theologie.* SBS 219. Stuttgart: Katholisches Bibelwerk.

———. 2011a. *Schriftgelehrte Traditionsliteratur.* FAT 77. Tübingen: Mohr (Siebeck).

———. 2011b. "The Quest for 'God:' Monotheistic Arguments in the Priestly Texts of the Hebrew Bible," 271–289 in Beate Pongratz-Leisten, ed., *Reconsidering the Concept of Revolutionary Monotheism*. Winona Lake, IN: Eisenbrauns.

———. 2011c."Literaturgeschichte des Alten Testaments: Aufgaben, Stand, Problemfelder und Perspektiven." *TLZ* 136: 243–262.

———. 2011d. *Jesaja 1-23*. ZBK 19/1. Zürich: Theologischer Verlag.

———, and Odil Hannes Steck. 2005. "Heilserwartungen in den Prophetenbüchern des Alten Testaments," 1–36 in Konrad Schmid, ed., *Prophetische Heils- und Herrscherwartungen*. SBS 194. Stuttgart: Katholisches Bibelwerk.

Schmidt, Ludwig. 1998. "Literatur zum Buch Numeri." *TRu* 63: 241–66.

———. 2004. *Das vierte Buch Mose: Numeri. Kapitel 10,11–36,13*. ATD 7/2. Göttingen: Vandenhoeck & Ruprecht.

———. 2005. "Neuere Literatur zum Buch Numeri (1996–2003)." *TRu* 70: 389–407.

Schmidt, Werner H. 1965. "Die deuteronomistische Redaktion des Amosbuches." *ZAW* 77: 168–93.

———. 1983. *Exodus, Sinai und Mose: Erwägungen zu Ex 1–19 und 24*. EdF 191. Darmstadt: Wissenschaftliche Buchgesellschaft.

———. 1979, ⁵1995. *Einführung in das Alte Testament*. Berlin and New York: de Gruyter. English: *Old Testament Introduction*. Translated by Matthew J. O'Connell. New York: Crossroad, 1984, 1990; de Gruyter, 1999.

Schmitt, Hans-Christoph. 1994. "Der heidnische Mantiker als eschatologischer Jahweprophet. Zum Verständnis Bileams in der Endgestalt von Num 22–24," 180–98 in Ingo Kottsieper et al., eds., *"Wer ist wie du, Herr, unter den Göttern?" Studien zur Theologie und Religionsgeschichte Israels. FS Otto Kaiser*. Göttingen: Vandenhoeck & Ruprecht.

Schmitt, John J. 1985. "The Motherhood of God and Zion as Mother." *RB* 92: 557–69.

———. 1991. "The Virgin of Israel: Referent and Use of the Phrase in Amos and Jeremiah." *CBQ* 53: 365–87.

Schniedewind, William M. 2004. *How the Bible Became a Book: The Textualization of Ancient Israel*. Cambridge and New York: Cambridge University Press.

Schoors, Antoon. 1998. *Die Königreiche Israel und Juda im 8. und 7. Jahrhundert v. Chr: Die assyrische Krise*. Biblische Enzyklopädie 5. Stuttgart: Kohlhammer.

Schreiner, Josef. 1995. *Theologie des Alten Testaments*. NEB Additional Volume 1. Würzburg: Echter Verlag.

Schreiner, Stefan. 1999. "Wo man Tora lernt, braucht man keinen Tempel. Einige Anmerkungen zum Problem der Tempelsubstitution im rabbinischen Judentum," 371–92 in Beate Ego et al., eds., *Gemeinde ohne Tempel: Community without Temple: Zur Substituierung und Transformation des Jerusalemer Tempels und seines Kults im Alten Testament, antiken Judentum und frühen Christentum*. WUNT 118. Tübingen: Mohr.

Schroer, Silvia. 2003. "Von zarter Hand geschrieben. Autorinnen in der Bibel?" *Welt und Umwelt der Bibel* 28: 28–29.

Schüle, Andreas. 2006. *Der Prolog der hebräischen Bibel: Der literar- und theologiegeschichtliche Diskurs der Urgeschichte (Genesis 1–11)*. ATANT 86. Zürich: Theologischer Verlag.

Schultze, Martin. 1870. *Geschichte der althebräischen Literatur für den denkenden Bibelleser*. Thorn: Lambeck.

Schwartz, Seth. 2005. "Hebrew and Imperialism in Jewish Palestine," 53–84 in Carol

Bakhos, ed., *Ancient Judaism in Its Hellenistic Context*. JSJSup 95. Leiden and Boston: Brill.

Schwienhorst-Schönberger, Ludger. 1990. *Das Bundesbuch (Ex 20,22–23,33): Studien zu seiner Entstehung und Theologie*. BZAW 188. Berlin and New York: de Gruyter.

———. 1994, ²1996 *"Nicht im Menschen gründet das Glück" (Koh 2,24): Kohelet im Spannungsfeld jüdischer Weisheit und hellenistischer Philosophie*. HBS 2. Freiburg: Herder.

———. 2004. *Kohelet*. HTKAT. Freiburg: Herder.

Scoralick, Ruth. 1995. *Einzelspruch und Sammlung: Komposition im Buch der Sprichwörter Kapitel 10–15*. BZAW 232. Berlin and New York: de Gruyter.

Seebass, Horst. 1996, 1997, 1999, 2000. *Genesis I; II/1; II/2; III*. Neukirchen-Vluyn: Neukirchener Verlag.

Segal, Michael. 2007. *The Book of Jubilees: Rewritten Bible, Redaction, Ideology, and Theology*. Supplements to the Journal for the study of Judaism 117. Leiden: Brill.

Seibert, Jakob. 1991. "Zur Begründung von Herrschaftsanspruch und Herrschaftslegitimation in der frühen Diadochenzeit," 87–100 in idem, ed., *Hellenistische Studien: Gedenkschrift für Hermann Bengtson*. Münchener Arbeiten zur Alten Geschichte 5. Munich: Editio Maris.

Seiler, Stefan. 1998. *Die Geschichte von der Thronfolge Davids (2Sam 9–20; 1Kön 1–2): Untersuchungen zur Literarkritik und Tendenz*. BZAW 267. Berlin and New York: de Gruyter.

Seitz, Christopher R. 1989. *Theology in Conflict: Reactions to the Exile in the Book of Jeremiah*. BZAW 176. Berlin and New York: de Gruyter.

Seow, Choon Leong. 1997. *Ecclesiastes: A New Translation with Introduction and Commentary*. AB 18C. New York: Doubleday.

Seybold, Klaus. 1986. *Die Psalmen: Eine Einführung*. UB 382. Stuttgart: Kohlhammer. English: *Introducing the Psalms*. Translated by R. Graeme Dunphy. Edinburgh: T & T Clark, 1990.

Shectman, Sarah, and Joel Baden. 2009. *The Strata of the Priestly Writings: Contemporary Debate and Future Directions*. ATANT 95. Zürich: Theologischer Verlag.

Siegert, Folker. 2001. *Zwischen Hebräischer Bibel und Alten Testament: Eine Einführung in die Septuaginta*. Münsteraner judaistische Studien 9. Münster: Lit.

Simon, Richard. 1685. *Histoire critique du Vieux Testament*. Rotterdam: Chez R. Leers.

Ska, Jean-Louis. 1997. "L'appel d'Abraham et l'acte de naissance d'Israël," 367–89 in Marc Vervenne and Johan Lust, eds., *Deuteronomy and Deuteronomic Literature*. FS C. H. W. Brekelmans. BETL 133. Leuven: University Press; Peeters.

Smelik, Klaas A. D. 1987. *Historische Dokumente aus dem alten Israel*. Göttingen: Vandenhoeck & Ruprecht.

Smend, Rudolf, Sr. 1882. "Über die Genesis des Judenthums." ZAW 2: 94–151.

Smend, Rudolf. 1982. "Theologie im Alten Testament," 104–17 in idem, *Die Mitte des Alten Testaments*. BEvT 99. Munich: Kaiser, 1986.

———. 1995. "Mose als geschichtliche Gestalt." *Historische Zeitschrift* 260: 1–19.

Smith, Morton. 1952. "The Common Theology of the Ancient Near East." *JBL* 71: 135–47.

Soggin, J. Alberto. 1968, 1969 (⁴1987). *Introduzione all'Antico Testamento*. Brescia: Paideia. English: *Introduction to the Old Testament: From Its Origins to the Closing of the Alexandrian Canon*. Translated by John Bowden. London: SCM; Philadelphia: Westminster, 1976.

Speyer, Wolfgang. 1970. *Bücherfunde in der Glaubenswerbung der Antike: Mit einem Ausblick auf Mittelalter und Neuzeit.* Hypomnemata 24. Göttingen: Vandenhoeck & Ruprecht.

Spieckermann, Hermann. 1982. *Juda unter Assur in der Sargonidenzeit.* FRLANT 129. Göttingen: Vandenhoeck & Ruprecht.

———. 1989. *Heilsgegenwart: Eine Theologie der Psalmen.* FRLANT 148. Göttingen: Vandenhoeck & Ruprecht.

———. 1992. "Stadtgott und Gottesstadt. Beobachtungen im Alten Orient und im Alten Testament." *Bib* 73: 1–31.

———. 1998. "*Ludlul bēl nēmeqi* und die Frage nach der Gerechtigkeit Gottes," 329–41 in Stefan M. Maul, ed., *Festschrift für Rykle Borger zu seinem 65. Geburtstag am 24. Mai 1994.* tikip santakki mala bašmu. Groningen: STYX = 103–18 in idem, *Gottes Liebe zu Israel: Studien zur Theologie des Alten Testaments.* FAT 33. Tübingen: Mohr (Siebeck), 2001.

———. 2000. "Ambivalenzen. Ermöglichte und verwirklichte Schöpfung in Genesis 2f," 363–76 in Axel Graupner et al., eds., *Verbindungslinien. FS Werner H. Schmidt.* Neukirchen-Vluyn: Neukirchener Verlag.

———. 2001. "Hiob/Hiobbuch." *RGG* 3: 1777–81.

Staiger, Emil. 1955. *Die Kunst der Interpretation: Studien zur deutschen Literaturgeschichte.* Zürich: Atlantis.

Steck, Odil Hannes. 1967. *Israel und das gewaltsame Geschick der Propheten.* WMANT 23. Neukirchen-Vluyn: Neukirchener Verlag.

———. 1968. "Das Problem theologischer Strömungen in nachexilischer Zeit." *EvT* 28: 445–58.

———. 1981. "Überlegungen zur Eigenart der spätisraelitischen Apokalyptik," 301–15 in Jörg Jeremias and Lothar Perlitt, eds., *Die Botschaft und die Boten: Festschrift für Hans Walter Wolff zum 70. Geburtstag.* Neukirchen-Vluyn: Neukirchener Verlag.

———. 1971. "Genesis 12,1-3 und die Urgeschichte des Jahwisten," 525–54 in Hans Walter Wolff, ed., *Probleme biblischer Theologie. FS Gerhard von Rad.* Munich: Kaiser = idem, *Wahrnehmungen Gottes im Alten Testament: Gesammelte Studien,* 117–48. TB 70. Munich: Kaiser, 1982.

———. 1972. *Friedensvorstellungen im alten Jerusalem.* Zürich: Theologischer Verlag.

———. 1978. "Strömungen theologischer Tradition im Alten Israel," 27–56 in idem, ed., *Zu Tradition und Theologie im Alten Testament.* BTSt 2. Neukirchen-Vluyn: Neukirchener Verlag = idem, *Wahrnehmungen Gottes im Alten Testament: Gesammelte Studien,* 291–317. TB 70. Munich: Kaiser, 1982.

———. 1980. "Weltgeschehen und Gottesvolk im Buche Daniel, 262–90 in idem, *Wahrnehmungen Gottes im Alten Testament: Gesammelte Studien.* TB 70. Munich: Kaiser, 1982.

———. 1985. *Bereitete Heimkehr: Jesaja 35 als redaktionelle Brücke zwischen dem Ersten und dem Zweiten Jesaja.* SBS 121. Stuttgart: Katholisches Bibelwerk.

———. 1989. "Zion als Gelände und Gestalt. Überlegungen zur Wahrnehmung Jerusalems als Stadt und Frau im Alten Testament." *ZTK* 86: 261–81 = idem, *Gottesknecht und Zion: Gesammelte Aufsätze zu Deuterojesaja,* 126–45. FAT 4. Tübingen: Mohr (Siebeck) 1992b.

———. 1991a. *Der Abschluss der Prophetie im Alten Testament: Ein Versuch zur Frage der Vorgeschichte des Kanons.* BTS 17. Neukirchen-Vluyn: Neukirchener Verlag.

———. 1991b. *Studien zu Tritojesaja*. BZAW 203. Berlin and New York: de Gruyter.

———. 1992a. "Der Kanon des hebräischen Alten Testaments," 11–33 in Wolfhart Pannenberg and Theodor Schneider, eds., *Verbindliches Zeugnis I*. Dialog der Kirchen 7. Freiburg: Herder; Göttingen: Vandenhoeck & Ruprecht.

———. 1992b. "Israel und Zion. Zum Problem konzeptioneller Einheit und literarischer Schichtung in Deuterojesaja," 173–207 in idem, *Gottesknecht und Zion: Gesammelte Aufsätze zu Deuterojesaja*. FAT 4. Tübingen: Mohr (Siebeck).

———. 1993. *Das apokryphe Baruchbuch: Studien zu Rezeption und Konzentration "kanonischer" Überlieferung*. FRLANT 160. Göttingen: Vandenhoeck & Ruprecht.

———. 1996. *Die Prophetenbücher und ihr theologisches Zeugnis: Wege der Nachfrage und Fährten zur Antwort*. Tübingen: Mohr.

———. 1997. "Der neue Himmel und die neue Erde. Beobachtungen zur Rezeption von Gen 1–3 in Jes 65,16b-25," 349–65 in Jacques van Ruiten and Marc Vervenne, eds., *Studies in the Book of Isaiah. FS Willem A. M. Beuken*. BETL 132. Leuven: Leuven University Press; Peeters.

———. 1998. *Die erste Jesajarolle von Qumran (1QIs^a): Schreibweise als Leseanleitung für ein Prophetenbuch*. SBS 173/1, 2. Stuttgart: Katholisches Bibelwerk.

———. [14]1999. *Exegese des Alten Testaments: Leitfaden der Methodik*. Neukirchen-Vluyn: Neukirchener Verlag. English: *Old Testament Exegesis: A Guide to the Methodology*. Translated by James D. Nogalski. Atlanta: Scholars Press, 1998.

———. 2001. *Gott in der Zeit entdecken: Die Prophetenbücher des Alten Testaments als Vorbild für Theologie und Kirche*. BTS 42. Neukirchen-Vluyn: Neukirchener Verlag.

———. 2003. "Zur konzentrischen Anlage von Jes 1,21-26," 97–103 in Irmtraud Fischer, Ursula Rapp, and Johannes Schiller, eds., *Auf den Spuren der schriftgelehrten Weisen. FS Johannes Marböck*. BZAW 331. Berlin and New York: de Gruyter.

Stegemann, Hartmut. 1987. "Die 'Mitte der Schrift' aus der Sicht der Gemeinde von Qumran," in Martin Klopfenstein et al., eds., *Mitte der Schrift? Ein jüdisch-christliches Gespräch*. Judaica et Christiana 11. Bern: Peter Lang, 149–183.

———. [2]1989. "Die Bedeutung der Qumranfunde für die Erforschung der Apokalyptik," 495–509 in David Hellholm, ed., *Apocalypticism in the Mediterranean World and the Near East*. Tübingen: Mohr.

———. [9]1999. *Die Essener, Qumran, Johannes der Täufer und Jesus: Ein Sachbuch*. Freiburg et al.: Herder. English: *The Library of Qumran, on the Essenes, Qumran, John the Baptist, and Jesus*. Grand Rapids: Eerdmans; Leiden: Brill, 1998.

Steinberg, Julius. 2006. *Die Ketuvim—ihr Aufbau und ihre Botschaft*. BBB 152. Hamburg: Philo.

Steiner, Margarete L. 1998a. "David's Jerusalem: Fiction or Reality? It's Not There: Archaeology Proves a Negative." *BAR* 24: 26–33.

———. 1998b. "The Archaeology of Ancient Jerusalem." *CurBS* 6: 143–68.

———. 2007. "The Notion of Jerusalem as a Holy City," 447–58 in Robert Rezetko et al., eds., *Reflection and Refraction. FS A. Graeme Auld*. VTSup 113. Leiden and Boston.

Steins, Georg. 1995. *Die Chronik als kanonisches Abschlussphänomen*. BBB 93. Weinheim: Beltz Athenäum.

Stemberger, Günter. 1996. "Öffentlichkeit der Tora im Judentum. Anspruch und Wirklichkeit." *JBTh* 11: 91–101.

Stern, Ephraim. 2001. *Archaeology of the Land of the Bible.* Vol. 2: *The Assyrian, Babylonian, and Persian Periods 732–332 BCE.* ABRL. New York: Doubleday.

———. 2004. "The Babylonian Gap: The Archaeological Reality." *JSOT* 28: 273–77.

Steymans, Hans Ulrich. 1995a. *Deuteronomium 28 und die adê zur Thronfolgeregelung Asarhaddons: Segen und Fluch im Alten Orient und in Israel.* OBO 145. Fribourg: Universitätsverlag; Göttingen: Vandenhoeck & Ruprecht.

———. 1995b. "Eine assyrische Vorlage für Deuteronomium 28,20-44," in Georg Braulik, ed., *Bundesdokument und Gesetz: Studien zum Deuteronomium.* HBS 4. Freiburg et al.: Herder.

———. 2006. "Die literarische und theologische Bedeutung der Thronfolgevereidigung Asarhaddons," 331–49 in Markus Witte, Konrad Schmid, Doris Prechel, and Jan Christian Gertz, eds., *Die deuteronomistischen Geschichtswerke: Redaktions- und religionsgeschichtliche Perspektiven zur "Deuteronomismus"-Diskussion in Tora und Vorderen Propheten.* BZAW 365. Berlin and New York: de Gruyter.

Stipp, Hermann-Josef. 1994. *Das masoretische und alexandrinische Sondergut des Jeremiabuches: Textgeschichtlicher Rang, Eigenarten, Triebkräfte.* OBO 136. Fribourg: Universitätsverlag; Göttingen: Vandenhoeck & Ruprecht.

———. 1995. "Ahabs Buße und die Komposition des deuteronomistischen Geschichtswerks." *Bib* 76: 471–497.

———. 2000. "Gedalja und die Kolonie von Mizpa." *ZAR* 6: 155–71.

———. 2003. "Vom Heil zum Gericht. Die Selbstinterpretation Jesajas in der Denkschrift," 323–54 in Franz Sedlmeier, ed., *Gottes Wege suchend: Beiträge zum Verständnis der Bibel und ihrer Botschaft. FS Rudolf Mosis.* Würzburg: Echter Verlag.

———. 2005. "'Meinen Bund hat er gebrochen' (Gen 17,14). Die Individualisierung des Bundesbruchs in der Priesterschrift." *MTZ* 56: 290–304.

———. 2011a. "Die Verfasserschaft der Trostschrift Jer 30-31*." *ZAW* 123: 184–206.

———. 2011b. *Das deuteronomistische Geschichtswerk.* Österreichische biblische Studien 39. Frankfurt: Peter Lang.

Stolper, Matthew W. 1985. *Entrepreneurs and Empire: The Murašu Archive, the Murašu Firm, and Persian Rule in Babylonia.* Uitgaven van het Nederlands Historisch-Archaeologisch Instituut te Istanbul 54. Istanbul: Nederlands Historisch-Archaeologisch Instituut te Istanbul.

Stolz, Fritz. 1983a. *Psalmen im nachkultischen Raum.* TS 129. Zürich: Theologischer Verlag.

———. 1983b. "Unterscheidungen in den Religionen," 11–24 in Hans Friedrich Geisser and Walter Mostert, eds., *Wirkungen hermeneutischer Theologie. FS Gerhard Ebeling.* Zürich: Theologischer Verlag.

———. 1988. *Grundzüge der Religionswissenschaft.* Göttingen: Vandenhoeck & Ruprecht.

———. 1996. *Einführung in den biblischen Monotheismus.* Darmstadt: Wissenschaftliche Buchgesellschaft.

———. 1997. "Religionsgeschichte Israels." *TRE* 28: 585–603.

Strecker, Georg. 1992. *Literaturgeschichte des Neuen Testaments.* UTB 1682. Göttingen: Vandenhoeck & Ruprecht.

Stuckenbruck, Loren T. 2004. "'Angels' and 'God': Exploring the Limits of Early Jewish Monotheism," 45–70 in idem and Wendy E. S. North, eds., *Early Jewish and Christian Monotheism.* JSOTSup 263. London and New York: T & T Clark International.

Süssenbach, Claudia. 2004. *Der elohistische Psalter: Untersuchungen zur Komposition und Theologie von Ps 42–83.* FAT II/7. Tübingen: Mohr (Siebeck).

Sweeney, Marvin A. 2001. *King Josiah of Judah: The Lost Messiah of Israel.* Oxford and New York: Oxford University Press.

Swete, Henry B. ²1914. *An Introduction to the Old Testament in Greek.* Cambridge: Cambridge University Press. Reprint Peabody, MA: Hendrickson, 1989.

Tadmor, Hayim. 1994. *The Inscriptions of Tiglath-Pileser III King of Assyria: Critical Edition, with Introductions, Translations and Commentary.* Fontes ad res Judaicas spectantes. Jerusalem: Israel Academy of Sciences and Humanities.

Tappy, Ron E. 1992; 2001. *The Archaeology of Israelite Samaria.* Vol. 1: *Early Iron Age through the Ninth Century BCE.* Vol. 2: *The Eighth Century BCE.* HSS 44, 50. Atlanta: Scholars Press.

Theissen, Gerd. 2007. *Die Entstehung des Neuen Testaments als literaturgeschichtliches Problem.* Heidelberg: Winter.

Thiel, Winfried. 1973. *Die deuteronomistische Redaktion von Jeremia 1–25.* WMANT 41. Neukirchen-Vluyn: Neukirchener Verlag.

———. 1981. *Die deuteronomistische Redaktion von Jeremia 26–45.* WMANT 52. Neukirchen-Vluyn: Neukirchener Verlag.

Thompson, Henry O., and Fawzi Zayadine. 1974. "The Works of Amminadab." *BA* 37: 13–19.

Tigay, Jeffrey H., ed. 1985. *Empirical Models for Biblical Criticism.* Philadelphia: University of Pennsylvania Press.

Tilly, Michael. 2005. *Einführung in die Septuaginta.* Darmstadt: Wissenschaftliche Buchgesellschaft.

Timm, Stefan. 2002. "Ein assyrisch bezeugter Tempel in Samaria?" 126–33 in Ulrich Hübner and Ernst Axel Knauf, eds., *Kein Land für sich allein: Studien zum Kulturkontakt in Kanaan, Israel/Palästina und Ebirnâri für Manfred Weippert zum 65. Geburtstag.* OBO 186. Fribourg: Universitätsverlag; Göttingen: Vandenhoeck & Ruprecht.

Toorn, Karel van der, ed. 1997. *The Image and the Book: Iconic Cults, Aniconism, and the Rise of Book Religion in Israel and the Ancient Near East.* CBET 21. Leuven: Peeters.

———. 2000. "Cuneiform Documents from Syria-Palestine. Texts, Scribes, and Schools." *ZDPV* 116: 97–113.

———. 2004. "From the Mouth of the Prophet: The Literary Fixation of Jeremiah's Prophecies in the Context of the Ancient Near East," 191–202 in John Kaltner and Louis Stulman, eds., *Inspired Speech: Prophecy in the Ancient Near East. FS Herbert B. Huffmon.* JSOTSup 378. Edinburgh: T & T Clark.

———. 2007. *Scribal Culture and the Making of the Bible.* Cambridge, MA, and London: Harvard University Press.

Tov, Emanuel. 1992. *Textual Criticism of the Hebrew Bible.* Minneapolis: Fortress.

———. 1998. "Rewritten Bible Compositions and Biblical Manuscripts, with Special Attention to the Samaritan Pentateuch." *DSD*: 334–54.

———. 2004. *Scribal Practices and Approaches Reflected in the Texts Found in the Judean Desert,* STDJ 54. Leiden and Boston: Brill.

———. 2006. "Hebrew Scripture Editions: Philosophy and Praxis," 281–312 in Florentino García Martínez et al., eds., *From 4QMMT to Resurrection. Mélanges qumraniens en hommage à Émile Puech.* STDJ 61. Leiden and Boston: Brill.

Trebolle Barrera, Julio C. 2002. "Origins of a Tripartite Old Testament Canon," 128–45 in Lee Martin McDonald and James A. Sanders, eds., *The Canon Debate*. Peabody, MA: Hendrickson.

Treves, Marco. 1988. *The Dates of the Psalms: History and Poetry in Ancient Israel*. Pisa: Giardini.

Troyer, Kristin de. 2005. *Die Septuaginta und die Endgestalt des Alten Testaments: Untersuchungen zur Entstehungsgeschichte alttestamentlicher Texte*. UTB 2599. Göttingen: Vandenhoeck & Ruprecht.

Tull, Patricia K. 2000. "Intertextuality and the Hebrew Scriptures." *CRBS* 8: 59–90.

Uehlinger, Christoph. 1994. "Die Frau im Efa (Sach 5,5-11). Eine Programmvision von der Abschiebung der Göttin." *BK* 49: 93–103.

———. 1995. "Gab es eine joschijanische Kultreform?" 57–89 in Walter Gross, ed., *Jeremia und die "deuteronomistische Bewegung."* BBB 98. Weinheim: Beltz Athenäum.

———. 1997. "Qohelet im Horizont mesopotamischer, levantinischer und ägyptischer Weisheitsliteratur der persischen und hellenistischen Zeit," 155–247 in Ludger Schwienhorst-Schönberger, ed., *Das Buch Kohelet: Studien zur Struktur, Geschichte, Rezeption und Theologie*. BZAW 254. Berlin and New York: de Gruyter.

———. 1998a. "'. . . und wo sind die Götter von Samarien?' Die Wegführung syrisch-palästinischer Kultstatuen auf einem Relief Sargons II. in Khorsabad/Dûr-Šarrukin," 739–76 in Manfred Dietrich and Ingo Kottsieper, eds., *"Und Mose schrieb dieses Lied auf . . .": Studien zum Alten Testament und zum alten Orient*. FS Oswald Loretz. AOAT 250. Münster: Ugarit-Verlag.

———. 1998b. "Bilderkult." *RGG* 1: 1565–70.

———. 1998c. "Bilderverbot." *RGG* 1: 1574–77.

———. 2001. "Bildquellen und 'Geschichte Israels.' Grundsätzliche Überlegungen und Fallbeispiele," 25–77 in Christof Hardmeier, ed., *Steine, Bilder, Texte: Historische Evidenz außerbiblischer und biblischer Quellen*. ABG 5. Leipzig: Evangelische Verlagsanstalt.

———. 2007a. "Spurensicherung: alte und neue Siegel und Bullen und das Problem ihrer historischen Kontextualisierung," 89–137 in Sylke Lubs et al., eds., *Behutsames Lesen: Alttestamentliche Exegese im interdisziplinären Methodendiskurs. FS Christof Hardmeier*. ABG 28. Leipzig: Evangelische Verlagsanstalt.

———. 2007b. "Das Hiob-Buch im Kontext der altorientalischen Literatur- und Religionsgeschichte," 97–162 in Thomas Krüger et al., eds., *Das Buch Hiob und seine Interpretationen: Beiträge zum Hiob-Symposium auf dem Monte Verità von 14.–19. August 2005*. ATANT 88. Zürich: Theologischer Verlag.

———, and S. Müller Trufaut. 2001b. "Ezekiel 1, Babylonian Cosmological Scholarship and Iconography: Attempts at Further Refinement," *TZ* 57: 140–71.

———, and Andreas Grandy. 2005. "Vom Toben des Meeres zum Jubel der Völker. Psalterexegetische Beobachtungen zu Psalm 46," 372–93 in Dieter Böhler et al., eds., *L'Ecrit et l'Esprit: Études d'histoire du texte et de théologie biblique en hommage à Adrian Schenker*. OBO 214. Fribourg: Universitätsverlag; Göttingen: Vandenhoeck & Ruprecht.

Ulrich, Eugene. 1992. "The Canonical Process, Textual Criticism, and Latter Stages in the Composition of the Bible," 267–91 in Michael Fishbane et al., eds., *Sha'arei Talmon: Studies in the Bible, Qumran, and the Ancient Near East Presented to Shemaryahu Talmon*. Winona Lake, IN: Eisenbrauns.

———. 1994. "An Index of the Passages in the Biblical Manuscripts from the Judean Desert (Genesis–Kings)." *DSD* 1: 113–29.

———. 1995. "An Index of the Passages in the Biblical Manuscripts from the Judean Desert (Part 2: Isaiah–Chronicles)." *DSD* 2: 86–107.

———. 2000. "Daniel, Book of," in Lawrence H. Schiffmann and James C. VanderKam, eds., *Encyclopedia of the Dead Sea Scrolls*. Oxford and New York: Oxford University Press, 1: 170–74.

———. 2003a. "From Literature to Scripture: Reflections on the Growth of a Text's Authoritativeness." *DSD* 10: 3–25.

———. 2003b. "The Non-attestation of a Tripartite Canon in 4QMMT." *CBQ* 65: 202–14.

———. 2010. *The Biblical Qumran Scrolls: Transcriptions and Textual Variants*. VTSup 134. Leiden et al.: Brill.

Ussishkin, David. 2005. "Big City, Few People: Jerusalem in the Persian Period." *BAR* 31: 26–35.

———. 2006. "The Borders and *de facto* Size of Jerusalem in the Persian Period," 147–66 in Oded Lipschits and Manfred Oeming, eds., *Judah and the Judeans in the Persian Period*. Winona Lake, IN: Eisenbrauns.

Utzschneider, Helmut. 2002. "Literaturgeschichte II. Altes Testament." *RGG* 5: 405–8.

———. 2006. "Was ist alttestamentliche Literatur? Kanon, Quelle und literarische Ästhetik als LesArts alttestamentlicher Literatur," 65–83 in idem and Erhard Blum, eds., *Lesarten der Bibel: Untersuchungen zu einer Theorie der Exegese des Alten Testaments*. Stuttgart: Kohlhammer.

Vanderhooft, David Stephen. 1999. *The Neo-Babylonian Empire and Babylon in the Latter Prophets*. HSM 59. Atlanta: Scholars Press.

VanderKam, James C. 2000. "Revealed Literature in the Second Temple Period," 241–54 in idem, *From Revelation to Canon: Studies in the Hebrew Bible and Second Temple Literature*. JSJSup 62. Leiden and Boston: Brill.

Vanoni, Gottfried. 1985. "Beobachtungen zur deuteronomistischen Terminologie in 2Kön 23,25–25,30," 357–62 in Norbert Lohfink, ed., *Das Deuteronomium: Entstehung, Gestalt und Botschaft*. BETL 73. Leuven: Leuven University Press.

Van Seters, John. 1981. "Histories and Historians of the Ancient Near East: The Israelites." *Or* 50: 137–85.

———. 1983. *In Search of History: Historiography in the Ancient World and the Origins of Biblical History*. New Haven: Yale University Press.

———. 1990. "Joshua's Campaign of Canaan and Near Eastern Historiography." *SJOT* 4: 1–12.

———. 1996. "Cultic Laws in the Covenant Code (Exodus 20,22–23,33) and Their Relationship to Deuteronomy and the Holiness Code," 319–45 in Marc Vervenne, ed., *Studies in the Book of Exodus: Redaction, Reception, Interpretation*. BETL 126. Leuven: Leuven University Press; Peeters.

———. 1999. *The Pentateuch: A Social-Science Commentary*. Sheffield: Sheffield Academic Press.

———. 2000. "The Court History and DtrH: Conflicting Perspectives on the House of David," 70–93 in Albert de Pury and Thomas Römer, eds., *Die sogenannte Thronfolgegeschichte Davids: Neue Einsichten und Anfragen*. OBO 176. Fribourg: Universitätsverlag; Göttingen: Vandenhoeck & Ruprecht.

———. 2003. *A Law Book for the Diaspora: Revision in the Study of the Covenant Code*. Oxford: Oxford University Press.

———. 2006. *The Edited Bible: The Curious History of the "Editor" in Biblical Criticism*. Winona Lake, IN: Eisenbrauns.

Vaughn, Andrew G., and Ann E. Killebrew, eds. 2003. *Jerusalem in Bible and Archaeology: The First Temple Period*. Leiden and Boston: Brill; Atlanta: Scholars Press.

Veenhof, Klaas R. 2001. *Geschichte des Alten Orients bis zur Zeit Alexanders des Grossen*. GAT 11. Göttingen: Vandenhoeck & Ruprecht.

Vegge, Tor. 2007. *Paulus und das antike Schulwesen: Schule und Bildung des Paulus*. BZNW 134. Berlin and New York: de Gruyter.

Veijola, Timo. 1975. *Die ewige Dynastie: David und die Entstehung seiner Dynastie nach der deuteronomistischen Darstellung*. Helsinki: Suomalainen Tiedeakatemia.

———. 1992a. "Das Bekenntnis Israels. Beobachtungen zur Geschichte und Theologie von Dtn 6,4-9." *TZ* 48: 369–81.

———. 1992b. "Höre Israel! Der Sinn und Hintergrund von Deuteronomium VI 4-9." *VT* 42: 528–41.

———, ed. 1996. *Das Deuteronomium und seine Querbeziehungen*. SESJ 62. Helsinki: Finnische Exegetische Gesellschaft; Göttingen: Vandenhoeck & Ruprecht.

———. 2000. "Die Deuteronomisten als Vorgänger der Schriftgelehrten. Ein Beitrag zur Entstehung des Judentums," 192–240 in idem, *Moses Erben: Studien zum Dekalog, zum Deuteronomismus und zum Schriftgelehrtentum*. BWANT 149. Stuttgart: Kohlhammer.

Veldhuis, Niek. 2003. "Mesopotamian Canons," 9–28 in Margalit Finkelberg and Guy G. Stroumsa, eds., *Homer, the Bible and Beyond: Literary and Religious Canons in the Ancient World*. Leiden: Brill.

Veltri, Giuseppe. 2003. "Philo von Alexandrien." *RGG* 6: 1286–88.

Vielhauer, Philipp. ⁶1997. "Die Apokalyptik," 492–508 in Wilhelm Schneemelcher, ed., *Neutestamentliche Apokryphen in deutscher Übersetzung*. Tübingen: Mohr (Siebeck). English: *New Testament Apocrypha*. English translation edited by Robert McLachlan Wilson. Vol. 2: *Writings Relating to the Apostles; Apocalypses and Related Subjects*. C. Apocalypses and Related Subjects, 542–602. Revised by Georg Strecker. Louisville: Westminster John Knox, rev. ed. 1991–92.

Vielhauer, Roman. 2007. *Das Werden des Buches Hosea: Eine redaktionsgeschichtliche Untersuchung*. BZAW 349. Berlin and New York: de Gruyter.

Vieweger, Dieter. 2003. *Archäologie der biblischen Welt*. UTB 2394. Göttingen: Vandenhoeck & Ruprecht.

Vincent, Jean Marcel. 1990. *Leben und Werk des frühen Eduard Reuss*. BEvT 106. Munich: Kaiser.

Vleeming, Sven P., and Jan Wim Wesselius. 1982. "An Aramaic Hymn from the Fourth Century B.C." *BibOr* 39: 501–9.

Volk, Konrad. 2000. "Edubba'a and Edubba'a-Literatur: Rätsel und Lösungen." *ZA* 90: 1–30.

Vos, Jacobus Cornelis de. 2003. *Das Los Judas: Über Entstehung und Ziele der Landbeschreibung in Josua 15*. VTSup 95. Leiden and Boston: Brill.

Vriezen, Theodoor Christiaan, and Adriaan S. van der Woude. 2005. *Ancient Israelite and Early Jewish Literature*. Translated by Brian Doyle. Leiden and Boston: Brill.

Wagner, Andreas. 1996. "Gattung und 'Sitz im Leben.' Zur Bedeutung der formgeschichtlichen Arbeit Hermann Gunkels (1862–1932) für das Verstehen der sprachlichen

Grösse Text," 117–29 in Susanna Michaelis, ed., *Texte: Konstitution, Verarbeitung, Typik*. Edition Linguistik 13. Munich and Newcastle: LINCOM Europa.

Wahl, Harald Martin. 1992. "Noah, Daniel und Hiob in Ezechiel XIV 12-20 (21-23): Anmerkungen zum traditionsgeschichtlichen Hintergrund." *VT* 42: 542–53.

Waltisberg, Michael. 1999. "Zum Alter der Sprache des Deboraliedes Ri. 5." *ZAH* 12: 218–32.

Wanke, Gunther. 1966. *Die Zionstheologie der Korachiten*. BZAW 97. Berlin: Topelmann.

Watts, James W., ed. 2001. *Persia and Torah: The Theory of Imperial Authorization of the Pentateuch*. SBLSymS 17. Atlanta: Scholars Press.

Weber, Beat. 2000. "Zur Datierung der Asaph-Psalmen 74 und 79." *Bib* 81: 521–32.

Weber, Otto. 1907. *Die Literatur der Babylonier und Assyrier: Ein Überblick*. Leipzig: J. C. Hinrichs.

Weinfeld, Moshe. 1972. *Deuteronomy and the Deuteronomic School*. Oxford: Clarendon Press.

Weinstein, James M. 1981. "The Egyptian Empire in Palestine: A Reassessment." *BASOR* 241: 1–28.

Weisberg, David B. 2002. "The Impact of Assyriology on Biblical Studies," xliii–xlviii in William W. Hallo, ed., *The Context of Scripture: Archival Documents from the Biblical World*. Leiden and New York: Brill.

Weippert, Helga. 1972. "Die 'deuteronomistischen Beurteilungen der Könige von Israel and Juda und das Problem der Redaktion der Königsbücher." *Bib* 53: 301–39.

———. 1988. *Palästina in vorhellenistischer Zeit*. Handbuch der Archäologie. Vorderasian II/1. Munich: Beck.

Weippert, Manfred. 1993. "Geschichte Israels als Scheideweg." *TRu* 58: 71–103.

———. 1990. "Synkretismus und Monotheismus. Religionsinterne Konfliktbewältigung im alten Israel," 1–24 in idem, *Jahwe und die anderen Götter: Studien zur Religionsgeschichte des antiken Israel in ihrem syrisch-palästinischen Kontext*. FAT 18. Tübingen: Mohr (Siebeck), 1997.

Wellek, René. 1979. "The Fall of Literary History," 418–31 in Richard E. Amacher and Victor Lange, eds., *New Perspectives in German Literary Criticism: A Collection of Essays*. Translated by David Henry Wilson et al. Princeton: Princeton University Press.

———, and Austin Warren. 1949. *Theory of Literature*. New York: Harcourt, Brace.

Wellhausen, Julius. 1880. "Geschichte Israels" 1880, 13–64 in idem, *Grundrisse zum Alten Testament*. Edited by Rudolf Smend. TB 27. Munich: Kaiser, 1965.

———. 1883; ⁶1927. *Prolegomena zur Geschichte Israels*. Berlin: G. Reimer. English: *Prolegomena to the History of Israel*. Atlanta: Scholars Press, 1994.

———. ³1899. *Die Composition des Hexateuchs und der historischen Bücher des Alten Testaments*. Berlin: G. Reimer.

———. 1904. *Israelitische und jüdische Geschichte*. Berlin: G. Reimer.

Welten, Peter. 1973. *Geschichte und Geschichtsdarstellung in den Chronikbüchern*. WMANT 42. Neukirchen-Vluyn: Neukirchener Verlag.

Wessetzky, Vilmos. 1984. "Die Bücherliste des Tempels von Edfu und Imhotep." *Göttinger Miszellen* 83: 85–89.

Westermann, Claus. 1977. *Der Aufbau des Buches Hiob: Mit einer Einführung in die neuere Hiobforschung von Jürgen Kegler*. CTM 6. Stuttgart: Calwer. English: *The Structure of the Book of Job: a Form-critical Analysis*. Translated by Charles A. Muenchow. Philadelphia: Fortress Press, 1981.

Wette, Wilhelm Martin Leberecht de. 1805. *Dissertatio critico-exegetica qua Deutero-nomium a prioribus Pentateuchi libris diversum, alius cuiusdam recentioris auctoris opus esse monstrator*. Jena: Literis Etzdorfii.

Wettengel, Wolfgang. 2003. *Die Erzählung von den beiden Brüdern: Der Papyrus d'Orbiney und die Königsideologie der Ramessiden*. OBO 195. Fribourg: Universitätsverlag; Göttingen: Vandenhoeck & Ruprecht.

White, John Bradley. 1980. "Universalization of History in Deutero-Isaiah," 179–95 in Carl D. Evans et al., eds., *Scripture in Context: Essays on the Comparative Method*. Pittsburgh Theological Monograph Series 34. Pittsburgh: Pickwick Press.

Whybray, Roger Norman. 1965. *Wisdom in Proverbs*. SBT 45. London: SCM Press.

———. 1968. "The Joseph Story and Pentateuchal Criticism." *VT* 18: 522–28.

Wiesehöfer, Josef. 1999. *Das frühe Persien: Geschichte eines antiken Weltreichs*. Munich: Beck.

Wildeboer, Gerrit. 1893. *De letterkunde des Ouden Verbonds naar de tijdsorde van haar ontstaan*. Groningen: Wolters. German: *Die Litteratur des Alten Testaments nach der Zeitfolge ihrer Entstehung*. Göttingen: Vandenhoeck & Ruprecht, 1895.

Wilke, Alexa F. 2006. *Kronerben der Weisheit: Gott, König und Frommer in der didaktischen Literatur Ägyptens und Israels*. FAT 2d series 20. Tübingen: Mohr (Siebeck).

Willi, Thomas. 1972. *Die Chronik als Auslegung*. FRLANT 106. Göttingen: Vandenhoeck & Ruprecht.

———. 2007. "Die Chronik: (k)ein Buch wie andere. Die biblischen Chronikbücher als Exempel alttestamentlicher Literaturwerdung," 89–137 in Sylke Lubs et al., eds., *Behutsames Lesen: Alttestamentliche Exegese im interdisziplinären Methodendiskurs. FS Christof Hardmeier*. ABG 28. Leipzig: Evangelische Verlagsanstalt.

Williamson, Hugh G. M. 2004. "In Search of the Pre-Exilic Isaiah," 181–206 in John Day, ed., *In Search of Pre-Exilic Israel: Proceedings of the Oxford Old Testament Seminar*. JSOTSup 406. London and New York: T & T Clark.

Willi-Plein, Ina. 1998. "Sacharja/Sacharjabuch." *TRE* 29: 539–47.

———. 1999. "Warum musste der Zweite Tempel gebaut werden?" 57–73 in Beate Ego et al., eds., *Gemeinde ohne Tempel. Community without Temple: Zur Substituierung und Transformation des Jerusalemer Tempels und seines Kults im Alten Testament, antiken Judentum und frühen Christentum*. WUNT 118. Tübingen: Mohr.

Wilson, F. M. 1987. "Sacred or Profane? The Yahwistic Redaction of Proverbs Reconsidered," 313–34 in Kenneth G. Hoglund et al., eds., *The Listening Heart: Essays in Wisdom and the Psalms in Honor of Roland E. Murphy*. JSOTSup 87. Sheffield: JSOT Press.

Wilson, Gerald Henry. 1985. *The Editing of the Hebrew Psalter*. Chico, CA: Scholars Press.

———. 1990. "A First Century C.E. Date for the Closing of the Hebrew Psalter?" 136–43 in Joshua J. Adler, ed., *Haim M. I. Gevaryahu: Memorial Volume*. English–French–German Section. Jerusalem: World Jewish Bible Center.

Wischnowsky, Marc. 2001. *Die Tochter Zion: Aufnahme und Überwindung der Stadtklage in den Prophetenschriften des Alten Testaments*. WMANT 89. Neukirchen-Vluyn: Neukirchener Verlag.

Witte, Markus. 1998. *Die biblische Urgeschichte: Redaktions- und theologiegeschichtliche Beobachtungen zu Genesis 1,1–11,26*. BZAW 265. Berlin and New York: de Gruyter.

————. 2006. "Vom Glauben in der (End-)Zeit. Ein exegetischer Spaziergang durch das Buch Habakuk," 323–37 in Gesche Linde et al., eds., *Theologie zwischen Pragmatismus und Existenzdenken*. Marburger theologische Studien 90. Marburg: Elwert.

————. 2010. "Von der Analyse zur Synthese: Historisch-kritische Anmerkungen zu Hermann Gunkels Konzept einer israelitischen Literaturgeschichte," 21–51 in Ute Eisen et al., eds., *Hermann Gunkel Revisited: Literatur- und religionsgeschichtliche Studien*. Exegese in unserer Zeit 20. Münster: Lit.

————, Konrad Schmid, Doris Prechel, and Jan Christian Gertz, eds. 2006. *Die deuteronomistischen Geschichtswerke: Redaktions- und religionsgeschichtliche Perspektiven zur "Deuteronomismus"-Diskussion in Tora und Vorderen Propheten*. BZAW 365. Berlin and New York: de Gruyter.

Wöhrle, Jakob. 2006. *Die frühen Sammlungen des Zwölfprophetenbuches: Entstehung und Komposition*. BZAW 360. Berlin and New York: de Gruyter.

Wolff, Hans Walter. 1951. "Das Thema 'Umkehr' in der alttestamentlichen Prophetie." *ZTK* 48: 129–48 = idem, *Gesammelte Studien zum Alten Testament*, 130–50. TB 22. Munich: Kaiser, 1964.

————. 1961. "Das Kerygma des deuteronomistischen Geschichtswerks." *ZAW* 73: 171–86 = idem, *Gesammelte Studien zum Alten Testament*, 308–24. TB 22. Munich: Kaiser, 1964.

————. 1985. "Haggai/Haggaibuch." *TRE* 14: 355–60.

Woude, Adriaan S. van der. 1992. "Pluriformity and Uniformity. Reflections on the Transmission of the Text of the Old Testament," 151–69 in Jan N. Bremmer and Florentino García Martínez, eds., *Sacred History and Sacred Texts in Early Judaism: A Symposium in Honour of A. S. van der Woude*. CBET 5. Kampen: Kok Pharos.

Wright, Jacob L. 2004. *Rebuilding Identity: The Nehemiah-Memoir and Its Earliest Readers*. BZAW 348. Berlin and New York: de Gruyter.

Wyrick, Jed. 2004. *The Ascension of Authorship: Attribution and Canon Formation in Jewish, Hellenistic and Christian Traditions*. Cambridge, MA: Harvard University Press.

Young, Ian. 1993. *Diversity in Pre-Exilic Hebrew*. FAT 5. Tübingen: Mohr (Siebeck).

————. 1998. "Israelite Literacy: Interpreting the Evidence." *VT* 48: 230–53, 408–22.

————. 2003. *Biblical Hebrew: Studies in Chronology and Typology*. JSOTSup 369. London and New York: T & T Clark International.

————. 2005. "Israelite Literacy and Inscriptions: A Response to Richard Hess." *VT* 55: 565–68.

————, and Robert Rezetko. 2008. *Linguistic Dating of Biblical Texts*. 2 vols., London: Equinox.

Younger, K. Lawson, Jr. 1990. *Ancient Conquest Accounts: A Study in Ancient Near Eastern and Biblical History Writings*. JSOTSup 98. Sheffield: JSOT Press.

————. 2002. "The 'Contextual Method': Some West Semitic Reflections," xxxv–xlii in William W. Hallo, ed., *The Context of Scripture: Archival Documents from the Biblical World*. Leiden and New York: Brill.

Zadok, Ran. 1979. *The Jews in Babylonia During the Chaldean and Achaemenian Periods According to the Babylonian Sources*. Haifa: University of Haifa.

Zahn, Theodor. 1890. *Geschichte des neutestamentlichen Kanons*. Leipzig: A. Deichert.

Zenger, Erich. 1968. "Die deuteronomistische Interpretation der Rehabilitierung Jojachins." *BZ* 12: 16–30.

————. 1994. "Mose/Moselied/Mosesegen/Moseschriften I." *TRE* 23: 330–41.

————. 1997a. "'Dass alles Fleisch den Namen seiner Heiligung segne' (Ps 145,21). Die Komposition Ps 145–150 als Anstoss zu einer christlich-jüdischen Psalmenhermeneutik." *BZ* 41: 1–27.

————. 1997b. "Priesterschrift." *TRE* 27: 435–46.

————. 1997c. "Die Provokation des 149. Psalms. Von der Unverzichtbarkeit der kanonischen Psalmenauslegung," 181–94 in Rainer Kessler et al., eds., *"Ihr Völker alle, klatscht in die Hände!" FS für Erhard S. Gerstenberger zum 65. Geburtstag.* Exegese in unserer Zeit 3. Münster: Lit.

————. 1998. "Der Psalter als Buch," 1–57 in idem, ed., Der *Psalter in Judentum und Christentum.* HBS 18. Freiburg: Herder.

————. 1999. "Die Psalmen im Psalter: Neue Perspektiven der Forschung." *TRev* 95: 443–56.

————. 2002. "'Es sollen sich niederwerfen vor ihm alle Könige' (Ps 72,11). Redaktionsgeschichtliche Beobachtungen zu Psalm 72 und zum Programm des messianischen Psalters 2–89," 66–93 in idem and Eckart Otto, eds., *"Mein Sohn bist du" (Ps 2,7): Studien zu den Königspsalmen.* SBS 192. Stuttgart: Katholisches Bibelwerk.

————. 2003. "Der Monotheismus Israels. Entstehung, Profil, Relevanz," 9–52 in Thomas Söding, ed., *Ist der Glaube Feind der Freiheit? Die neue Debatte um den Monotheismus.* QD 196. Freiburg: Herder.

————. ⁵2004. *Einleitung in das Alte Testament.* Stuttgart: Kohlhammer.

————. ed. 2010. *The Composition of the Book of Psalms.* BETL 238. Leuven: Leuven University Press; Peeters.

Zevit, Ziony. 2001. *The Religions of Ancient Israel: A Synthesis of Parallactic Approaches.* London and New York: Continuum.

————. 2002. "Three Debates about Bible and Archaeology." *Bib* 83: 1–27.

Zimmer, Tilmann. 1999. *Zwischen Tod und Lebensglück: Eine Untersuchung zur Anthropologie Qohelets.* BZAW 286. Berlin and New York: de Gruyter.

Zimmerli, Walther. 1969. "Sinaibund und Abrahambund. Ein Beitrag zum Verständnis der Priesterschrift." *TZ* 16 (1960): 268–80 = idem, *Gottes Offenbarung: Gesammelte Aufsätze zum Alten Testament,* 205–17. TB 19. Munich: Kaiser, 1963.

————. 1969. *Ezechiel.* BK XIII/1.2. Neukirchen-Vluyn: Neukirchener Verlag.

Zobel, Konstantin. 1992. *Prophetie und Deuteronomium: Die Rezeption prophetischer Theologie durch das Deuteronomium.* BZAW 199. Berlin and New York: de Gruyter.

Zunz, Leopold. ²1892. *Die gottesdienstlichen Vorträge der Juden, historisch entwickelt: Ein Beitrag zur Alterthumskunde und biblischen Kritik, zur Literatur- und Religionsgeschichte (1832).* Edited by Nehemiah Brüll. Frankfurt: J. Kauffmann.

Zwickel, Wolfgang. 1999. *Der salomonische Tempel.* Kulturgeschichte der antiken Welt 83. Mainz: von Zabern.

Index of Biblical Passages

Old Testament		8:22	157	18	86, 123		
Genesis		9	147, 149,	18:10b-15	85, 86		
1–11	155, 192		202	18:11	86		
1–6	147	9:6	80	18:14b	123		
1–3	147	10	124, 157	19:30-38	86		
1	147, 151,	10:4	198	20:9	118		
	156, 158,	10:5	124	21	86		
	174, 199,	10:9	56	21:2	86		
	204, 222	10:20	124	24	161		
1:2	111	10:31-32	124	25–35	58, 59, 123		
1:28	80, 149	11	24, 155, 157,	25	59		
1:31a	148		199, 221	26	123		
2–8	156	11:1-2	157	27	59		
2–4	157	12–50	123	27:11	59		
2–3	155, 157,	12–36	40, 120, 121	27:29	59		
	158	12:1-3	123, 124	27:39-40	59		
2:1	148, 149	12:1	124	27:43	58		
2:2a	148	12:7	180	28:10	58		
2:3a	148	12:7a	180	28:10-22	59		
2:5-9	158	12:10-20	161	28:13-15	123, 124		
2:16-17	158	13	86, 123	28:20-22	59		
3:22	158	13:2	86	29–31	59		
3:24	158	13:5	86	29:4	58		
4	155, 157	13:14-17	123, 124	32–33	59		
4:16	157	13:18	86	32:23-32	161		
5	24, 178,	15	161	32:23-33	59		
	199, 221	17	147, 149,	35:6-7	59		
6–9	147, 155,		161, 176	35:11	151		
	157, 202	17:2	80	37–50	118, 120,		
6:5-8	156, 157	17:6-7	176		121, 122,		
6:5	157	17:6	151		123		
6:6	156, 157	17:7	150, 152,	37–40	121		
6:7	156, 157		177	37:10	122		
6:13	149	17:9-14	152	46:2-4	123, 124		
8:20-22	156, 157	17:16	151	46:2	124		
8:21	156, 157	18–19	86, 123	47:28	221		

50	161	7:8-13	82	29:45-46	152, 176, 177
50:13-16	161	7:14-24	82		
50:14	121	8:15	120	29:46	177
50:19-20	121	11:1-3	81	32–34	125
50:24	180	12:12	151	32	109, 118, 119
50:25	37	12:35-36	81		
		12:40-41	221	32:4	118
Exodus		12:40	24	32:4b	118
1–2	82	13:19	37	32:13	180
1	80, 121	14	135	32:21	118
1:6-8	80, 121	15	82, 83	32:30-31	118, 119
1:7	80	15:8	82	33:1	180
1:8	80	15:13	82	34	97
1:9	80	15:21b	83	34:12	120
1:20	80	16	141	34:13-15	120
2—2 Kings 25		17:8-16	198	34:27-28	228
	117, 118	17:14	32, 228	34:28	32
2	42, 80, 81, 83, 118, 161	19– Numbers 10	125	35–40	125, 147
				39:32a	148
2:1	80	19–24	125, 126	39:43a	148
2:6	80	19	125	39:43b	148
2:23a	82	20–23	96, 97, 126	40:33b	148
2:23aα	82				
3–4	82, 161	20	138, 139	Leviticus	
3:1—4:18	82	20:5	120	1–7	156
3:1—4:17	82	20:22—23:33	96	17–26	96, 176
3:7-10	82	20:22—21:1	98	17:16-26	177
3:7	82	20:23	99	26	162, 176
3:9	82	20:24	100	26:3	176
3:16-18	82	21–23	99	26:9-13	176
3:18	82	21	101	26:9	176
4:1-9	82	21:2-7	100, 101	26:11-13	176
4:1-5	82	21:2	99	26:11	177
4:1	82	21:6	102	26:34-35	220
4:9	82	21:12-14	102	27:34	178
4:19	82	22:4-5	97		
4:24-26	161	22:6-8	97	Numbers	
5–11	161	22:20-23	98	1–10	125
5:2-3	120	22:24-26	98, 99	1:1	178
6	82, 147, 161	23:13b	99	10	125
6:2-8	82, 176	23:31b-33	99	11	141
6:2-3	151	23:32	120	14	141
6:4-7	177	23:33	120	16	141
6:7	177	24	126, 222	21:14	14
6:9a	82	24:4	32, 228	22–24	178, 197
6:9b	82	24:7	96	24:23-24	197
6:20	80	25–40	131, 149	32:11	180
7–12	120	25–31	125, 147	33:2	32, 228
		25:8	152		

Deuteronomy		28	101, 150	1:1	72
1:8	180	28:11	180	4–6	61, 109, 117
1:35	180	30	159, 174		
4–6	137	30:1-2	174	4:22	117
4	174	30:2	174	5:3-4	117
4:5-6	189	30:6	146	7:3	174
4:30	174	30:7	174	7:16	60
5	138, 139	30:8-10	175	8–12	73
5:6-7	134	30:10	174	8	109, 117
5:7	120	30:20	180	9–11	117
6–28	138	31:7	180	9:1-10	62
6:4-9	138, 188	31:9	228	9:9	37
6:4	102, 110, 137	31:20-21	180	9:16	62
		34	149	10:12	56
6:5-8	188	34:4	180	10:25	34
6:5	137	34:10-12	40, 179, 218	11:1-15	62
6:10	180	34:10	179, 180	12	109, 117
6:18	180	34:11-12	180	12:14-15	174
6:23	180			13–14	62
7:1-6	178	Joshua		14:47	60
7:13	180	1	218	14:49-51	60
8:1	180	1:7-8	40, 179, 218	15	198
9:5	180	1:13	218	16	61, 62
10:11	180	6	83	17	62, 63
11:9	180	9–10	83	17:7	62
11:21	180	10:13	14	24:14	56
12–26	138	15	61	27	63
12	102	18–19	58	30:27-31	60
12:1	138	18:1	149		
12:13-14	100	19:51	149	2 Samuel	
12:29-31	120	24	161	1:18	14
13	101	24:32	37	2:9	60
13:17	233			3:2-5	60
15	101	Judges		5 (7–8)	61
15:12-18	100, 101	1:29-40	198	5:13-16	60
15:17	102	2:11-12	174	6 (7 or 9)	61
16–18	138	3–9	78, 79, 81	7	117, 195
16:21	167	3:7-11	79	7:12-17	195
17:18	34, 99	3:12-14	79	7:16	195
18:15	180	8:21	56	8:16-18	60
19:1-13	102	9	79	8:17	35
19:8	180			11:1-27	62
20:16-17	120	Ruth		12:24b	62
25:17-19	198	4:18-22	152	13:13	62
25:19	120			15:1-6	62
26:3	180	1 Samuel		15:13	62
26:5-9	122	1	72	18:1-19	62
26:15	180	1:1-20	62	18:9a	62

20:1-22	62
20:23-26	60
21:15-22	62
21:19	62
23:8-39	62
23:13-17	198
23:24-39	60
1 Kings	
1–2	62
1:20	61
1:27	61
2	61, 62
2:1-4	61
2:5-9	61
2:10-12	61
3–10	71
4	61
4:1-6	60
4:3	35
5:14	71
6–8	42
6–7	71
6:1	24, 221
8	110
8:8	78
8:12-13	55
8:14-21	110
8:21	196
8:22	110
8:30	110
8:38-39	110
8:44-45	110
8:46-53	174
8:53 LXX	14, 55
9:15	50
9:17-18	60
9:21	78
10:12	78
10:23-24	71
11:41	14, 60
12—2 Kings 23	78
12	62, 109, 118, 119
12:26-27	55
12:28	118
12:28b	118

14:19—2 Kings 15:26	58
14:19	14
14:22 LXX	76
14:29	14, 60
14:30	53
15:1-3	76
15:7	53
15:9	116
15:11-14	76
15:16	53
15:25-26	74
15:32	53
15:33-34	74
16:18-19	74
16:25-26	74
16:29-31	75
16:34	58
17–19	60
19:8	125
19:19	78
21	60
22:28	88
22:41-43	76
22:51-52	75
2 Kings	
1–9	60
1	54
2:11-12	208
3:1-3	75
3:4	58
8:16-19	76
8:22	78
8:25-27	76
10:28-31	75
12:2-3	77
13	60
13:1-2	75
14:1-4	77
14:23-24	75
15:1-4	77
15:8-9	75
15:9	116
15:17-18	75
15:20	65
15:23-24	75
15:27-28	75

15:32-35	77
16:1-4	76, 77
17	78, 118, 119
17:1-2	75, 76
17:7-20	119
17:7-8	119
17:7	76
17:9-20	109
17:13	174
17:19	78
17:21-23	119
17:21	118, 119
18–20	92, 115, 116
18:1-6	77
18:4	78
18:9—19:9	116
18:13-16	66
18:13-19	115
18:14-16	115
18:17-19	115
18:14-16	66
19:9	115, 116
19:32-37	116
19:36	115, 116
21	78, 196
21:1-3	76, 77
21:1	196
21:2	78
21:3	167
21:19-22	76, 77
22–23	74, 101, 228, 229
22	34, 66
22:1-2	77, 96
22:3	36
22:8-13	229
23–24	78
23	67, 78, 116
23:4	167
23:8	78
23:25	174
23:26	78
23:32	78, 116, 117
23:37	78, 116, 117
24–25	109, 116, 117, 127
24:3	78

2 Kings (*continued*)
24:5	60
24:6	129
24:9	78, 116, 117
24:14	105, 171
24:19	78, 116, 117
25	117, 118, 162
25:8-12	106, 162
25:9	162
25:12	162
25:13-21	162
25:27-30	118, 161

1 Chronicles
1–9	195
3:16-19	143
10	195
11–29	195
17	195
17:5	196
17:11-15	195
17:14	195
17:21	196
25:8	35

2 Chronicles
5:10	196
6:5	196
6:11	196
7:22	196
17:7-9	34
20:7	85
20:10	196
26:14	194
33:11-16	197
35:20-24	105
35:25	111
36	117
36:11-14	197
36:17-21	106
36:21	220
36:23b	17

Ezra
1–6	143, 162, 163
2	143

5:1   164
5:11-16   167
5:14-16   143
6:14   163, 164
7–10   162
7   179
7:6   35
7:7   145
7:12-26   35
7:27   163
9   146
9:9   145
10   178

Nehemiah
1–7	162
1:1	145
2:1	145
2:11-15	144
5	145
7	143
8–10	163
8:1-2	34
8:5-8	230
9	125, 146
11–13	163
13:2-3	35

Esther
2:5	199
3:1	199

Job
1–2	154
1:17	154
3–31	154
3–27	154, 155
3	155
5	190
7	155
7:17-18	155
7:17	155
16:12	155
23:9-10	155
27	189
28	189
28:20-23	190
28:28	190

29–31   155, 189
32–37   154, 189, 190
38–41   154, 155
42   199
42:7   154

Psalms
1–41	215
1–2	214
1	40, 54, 199, 213, 214
1:2	38, 214
2–89	192, 214, 215
2	55
2:1-2	192
2:1-9	55
2:7	195
2:9	192
3–41	153
3–14	114
3–7	114
3:9	115
6	59, 112
8	114, 155
8:4-5	155
9–14	114
13	55, 112
14:7	115
18:33-46	55
18:51	192
20	153
20:7	192
21:2-7	55
21:9-13	55
24	69, 70, 229
24:7-10.	70, 228
28:8-9	192
29	53, 70
41	215
41:14	214, 215
42–83	153
42–72	215
42–48	153
44	113
45	53
46	69

47:10	85	119:99	35	16:9	191
48	69, 113, 128	120–134	153	16:10-15	71
48:2-7	128	136	54	19:21	191
48:9	128	137	54, 113	20:24-28	71
48:13-15	128	137:9	155	20:24	191
49	54, 192	139:8-10	155	21:1-2	71
56:8	55	145	153, 160	21:2	191
59:6	55	145:1	153	21:30	191
59:9	55	145:13	153	21:30-31	71
60	71	145:15-16	153	22:17—24:22	72
68	53, 70	146–150	214, 215	24:21-22	191
72	55, 70, 71,	146	160	25:1	71
	215	146:5-10	153	25:6-7	71
72:1-7	55	147	160		
72:1	71	147:7-9	153	Ecclesiastes	
72:8	70, 206	149	214, 216	1:9-11	191
72:12-14	55	149:5-9	216	2:13-16	191
72:16-17	55	150	216	3:11-13	190
72:17	124	150:6	215	3:19-22	214
72:18-19	214, 215			3:19	192
73–89	215	Proverbs		9:1	192
73–83	153	1–9	42, 186, 187,		
73	54, 192		188, 189,	Isaiah	
74	216		191	1–62	202, 203,
78	54	1:7	186		204
84–85	153	1:20-23	189	1–39	40, 91, 147,
84:9-10	192	3:13-18	188		174, 202,
87–88	153	3:16-18	191		203
89	215	5:12-14	35	1–35	207
89:51-52	192	6	188	1–11	91, 93, 94
89:53	214, 215	6:20-22	188	1	137, 162
90–106	215	8:15-16	189	1:1	175, 208
90	113	8:22-31	187	1:2-9	162
93–100	215	8:32-33	187	1:7	162
93	69, 153	8:35	187	1:8	162
96–99	153	9:10	186	1:10-15	162
102	54	9:17	187	1:21-26	92, 93
104	54, 192	10–29	71	1:27-28	92, 93
105:6	85	10	56	5	94
105:9	85	10:1-5	56, 57	5:8-24	93
105:42	85	10:1	57	5:25-30	93
106	215	10:2	57	5:25	94, 95
106:48	214, 215	10:3	57	6–8	92, 93
107–150	146, 215	10:4	57	6	92, 95, 166,
110	216	10:5	57		203
110:1-3	55	14:28	71	6:9-10	92, 94
110:2-5	216	14:35	71	7:14	96
119	54, 214	16:1	191	8:1-4	92

Isaiah (continued)
8:1   88
8:5-8   92
8:16-18   88
8:23   93, 96
9–10   94
9:1-6   93, 96, 168
9:1-6a   96
9:1   168, 169
9:5   96
9:7-20   93
9:7-8   94
9:7   68, 95
9:11   94, 95
9:12   94
9:16   94, 95
9:20   94, 95
10:1-4   93
10:4   93, 94, 95
11:1-5   93, 189, 206
11:11-16   203
12   91
13–23   91
13   208
14:24-27   95
14:26-27   95
16:13-14   23
16:13   23
16:14   23
17   92
17:1-6   92
24–27   92, 202
24:4-6   202
25:8   214
26:19   214
26:20-21   202
27:12-13   203
28–32   91
29:22   85
33–35   92
33   203
34:1   200
34:2-4   178, 200, 203
34:4   31
34:5-6   200
34:5   200
35   37, 203

36–39   92, 115, 116, 207
36   115
36:1   66
40–66   131, 132, 133, 134, 136, 137, 147, 167, 207
40–55   15, 124, 131, 136, 167, 168, 202, 203
40–52   167
40–48   132
40   203
40:1-5   132
40:1-2   206
40:2   113
40:3   166, 168
40:3-4   165
40:6-8   203
40:19-20   136
41:6-7   136
41:8-10   136
41:8   85
42–55   136
42:1-4   167
42:5-7   167
42:17   136
43   204
43:12-13   132
43:16-21   136, 204
44:9-20   136
45:1-2   131, 132
45:1   133, 145, 146, 160, 168
45:3   160
45:4   160
45:5   110
45:6-7   134, 135
45:6   134
45:16-17   136
45:20b   136
45:21   132
46:5-8   136
47   108, 143

48:3   132
48:5   132
48:22   136
49:14-26   136
51:1-11   203
51:2   85
51:9-10   136
51:17   136
51:19-23   136
52:1-2   136
52:7-10   132
52:7   165, 166
54:1   136
56–59   137, 145, 168, 169, 167, 168, 192, 202, 203, 204
56   167
56:1-9   233
56:1-7   168
57:14   168
57:20-21   204
60–62   168
60–61   206
60   169
60:1-12   168
60:7-13   163
62:10-12   203
63–66   168, 169
63–64   137
63:7—64:11   204
63:16   85
65–66   137, 175
65   193, 204
65:1-15   204
65:13-17   204
65:17-25   193, 204
65:17   191
66:1   205
66:18-24   208

Jeremiah
1–25   129
1–24   171
1   166
1:11-14   171
2:19-25   127

2:32-33	127	29:16	171, 173	Ezekiel	
3:1—4:2	175	30–33	171	1–3	31, 131
4–10	109, 113,	30–31	169	4–24	130
	126, 129,	30:18	233	7:2-3	150
	133	31	159	8–11	131
4:13-15	127	31:31-34	74	11	171
4:14	126	32	35, 129, 159,	11:13-21	172
4:29-30	127		173	11:23	131
6	128	32:23	179	16:44	56
6:22-26	128	32:37	173	17	127
6:22-24	108	32:40	146	17:11-16	127
8:18-23	130	33:14-16	205, 206	19	130
9:12	179	33:14-26	24, 205	20	82
10:11	30	33:14	206	28	158
10:12-16	108	33:16	206	28:17	158
13	129	33:26	85	31	130, 172
16	129	36	31, 35, 36	33:22-29	172
16:11	179	32		33:24	85, 87
18	129	36:23	32	36	130, 159
21–23	109, 129	36:32	23, 35, 87	36:26	146
22:18-19	129, 175	37:3-10	116	37	214
22:24-26	164	37:5	116	39:25-29	173
22:24	164	41:5	111	40–48	131, 149,
22:30	164	43	35		173
23	173	43:10	134, 169		
23:3	170	45	35	Daniel	
23:5-6	205, 206	45:4-5	200	1–6	134, 146,
23:7-8	173	46–51	200		159, 160,
24	74, 166, 170,	46–49	129		185, 199,
	171, 173	48:40-41	38		208, 219
24:1-10	170	49:7-22	38	1–4	146
25	201	49:30	38	1	159
25:8-11	38	49:32	38	2–7	159
25:9	134, 169	50–51	108, 143,	2	159, 185,
25:11	169		169		208, 219
25:12	105	50:13	38	2:47	159
25:15-29	38	50:40	38	3:28-29	159
25:27-31	178, 201	50:41-43	108	3:31-33	160
25:27	201	50:44-46	38	3:35	85
26:17-19	88	51:15-19	108	4:1-3	160
27–28	129	52:28-30	105, 106	4:34	160
27	129, 169			4:37	160
27:6	134, 146,	Lamentations		6:25-28	160
	168, 169	1–4	111	6:26-29	160
27:8	168, 169	1:1-8	113	7	159, 185,
29:1	88	1:10	169		208, 219
29:10	105, 169,	3	111	7:7	219
	206	5	111, 112	7:8	219
29:14	173	5:1-18	112	8–12	159, 219
		5:19-21	112		

Daniel (*continued*)

8–9	166, 219	
9	46, 73, 159,	
	174, 219,	
	220, 221	
9:2	219	
9:24-27	220	
9:26-27	159	
10–12	219	
11:30	198	
11:34	214	
11:45	219	
12:2-3	214	

Hosea

1–3	89
1:1	208
1:2-9	89
1:2	80
2:1-3	89
2:4-15	89
2:15	89
2:16-25	89
2:18	89
2:23	89
3:1-4	89
3:5	89
4–9	89
4:1	89
4:15	88, 89
5:1	89
5:5	89
5:8	89
7:10	88
8:1	89, 179
8:14	88
9:1	89
11:1	89
11:10	88

Joel

2	208
3:12-16	201
4:12-16	201

Amos

1:1	90, 91, 94
1:9-12	91
2:4-5	91

2:4	179
2:6-8	98, 99
2:10-12	91
2:13	90, 94
3–6	37, 90, 91
3:1	37, 90, 91
3:7	91
4:6-12	94
4:6	94
4:8	94
4:9	94
4:10	94
4:11	94
5:1	37, 90, 91
5:4	94
5:5	94
5:6	94
5:14	94
5:25-26	91
7–9	90, 95, 166
7:9	85, 86
7:12	55
7:14	90
7:16	85, 86
8:2-3	90
8:2	149
9:1	90, 94

Obadiah

1-4	38
8-9	38

Micah

1:2	88
3:12	88
7:12-13	201
7:20	85

Habakkuk

2:2	37

Zephaniah

3:8	201

Haggai

2:2	143
2:6	164, 165
2:21-23	117, 164,
	165

2:22	164

Zechariah

1–8	143, 163,
	165, 166,
	206
1:3	175, 208
1:7-15	165
1:8-13	165
1:14-15	165
2:1-4	165
2:5-9	165
3–4	165
4:1-6a	165
4:6b-10a	165, 166
4:10b-14	165
5:1-4	165
5:5-11	165, 166,
	167
5:11	167
6:1-8	165
6:9-15	165
7–8	165
9–14	206
9–11	206
9	206
9:1–8	206
9:1	208
9:9-10	206, 207
9:13	206
11:13	206
12–14	206
12:1	208
14:5	90
14:16-21	208
14:20-21	206

Malachi

1:1	208
3	218
3:1	208
3:7	175, 208
3:22-24	40, 179, 208
3:22	218

Sirach

Prologue	225
1:1	188
1:8	188

10	216	1:54-59	212	Luke		
10:8	216	6:53	138	16:16	226	
10:14-17	216	6:49	138	16:29	226	
24	189, 220			16:31	226	
24:1-8	217	2 Maccabees		24:22	227	
24:19-23	217	2:13-15	34, 35	24:27	227	
36	214, 216	2:15	34	24:44	227	
36:1-5	217	4:14	211			
38–39	35	6:1-9	212	Acts		
44–50	218	6:2	212	19:9	35	
46:11-12	217			26:22	227	
47	194	**New Testament**		28:23	227	
49:10	207	Matthew				
50:27-29	23	23	35			
51:23	35					
		Mark				
1 Maccabees		11:27-33	35			
1:41-51	212					
1:41-59	212					

Index of Authors

Albertz, Rainer, 97
Alt, Albrecht, 97, 102, 123, 137

Barth, Hermann, 95
Bewer, Julius A., 7
Blum, Erhard, 20, 27, 94, 122, 179
Budde, Karl, 6, 7

Cassel, David, 5
Creelman, Harlan, 7
Cross, Frank Moore, 74

Dietrich, Walter, 11, 62
Donner, Herbert, 36
Droysen, Johann Gustav, 184
Duhm, Bernhard, 36, 54, 168, 202

Engnell, Ivan, 54

Finkelstein, Israel, 24
Fohrer, Georg, 10
Frei, Peter, 179
Fürst, Julius, 4, 5

Gottwald, Norman K., 10
Graf, Karl Heinrich, 5
Gressmann, Hugo, 8
Gunkel, Hermann, 6, 7, 9, 38, 39, 41

Halbe, Jörn, 96
Hardmeier, Christof, 115, 116
Hempel, Johannes, 6, 7, 8
Herder, Johann Gottfried, 4
Hupfeld, Hermann, 4

Japhet, Sara, 162
Jauss, Hans Robert, 9

Kaiser, Otto, 10
Kautzsch, Emil, 6
Keel, Othmar, 126
Klostermann, August, 35, 176
Koch, Klaus, 9
Köckert, Matthias, 122
Kratz, Reinhard, 14, 51, 62, 97
Kuenen, Abraham, 5, 6

Lambert, Wilfred, 108
Lemche, Niels Peter, 11
Levin, Christoph, 12
Lods, Adolphe, 8
Lohfink, Norbert, 176
Lowth, Richard, 4

Maier, Ernst H., 4
Marx, Karl, 3
Meinhold, Johannes, 7

Noth, Martin, 74, 174

Otto, Eckart, 97
Osumi, Yuichi, 97

Perkins, David, 1
Plöger, Otto, 152
Pohlmann, Karl-Friedrich, 130, 171

Rad, Gerhard von, 9, 13, 22, 27, 28, 122, 123
Rendtorff, Rolf, 122
Reuss, Eduard, 5, 6
Rost, Leonhard, 61
Rothenbusch, Ralf, 97

Schniedewind, William, 24

Schoors, Antoon, 11
Schwienhorst-Schönberger, Ludger, 97
Silberman, Neil Asher, 24
Simon, Richard, 4
Spinoza, Baruch, 4
Staigers, Emil, 9
Steck, Odil Hannes, 56, 203
Steins, Georg, 194

Thiel, Winfried, 129

Van Seters, John, 36, 37, 61
Vanoni, Gottfried, 116

Warren, Austin, 1
Weber, Max, 3
Weippert, Manfred, 10
Wellek, René, 1
Wellhausen, Julius, 4, 5, 6, 8, 27, 28, 33, 74, 85, 121, 149
Wette, W. M. L. de, 101
Wildeboer, Gerrit, 5, 6
Wolff, Hans Walter, 174
Woude, Adriaan S. van der, 21

Zimmerli, Walter, 28, 150
Zunz, Leopold, 162

CPSIA information can be obtained
at www.ICGtesting.com
Printed in the USA
LVHW081951180220
647368LV00006B/23/J